An Introduction to Pidgins and Creoles

This textbook is a clear and concise introduction to the study of how new languages come into being.

Starting with an overview of the field's basic concepts, it surveys the new languages that developed as a result of the European expansion to the Americas, Africa, Asia and the Pacific. Long misunderstood as 'bad' versions of European languages, today such varieties as Jamaican Creole English, Haitian Creole French and New Guinea Pidgin are recognized as distinct languages in their own right.

John Holm examines the structure of these pidgins and creoles, the social history of their speakers, and the theories put forward to explain how their vocabularies, sound systems and grammars evolved. His new findings on structural typology, including non-Atlantic creoles, permit a wide-ranging assessment of the nature of restructured languages worldwide.

This much-needed book will be welcomed by students and researchers in linguistics, sociolinguistics, western European languages, anthropology and sociology.

JOHN HOLM is Chair of English Linguistics at the University of Coimbra, Portugal. He is the author of *Pidgins and creoles* (2 volumes) and has co-edited a number of books, including *Focus on the Caribbean* and *Atlantic meets Pacific: a global view of pidginization and creolization.*

CAMBRIDGE TEXTBOOKS IN LINGUISTICS

General editors: S. R. ANDERSON, J. BRESNAN, B. COMRIE, W. DRESSLER,
C. J. EWEN, R. HUDDLESTON, R. LASS, D. LIGHTFOOT, J. LYONS,
P. H. MATTHEWS, R. POSNER, S. ROMAINE, N. V. SMITH, N. VINCENT

AN INTRODUCTION TO PIDGINS
AND CREOLES

AN INTRODUCTION TO PIDGINS AND CREOLES

JOHN HOLM

UNIVERSITY OF COIMBRA, PORTUGAL

CAMBRIDGE UNIVERSITY PRESS

PUBLISHED BY THE PRESS SYNDICATE OF THE UNIVERSITY OF CAMBRIDGE
The Pitt Building, Trumpington Street, Cambridge, United Kingdom

CAMBRIDGE UNIVERSITY PRESS
The Edinburgh Building, Cambridge CB2 2RU, UK   http://www.cup.cam.ac.uk
40 West 20th Street, New York NY 10011–4211, USA   http://www.cup.org
10 Stamford Road, Oakleigh, Melbourne 3166, Australia

First published 2000

Printed in the United Kingdom at the University Press, Cambridge

Typeset in 9½/13pt Times   [GC]

A catalogue record for this book is available from the British Library

Library of Congress cataloguing in publication data

Holm, John A.
An introduction to pidgins and creoles / John Holm.
   p.   cm. – (Cambridge textbooks in linguistics)
Includes bibliographical references (p.) and index.
ISBN 0 521 58460 4. – ISBN 0 521 58581 3 (paperback)
1. Creole dialects.   2. Pidgin languages.   I. Title.   II. Series.
PM7801.H65   2000
417′.22 – dc21   99-23499 CIP

ISBN 0 521 58460 4 hardback
ISBN 0 521 58581 3 paperback

CONTENTS

Contents

PREFACE

I am finishing this book at the University of Coimbra, the first and oldest university of Portugal, where I first came as a student of Portuguese in 1988 in order to gain better access to the literature on the Portuguese-based creoles and the Brazilian vernacular. This seems entirely proper, since it was a Fulbright award in 1993–1994 that first allowed me to teach here and to begin work on this book. I am grateful to the J. William Fulbright Foreign Scholarship Board, to the colleagues who were so helpful, especially Ana Luis and Clara Keating, and to those professors – Maria Irene Ramalho de Sousa Santos, Martin Kayman and Jorge Morais Barbosa – whose extraordinary efforts led to the creation of the chair I now hold here.

It is an honour to be part of one of the great medieval universities of Europe, but that is not the whole story of this book. From 1980 until 1998, I taught at the City University of New York (CUNY). Few people outside that institution can appreciate the riches of its cultural diversity, such as the thousands of its students who speak creole and semi-creole languages. Mitchell (1997) notes that 'More students of color earn their bachelor degrees from the City University of New York than any other institution in the country.' Although many of these students speak standard English as their first language, many also speak Creole English or French, African American Vernacular English or nonstandard Caribbean Spanish. Appropriately, the Ph.D. Program in Linguistics at the CUNY Graduate Center has long supported research and teaching in creole linguistics.

Within that program, I was able to organize two major research projects that contributed to this book and benefited from the collaboration of students at CUNY as well as colleagues at other universities. The first was on comparative creole syntax, a study of some 100 grammatical structures that many creoles share, but which most of their lexical-source languages do not. This study in creole typology was the cumulative result of several graduate seminars; a number of the participants were native speakers of either the creoles they worked on or their lexical source languages. They included the following scholars (all then at CUNY unless otherwise indicated): Dwijen Bhattacharjya [Nagamese, or creolized Assamese], Daniel Chapuis [Dominican and Seychellois Creole French], Michel DeGraff [Haitian Creole French], Christa de Kleine [Negerhollands Creole Dutch], Nicholas Faraclas (University of Papua New Guinea) [Tok Pisin Pidgin/Creole English), Kate Green [Palenquero Creole Spanish], Mary Huttar (Summer Institute of Linguistics) [Ndyuka Creole English], Gerardo Lorenzino [Angolar Creole Portuguese], Heliana Mello [Cape Verdean Creole Portuguese], Abigail Michel [Papiamentu Creole Spanish], Jonathan Owens (University of Bayreuth) and Cornelia Khamis (University of Hamburg) [Nubi Creole Arabic], Peter Patrick (University of Essex) [Jamaican Creole English], Salvatore Santoro [Zamboangueño Creole Spanish], Miki Suzuki [Guiné-Bissau Creole Portuguese] and Sorie Yillah [Sierra Leonean Krio]. This research on creole syntax provided much of the new information in chapter 6 of the present volume and also led to a number of joint publications (Holm *et al.* 1994, 1997, 1998, 1999, fc.; Holm and Patrick fc.). I am indebted to all of these scholars for their indispensable contributions.

The second was a series of graduate seminars on semi-creolization, which has helped to redefine the theoretical boundaries of creole linguistics. A number of talented doctoral students participated, some of whom were again native speakers of the semi-creoles they described or their lexical-source languages. These seminars were extraordinarily productive, leading to conference papers and journal articles (e.g. Craig 1991 on American Indian English) and dissertations (e.g. Mello 1997a on Brazilian Vernacular Portuguese and Green 1997 on non-standard Dominican Spanish); two of the dissertations are still in progress (Chapuis fc. on Réunionnais and Slomanson fc. on Afrikaans). Their work helped to identify the remaining problems in developing a usable theoretical model for semi-creolization by tracing the genesis of a number of partially restructured languages, comparing them, and looking for the relationship between the social history of their speakers and the linguistic outcome. The results are described more fully in Holm (1992a, 1998a, 1998b, fc.).

Thanks to these two projects, this book contains much fresh material. However, it also rests on the foundation of my earlier volumes in the Cambridge Language Surveys series: *Pidgins and creoles* (vols. I and II), and on all the help that generous colleagues gave me during their preparation. I hope they will understand if I do not reproduce here an honour roll that occupies pages in that earlier book, but I do thank them all once more. For their help in preparing this new book, I am indebted to Michel DeGraff, Christa de Kleine, Nicholas Faraclas, Frans Hinskens, Gerardo Lorenzino, Philippe Maurer, Abigail Michel, Jonathan Owens, Peter Patrick and Armin

Schwegler, as well as my editors at Cambridge University Press, particularly Suzanne Romaine. For technical assistance in the preparation of this volume, I would like to thank Taka'aki Hashimoto.

This book has also profited from my being able to attend international conferences on creole linguistics over the past several years, and I would like to express my appreciation here for travel grants from the Deutsche Forschungsgemeinschaft to attend the International Symposium on Degrees of Restructuring in Creole Languages at the University of Regensburg (1998); from the University of Heidelberg's Graduierten Kolleg to participate in a workshop on comparative creole syntax (1997); from the German government to attend the Second Colloquium on Creoles based on Spanish and Portuguese (Berlin, 1996); from the Colombian government to attend the First International Colloquium on Cartagena, the Afro-Caribbean and Palenque (Cartagena, 1996); from the Associação Brasileira de Lingüística to attend their national conference (Florianópolis, 1999); and from the American Council of Learned Societies to attend the joint meeting of the Society for Caribbean Linguistics and the Society for Pidgin and Creole Linguistics at the University of Guyana (1994).

Finally, for his patience and encouragement over the past twenty-five years, a most important contribution to the writing of this book, I would like to thank my partner and friend, Michael Pye.

TABLES

ABBREVIATIONS AND SYMBOLS

A	Arabic
AAVE	African American Vernacular English
ACC	accusative case
ADJ	adjective
AN	Angolar CP
ANT	anterior marker
As	Assamese
ASP	aspectual
BVP	Brazilian Vernacular Portuguese
C	consonant; complement
CA	Creole Arabic
CAs	Creole Assamese
CD	Creole Dutch
CE	Creole English
CF	Creole French
COMP	completive marker; complementizer; comparative marker
COND	conditional
CONT	continuous; durative
COP	copula
CP	Creole Portuguese
CS	Creole Spanish
CTF	counterfactual
CV	Cape Verdean CP

D	Dutch
DEF	definite article
DEM	demonstrative
DET	determiner
DIM	diminutive
DM	Dominican CF
E	English
EMPH	emphatic
F	French
FEM	feminine
FUT	future marker
GB	Guiné-Bissau CP
GC	Guyanese CE
GU	Gullah CE
HA	Haitian CF
HAB	habitual marker
HL	highlighter
IMP	impersonal
IND	indefinite
INF	infinitive marker
INT	intensifier
IP	immediate past marker
IRR	irrealis marker
JC	Jamaican CE

Abbreviations and symbols

KR	Krio CE		R	rare
			REAL	realis
LOC	locative		REL	relative, relativizer
			RP	relative pronoun
MASC	masculine			
MC	Mauritian CF		S	Spanish; subject
MOD	modal		SC	Seychellois CF
			sg	singular
N	any nasal		SOV	subject-object-verb
NB	Nubi CA		SPEC	specific
NEG	negator		SR	Sranan CE
NG	Nagamese CAs		SRP	subject referencing pronoun
NH	Negerhollands CD		ST	Sãotomense CP
NOM	nominative case		SVO	subject-verb-object
NP	noun phrase			
			t	trace (original position of an element)
OBJ	object			
			TMA	tense–mood–aspect marker
P	Portuguese; pidgin		TP	Tok Pisin P/C E
PASS	passive		TR	transitivizer
p.c.	personal communication			
PERF	perfect		V	verb; vowel
PL	Palenquero CS		VP	verb phrase
pl	plural			
PLUR	plural marker		ZM	Zamboangueño CS
POL	polite			
POSS	possessive		1s	first person singular
PP	Papiamentu CS		2s	second person singular
PRES	present (tense)		3s	third person singular
PRO	pronoun; pronominalizing suffix		1p	first person plural
			2p	second person plural
PROG	progressive marker		3p	third person plural
proP	pro-predicate		<	derived from
PROX	proximal future		( )	optional
PT	participle		−	negated (TMA marker)
			+	presence attested
QM	question marker		0	absence attested
QUOT	quotation complementizer		?	presence unknown
QW	question word; interrogative			

For my cousin Kevin in Barbados
and my godson Ricky in Brooklyn

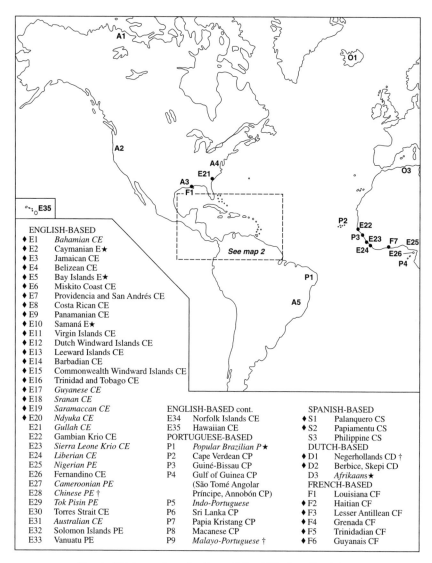

ENGLISH-BASED
- ♦ E1   *Bahamian CE*
- ♦ E2   *Caymanian E*★
- ♦ E3   *Jamaican CE*
- ♦ E4   *Belizean CE*
- ♦ E5   *Bay Islands E*★
- ♦ E6   *Miskito Coast CE*
- ♦ E7   *Providencia and San Andrés CE*
- ♦ E8   *Costa Rican CE*
- ♦ E9   *Panamanian CE*
- ♦ E10 *Samaná E*★
- ♦ E11 *Virgin Islands CE*
- ♦ E12 *Dutch Windward Islands CE*
- ♦ E13 *Leeward Islands CE*
- ♦ E14 *Barbadian CE*
- ♦ E15 *Commonwealth Windward Islands CE*
- ♦ E16 *Trinidad and Tobago CE*
- ♦ E17 *Guyanese CE*
- ♦ E18 *Sranan CE*
- ♦ E19 *Saramaccan CE*
- ♦ E20 *Ndyuka CE*
- E21 Gullah CE
- E22 Gambian Krio CE
- E23 *Sierra Leone Krio CE*
- E24 *Liberian CE*
- E25 *Nigerian PE*
- E26 Fernandino CE
- E27 *Cameroonian PE*
- E28 *Chinese PE* †
- E29 *Tok Pisin PE*
- E30 Torres Strait CE
- E31 *Australian CE*
- E32 Solomon Islands PE
- E33 Vanuatu PE

ENGLISH-BASED cont.
- E34 Norfolk Islands CE
- E35 Hawaiian CE

PORTUGUESE-BASED
- P1   *Popular Brazilian P*★
- P2   Cape Verdean CP
- P3   Guiné-Bissau CP
- P4   Gulf of Guinea CP
       (São Tomé Angolar
       Príncipe, Annobón CP)
- P5   *Indo-Portuguese*
- P6   Sri Lanka CP
- P7   Papia Kristang CP
- P8   Macanese CP
- P9   *Malayo-Portuguese* †

SPANISH-BASED
- ♦ S1   Palanquero CS
- ♦ S2   Papiamentu CS
- S3   Philippine CS

DUTCH-BASED
- ♦ D1   Negerhollands CD †
- ♦ D2   Berbice, Skepi CD
- D3   *Afrikaans*★

FRENCH-BASED
- F1   Louisiana CF
- ♦ F2   Haitian CF
- ♦ F3   Lesser Antillean CF
- ♦ F4   Grenada CF
- ♦ F5   Trinidadian CF
- ♦ F6   Guyanais CF

Map 1. Pidgins and creoles (from Holm 1988–9: xviii–xix)

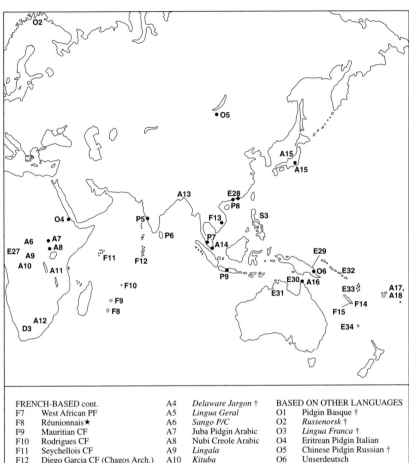

FRENCH-BASED cont.		A4	*Delaware Jargon* †	BASED ON OTHER LANGUAGES	
F7	West African PF	A5	*Lingua Geral*	O1	Pidgin Basque †
F8	Réunionnais ★	A6	*Sango P/C*	O2	*Russenorsk* †
F9	Mauritian CF	A7	Juba Pidgin Arabic	O3	*Lingua Franca* †
F10	Rodrigues CF	A8	Nubi Creole Arabic	O4	Eritrean Pidgin Italian
F11	Seychellois CF	A9	*Lingala*	O5	Chinese Pidgin Russian †
F12	Diego Garcia CF (Chagos Arch.)	A10	*Kituba*	O6	Unserdeutsch
F13	Vietnamese PF†	A11	*Swahili P/C*		
F14	New Caledonian PF†	A12	*Fanakalo*		
F15	Tayo CF	A13	Naga Pidgin	†	Extinct
AFRICAN-,ASIAN-,AUSTRONESIAN-		A14	Baba Malay	★	Semi-creole
AND AMERINDIAN-BASED		A15	Pidgin Japanese †	*Italics*	Spoken over a wider area
A1	*Eskimo Trade Jargon* †	A16	Hiri Motu	♦	Shown on map 2
A2	*Chinook Jargon* †	A17	Pidgin Fijian		
A3	*Mobilian Jargon* (†)	A18	Pidgin Hindustani		

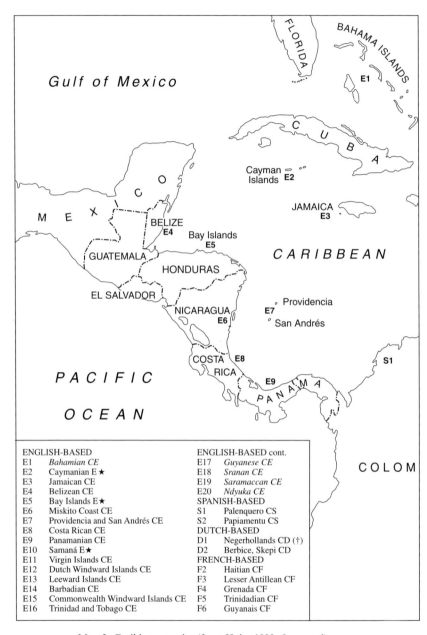

Map 2. Caribbean creoles (from Holm 1988–9: xx–xxi)

ENGLISH-BASED
E1	*Bahamian CE*
E2	Caymanian E ★
E3	Jamaican CE
E4	Belizean CE
E5	Bay Islands E ★
E6	Miskito Coast CE
E7	Providencia and San Andrés CE
E8	Costa Rican CE
E9	Panamanian CE
E10	Samaná E ★
E11	Virgin Islands CE
E12	Dutch Windward Islands CE
E13	Leeward Islands CE
E14	Barbadian CE
E15	Commonwealth Windward Islands CE
E16	Trinidad and Tobago CE

ENGLISH-BASED cont.
E17	*Guyanese CE*
E18	*Sranan CE*
E19	*Saramaccan CE*
E20	*Ndyuka CE*

SPANISH-BASED
S1	Palenquero CS
S2	Papiamentu CS

DUTCH-BASED
D1	Negerhollands CD (†)
D2	Berbice, Skepi CD

FRENCH-BASED
F2	Haitian CF
F3	Lesser Antillean CF
F4	Grenada CF
F5	Trinidadian CF
F6	Guyanais CF

ATLANTIC

OCEAN

VIRGIN
ISLANDS   Anguilla
E11, D1   St. Martin
HAITI   DOMINICAN   E12   Antigua
F2   REP.   Saba   E13   Montserrat
              PUERTO   St. Kitts   Guadeloupe
              RICO   Nevis
                       LEEWARD   Dominica   F3
SEA   ISLANDS   Martinique
                       WINDWARD   St. Lucia
                       St. Vincent   Barbados
                       ISLANDS   E15   E14
                                  F 4
                              Grenada
        Aruba   S2   Bonaire   Tobago
                 Curaçao
                                       Trinidad
                                       E16, F5

E10

       VENEZUELA   E17   D2
                          GUYANA   E18   F6
                             E19   E20   FRENCH
                             SURINAME   GUIANA
BIA

†   Extinct
★   Semi-creole
Italics   Spoken over a wider area

| 0 | 500 | 1000 *km* |
| 0 | | 500 *miles* |

I
Introduction

1.0 Pidgins and creoles and linguistics

What earlier generations thought of pidgin and creole languages is all too clear from their very names: *broken English, bastard Portuguese, nigger French, kombuistaaltje* ('cookhouse lingo'), *isikula* ('coolie language'). This contempt often stemmed in part from the feeling that pidgins and creoles were corruptions of 'higher', usually European languages, and in part from attitudes toward the speakers of such languages who were often perceived as semi-savages whose partial acquisition of civilized habits was somehow an affront. Those speakers of creole languages who had access to education were duly convinced that their speech was wrong, and they often tried to make it more similar to the standard. With few exceptions, even linguists thought of pidgin and creole languages as 'aberrant' (Bloomfield 1933:471) if they thought of them at all – that is, as defective and therefore inappropriate as objects of serious study. The analogy seemed to be that broken English, for example, was of as little interest to the linguist as a broken diamond would be to a gemologist.

It is only comparatively recently that linguists have realized that pidgins and creoles are not wrong versions of other languages but rather *new* languages. Their words were largely taken from an older language during a period of linguistic crisis to fill an urgent need for communication. This makes them appear to be deformed versions of that older language. If, however, one examines them as linguistic *systems*, analysing the structure of their phonology, syntax and word formation, it becomes evident that these systems are quite different from those of the language from which they drew their lexicon (their *lexical source* or *base language*). Their systems are so different, in fact, that they can hardly be considered even dialects of their base language. They are new languages, shaped by many of the same linguistic forces that shaped English and other 'proper' languages.

Pidgins and creoles were largely ignored by earlier linguists not only because of this misunderstanding of their identity, but also because of the prevailing notion of what language was and why it was worth studying. In western Europe, this notion had grown out of the Roman tradition of rhetoric: the cultivation and refinement of language for public speaking and writing. During the millennium in which western Europeans retained Latin as their medium of writing, it was a foreign language that had to be taught prescriptively, with definite rules as to what was right and wrong. As western European languages came to replace Latin in serious writing, the idea that there could be only one correct form was transferred to them after an initial period of flux. The rise of modern European states reinforced the idea of a language – a relatively uniform variety used by the educated and ruling classes in speaking and writing – as opposed to a dialect – the uncultivated speech of the masses, changing from one locality to another. The appearance of uniformity of written languages was further reinforced by the advent of printing, which hastened the standardization of orthographic conventions.

Written languages were usually studied for quite practical reasons: access to the learning stored in their literature. Languages were regarded as relatively fixed and stable entities, although dialect studies such as Dante's *De vulgari eloquentia* reflected the understanding that languages change over time as well as space. In 1863 the German linguist, August Schleicher, described languages as 'natural organisms that come into being, develop, age, and die according to laws that are quite independent of man's will' (cited by Arens 1969:259). Such a reification of language is at odds with the more current notion of language as an individual's set of habits for communicating that have largely been determined by his or her social experience, guided by an innate ability to decipher and learn the language habits of other humans. These habits for encoding one's thoughts and perceptions into verbal symbols in order to communicate them can shift to some degree with one's social circumstances; similarly, the most frequent language habits of the aggregate of individuals forming the society can also shift (Hudson 1980). Since individuals use language to communicate not only their meaning but also their social identity, they can shift their habits to signal a shift in their social allegiances; similarly, an entire speech community can shift language habits to signal a more focused or cohesive identity (Le Page and Tabouret-Keller 1985). Such an understanding of language as a dynamic part of the interrelationship between the individual and society has allowed linguists to deal with aspects of language that do not fit a static model of artificial homogeneity based on standardized languages. Thus it is only relatively recently that linguists have begun to study language that appears to lack order: the speech of very young children, foreigners, aphasics and linguistically heterogeneous communities.

The more social view of language began with a nineteenth-century philologist who realized that some Western European languages had not only ancestors but also descendants in the form of creoles. This early creolist was Hugo Schuchardt, a student of Schleicher's who rejected his idea of language as a natural organism that followed natural laws such as regular sound changes, which the Neogrammarians held to be without exception. Schuchardt's interest in challenging this theory led him to the creoles, in which sound changes were often irregular because language mixing had disrupted the internally motivated historical sound changes that might be expected in languages in isolation. Schuchardt came to realize that individuals play an important role in the social process leading to language mixture: 'Old and new forms are distributed . . . within a single dialect according to sex, education, temperament, in short in the most diverse manner' (1885:18, cited by Fought 1982:425). Schuchardt's concern with the social matrix of language change marks him as nearly a century ahead of his time, but his work received only limited attention from his contemporaries. Most linguists continued to consider pidgins and creoles freakish exceptions that were irrelevant to any theory of 'normal' language. Yet Reinecke (1937:6) realized that, because of their very nature, pidgins and creoles could offer important insights into the study of language: 'What some Germans have ambitiously called the sociology of language (*Sprachsoziologie*) is still in its infancy . . . Among the localities most suitable for special studies are those in which the marginal languages are spoken. Changes there have been very rapid and pronounced. Languages can be observed taking form within a man's lifetime.'

Since the establishment of pidgin and creole studies as an academic discipline in the late 1950s and early 1960s, it has become clear that the linguistic forces that shape pidgins and creoles are exceptional only in that they are indeed 'very rapid and pronounced'. Moreover, research on the processes of pidginization and creolization has led to important advances in a number of areas of applied and theoretical linguistics. Studies of creole continua (2.11) led to the development of implicational scaling in linguistics. Labov's work on African American Vernacular English (a semi-creole: see 1.3) laid the foundation for modern sociolinguistics, which has in turn cast new light on language change as being socially motivated. Pidginization and creolization have become important to historical linguists as extreme examples of contact-induced language change which challenge the validity of some traditional assumptions about the genetic relatedness of languages, particularly the family-tree model, and concepts like glottochronology (2.9). This has brought us closer to a method for establishing whether a language was previously creolized, using both linguistic and sociohistorical data (e.g. Rickford 1977,

Mello 1997a). A better understanding of pidginization has also contributed to our understanding of the acquisition of second languages (e.g. Andersen 1983, Romaine 1988), while first-language acquisition theory has been challenged by the concept of the innate bioprogram (2.12) as developed by Bickerton (1981) in the context of creolization theory and having, he claimed, implications for the origin of all languages and even language itself. Finally, work on the role that language universals might play in pidginization (Kay and Sankoff 1974) as well as creolization has focused attention on the very nature of universals, thus contributing to grammatical theory.

The practical value of pidgin and creole studies is also considerable. Because these languages were not traditionally written, their speakers have usually had to learn literacy in a foreign or quasi-foreign language, often the lexical source language. Yet because the restructured variety's separate identity or very existence frequently received no official acknowledgement the (quasi-)foreign language of literacy and instruction was taught as the child's mother tongue – that is, not taught at all. This has caused serious educational problems for the millions who speak creoles in the Caribbean area, and for the scores of millions who speak post-creoles and semi-creoles (1.3) in such countries as the United States, Brazil and Australia. Creolists from Caribbean countries have taken the lead in applying the results of their linguistic research to practical problems in education, and they are not alone. However, there is still an enormous amount of work to be done simply to describe these restructured varieties so educators can understand clearly what the first language of their pupils actually is.

In Papua New Guinea in the South Pacific area, Tok Pisin (an English-based pidgin) is now used in the House of Assembly and in news broadcasts because of its nationwide currency. Scholars of pidgin and creole languages have taken an active and influential role in language planning there. Other creoles are also acquiring such status in the Cape Verde Islands, Guiné-Bissau, the Seychelles, Haiti and the Netherlands Antilles, and creolists from these and other countries are engaged in practical projects from lexicography to the preparation of teaching materials.

1.1 Pidgins

There are problems in defining the most basic concepts in language: *word*, *sentence*, *dialect* and even *language* itself. Our definitions, like our grammars, often leak: they fail to account for the endless variety of reality. Yet a clear understanding of concepts is important: they are the building blocks we use to construct our theories to account for that reality. The definitions below are presented as straightforwardly as possible in an effort to make them intelligible and useful; their problems and weaknesses will be briefly indicated in the ensuing discussion, and it is hoped that the material that follows in the selected case studies in chapter 3 and broader surveys (e.g. Holm 1988–9, vol. II) will make clear the full implications of their problematical aspects.

A *pidgin* is a reduced language that results from extended contact between groups of people with no language in common; it evolves when they need some means of verbal communication, perhaps for trade, but no group learns the native language of any other group for social reasons that may include lack of trust or close contact. Usually those with less power (speakers of *substrate* languages) are more accommodating and use words from the language of those with more power (the *superstrate*), although the meaning, form and use of these words may be influenced by the substrate languages. When dealing with the other groups, the superstrate speakers adopt many of these changes to make themselves more readily understood and no longer try to speak as they do within their own group. They cooperate with the other groups to create a make-shift language to serve their needs, simplifying by dropping unnecessary complications such as inflections (e.g., *two knives* becomes *two knife*) and reducing the number of different words they use, but compensating by extending their meanings or using circumlocutions. By definition the resulting pidgin is restricted to a very limited domain such as trade, and it is no one's native language (e.g. Hymes 1971:15ff.).

Although individuals can simplify and reduce their language on an *ad hoc* basis (for example, New Yorkers buying sunglasses in Lisbon), this results not in a pidgin but a *jargon* with no fixed norms. A pidgin is more stable and has certain norms of meaning, pronunciation and grammar, although there is still variation resulting from the transfer of features from speakers' first languages. It has been suggested that such stabilization requires *tertiary hybridization*, in which two or more groups of substrate speakers adopt the pidgin for communicating with each other (Whinnom 1971). If superstrate speakers become the least important part of this pidgin triangle and close contact in the pidgin is established and maintained between speakers of different substrate languages over an extended period of time, an *expanded pidgin* results: the simpler structure of the earlier pidgin is elaborated to meet more demanding communicative needs (Mühlhäusler 1986:5).

This description distinguishes pidgins from the imperfect speech of foreigners in other social situations, when native speakers of the target language do not try to follow the foreigners' imperfect version of it, and this does not become established or stabilized. However, two further stipulations are needed

5

to distinguish pidgins from other kinds of contact language. First, social distance must be maintained between speakers of the superstrate and the other languages; otherwise, if the substrate speakers so desired, they could eventually acquire enough information about the superstrate language to speak it in a non-pidginized form (Valdman 1978:9–10). Secondly, it must be assumed that the languages in contact are not closely related, in which case *koineization* or a kind of dialect levelling would result (1.3). Finally it should be noted that contact languages can evolve between trading partners of approximately equal power, such as Russenorsk (Broch and Jahr 1984). Such varieties, if they are indeed stable pidgins rather than jargons, tend to draw their vocabulary more equally from both languages – sometimes even to refer to the same things.

The following is a text of Melanesian Pidgin English, Tok Pisin (cf. 'talk pidgin') used in Papua New Guinea. It is from Hall (1966:149):

> naw mi stap rabawl. mi stap lɔng bɪglajn,   mi katim kopra. naw
> Then I   stay Rabaul. I   was in   workgroup, I   cut   copra. Then
>
> wənfɛlə mastər   bilɔng kampani ɛm i-kɪčɪm mi mi kʊk lɔng ɛm
> a   white man from   company he take   me I cook for him
>
> gɛn. mastər king. mi stap. naw ol mastar   i-kɪk
> again. Mister King. I   stay. Then all white men were playing football.
>
> i-   kɪkɪm ɛm. naw lɛg bilɔng ɛm i-swelap.
> They kick   him. Then leg of   him swell up.

One of the most striking features of this text is the absence of complex phrase-level structures such as embedding. However, this recording was made by Margaret Mead over sixty years ago, when Tok Pisin was not yet widely spoken in an expanded form. Today embedded structures such as relative clauses are found not only in the speech of Tok Pisin's native speakers (often children of interethnic marriages growing up in a multi-ethnic urban setting) but also in the speech of adults who are not native speakers (Sankoff and Brown 1976; cf. Tok Pisin text in section 3.12).

1.2 Creoles

A *creole* has a jargon or a pidgin in its ancestry; it is spoken natively by an entire speech community, often one whose ancestors were displaced geographically so that their ties with their original language and sociocultural identity were partly broken. Such social conditions were often the result of slavery. For example, from the seventeenth to the nineteenth century, Africans of diverse ethnolinguistic groups were brought by Europeans to colonies in the New World to work together on sugar plantations. For the first generation of slaves in such a setting, the conditions were often those that produce a pidgin. Normally the Africans had no language in common except what they could learn of the Europeans' language, and access to this was usually very restricted because of the social conditions of slavery. The children born in the New World were usually exposed more to this pidgin – and found it more useful – than their parents' native languages. Since the pidgin was a foreign language for the parents, they probably spoke it less fluently; moreover, they had a more limited vocabulary and were more restricted in their syntactic alternatives. Furthermore, each speaker's mother tongue influenced his or her use of the pidgin in different ways, so there was probably massive linguistic variation while the new speech community was being established. Although it appears that the children were given highly variable and possibly chaotic and incomplete linguistic input, they were somehow able to organize it into the creole that was their native language, an ability which may be an innate characteristic of our species. This process of *creolization* or *nativization* (in which a pidgin acquires native speakers) is still not completely understood, but it is thought to be the opposite of pidginization: a process of expansion rather than reduction (although a pidgin can be expanded without being nativized). For example, creoles have phonological rules (e.g. assimilation) not found in early pidgins. Creole speakers need a vocabulary to cover all aspects of their life, not just one domain like trade; where words were missing, they were provided by various means, such as innovative combinations (e.g. Jamaican Creole *han-migl* 'palm' from English *hand* + *middle*). For many linguists, the most fascinating aspect of this expansion and elaboration was the reorganization of the grammar, ranging from the creation of a coherent verbal system to complex phrase-level structures such as embedding.

There are many questions about the process of creolization that remain unresolved. Is it qualitatively different from the expansion of a pidgin that does not acquire native speakers? How crucial is the uprooting of those who begin the new speech community? There are creoles whose speakers were never uprooted, such as the Portuguese-based varieties in Asia (Holm 1988–9:284–98), although in a sense the Portuguese fathers of the first generations were indeed uprooted and their racially mixed progeny formed not only a new speech community but also a new ethnic group. It has been proposed (Gilman 1979) that the significant difference between creoles and extended pidgins is not nativization, since the designation of what is a 'first' as opposed to a 'primary' language is arbitrary and irrelevant in many multilingual contexts, but rather whether the language is one of ethnic reference. However, this does not decide the issue of whether the differences between creoles and extended pidgins are entirely social rather than linguistic. The restructured Portuguese of Guiné-Bissau is an extended pidgin for most of its speakers in that country, but a language of ethnic reference for a group in neighbouring Senegal; despite recent research (Peck 1988, Kihm 1994, Couto 1996), it is still not clear whether there are any significant linguistic differences between the two. Singler (1984:68) argues that 'The evidence from other West African pidgins and, especially, from Tok Pisin argues for the rejection of the centrality of nativization in the expansion of fledgling pidgins and the recognition of the fundamental commonality of creoles with extended pidgins.' Mühlhäusler (1982:452) found that 'The structural consequences of creolization of Tok Pisin are less dramatic than in the case of creolization of an unstable jargon. Both Sankoff's and my own findings indicate that, instead of radical restructuring, the trends already present in expanded Tok Pisin are carried further in its creolized varieties.'

Some linguists distinguish between the creolization of an extended pidgin, which is both socially and linguistically gradual, and the creolization of an early pidgin or even an unstable jargon, called *early* creolization (Bickerton in Bickerton *et al.* 1984) or *abrupt creolization* (Thomason and Kaufmann 1988). If Caribbean and other creoles did indeed grow out of nativized varieties of unstable pre-pidgin jargons, then the classical definition of a creole as 'any language with a pidgin in its ancestry' is technically wrong. The crucial element would seem to be a variety that has been radically reduced (a jargon or a pidgin) rather than one that has stabilized (a pidgin but not a jargon). However, our knowledge of the earlier stages of particular creoles is usually quite sketchy and based on speculation rather than direct evidence. It may be prudent to reserve judgement on this issue.

There are other major issues regarding creolization that remain unresolved. To what extent did adult speakers of the pidgin or jargon help their creole-speaking children organize their speech? To what extent did these adults draw on their native languages to do this? What was the role of universal trends in the acquisition of a first or second language? These issues will be discussed in detail in chapter 2, and a number of them will be illustrated in chapter 3 in actual case studies.

The following text (Park 1975) is in Ndyuka, an English-based creole spoken in the interior of Suriname in northern South America (see section 3.9):

> Mi be go   a onti   anga wan dagu fu mi.   A be   wan bun
> I   had gone hunting with a   dog of mine. He was a   good
>
> onti   dagu. Da   fa mi waka so, a tapu   wan kapasi   na a
> hunting dog. Then as I   walked so, he cornered an   armadillo in the

olo. A lon go   so, a tyai   wan he kon   na   a   olo.
hole. He ran away so, he brought a   capybara into the hole.

Note that unlike the pidgin text in Tok Pisin, the above creole text has an embedded subordinate clause, 'fa mi waka so'.

Before leaving our discussion of the terms *pidgin* and *creole*, a word about their origin may be of interest. The etymology of *pidgin* is uncertain, and an entire article has been devoted to it (Hancock 1979a). The *Oxford English Dictionary* derives it from the English word *business* as pronounced in Chinese Pidgin English, which was of course used for transacting business. Other possible sources include the Hebrew-derived *pidjom* 'exchange, trade, redemption'; a Chinese pronunciation of the Portuguese word *ocupação* 'business'; or a South Seas pronunciation of English *beach* as *beachee*, from the location where the language was often used (Mühlhäusler 1986:1). Lest we run out of alternatives, I have suggested Portuguese *baixo* 'low,' used to distinguish pidgin Portuguese (*baixo português*) from standard Portuguese in Portugal's Asian empire during the sixteenth and seventeenth centuries. *Baixo português* was in fact the trade language that preceded pidgin English on the coast of China, and there are no more phonological problems (and certainly fewer semantic ones) in deriving *pidgin* from /baišu/ rather than /bɪznɪs/.

The origin of the term *creole* is more certain. Latin *creāre* 'to create' became Portuguese *criar* 'to raise (e.g. a child)', whence the past participle *criado* '(a person) raised; a servant born into one's household'. *Crioulo*, with a diminutive suffix, came to mean an African slave born in the New World in Brazilian usage. The word's meaning was then extended to include Europeans born in the New World. The word finally came to refer to the customs and speech of Africans and Europeans born in the New World. It was later borrowed as Spanish *criollo*, French *créole*, Dutch *creools* and English *creole*.

1.3   Other terms

In addition to those terms in italics introduced in the preceding two sections, there are some other terms to be explained here that will recur in the following chapters. They are largely confined to (or have a particular meaning in) pidgin and creole linguistics (sometimes shortened to *creolistics*; cf. French *créolistique* or German *Kreolistik*). Terms having to do with theory (e.g. *relexification, bioprogram*) are explained in chapter 2 and can be found in the index.

In some areas where the speakers of a creole remain in contact with its lexical donor language (e.g. in Jamaica, where English is the official language), there has been a historical tendency for the creole to drop its most noticeable non-European features, often (but not always) replacing them with European ones – or what are taken to be such. This process of *decreolization* can result in a *continuum* of varieties from those farthest from the superstrate (the *basilect*) to those closest (the *acrolect*), with *mesolectal* or intermediate varieties between them. After a number of generations some varieties lose all but a few vestiges of their *creole features* (those not found in the superstrate) through decreolization, resulting in *post-creole* varieties such as (according to some) African American Vernacular English or Brazilian Vernacular Portuguese. However, others say that these particular varieties are rather the products of *semi-creolization*, which occurs when people with different first languages shift to a typologically distinct target language (itself an amalgam of dialects in contact, including fully restructured varieties) under social circumstances that partially restrict their access to the target language as normally used among native speakers. The processes that produce a semi-creole include *dialect levelling* (see *koineization* below), preserving features that may be archaic or regional in the standard language; *language drift*, following internal tendencies within the source language, such as phonotactic, morphological or syntactic simplification; *imperfect language shift* by the entire population, perpetuating features from ancestral languages or *interlanguages* (see below) in the speech of monolingual descendants; and *borrowing* features from fully pidginized or creolized varieties of the target language spoken by newcomers, or found locally but confined to areas where sociolinguistic conditions were favourable to full restructuring; and in some cases *secondary levelling*, corresponding to the *decreolization* which full creoles can undergo. These processes result in a new variety with a substantial amount of the source language's structure intact, including the inflections not found in basilectal creoles, but also with a significant number of the structural features of a creole, such as those inherited from its substrate or the interlanguages that led to its preceding pidgin (Holm 1998a, 1998b, fc.).

The term *creoloid* has been used for so many different kinds of vaguely creole-like languages that its usefulness has become rather limited; here it will be used only to mean languages that superficially resemble creoles in some way (e.g. by being morphologically simpler than a possible source language), but which, on close examination, appear never to have undergone even partial creolization. This may have been caused by the language shift of an entire speech community, such as the adoption of Old High German by Romance-speaking Jews, producing Yiddish, or the adoption of English by Puerto Ricans in New York, producing Nuyorican. These *xenolects* or slightly foreignized varieties spoken natively, akin to what Siegel (1997) calls *indigenized varieties* that have taken root abroad (such as Singapore English), are not creoles or even semi-creoles because they have undergone significantly less restructuring. Nor are *interlanguages* (intermediate varieties of a target language spoken by foreign learners) to be considered pidgins (since they lack shared norms or stability) or even jargons (since they are targeted toward the native-speaker's variety and are not confined to a particular domain). As mentioned above, contact of closely related languages can result in *koineization*, in which dialect levelling produces some morphological simplification but leaves intact many fairly complex grammatical features common to both language varieties. This is particularly true in new speech communities overseas, as in the case of the closely related languages of northern India that formed new varieties of Hindustani or Bhojpuri in Trinidad, Guyana, Suriname, Mauritius and Fiji, spoken by the descendants of contract labourers (Siegel 1987). There is also a tendency toward simplification in isolated overseas enclave varieties such as Missouri French, particularly when they are used by a dwindling number of speakers who are bilingual in the surrounding language (Maher 1985). However, *language death* or *attrition* can also take place in a language's original location if it gradually loses speakers to an encroaching language and is finally spoken only by bilinguals who lack native-speaker competence in the dying language.

Finally there are *mixed languages* that are none of the above, both in the trivial sense that practically all languages are mixed to some degree by contact with other languages and also in a miscellaneous category of very mixed languages whose genesis had to be quite different from that of pidgins or creoles. For example, there is the strange case of Mbugu or Ma'a in Tanzania, a Cushitic language that acquired Bantu grammar, apparently under duress (Goodman 1971, Thomason 1997a). Then there is Anglo-Romani: basically English syntax, phonology and function words holding together Romani or Gypsy lexical items, used principally between English-speaking Gypsies in the presence of English-speaking non-Gypsies in order to maintain secrecy (Hancock 1984). Another case of language mixing is Michif, spoken on the Turtle Mountain Indian reservation in North Dakota in the United States (Bakker and Papen 1997). It consists largely of perfectly formed Cree verb phrases and perfectly formed French noun phrases, e.g. 'Nkii-cihtaan dans la ligne', literally 'I-PAST-go to the-FEMININE state-line' (Richard Rhodes p.c.). Thomason (1984) hypothesizes that Michif was created by racially mixed bilinguals (cf. French *métis* 'half-breed', whence *Michif*) in order to assert a social identity distinct from that of speakers of either French or Cree. Such *bilingual mixtures* (Thomason 1997c) are said to result from *language intertwining* (Bakker and Muysken 1994).

This inventory of non-pidgins and non-creoles is by no means exhaustive, but it helps to define the subject at hand by specifying what pidgins and creoles are not.

1.4 Scope of the book

As an introduction to the study of pidgin and creole languages, the present work attempts to bring together the most important information relating to this field as objectively as possible, avoiding tendentiousness in matters of theory. However, decisions as to what data are important enough to be included, even before any question of their interpretation, always imply a theoretical position. To be explicit, this book reflects the belief that while universal tendencies in adult second-language acquisition carried over into pidginization and creolization (2.12) play a role in shaping creole languages (e.g. the nearly complete reliance on free rather than inflectional morphemes to convey grammatical information), a significant number of the features in a creole language that are not attributable to its superstrate can be traced to parallel features in its substrate languages. Together with creole-internal innovations, borrowings from adstrate languages (those which are neither superstrate nor substrate) and the convergence of all or some of the above, these account for the features that distinguish creoles from their lexical source languages.

This moderate substratist position (2.13) has influenced the choice of which languages provide most of the linguistic features compared in chapters 4 to 6. These are the *Atlantic creoles*, a term first applied to the English-based creoles of the Caribbean area and coastal West Africa (Hancock 1969) and later extended to include the other creoles in these areas, those whose lexicons are based on Portuguese, Spanish, Dutch and French. The Atlantic creoles share many structural features on all linguistic levels that are not found in their European lexical source languages, as chapters 4 to 6 will demonstrate. Many of these features can be attributed to the substratum of African languages that these creoles share. To highlight this, the features of Atlantic creoles of different lexical bases (particularly Angolar CP, Papiamentu CS, Negerhollands CD, Haitian CF and Jamaican CE) are contrasted in chapter 6 with those of two non-Atlantic varieties (Tok Pisin and Nubi Arabic).

It might be asked why the comparison of linguistic features draws mainly on the Atlantic creoles rather than more equally on all creoles and pidgins. The main reason is that it has been demonstrated (e.g. Holm 1988–9) that the Atlantic creoles form a natural group with many comparable features because of similarities in their genesis and development. However, no claim is being made that their common features are necessarily traits of all creoles (the fundamental flaw in the work of extreme universalists) – much less traits of all pidgins.

The development of the discipline has imposed a logical order in comparative work. Not until a number of individual varieties had been adequately described could we start comparing varieties in the same lexical groups and not until comparative studies within lexical groups had been done could we start comparative work for larger groupings. The present work builds on the cross-lexical-base comparative work on the Atlantic creoles, comparing the structure of that group with that of other varieties. The agenda in pidgin and creole studies is still a long and demanding one. As contact linguistics increasingly influences the central concerns of general linguistics, the next generations do not need to fear a dearth of important, fascinating research yet to be done.

Having identified as precisely as is possible at this point what pidgin and creole languages are, we will now look at how they came to be studied and the problems they have posed for linguistic theory.

2
The development of theory

2.0 Introduction

This chapter traces the development of the major ideas that have shaped the study of pidgin and creole languages. It also gives an overview of the history of the discipline itself, but its primary objective is to provide a better understanding of the climate of ideas in which the main theoretical advances were made.

2.1 Before European expansion

Although most of the known pidgin and creole languages arose after western Europeans began establishing overseas colonies in the fifteenth century, there is ample reason to believe that more existed in earlier times than the two that have been documented: Lingua Franca and Pidgin Arabic (see below). Indeed, language contact seems likely to be nearly as old as language itself. However, languages have not been recorded in writing until the last few millennia and mixed languages have usually been among the last to be written down. Zyhlarz (1932–3) considered the language of ancient Egypt, first recorded in hieroglyphs in the third millennium BC, to have grown out of a trade language, i.e. a pidgin that developed among several Afro-Asiatic languages which came into contact in the Nile valley. If this is the case, it was essentially a creole language (Reinecke *et al.* 1975:53). In any case the languages of ancient empires from China to Sumer expanded along with their military, commercial and cultural influence and it is quite likely that this happened via pidginized varieties, although no known records of such speech remain. In classical Greek drama, foreigners are sometimes represented as speaking broken Greek (Hall 1966:3); Hesseling (1928) explained the peculiar characteristics of the Tsakonian dialect of Greek by postulating that it had been creolized (Muysken and Meijer 1979:ix). It seems probable that contact varieties – and possibly fairly stable pidgins – accompanied the colonial expansion of not only the Greeks but also the Phoenicians, Carthaginians and Romans. Hancock (1977) speculated about the possible restructuring of trade languages such as that used in Britain during Roman times, but these remain undocumented and the few references to them in old writings are unclear. There are also reports of a simplified Latin used by Jewish traders (Whinnom 1977:304), but again there are no extant specimens.

The earliest known record of any pidgin is a brief text of restructured Arabic apparently used along a trade route in central Mauritania during the eleventh century (Thomason and Elgibali 1986). In a manuscript completed in 1068 AD, the geographer al-Bakri cites a traveller's complaint that in the town of Maridi 'The Blacks have mutilated our beautiful language and spoiled its eloquence with their twisted tongues', followed by a ten-sentence sample of their speech. The version of the manuscript containing this passage was uncovered by Elgibali in a library in Egypt in 1982.

Lingua Franca, a pidgin with a lexicon drawn mainly from the southern Romance languages, was used along the southern and eastern coasts of the Mediterranean from the time of the Crusades until the beginning of the twentieth century for communication among Europeans, Arabs, Turks and others (Schuchardt 1909). It may already have been in use at the time the Maridi Arabic text was recorded, but it was not documented until later. Around 1204 a version of the Apostles' Creed in a pidginized Latin resembling later Lingua Franca was recorded in Constantinople (Kahane *et al.* 1958). The first known text of what is clearly Lingua Franca was written in Djerba, Tunisia, in 1353 (Grion 1891, Whinnom 1977:306).

The question has arisen whether contact-induced restructuring may have played a role in the development of early Germanic languages (Feist 1932) and modern European languages. The Romance languages that grew out of Latin offer no clear evidence of prior creolization: the basic structure of their linguistic systems indicates no abrupt break with that of Latin. Jespersen (1922:236) found that 'no cataclysm such as that through which English has become Beach-la-mar need on any account be invoked to explain the perfectly natural change from Latin to Old French and from Old French to modern French'. While there is evidence to suggest language contact and mixture, such as the front rounded vowels found in French and Germanic languages but not in Latin, such innovations may also have resulted from language-internal processes rather than borrowing.

Such considerations also cast light on the question of the possible role that creolization may have played in the emergence of Middle English, which evolved after the Norman French conquered England's Anglo-Saxon-speaking inhabitants in the eleventh century. The massive loss of inflectional endings and other features of Middle English morphosyntax suggest the profound impact of language contact. Adam (1883:10) compared Middle English to the

Caribbean creoles when he suggested that the speakers of African substrate languages 'mounted a resistance comparable in some measure to that of the Anglo-Saxons who, after the Norman conquest, made their grammar and phonology prevail over that of their conquerors' despite the massive borrowing of French vocabulary into Middle English. However, most linguists (e.g. Domingue 1977, Thomason and Kaufman 1988) stop short of claiming that Middle English resulted from creolization. The similarities of the sociolinguistic situation in England during this period and that in the Caribbean later on are outweighed by the differences: the English peasants always had a means of communicating among themselves without recourse to a pidgin, although communication between them and their French overlords may well have involved pidginized varieties of either Anglo-Saxon or Norman French during the initial period of contact. Still, the similarity of the linguistic outcome of this situation and that in the Caribbean led an early creolist to speculate that English might have already been 'thoroughly creolized in its grammar' (Van Name 1869–70:125).

2.2 Early European expansion

The earliest known text of a restructured variety of a European language spoken by sub-Saharan Africans is in a Portuguese poem published in 1516 (Teyssier 1959). Naro (1978) identifies this as a pidgin, although it may have been a less stable variety of foreigners' Portuguese. The earliest known record of the Spanish word *criollo* (whence *creole*) is in a book published in 1590 (Corominas 1967:178) and translated into English in 1604: 'Some Crollos [*sic*], for so they call the Spaniards borne at the Indies' (*Oxford English Dictionary*). The meaning of the word was extended to both whites and blacks born in the New World or other colonies, and eventually came to refer to their customs and language. The first known use of the word in the latter meaning is in the 1685 diary of the French navigator Le Courbe, who used the term *langue créole* for a restructured variety of Portuguese used by Senegalese traders: 'These Senegalese, besides the language of the country, also speak a certain jargon which resembles but little the Portuguese language and which is called the creole language like the Lingua Franca of the Mediterranean Sea' (cited by Chaudenson 1979:9). John Barbot, reporting a voyage completed in 1682, referred to Africans' use of 'Lingua Franca or broken Portuguese' (cited by Dillard 1979:264).

This early period of commercial and colonial expansion brought Europeans into contact with a great number of new languages completely unrelated to their own, a fact which had an important impact on the course of philology by the eighteenth century. During the early period of contact, however, these languages were the object of interest and study mostly for their practical use in trade and in establishing outposts and colonies as well as in spreading Christianity. Lists of words and phrases were collected from the time of the first explorers, and later travellers sometimes noted the contact languages that were emerging around them. In 1640 Jacques Bouton, a Frenchman in Martinique, noted that the Carib Indians there used a jargon of French mixed with Spanish, English and Dutch, and he recorded a sample. Not long afterwards Père Chévillard, a priest on the same island, noted that the Africans were 'attentive observers who rapidly familiarized themselves with the language of the European, which was purposely corrupted to facilitate its comprehension' (from a 1659 document cited by Goodman 1964:104). Pierre Pelleprat, a contemporary, wrote that the changes in the language were initiated by the Africans and then repeated by the Europeans: 'We adjust to their way of talking, which is usually with the infinitive of the verb, for example *moi prier Dieu* ["I prayed to God"]' (1655, cited by Goodman 1964:105).

The earliest known attestation of any creole language is from Martinique, dated 1671 (Carden *et al.* 1990, published in McWhorter 1998:800). It includes unequivocal features of modern Caribbean Creole French such as the preverbal anterior marker *té* and the post-nominal determiner *là*:

> Moi té   tini   peur bête   là
> I   ANT have fear   animal DET

The earliest known Portuguese creole text is a 33-sentence conversation in Malayo-Portuguese (reproduced in part in Holm 1988–9:294–5) published in 1692 by Georg Meister, a German who had been in the East Indies with the Dutch. His spelling reflects his Thuringian dialect of German and a smattering of Latin and French, but no knowledge of European Portuguese. As Hancock (1977:277) has noted: 'In the few instances where the early forms of modern creoles have been recorded, it appears to have been by speakers of languages lexically unrelated to them.' Such speakers were apparently more willing to deal with the creoles as autonomous systems, and their representation of creole sounds was usually less obscured by the orthography of the lexical source language.

The earliest known recordings of a North American pidgin are also from this period. Samples of Delaware Jargon were collected by a Swede, Campanius Holm, in New Sweden in the 1640s, and the Englishman William Penn published some phrases in 1683 (Thomason 1980). The translation of the text published by Thomas (1698) reflects the English of the period: '*Hitah ta-koman* "Friend, from whence com'st?"'

2.3 The eighteenth century

During the eighteenth century the Caribbean creoles came to be recognized as varieties that were clearly distinguishable from their European lexical source languages, at least on a practical level by the Europeans who came into regular contact with them. It gradually became clear that somehow foreigners' speech ('broken English', for example) had taken root and become the local language of blacks, influencing the speech of local whites as well. Another attestation of creole French is found in Père Labat's *Nouveau voyage aux Iles de l'Amérique, 1693–1705*, in which a black woman on Martinique is quoted accusing a certain man of being the father of her child: 'Toi papa li' 'You are its father' (cited by Goodman 1964:106). This was followed in 1718 by the earliest known text of an English-based creole, Sranan, in J. D. Herlein's *Beschryvinge van de volks-plantinge Zuriname* (reproduced in Rens 1953:142):

Oudy.	Howdy.
Oe fasje joe tem?	How fashion you stand?
My bon.	Me good.
Jou bon toe?	You good too?
Ay.	Aye.

The spread of Britain's commercial empire during this period led to the emergence of restructured varieties of English in Africa and Asia as well. The first published reference to a local West African variety of English is in Francis Moore's 1734 *Travels into the inland parts of Africa*: 'The English have in the River Gambia much corrupted the English language, by Words or Literal Translations from the Portuguese or Mundingoes' (p. 294; cited by Hancock 1969:13). In his book, *A voyage to the East Indies in 1747 and 1748*, C. F. Noble gave the first report of a 'broken and mixed dialect of English and Portuguese' in China (p. 244, cited by Bauer 1975:96).

The first serious study of creole languages began in the 1730s when Moravian missionaries were sent to convert the slaves on St Thomas (1732) and in Suriname (1735). The Church of the United Brethren, often called the Moravian Church because of its origins in Czech Protestantism under Hus, was granted lands in Herrnhut, Saxony, in 1722 under the patronage of Count Nikolaus von Zinzendorf. On attending the coronation of Christian VI of Denmark in 1731, Zinzendorf met an old slave named Andres from St Thomas in the Danish West Indies. Deeply moved by the slave's account of the miserable existence of his people and their desire to become Christians, the count organized a Moravian mission to St Thomas and visited the island himself in 1739 to reassure the hostile slave owners regarding the intentions of the missionaries (Stein 1986a). At first the German-speaking missionaries attempted to use Dutch with the slaves, who spoke Negerhollands, a Dutch-based creole (section 3.6). When this proved unsuccessful, they began learning Negerhollands, which they called *carriols* in the early years (cf. Dutch *creools*, apparently with an epenthetic vowel), one of the earliest known uses of the word referring to a West Indian language. The Moravians were also among the first to treat a creole as an autonomous language to be studied and written as a linguistic system independent of its lexical donor language. They taught the slaves to read and write in the creole, leading to a series of remarkable letters such as the count's farewell address to them and their response (Zinzendorf 1742). The ensuing literature, including grammars, dictionaries and translations of the gospels as well as original sermons and songs (Stein 1986b), has been preserved in the archives in Herrnhut. Although influenced by the second-language version of the creole spoken by the missionaries, this literature, particularly the letters written by the slaves, offers invaluable insights into the structure of the creole as used by the first generations of its speakers. For example, the earliest letters from the 1740s show no evidence of the creole's preverbal markers *le* and *ka* (6.1.3) or the plural marker *sender* (6.4.2), and there is alternation of Dutch *ik* and Negerhollands *mi* for 'I', suggesting that the creole's structure was not yet stable (Stein 1986a:9). These early texts have now been published (van Rossem and van der Voort 1996).

The first published grammar of any creole language was Jochum Melchor Magens' *Grammatica over det Creolske sprog, som bruges paa de trende Danske Eilande, St. Croix, St. Thomas og St. Jans i Amerika* (Copenhagen, 1770). Writing for the competing Danish Lutheran missionaries, Magens was a native speaker of the acrolectal (1.3) creole spoken by whites, and he had studied philology in Denmark. His work contained a 24-page grammar on a Latin model and 43 pages of dialogue translated into Danish, as well as 3 pages of proverbs.

In 1777 the Moravian missionary Christian Oldendorp published a history of the mission containing a dozen pages on the creole. However, Stein (1986b) and Gilbert (1986b) have examined the original manuscript version, which contains 53 pages of grammatical and sociolinguistic information as well as a 189-page German–Negerhollands dictionary and 13 pages of texts. Oldendorp's comments on the use of European languages in the West Indies merit quotation in full for the light they throw on the thinking of this period:

> In the West Indies, the European languages tend to deviate to an extreme extent. For the most part, only those people who learned to speak them in Europe can talk the pure European form of the language. On the other hand, the people who were born here – the

Crioles – do not speak the same kind of language. They change it more or less; they employ words taken from elsewhere, arising from the collision of the people of many nations. They have lived together for a long time, or at least have been in constant contact, so that some features of their languages have been passed from one to the other . . . Hence, there is a criole English, a criole French, and so on. Blacks in these places speak Criole, too. Except for those who have learned the European languages in their youth, from whites for the most part, Blacks generally corrupt the European languages still more, due to their Guinea dialect and to the words which they mix in with their speech. (Oldendorp ms., translated by Gilbert 1986b)

Thus Oldendorp considered all European languages spoken natively by West Indians to have been influenced by the high degree of language contact in the Caribbean area. He attributed the even greater divergence of the speech of blacks from the standard languages to the influence of their African languages. It is clear from the following that he considered creole to be 'the language of blacks' and understood how it was acquired by whites: 'Since the white children are taken care of by black women and grow up among black children, they first learn creole, or the language of blacks, and sometimes they never learn another properly. However, this language is spoken better [*feiner*] by the whites than the blacks' (Oldendorp 1777, quoted by Stein 1984:92). The Moravians did similar work on two varieties of creole English in Suriname: Sranan, spoken on the coast, and Saramaccan, spoken in the interior (Arends and Perl 1995). Besides their translations of the Bible from the 1770s onwards, C. L. Schumann wrote a 55-page manuscript dictionary of Saramaccan in 1778 (reproduced in Schuchardt 1914a) and a 135-page manuscript dictionary of Sranan in 1783 (reproduced in Kramp 1983). Like Oldendorp, Schumann distinguished between the creole as spoken by whites and by blacks. In 1778 Pieter van Dyk published a 112-page book on the 'Bastert Engels' of Suriname, with parallel columns in Sranan and Dutch – the first book published on a creolized variety of English. As on St Thomas, the Moravians developed a literary variety of the creole for translating the scriptures. Moreover, the German speakers' errors in phonology and syntax were often not corrected but rather imitated by the native speakers of the creole, laying the foundations for a special variety of Church Creole which is still used on solemn occasions (Voorhoeve 1971).

In 1780 the Dutch published the first grammar and dictionary of Malayo-Portuguese – the earliest such work on any variety of restructured Portuguese (Whinnom 1965:513). The earliest published text of Haitian Creole French appears in a 1785 book describing the colony, written by a Swiss traveller, Justin Girod-Chantrans (Valdman 1978:98). It was followed by a guide book to Haiti (Ducoeurjoly 1802) with 24 pages of conversations in Creole along with the first French–Creole vocabulary, 72 pages in length, intended for travellers.

It should be remembered that at this time the highly inflected grammars of Greek and Latin were still held up as ideals against which the grammars of other languages were measured – and usually found deficient. The standard varieties of European languages were still being codified: uniformity, logic and consistency were prized by eighteenth-century neoclassicists, and this was reflected in the increasing rigidity of orthography and the growing authority accorded dictionaries and grammars. At the same time philosophers of language marvelled at the diversity of the languages that Europeans were coming into contact with around the globe, a diversity that challenged the traditional monogenetic theory of the common origin of all languages. The growing British colonial involvement in India spurred an interest in Hindi and the great work of the Sanskrit scholar Panini. As Robins (1967:134) remarks:

> If any single year can, albeit artificially, be taken to mark the start of the contemporary world of linguistic science, it is the year 1786 . . .
> [when] Sir William Jones of the East India Company read his famous paper to the Royal Asiatic Society in Calcutta, wherein he established beyond doubt the historical kinship of Sanskrit, the classical language of India, with Latin, Greek, and the Germanic languages.

This discovery led to the comparative historical work on the interrelationship of the Indo-European languages which dominated European philology for so much of the following century. Moreover, Jones raised the question of the role of language contact in language change: 'both the Gothick and the Celtick, though blended with a different idiom, had the same origin with the Sanscrit' (quoted by Hancock 1977:277).

2.4 The early nineteenth century

While the Moravians continued their work in the Caribbean, other missionaries took up the study of other creole languages. Ceylon became British in 1796, and in 1818 the Wesleyan Mission Press began publishing works in Indo-Portuguese. In 1825 a short catechism was published in Papiamentu, beginning the strongest and longest literary tradition of any creole language. In 1829 the British and Foreign Bible Society in London published the first complete edition of *Da Njoe Testament* in Sranan Creole English for the Moravians in Suriname. The founder of an Edinburgh newspaper attacked the translation and rebuked the Moravians for 'putting the broken English of the Negroes . . . into a written and permanent form', which would 'embody their barbarous, mixed, imperfect phrase in the pages of schoolbooks' (quoted by Reinecke 1983). While he would approve the translation of the Bible into 'the spoken [native] language of a district, however defective and uncouth', he opposed its translation into 'the blundering phraseology of foreigners when attempting to leave off their original tongue, and to adopt that which is used by the people among whom they have come to dwell . . . Why are not the children taught English?' The philologist William Greenfield replied in a monograph (1830), outlining the history of Sranan and emphasizing that it was an established and rule-governed language heavily influenced by Dutch: 'it is obvious that it can no longer be denominated "broken English" or English attempted to be spoken by the Negroes endeavouring to leave off their own tongue' (17). He went on to argue for the autonomy of Sranan, using the paradigms of traditional grammar to show how English, Sranan and Dutch handle articles and nouns, pronouns, verbs and the comparison of adjectives. He concluded: 'Negro-English differs as much from the English and Dutch as these languages do from each other' (32). Since a critic had suggested that a comparison with creole Dutch would prove that Sranan was in fact English, Greenfield provided parallel columns of the first chapter of the Gospel of John in Sranan, English, Dutch and Negerhollands Creole Dutch – the first published comparison of creole languages. He went on to stress that the origin of Sranan was not so different from that of languages like English, once despised as 'a barbarous jargon neither good French nor pure Saxon' (50–1): 'The process by which they have been framed is precisely that which is presented by the Negro-English, i.e. by corruption and inter-mixture, and the subsequent invention of new terms, by compounding or otherwise changing those already existing' (48–9). He dismissed the idea that Sranan had resulted from the inferior ability of Africans to learn English: 'The human mind is the same in every clime; and accordingly we find nearly the same process adopted in the formation of language in every country. The Negroes have been proved to be in no degree inferior to other nations in solidity of judgment or fertility of imagination' (51).

Unfortunately Greenfield's monograph was soon forgotten, in part be-cause his ideas on both language and race were much ahead of their time. Despite agitation for the abolition of slavery in Britain and elsewhere, many clung to the racist belief that the intelligence of blacks was inferior and that this justified their 'protection' under that institution. With no understanding of the social factors determining language acquisition in cases of pidginization and creolization, many white speakers of the lexical source languages took the divergences they heard in the creoles as proof of the blacks' incapacity to learn languages properly. This attitude was reinforced by more general attitudes toward language: 'one notices from Grimm on a definite admiration for flexional morphology' (Robins 1967:181). For example, in the nineteenth century, declensions were artificially preserved in written Dutch: 'Is not inflection the mark of a civilized language and its loss a sign of decadence?' (Brachin 1985:34). The lack of such inflections in many African languages, about which European scholars still knew relatively little, was accepted as evidence of their primitive state of development. Describing Guinea Creole Portuguese, the French military officer Bertrand-Bocandé (1849:73) remarked:

> It is clear that people used to expressing themselves with a rather simple language cannot easily elevate their intelligence to the genius of a European language. When they were in contact with the Portuguese and forced to communicate with them speaking the same language, it was necessary that the varied expressions acquired during so many centuries of civilization dropped their perfection to adapt to ideas being born and to barbarous forms of language of half-savage peoples. (Cited in English by Meijer and Muysken 1977:22)

Regrettably it cannot be claimed that such notions are no longer current, although they are more seldom encountered in print. Western thought has long rested on some basic racist assumptions and these have shaped the thinking of linguists as well as others. The 'thick lips and thick minds' theory of the origin of black speech varieties (Dillard 1972:11) has a long history, even in the work of creolists who were enlightened for their times. Wullschlägel (1856:viii) explained the phonological differences between Sranan words and their English etyma as the result of 'the Negroes . . . trying to adapt them to their speech organs'. Even Schuchardt (1887:138) suggested that the preference for labial sounds in Cape Verdean Creole Portuguese could be explained by 'the well developed lips of the Negroes', and Saint-Quentin (1872:lviii) referred to their 'limited intelligence'. As late as 1913 van Ginneken asserted that creoles maintained the 'inner form' of African languages because blacks, no matter how acculturated they might appear to be to European ways, could never give up their 'Negro way of thinking [negergedachten]' (p. 245).

In the early nineteenth century the Romantic movement placed a high value on everything connected with 'the people'; in Europe this helped focus linguistic attention on the dialects of rural peasants (Robins 1967:186), but overseas it seems to have done little to foster interest in colonial creoles until, possibly, the latter part of the century. It was a French priest, l'Abbé Goux, who published the first systematic treatment of a French-based creole in 1842 (Goodman 1964:109), a fourteen-page description of Lesser Antillean Creole attached to a *Catéchisme en langue créole*. Although a fable in Mauritian

Creole had appeared in an 1818 travelogue, it was not until 1846 that literature in French-based creoles really began with *Les Bambous*, a verse adaptation of some of La Fontaine's fables by François Marbot, a native of Martinique (Goodman 1964:108). The first detailed grammar of a French-based creole was a book on the variety spoken in Trinidad (Thomas 1869), written by a school teacher and clergyman who lived on that island but who may not have been a native speaker (Goodman 1964:109). Besides the grammar, the book includes a collection of idioms, proverbs and short texts. The first study of the creole of French Guiana was by a native speaker, Auguste de Saint-Quentin (1872). Goodman (1964:110) notes that 'His treatment of the grammar is concise and almost as lucid and thorough as that of the phonology, describing it in terms of its own structure without gratuitous references to standard French.' The 1880s brought a number of works on the creole French dialects, notably those of Mauritius (Baissac 1880) and Louisiana (Mercier 1880, Fortier 1885).

This period also brought the first longer descriptions of two English-based creoles: a 68-page *Kurzgefasste Neger-Englische Grammatik* on Sranan (Anonymous 1854; by H. R. Wullschlägel according to Schuchardt (1980:102)) and substantial dictionaries of the same language (Focke 1855 and Wullschlägel 1856), as well as a study of Jamaican Creole (Russell 1868), the first description of any West Indian variety of Creole English. This period also brought the first dictionary of Papiamentu (van Ewijk 1875), which – like the Sranan dictionaries – was needed for quite practical reasons by Dutch speakers.

2.5 Van Name

Addison Van Name's 'Contributions to creole grammar' (1869–70) has been said to represent the beginning of the scientific study of creole languages (Stolz 1986:14). It is the first comparative study of creoles from all four lexical bases found in the Caribbean (French, Spanish, Dutch, English), based on earlier studies (e.g. Oldendorp 1777, Wullschlägel 1856, Thomas 1869) and work with informants. Van Name, a librarian at Yale University, was apparently trained in philology and familiar with a number of European languages. His description of the four lexical groups in some forty pages is remarkably clear, compact and well informed. Reinecke (1937:16) found Van Name's observations 'much more sound than many written later'; indeed, one is hard put to think of a single recent article that would serve as a better introduction to comparative creole studies.

Van Name was the first to remark on a number of syntactic features common to many Caribbean creoles, e.g. the use of the third person plural pronoun to indicate plurality (cf. section 6.4.2), the serial use of the verb meaning 'give' (6.3.1) or the use of the word for 'body' as a quasi-reflexive pronoun (6.4.5). He also noted lexical similarities such as the words for 'it has' meaning 'there is' (cf. 6.2.3), or those for 'too much' meaning 'very', as well as phonological similarities such as the regressive nasalization of vowels (cf. 5.4). Van Name had a surprisingly good feel for the languages and questioned the authenticity of the passive construction in Negerhollands (p. 163; cf. 4.3.2). Yet in some respects he was rather naive; he thought that the French 'Creole has in some cases recovered a final consonant, especially *t*' (p. 131 – actually an archaic or regional feature; cf. 4.2.1) and that Papiamentu Creole Spanish 'dipthongs [*sic*] *ie* and *ue* usually return to *e* and *o*, their Latin originals' (p. 150 – actually Portuguese influence).

The more general statements that Van Name made about the origin of the creoles (pp. 123–6) are few but provocative, frequently touching on issues that are still being debated. It is clear that he understood creolization to have been preceded by pidginization: 'The language spoken by the first generation of blacks was a broken French or Spanish, as the case might be, which, in the course of time, developed into a well defined Creole' (p. 124). Gilbert (1986a:17) has asserted that the 'distinction between pidgins and creoles [was] proposed by Robert Hall in 1966', but it should be borne in mind that the first attested English use of the word *pigeon* in the sense of 'pidgin' was in 1859, not long before Van Name's article. Although the word with its current linguistic meaning was apparently not known to him, its referent clearly was, as was its relationship to creolization. Van Name understood the pidginization/ creolization process to represent accelerated language change:

> The changes which [creoles] have passed through are not essentially different in kind, and hardly greater in extent than those, for instance, which separate the French from the Latin, but from the greater violence of the forces at work they have been far more rapid . . . here two or three generations have sufficed for a complete transformation.
> (1869–70:123)

It is precisely this unresolved relationship of creolization to other kinds of language change that began attracting historical linguists to creole studies in the 1980s (e.g. Boretzky 1983, Thomason and Kaufman 1988). Regarding the actual kinds of changes that creolization causes, Van Name wrote: 'The process has to be sure been mainly, but not altogether, one of decay; the extent of the loss has made some compensation necessary, and we find, if not many new formations, numerous instances of old material put to new uses' (1869–70:123). While Van Name's predecessors saw creoles as the result of the reduction of the lexical source language, Van Name realized that they were also the products of innovation and restructuring. He also grasped the importance of certain social factors in creolization:

> Of the causes which have contributed to the formation of these dialects the chief are: first, the mature age of the slaves, who were brought from Africa at a time of life when the vocal organs are no longer flexible, and when the intellectual effort necessary for the mastery of a new language is even under the most favorable circumstances very considerable and here quite out of the question; secondly, the fact that they constituted the great body of the population, the whites being in a minority seldom as large as one-fourth. (124)

Regarding the genetic relationship of the creoles, he wrote:

> It is scarcely necessary to remark that these languages are not of mixed blood, half African and half European, for languages do not mingle so readily as races. Even in the Creole vocabularies, the proportion of African words is very small . . . Still more remote must be the influence of African on Creole grammar. It is rather in the phonetic structure of the Creole, in the dislike of an accumulation of consonants, the preference, especially marked in the Negro English of Surinam, for a final vowel, that such influence may with more likelihood be traced.
>
> (124)

This appears to be the first salvo in a battle that is not yet over – whether the Atlantic creoles are European or African languages – the most extreme positions on which were taken by Faine (1936) and Sylvain (1936) respectively. Van Name's position is similar to that of Hall *et al.* (1953), who considered Haitian Creole French to be genetically derived from French rather than African languages, although Hall did not deny influence from the latter. Moreover, Van Name held the belief, now shared only by Bickerton (1981:121ff.) that a creole could differ genetically on different linguistic levels, e.g. having African traits on the levels of phonology and lexicon, but not syntax. Van Name's position appears to have been based on his impressions of what *seemed* African rather than firm knowledge of African languages. He also went by logic: 'In this tendency to nasalization in the French creoles, we may perhaps recognize an African trait, since it has found its way into the Spanish, English and Dutch Creole' (129). However, he did not extend this logic to identifying as African those syntactic features that are found throughout the creoles but not in their European lexical source languages (e.g. the third person plural pronoun used to mark plurality). Van Name repeatedly comments on features such as vowel harmony, without indicating any awareness of parallels in African languages: 'Some Papiamentu sound changes are apparently due to attraction by an accented vowel in a preceding or following syllable; thus *aña (año), caya (calle), bichi (bicho), bini (venir)'* (p. 150). Finally, it should be noted that Van Name was probably the first linguist to quantify variable features: he reported (p. 135) that French creole nouns agglutinated the final *-s* of French plural articles (e.g. *zami* 'friend' from *les amis*) at a rate varying from creole to creole, e.g. 10 to 1 (40 out of 44 occurrences) in Ducoeurjoly's text of Haitian, but 2 to 1 in Trinidadian.

2.6 Schuchardt and his contemporaries

Creole studies blossomed in the 1880s, when there was a surge in the study of individual varieties, e.g. the studies of French creoles mentioned above, and the first studies of African American Vernacular English (Harrison 1884) and West African Pidgin English (Grade 1889), as well as a number of Portuguese-based creoles (Coelho 1880–6). More importantly, there was a surge in thinking about theoretical problems connected with the origin of creole languages, leading to the emergence of two theories which still dominate debate in the field, that of the universalists and that of the substratists.

Adolpho Coelho was a Portuguese philologist who was a member of the Geographical Society of Lisbon, founded in 1878 just before the partitioning of Africa, a time of heightened interest in Portugal's overseas colonies. The society sponsored exploratory expeditions to the colonies and published a bulletin of its findings. These included Coelho's articles, printed between 1880 and 1886, about the varieties of creole Portuguese spoken in some of the colonies. Although much of the material came from the Cape Verde Islands, it included samples of the folk speech of São Tomé, Goa, Macao and even independent Brazil, sent to him by correspondents or gleaned from other writings. Coelho's efforts led to a number of further studies of these varieties by other Portuguese philologists over the next fifty years, also done in the traditional manner of European dialectology of the period. However, Coelho is mainly remembered as the first to articulate a theoretical position on the origin of creoles which came to be called the universalist theory:

> The Romance and creole dialects, Indo-Portuguese and all the similar formations represent the first stage or stages in the acquisition of a foreign language by a people that speaks or spoke another . . . They owe their origin to the operation of psychological or physiological laws that are everywhere the same, and not to the influence of the former languages of the peoples among whom these dialects are found.
>
> (1880–6:193, 195)

In other words, Coelho attributed the present form of the creoles to certain universal tendencies in second language learning by adults (e.g. simplification) rather than to the influence of substrate languages. He illustrated this with the following:

> For example, one seeks in vain in Indo-Portuguese any influence from Tamil or Sinhalese. The formation of the plural by reduplication of the singular in the Macao dialect could be attributed to Chinese influence, but this process is so basic that little can be established by it. In the dialect of the island of Sant' Iago *muito muito* is the superlative.
>
> (1880–6)

Coelho supported his hypothesis by pointing to certain widespread features such as the preverbal progressive marker *ta* and a number of common lexical items like *papia* 'speak' and *misti* 'need' (found in Papiamentu and a number of Portuguese-based creoles) or the preverbal anterior marker *te* (found in both Haitian and Louisiana Creole French). Meijer and Muysken (1977:25) conclude that 'His analysis was not detailed enough, however, to warrant calling him a major precursor of modern creole studies', but Gilbert (1986a:16) sees the ideas 'first hinted at by Coelho appearing in modern form in Bickerton's LBH [Language Bioprogram Hypothesis]' (section 2.12).

   Coelho's extreme universalist position (allowing for no substrate influence) was diametrically opposed to the extreme substratist position proposed in 1883 by the French philologist Lucien Adam (Kihm 1984). Adam wrote *Les idiomes négro-aryen et maléo-aryen* after serving as a magistrate for three years in French Guiana; he compared its creole to that of Trinidad (using Saint-Quentin 1872 and Thomas 1869) and to several West African languages, and compared Mauritian Creole French (using Baissac 1880) to the Malagasy language of Madagascar. He concluded that:

> the Guinea Negroes, transported to those [Caribbean] colonies, took words from French but retained as far as possible the phonology and grammar of their mother tongues . . . Such a formation is surely a hybrid . . . The grammar is no other than the general grammar of the languages of Guinea . . . I have been able to confirm that the phonology of this third colonial language [Mauritian Creole French] is of Malagasy provenance and that Mauritian speech constitutes a Malayo-Aryan language. (1883:4–7)

As Goodman (1964:113) points out, Adam was the first to bring to light certain parallels between an Atlantic creole and various African languages, such as the formation of the plural with the third person plural pronoun, the postposed definite article *la* (apparently the convergence of French and Ewe function words) and some phonological features: 'A great many of his parallels, however, are of a much more general nature and thus far less convincing, since they could be true of any number of languages'. For example, Goodman notes that Adam sometimes attributed the same feature (e.g. the lack of grammatical gender) to Malagasy in the case of Mauritian but to West African languages in the case of the American creoles (although there is nothing illogical about this: chance similarities in two unrelated substrata could well have produced the same effect in the resulting creoles). More problematical, some of the Mauritian features which Adam attributed to Malagasy influence are also found in the Caribbean creoles, such as *fin* as a preverbal marker of completive aspect, or the word *corps* 'body' as a quasi-reflexive pronoun.

Tension between the opposing theories of Coelho and Adam – as well as many new ideas – can be found throughout the work of the German linguist Hugo Schuchardt, who published some 40 articles and reviews on pidgins and creoles totalling almost 700 printed pages between 1880 and 1914. Widely acknowledged as the father of creole studies, Schuchardt has been described as having 'the richest and most complete perception of creoles of any single scholar up to the present' (Meijer and Muysken 1977:28). Fought (1982:419) is of the opinion that 'By any fair measure . . . Schuchardt must be counted among the major figures in linguistics . . . his work contributed significantly to the emergence of sociolinguistics, both directly and by way of his strong influence within dialectology, particularly in Romance'. Schuchardt (1842–1927) studied under August Schleicher, whose *Stammbaum* theory or genealogical tree model for the interrelationship of Indo-European languages made him one of the leading linguists of the mid nineteenth century. Along with Johannes Schmidt, another of Schleicher's students, Schuchardt developed the *Wellentheorie*, or theory of waves of linguistic innovation – such as sound changes that spread over a given area from dialect to dialect or, in a language contact situation, from language to language (Robins 1967:179; Fought 1982:424–7). Schuchardt particularly stressed the role of individuals in the social process leading to language mixture, adumbrating the modern sociolinguistic theories of variation: 'Old and new forms are distributed . . . within a single dialect not only according to age, but also according to sex, education, temperament, in short in the most diverse manner' (1885:18, cited by Fought 1982:425). One of the factors that led to Schuchardt's interest in creole languages was his opposition to the Neogrammarians' law of the absolute regularity of sound change. Creoles result from language contact, which disrupts the historical sound changes that might be expected in languages in isolation. Coelho's publications caught Schuchardt's interest and he took on the task of analysing the material from Coelho's correspondents and later his own. Between 1882 and 1885 Schuchardt wrote to some 343 colonial administrators, missionaries, journalists and other educated people living in areas he considered likely to have pidgin or creole languages (Gilbert 1984). His records indicate that he received 124 replies to his inquiries about local language varieties, effectively charting – however roughly – the geographical distribution of the major pidgin and creole languages. Reinecke (1937:21) notes that 'At first Schuchardt apparently did not differentiate between the "creole languages" on sociological or historical grounds. Any more or less broken European language spoken overseas by a whole community was a creole language. However, as his grasp of the field increased and his views matured, he grasped but did not emphasize the difference between the several varieties of "creole language".' At the beginning, for example, Schuchardt (1881:581) suggested including Chinese Pidgin English among the creole languages, and Coelho (1880–6) looked for creoles in not only Curaçao and Cuba, but also Ecuador and Chile, perhaps misled by the Spanish meaning of the word *criollo*: New World white.

Schuchardt's major work was on the Portuguese-based creoles – those of São Tomé (1882a), Annobón (1888a), Senegal (1888b), Cape Verde (1888c) and Príncipe (1889a), as well as Indo-Portuguese (1882b, 1883a, 1889b,c) and Malayo-Portuguese (1890). However, he also published on Philippine Creole Spanish (1883b), Vietnamese Pidgin French (1888d), Melanesian Pidgin English (1883c, 1889e), American Indian English (1889d), Saramaccan Creole English (1914a), Atlantic Creole English (published posthumously by Gilbert 1985) and Lingua Franca (1909), as well as Negerhollands Creole Dutch (1914b).

Schuchardt's position on the origin of creole features lay somewhere between Coelho's extreme universalist theory and Adam's extreme substratist theory. As Gilbert (1980:6) points out, Schuchardt generally tried to account for particular creole features on a case-by-case basis. Bickerton (1979a:ix) claimed that there was a 'complete absence of any kind of consistent theory in Schuchardt's work. He does not even make a clear distinction – to the modern scholar, the most basic and essential in the field – between native creole and nonnative pidgin.' Yet in the very volume that Bickerton was introducing, Schuchardt (1909:442, translated 1979:27) does indeed make this distinction, noting that the New World creoles 'evolved from communicative languages – both of which certainly have adjacent mother tongues – into mother tongues'. If Bickerton did not understand this passage, the problem may lie in Markey's translation of Schuchardt's *Vermittlungssprachen* as 'communicative languages', which does not correspond to any particular English concept. Reinecke (1937:22) had translated the term as 'interlanguages' and Gilbert (1980:68) as 'go-between languages'. The basic idea of *vermitteln* is to act as an intermediary, and the compound *Vermittlungssprache* is made clear by the following phrase 'die ja beiderseits Muttersprachen neben sich haben', aptly translated by Gilbert as 'where both sides retain their mother tongues'. Several lines later Schuchardt states that these *Handelssprachen* (Markey's 'commercial languages', Gilbert's 'trade languages') should not be called creoles, thus making an explicit distinction between *Vermittlungssprache* and *Kreolisch*. If Schuchardt's distinction between pidgins and creoles seems blurred to modern creolists, even those who read him in the original German (e.g. Meijer and Muysken 1977:42), this is probably partly because he did not always use the modern German terms for these concepts and partly because, as indicated above, he and his contemporaries did not always have the relevant sociolinguistic information to determine the status of particular varieties, especially at the beginning when they were dealing with quite fragmentary data. Moreover, it was not Schuchardt's style to make explicit pronouncements on theory, although he clearly recognized the importance of theoretical orientation, and his own understanding of the basic issues in the origin and development of pidgin and creole languages deepened and matured throughout his long career. However, much of his thinking has to be inferred from what he did and how he did it.

Schuchardt's first article on a creole language – São Tomé's Creole Portuguese (1882a) – has not yet been translated into English, but it is an extraordinary piece of work that illustrates the originality of his thinking. As he had remarked in his review of Coelho (Schuchardt 1881), the study of creole languages that he had begun ten years earlier for the light they might cast on the origin of the Romance languages led him to believe that more extensive data allowing comparisons of the creoles would eventually refute or at least limit Coelho's extreme universalist hypothesis (1881:581). Although Schuchardt did not explicitly formulate a substrate theory in the first of his 'Kreolische Studien' (1881), as Adam did the following year, it is clear from his methodology that his working hypothesis was indeed the importance of substrate influence. He cites a number of books on African languages to compare particular forms to those of the creole, concluding that the considerable grammatical differences between São Tomé and Cape Verdean Creole Portuguese may be due to the differences between their substrate languages, which he believed to belong to the Bantu and West Atlantic groups respectively (1882a:914). He also cites Van Name (1869–70) and remarks on the similarity of São Tomé phonology to that of the Caribbean creoles (1882a:895ff.). He hypothesizes some means of borrowing or diffusion among creoles of different lexical bases: 'From Creole Portuguese comes the completely equivalent progressive marker *ca* in the Creole French of Trinidad, Martinique, and Cayenne' (p. 911). He hints at the possibility of relexification: considering the phonotactics of Sranan Creole English and São Tomé Creole Portuguese, he suggests that 'one can only think that Negro English was somehow grafted onto [*gepfropft auf*] Negro Portuguese' (p. 901). Such thinking fitted a view of language reflected throughout Schuchardt's work: the Humboldtian concept of a language's inner (grammatical) form as opposed to its outer (lexical) form, with creoles retaining the inner form of their substrate while adopting the outer form of their lexical source language. Finally, Schuchardt introduces the first of his creole studies with what is probably one of the earliest sociolinguistic histories of a creole, relating what he has been able to find out about São Tomé's social history to linguistic features of the creole, such as the derivation of *kitó* 'pocketknife' from the *couteau* of the French corsairs who attacked the island in the sixteenth century.

Meijer and Muysken (1977:32) consider the influence of substrate languages to have been Schuchardt's main interest. Features of the Atlantic creoles which he attributed to such influence include verb-fronting (section 6.2.4), serial verbs (6.3), comparative structures (6.3.3), certain features of the verbal system (6.1.1–6.1.3), the alternation of /l/ and /r/ (5.6.4), semantic influence (4.3.2) and idioms (4.3.4). However, Schuchardt was always careful to distinguish between such features and those that he considered likely to have arisen from universal processes of creolization. Meijer and Muysken (1977:34–5) have compiled a very interesting list of such features, which includes various kinds of replacement: of bound grammatical morphemes by free morphemes, of inflected verb forms by infinitives, of unstressed weak forms (e.g. definite articles) by stressed strong forms (e.g. demonstratives), of tense and aspect inflections by preverbal markers – as well as a number of other features such as the deletion or moving of preverbal pronoun clitics. Gilbert (1983) notes that Schuchardt resisted Coelho's universalist explanation of the similarity of the creoles, favouring 'cultural, social, and historical explanations. Only when these did not suffice, did he talk about universal processes of simplification.' Schuchardt understood the similarities of the Atlantic creoles of all lexical bases to stem not from a single common ancestor (cf. monogenesis, 2.10) but rather from their parallel development: 'There exists no common Negro creole from which they could have issued . . . We have no divergence but rather parallelism. They are fashioned out of the same material according to the same plan, in the same style' (1914a or 1980:95).

Schuchardt had a clear understanding of the pidgin–creole life cycle:

> Go-between languages, auxiliary languages, languages of exigency are
> created everywhere and at all times. Most of them disappear again
> along with the condition that spawned them. Others endure and are

> stabilized without further substantial development. Some do this by
> edging out and replacing the languages which were once also used
> alongside them. It is in this manner, chiefly, that the Negro creole
> dialects have come into being, promoted by the rather great variety
> of languages within the slave populations. (1914a or 1980:91)

Schuchardt saw in addition the possibility of decreolization as part of this life
cycle in a passage that also adumbrates the creole continuum (2.11) and the
relationship of post-creole varieties like African American Vernacular English
to their creole origin: 'The Negro English that is most widely known is spoken
in the southern United States . . . those variants which still show a creole-like
character are increasingly falling into disuse by being accommodated to the
English of the whites by means of an intermediate speech variety' (published
posthumously by Gilbert 1985:42).

Schuchardt is sometimes credited (or blamed) for the 'baby talk' theory
of the origin of pidgins. As elaborated by Bloomfield (1933:472), this is as
follows:

> Speakers of a lower language may make so little progress in learning
> the dominant speech, that the masters, in communicating with them
> resort to 'baby talk'. This 'baby talk' is the masters' imitation of the
> subjects' incorrect speech . . . some of its features are based not upon
> the subjects' mistakes but upon grammatical relations that exist within
> the upper language itself. The subjects, in turn, deprived of the correct
> model, can do no better now than to acquire the simplified 'baby talk'
> version of the upper language. The result may be a conventionalized
> jargon.

This theory was refuted by DeCamp (1971a:19) and others as a sole explanation for pidginization and creolization since it did not account for the similarities among the creoles or the mutual intelligibility of the French creoles;
that is, it did not allow a role for the Africans, for example, in the creation
of the Caribbean creoles. However, Meijer and Muysken (1977:30) hold
that Schuchardt's views on simplification 'can certainly not be reduced to
the "baby talk" theory . . . Although this theory constitutes an important
element in his work on pidginization, alternative theories receive equal attention.' Schuchardt did in fact maintain that creoles are shaped by the 'foreigner
talk' of the native speakers of the lexical source language: 'All mutilation of
a language issues from those who have inherited it as their mother tongue, in
much the same way as the language of a child depends on the language of its
nurse' (1909:443 or 1980:69). Elsewhere, however, Schuchardt suggests that
restructuring results from a more collaborative effort:

> For the master and the slave it was simply a matter of mutual comprehension. The master stripped off from the European language everything that was peculiar to it, the slave suppressed everything in it that was distinctive. They met on a middle ground . . . [but] to a lesser extent at the very beginning. The white man was the teacher of the black man. At first the black man mimicked him. (1914a or 1980:91–2)

The explanation for this apparent contradiction would seem to lie in the different stages in question: at the very beginning of pidginization Europeans initiated the simplification of their language to facilitate comprehension, but, later on, the Africans introduced changes of their own, e.g. in speaking to Africans of other language backgrounds.

Toward the end of his career Schuchardt engaged in a polemic with the French linguist Antoine Meillet regarding the nature of mixed languages. This lasted throughout the war years and beyond (1914–21) and was later taken up again by Hall and Taylor (2.9) in their debate on the genetic identity of mixed languages. Meillet doubted that any languages were mixed to the degree that this changed their genetic identity despite substrate features that might well be present (e.g. Gaulish features in French). He feared that linguistic theory could not cope with languages having more than one genetic identity:

> If we have been able to succeed in reconstructing the history of some languages by comparison, it is because we were sure that each new system had to be explained as coming from a single system. In the case where one would have to take account of two initial systems and of their reactions to each other, the present methods would not be sufficient. For the right that one would have of choosing between two series of original forms would cause such an arbitrariness that every proof would become almost unrealizable. In spite of the hypotheses made in this direction, linguists have, fortunately, never yet been surely in the face of such a difficulty. If the difficulty really happens to occur, linguistics will have to work out new methods more delicate than those which are described here in order to overcome it, and it would remain to test them. (Meillet 1967:102)

Of course Schuchardt believed that creoles were truly mixed languages that were related to more than one family, so that Meillet's concept of genetic relationship, which could not handle such double identity, had to be untenable (Hall 1958:370).

Schuchardt's work remains a rich source of information and insights in many areas of creole linguistics. He was not only the founder of the discipline but also the first to grasp that 'The importance for general linguistics of the creole dialects has not yet been fully appreciated' (1914a or 1980:91).

2.7 Hesseling and his contemporaries

The Dutch linguist Dirk Christiaan Hesseling published on creole languages and creolization between 1897 and 1934, bridging the work of Schuchardt and Reinecke, the first modern creolist. Hesseling was a Greek scholar whose interest in the development of koine Greek from the older Attic dialects led to his interest in language mixing and creolization. After reading Schuchardt's 1891 study of Malayo-Portuguese, Hesseling developed a theory (1897, 1899) that this creole, which was spoken by slaves taken by the Dutch from the East Indies to their colony in South Africa during the seventeenth and eighteenth centuries, had influenced the development of Afrikaans. He believed the influence of the indigenous people in South Africa to have been rather limited in comparison to that of the Asian slaves, and that Afrikaans had stopped halfway in the process of creolization because of its particular sociolinguistic conditions. Hesseling's theory, modified and expanded by Valkhoff (1966, 1972), found few supporters in South Africa. Hesseling's interest in Afrikaans led him to work on Negerhollands Creole Dutch (1905), Dutch in Ceylon (1910), Papiamentu Creole Spanish (1933a) and a general theory of creolization (1933b, 1934).

DeCamp (1971a:22) suggested that Hesseling might be viewed as a precursor of the monogeneticists (2.10). Although Meijer and Muysken (1977:39) agreed that his view of the origin of Afrikaans might be so interpreted, they felt that the rest of his work did not support such a conclusion. Indeed, Hellinger (1985:40) points out Hesseling's observation that 'Similar causes in Indonesia and on the Cape produced convergent results' (1897 or 1979:11), a distinctly polygenetic view.

Hesseling was more sympathetic than Schuchardt to the idea of universal processes of creolization akin to adult second language acquisition. Unlike Schuchardt, he considered the speech of non-native speakers of the lexical source language to be more influential in the pidginization/creolization process than that of the native speakers. Although he often pointed out substrate features in the creoles, he did not believe that the creoles' grammar was simply that of their substrate languages. Moreover, Hesseling did not always agree with Schuchardt as to whether specific creole features should be attributed to universals or to substrate influence (Meijer and Muysken 1977:39). Muysken and Meijer (1979:xi) point out that Hesseling considered highly idiosyncratic factors to operate in the genesis of creoles, as well as in language change in general – the result of particular sociocultural circumstances, accidental phonetic resemblances between words, or idiosyncratic connotations. Hesseling maintained a distinction between a *gemengde taal* or language that has undergone mixing (i.e. practically any language) and a *mengeltaal* or mixed language (i.e. one whose grammar has been affected, or whose lexicon shows massive borrowing). A creole is a *mengeltaal* that results when there is a clash of languages and these languages are dissimilar. If either of these two conditions does not obtain, then simplification rather than creolization results (1934:319–21).

The Danish linguist Otto Jespersen dealt with language mixture in an often-cited chapter on 'Pidgins and congeners' in his book *Language* (1922). Comparing Melanesian and Chinese Pidgin English with Mauritian Creole French and Chinook Jargon, Jespersen generally agreed with Schuchardt as to the origin and basic nature of pidgins and creoles, although he discounted the role of substrate influence and maintained that more universal processes of language acquisition determined the speech of those who pidginized a language 'as if their minds were just as innocent of grammar as those of very small babies' (228). However, Jespersen also took sociolinguistic factors into account to explain the limited nature of such language acquisition: 'My view, then, is that Beach-la-mar as well as Pidgin is English, only English learnt imperfectly, in consequence partly of the difficulties always inherent in learning a totally different foreign language, partly of the obstacles put in the way of learning by the linguistic behaviour of the English-speaking people themselves' (225). Regarding this last point, Vendryes (1921) had asserted that 'Creole . . . is the speech . . . of a subordinate class whose superiors have never troubled nor desired to make them speak any language correctly.'

Hellinger (1985:43) sees Jespersen's ideas as foreshadowing those of Schumann (1978) and Bickerton (1977b), summed up in his observation that 'in all these seemingly so different cases the same mental factor is at work, namely imperfect mastery of a language' (Jespersen 1922:233ff.).

2.8 Reinecke and his contemporaries

Hellinger (1985:45) has suggested that in the 1930s the centre of gravity of creole studies shifted from the Old World to the New. Along with this came another shift from armchair creolists, who had almost no direct contact with the object of their study, to creolists who actively pursued fieldwork. A student of Hesseling, Jan de Josselin de Jong, collected texts of Negerhollands in phonemic spelling on St Thomas and St John, which he published in 1926. Other early fieldworkers came from the tradition of anthropology, such as Franz Boas, who studied Chinook Jargon (1933), or the folklorist Elsie Clews Parsons, whose massive collection of texts in the English- and French-based creoles of the Caribbean area (1933–43) reflects a keen interest in language. Although Melville and Frances Herskovits were anthropologists, one of their primary concerns was with the pidgin and creole languages of West Africa and the Caribbean as cultural artefacts. The Herskovitses (1936) concluded that from the Sea Islands of South Carolina to Suriname in South America 'Negroes have been using words from European languages to render literally the underlying morphological patterns of West African tongues' (p. 131). They were among the first to point out the similarity of idioms (i.e. turns of speech as opposed to purely grammatical constructions) in certain West African languages and the Caribbean creoles. Perhaps most importantly, their anthropological perspective lent a new dimension to their understanding of creolization as a general cultural phenomenon rather than one confined to language.

Substrate influence, for which the Herskovitses adduced considerable linguistic and cultural evidence, had become a perennial point of controversy in creole studies. Lou Lichtveld, a Dutch linguist from Suriname, described Sranan Creole English as having 'almost all the outer and inner characteristics of an African language' (1927:391). L. Göbl-Gáldi's 'Problems of Substrate in Creole French' (1933) points to not only substrate influence but also retentions from archaic and regional French, as well as innovations due to development within the creoles themselves (a source of change apparently not mentioned earlier in the literature). Göbl-Gáldi (1934) also attempted the first comparative structural study of the French-based creoles, or indeed of any lexical-base group, which was not superseded until that of Goodman (1964). It was not until much later that Hancock did the first comparative studies for subgrouping the English-based creoles, based on lexicon (1969) and syntax (1987), while Alleyne's comparison (1980) included phonology. A preliminary comparative study of the Portuguese-based creoles was done by Ivens Ferraz (1987).

After Göbl-Gáldi's careful and balanced approach to the issue of substrate influence, the next two works on creole French took extreme and diametrically opposed positions. The first was by Suzanne Sylvain (1936), a native speaker of Haitian Creole French who was also a linguist trained in African languages. Goodman (1964:116) describes her study of Haitian morphosyntax as 'surely the finest description of any creole dialect up to that time'. However, after her thorough and even-handed treatment of what she identified as the French and African features of the creole, she concluded quite surprisingly that 'we are in the presence of French which has been cast in the mould of African syntax or, since languages are generally classified according to their syntactic ancestry, an Ewe language with French vocabulary' (1936:178). Since this sentence is so often cited, it seems only fair to quote a personal communication about it from Robert A. Hall, Jr (1985): 'Suzanne told me, when

I discussed the matter with her in Haiti in '49, that this was not her own opinion but that of her mentor ... [who] had required her to put it in at the end.'

The second work, by Jules Faine (1936), was also by a Haitian, but this time an amateur philologist who claimed that African influence on Haitian was negligible: 'at least three quarters [of the creole] is from the Norman dialect of the sixteenth and seventeenth centuries, which has been preserved in a very pure state' (1936:1). This view is widely held in the Caribbean areas where French creoles are spoken; indeed, it had been asserted without support in the first doctoral dissertation on a creole language, written by a Guadeloupean (Poyen-Bellisle 1894:12). As Goodman notes (1964:126ff.), 'Faine could scarcely have chosen a less likely candidate than Norman among northern French dialects as the source of Creole phonology' and his evidence on other linguistic levels is equally unconvincing. Whatever his book's reception, Faine remained undaunted and in 1939 published *Le créole dans l'univers*, a comparison of Haitian and Mauritian Creole French, claiming that the French creoles came not from a single dialect of French but rather from a composite forming a nautical patois.

The American linguist Leonard Bloomfield devoted several brief but often-cited passages to pidgins and creoles in his popular book, *Language* (1933). Besides contributing to the theory of baby talk (section 2.6), he gave a clear definition of pidgins and creoles (without using those terms), noting that creolization occurs 'especially when the subject group is made up of persons from different speech communities, who can communicate among themselves only by means of the jargon' (1933:473). He went on to touch on the speech of American blacks and decreolization (2.11), concluding with some brief passages of Sranan.

John Reinecke is considered by many to be the father of modern creole studies. An American mainlander who settled in Hawaii (Sato and A. Reinecke 1987), John Reinecke's master's thesis (1935, published 1969), is still the best source of information on the development of Hawaiian Creole English. His 1937 doctoral dissertation, done at Yale University's Department of Race Relations, was entitled *Marginal languages: a sociological survey of the creole languages and trade jargons*. It is a remarkably complete guide to what was known about creole linguistics at that time. Reinecke spent a good part of the rest of his life at the scholarly tasks that would put the discipline on a solid footing, particularly the compilation of the comprehensive *Bibliography of pidgin and creole languages* (Reinecke *et al.* 1975). It is instructive to consider Reinecke's assessment of the field at the time he entered it:

38

many of the problems that concern creolists today had been stated or
at least adumbrated. But if no longer in their infancy, creole studies
in the 1930s had not passed their adolescence, either quantitatively or
qualitatively . . . For the most part, creole studies were peripheral to
the main theoretical concerns of linguistics; they were a field cultivated
mainly by amateur or semi-amateur aficionados . . . The amount of
information on any one pidgin or creole ranged from bare mention
to two or three tolerably adequate sketches of it. Except for a few
glances at Chinook Jargon, creole studies were Eurocentric, concerned
with languages of European lexicon and especially with that classic
area of plantation creoles, the Caribbean . . . Creole studies were
compartmentalized: Guthrie [1935 on Lingala] and Jacobs [1932 on
Chinook Jargon] and Sawyerr [1940 on Kriol], for instance, might
almost have been writing on three different planets for aught each
knew and cared about the others' work. The inaccessibility of much of
the writing, unpublished theses in particular, hindered the development
of a wide perspective among creolists. (1977:vii–viii)

Reinecke interspersed these remarks with observations on how short the
current state of the discipline fell from the ideal, yet one is struck by how
much his own efforts had helped advance the field. His dissertation, which
has circulated widely in its microfilm form since the 1960s although it has
never been published as a book, represents a monumental effort to provide
an overview of what he felt should be the scope of the discipline. The first 150
pages deal with the development of the theory of restructured languages
(surveying the literature up to 1937) and their classification, as well as sociolinguistic issues regarding their relation to standard languages, education and
national and ethnic identity. The next 716 pages provide a survey of over 40
pidgin and creole languages, including a number with non-European-derived
lexicons that were brought within the scope of the discipline for the first time,
e.g. pidginized varieties of Eskimo, Mobilian and other Amerindian languages; Lingua Geral; Pidgin Assamese; Pidgin Japanese; restructured Arabic;
Lingala; and Fanakalo. Each variety is discussed within the context of its
sociolinguistic history (which has since become an integral part of pidgin and
creole studies), followed by an examination of its distinctive linguistic features
and then a full bibliography.

Gilbert's statement (1986a:19) that 'Reinecke . . . never attempted a comprehensive explanation of the problems of linguistic similarity and simplification' within the creoles rather misses the point of his dissertation, which
was to identify the *socio*linguistic patterns that result in pidginization and
creolization. The German sociologist Ernst Schultze (1933) was the first to
identify the value of such an approach, but he lacked Reinecke's background

in linguistics, which was necessary to analyse the effects that such socio-linguistic patterns had on language.

Reinecke realized that 'A valid classification must be built on a complete and detailed knowledge of all the dialects' (1937:57), yet he doubted that it would be possible to do this 'on a purely linguistic basis on such points as degree of breakdown of the grammatical structure, size and flexibility of the vocabulary, stability of the dialects and degree of language mixture . . . [although] such features will be discussed later, to see if it is possible to correlate them with the social characteristics of the marginal languages' (p. 57). Instead, he proposed classifying them 'on the basis of the circumstances of their formation, their functions, and their development as fixed and recognized dialects'. Thus he arrived at the following categories, each defined in detail and illustrated with a number of examples: (1) plantation creole dialects (e.g. those of the Caribbean area and the islands off West Africa); (2) settlers' creole dialects (e.g. creole Portuguese in Guiné-Bissau and Asia); and (3) trade jargons (i.e. pidgins).

Reinecke's sociological distinction between plantation and settlers' creoles was largely ignored by later creolists since it did not seem to correspond to any discernible linguistic differences between such creoles. However, it is logical to expect both social and linguistic differences between creoles that remain in contact with their substrate languages (Reinecke's settler creoles like Indo-Portuguese) and those that do not (plantation creoles like São Tomé Creole Portuguese). Much recent theorizing about the sociology of creolization has considered only the latter situation, leading to assertions such as the claim that creoles became established as community languages because pidgin speakers had no other means of understanding one another. While this was indeed the case on São Tomé, it was clearly not the case with Indo-Portuguese, whose Indian-born speakers were always bi- or multilingual in the local languages that formed the creole's substrate. The establishment of settlers' creoles as community languages would seem to have much more to do with their association with a particular social identity (e.g. that of Eurasians). This seems likely to have been a key factor in the establishment of plantation creoles as well, which functioned as the badge of a local social identity. Linguistically, creoles that remain in contact with their substrate languages can be expected to be more influenced by them, particularly if the superstrate language is withdrawn and the substrate language is raised in prestige, as happened in the case of the Indo-Portuguese creole of Sri Lanka. This variety now has a great number of morphological and syntactic features with Tamil and Sinhalese counterparts that are not found in earlier texts (Smith 1979). Such linguistic change in the direction of the substrate could not occur in a plantation creole. Those tracing the nativization of extended pidgins in such places as Papua New Guinea and Nigeria need to bear Reinecke's distinction in mind. Its usefulness was later taken up or rediscovered by Chaudenson (1979:21) and Bickerton (1986), who distinguish 'créoles exogènes' or 'plantation creoles' from 'créoles endogènes' or 'fort creoles', respectively.

Reinecke also made a distinction within the plantation creoles (which he also proposed calling 'African creole dialects' – 1937:60) of 'maroon creoles' such as Saramaccan and Ndyuka Creole English, Annobonese Creole Portuguese and Jamaican Maroon Creole English. Moreover, Reinecke was the first to propose a mechanism for the partial restructuring of languages, the process that Hesseling (1897) had proposed (but not named) as responsible for Afrikaans, which Reinecke referred to as 'semi-creolized' (1937:559):

> In several instances the slaves were so situated among a majority or a large minority of whites (and there were other reasons as well for the result), that they, or rather their creole children, learned the common language, not a creole dialect; or the plantation creole dialects that had begun to form never crystalized, never got beyond the makeshift stage. This happened in . . . Brazil, Cuba and the Spanish-speaking Caribbean countries in general, and in the southern United States in general.
>
> (p. 61)

Reinecke further distinguished between settlers' creole dialects and language enclaves of settlers in Europe and North America:

> There are two main differences between these two types of settlement. On the one hand the European and American *Sprachinseln* are either numerous enough usually to keep their language uncorrupted to any great extent, or are so like the surrounding population as to be readily assimilated before their home language has time to break down structurally; while the creole settlements are at the same time small and slowly assimilable by the natives. On the other hand the settlers in Europe and America, set down in a social organization similar to their own, are assimilated rather than assimilators, so that their language remains unsimplified – they have not to speak it in a simplified form with a half-assimilated clientele or native traders. (p. 63)

Reinecke distinguished several other varieties which he considered to lie beyond the scope of pidgin and creole studies: colonial dialects (unrestructured varieties of European languages in the New World, Australia, etc.), foreigners' mixed speech (e.g. the English of foreigners in Hawaii), dying minor languages (e.g. New Jersey Dutch), 'babu' language (a school-taught foreign language that becomes a secondary language) and lingua francas that have not been restructured.

Although not all of these distinctions have been accepted and although Reinecke did not contribute directly to the theoretical debates among those who followed, he was surely a major figure in the founding of modern pidgin and creole studies: he not only staked out the full scope of the discipline but also established its sociological foundations, ensuring that it would be a part of what was to become sociolinguistics.

2.9 Hall and Taylor

Creolist works of the 1930s were not widely read at the time; they had no discernible effect on general linguistics, and they formed no recognized field of study within linguistics. It was in no small measure due to the efforts of Robert Hall and Douglas Taylor that there was a revival of interest in pidgin and creole languages after the Second World War that blossomed into the establishment of a new academic field in the late 1950s.

The war brought Americans suddenly into contact with a number of 'exotic' languages in Asia and the Pacific. The challenge they presented to linguistics and language teaching had a profound effect on both, and resulted in the description of a number of languages that had never been systematically studied before. One of these was the Pidgin English of Melanesia, described in structuralist terms by Hall and others in a book published for the United States Armed Services Institute in 1943. Hall, who emerged as a major figure in Romance and general linguistics, pursued his interest in pidgin and creole languages by studying Sranan Creole English (1948) and Haitian Creole French (Hall *et al.* 1953), becoming an authority on the latter. As the first creolist with any extensive first-hand knowledge of a pidgin, he was in a good position to develop a theory of the life cycle of pidgins (1962). Although Hall makes it clear that the distinction between pidgins and creoles regarding native speakers had already been established (1962:151, fn. 3), his account of creolization made it implicit that creoles *always* have a preceding phase as a pidgin. This position became widely accepted, but Alleyne (1980:126) objected that 'the existence of a prior "simplified pidgin" remains purely speculative' in the case of the Caribbean creoles, and Mühlhäusler (1986:8) hypothesized that creoles may have evolved from pre-pidgin (i.e. unstable) jargons.

Hall and Taylor were the first modern linguists to make their colleagues aware of the theoretical importance of restructured languages. Hall's involvement in more general linguistic theory led him to use data from pidgin and creole languages to test the validity of various hypotheses. In 1959 he cast doubt on the usefulness of glottochronology, a lexico-statistical technique to establish the number of years that two related languages have been separated, by applying it to the lexicon of Melanesian Pidgin English: 'even from this single instance it would seem that the "normal" rate of lexical replacement assumed for glottochronology is not valid in case pidginization has intervened'.

The issue of the importance of substrate languages emerged yet again in the 1950s, the revival of the debate becoming something of a rite of passage for each succeeding generation of creolists. This time, however, the polemic took a more sophisticated form, focusing on the validity of the concept of genetic relatedness. Moreover, the question was no longer whether or not creoles had features that could be traced to their substrata (it was agreed that they did), but rather how these features should affect the genetic classification of the creoles. Hall favoured classifying them as dialects of their European lexical source languages, while the case for classifying them as genetically distinct was advanced by Taylor, an English linguist who had settled in Dominica and was studying the Lesser Antillean CF spoken there.

Hall noted that creolists were retesting the notion of the substratum as developed in Romance linguistics in his review of Turner's (1949) book on the African features in Gullah CE, a landmark study based on the fieldwork that Turner had begun in the 1930s under the influence of Herskovits: 'The theory of linguistic substratum, at one time almost wholly discredited by the excesses of its proponents, is now being reinterpreted and, one might say, rehabilitated in the light of the more realistic picture of linguistic transfer afforded by pidgin and creolized languages' (Hall 1950:54). Hall questioned not the existence but rather the importance of substrate influence in the creoles and cautioned against extreme positions on this issue:

> In summary, anyone with some knowledge of pidgin and creole
> languages cannot deny the existence of the influence of the substrata.
> However, our experience with such languages leads us to be rather
> conservative or 'eclectic' regarding the possibility of such influence
> . . . Each presumed case for substrate influence should be judged
> independently on its own merits; thus we shall avoid the exaggerations
> of both those who see signs of the substrate everywhere and those who
> deny it completely. (Hall 1955:9, my translation)

In the same article (p. 2), Hall dubbed these the *sostratomani* ('substrato-maniacs') and *sostratofobi* ('substratophobes') respectively; Bickerton (1981) revived only the former term.

The following year Taylor published an article which took up the question of the classification of creolized languages. Noting that Hall *et al.* (1953) had classified Haitian as a Romance language (principally on the basis of lexical and phonological correspondences with French) but that one of the co-authors (Sylvain 1936) had also classified Haitian as an African language (principally on the basis of syntactic similarities to Ewe and other Niger-Congo languages), Taylor questioned the suitability of the concept of genetic relatedness when it came to pidgins and creoles, particularly since Meillet had specified that such relatedness implied continuity. Moreover, Taylor asserted that the Caribbean creoles were related to one another across lexical boundaries in ways their lexical source languages were not because of the important role that substrate languages had played in forming the creoles' syntax. Taylor based this assertion on the work of the Dutch linguist Jan Voorhoeve (1953), who had compared the verbal systems of Sranan Creole English and Lesser Antillean Creole French, which he called 'a related language' – the first time a relationship had been claimed to exist between two languages without reference to their lexicons. Taylor concluded that 'Languages originating in a pidgin or jargon, while genetically "orphans", may be said to have two "foster-parents": one that provides the basic morphological and/or syntactic pattern, and another from which the fundamental vocabulary is taken' (1956:413). Hall (1958) replied that although traditional historical linguists had assumed that the languages they compared were 'pure' and that their change was gradual, neither of these two factors is essential to the validity of the concept of genetic relatedness:

> No linguistic relationship is 'pure', whether the change be gradual or brusque . . . no one considers that the basic relationship of the language is changed by the presence of structural borrowings; we do not classify Alsatian German with the Romance languages because it has nasalized vowels. The question now arises: how far can structural borrowings go before they affect our classification of a language? (p. 370)

Taylor's (1963) response was one of the earliest affirmations of the monogenetic theory, so it is discussed in the following section.

2.10 Monogenesis

With the emergence of creole studies as a recognized branch of linguistics in the late 1950s and early 1960s, the number of researchers in this area swelled from perhaps a dozen to hundreds in the 1970s (DeCamp 1977:7). For this reason it becomes more convenient to discuss periods in terms of ideas rather than the many individuals who advanced them.

The early growth of creole linguistics was probably related to the movement toward independence in the British West Indies, which helped shift the perspective on language from that of the colonizer to that of the colonized. The participants at the first conference on creole languages, held at the University College of the West Indies in Jamaica in 1959, observed that to 'try to deal with people without understanding their native language was bound to be ineffective; to try to form a Federation of the West Indies while ignoring the language problems of the peoples comprising that Federation was to overlook a most important factor' (Le Page 1961:117).

A growing interest in Caribbean creoles is indicated by the appearance of two pioneering master's theses written by English-speaking West Indians: a Jamaican, Beryl Loftman (later Bailey) (1953), and a Guyanese, Richard Allsopp (1958). Both went on to write doctoral dissertations and become leading figures in creole studies. Robert Le Page, an English linguist teaching in Jamaica, was a major force in establishing academic recognition of creole linguistics. In 1951 he began a survey of the varieties of English spoken in the British West Indies by sending a questionnaire to local teachers regarding language usage and eliciting the local equivalents of a number of sentences in standard English. Despite a limited response and certain problems with this method, Le Page was able to organize this and other information he had gathered into his ground-breaking 'General outlines of Creole English dialects in the British Caribbean' (1957–8). This was to provide a basis for bringing the teaching of English 'into line with the needs of the Caribbean, rather than with the needs of . . . England' (Le Page 1955:46).

University College of the West Indies became the first centre for creole studies. Le Page cooperated with two visiting linguists from the United States, David DeCamp (who was working on dialect geography in Jamaica) and Frederic Cassidy (a lexicographer doing fieldwork for his important 1961 study, *Jamaica talk*). Cassidy, born and partly raised in Jamaica and fully bidialectal, joined forces with Le Page to compile the *Dictionary of Jamaican English* (1967, 1980), the first comprehensive etymological dictionary of any creole and a model for those that followed.

The first conference that Le Page convened in Jamaica in 1959 was small, including only the above scholars and Hall, Taylor and Voorhoeve, as well as Allsopp and several other graduate students (including Morris Goodman and David Lawton), two American dialectologists (A. H. Marckwardt and E. Bagby Atwood) and an Africanist (Jack Barry). M. Pradel Pompilus of Haiti and R. W. Thompson of Hong Kong University sent papers read in their absence.

> The conference sessions were held in one small room. In spite of the size of the group, never before had so many creolists, representing different continents and different languages, confronted each other face to face. The proceedings of the conference (Le Page 1961) formed the basis of much of the discussion and research of the following decade. As discussions of the applicability of such concepts as generative grammar, diglossia, continuum and comparative-historical

45

> reconstruction progressed, the participants began to think of
> themselves more as creolists than just as students of Haitian French
> or Jamaican English. (DeCamp 1977:12)

Among the most consequential ideas to surface at this conference was mono-genesis, the idea that many of the world's pidgins and creoles could be traced to a common origin, the Portuguese-based pidgin that arose in the fifteenth century in Africa, perhaps from the Lingua Franca, and that was eventually relexified (or translated word for word) into the pidgins of other European lexical bases that gave rise to the modern creoles. The nub of this idea origi-nated in Whinnom's 1956 book on Philippine Creole Spanish, which, he sug-gested, grew out of the creole Portuguese of the Indonesian island of Ternate which had been transported to the Philippines in the seventeenth century: 'The similarities in grammar and syntax, and even of vocabulary between the Spanish contact vernaculars in the Philippines and Indo-Portuguese are so many – and they are not attributable to a common substratum – that we can be quite certain that Ternateño did develop out of the common Portuguese pidgin of the Eastern Seas' (Whinnom 1956:9, fn. 21). Whinnom went on to remark that this Portuguese pidgin 'may not have been a "pure" contact vernacular, but a kind of imitation Sabir, the Lingua Franca of the Mediter-ranean' (9–10). In a 1957 review of Whinnom's book, Taylor pointed out that many of the features of Philippine CS were also found in the Caribbean creoles, e.g. the preposition *na* (4.4.1), compound prepositions (6.5.2), com-pletive *cabá* (6.1.5) and other preverbal markers such as Papiamentu CS nonpunctual *ta*, anterior *taba(ta)* and future *lo*. Thompson took these up in his 1959 conference paper, concluding that the pidgin Portuguese used by slavers, 'much influenced, no doubt, by the West African substratum, may have been the pattern for all the West Indian Creoles just as, in the Eastern and Pacific worlds Portuguese Creole dialects, well known to Europeans of many nationalities, may have provided the models for the two great branches of pidgin English, China Coast pidgin and Neo-Melanesian' (1961:113). Responding to an earlier version of Thompson's paper, Taylor (1959:488) construed this as a suggestion that the Portuguese pidgin had changed 'its vocabulary under the pressure of various other national languages but not – or to a much lesser extent – its grammatical structure'. Accepting the possib-ility of a massive shift from Portuguese to Spanish lexicon in the cases of Philippine CS and Papiamentu, Taylor (1960:156) went on to suggest that it may have been possible that both Sranan and Saramaccan Creole English 'began as an Afro-Portuguese pidgin that was later anglicized', an idea later expanded by Voorhoeve (see below). Stewart (1962:46) christened this kind of vocabulary shift 'relexification', a term taken up by Whinnom (1965:517) and others as an essential element of what was becoming the formal theory of monogenesis.

Yet there was disagreement among proponents of this theory as to how important the African substratum had been in shaping pidgin Portuguese. Taylor (1963:813) argued that it was indeed important, while Whinnom (1965:522) responded that the pidgin's simplicity suggested that the Lingua Franca was a more important model. Hellinger (1985:61) interprets the strong version of the monogenetic theory as claiming that *all* pidgin and creole languages can be traced to a single proto-pidgin, which she refutes by pointing to pidgins lexically based on African languages in whose genesis no European language was involved. However, Whinnom (1965:521) had explicitly excluded from his claim pidgins not lexically based on European languages. Many of the objections of other linguists to the monogenetic theory also hinge on its scope, i.e. whether it served as a plausible explanation for the similarity of all European-based pidgins and creoles, or just the Atlantic creoles, or just the creoles of a particular European lexical base. One of the original arguments for a common origin had been the considerable mutual intelligibility of the French-based creoles from Louisiana to Cayenne (Stewart 1962:45). This could have resulted from the relexification of a single pidgin in Africa which then spread by diffusion (true monogenesis) or parallel relexification in both Africa and various parts of the New World (actually polygenesis). Goodman (1964) did not refer to the role of pidgin Portuguese in the formation of the French creoles and later (1987) argued against it, but he did support the idea of monogenesis within the lexical base, growing out of a French-based pidgin in West Africa (1964:130). Stewart (1967) suggested a similar diffusionist model for the origin and spread of restructured English on both sides of the Atlantic. Based on their lexical similarities as opposed to standard English, Hancock too (1969:7, 12) posited a single origin for the English-based Atlantic creoles, but also hesitated to connect these to pidgin Portuguese via relexification.

Hancock's paper had been presented at the second conference on creolization held in Mona, Jamaica, in 1968. The proceedings, edited by Hymes (1971), became an enduring textbook for the emerging discipline of creole linguistics. At this conference there was a considerable amount of theoretical debate regarding monogenesis. The Trinidadian linguist Mervyn Alleyne (1971:170) rejected Whinnom's hypothesis that ' "pidgins" or "creoles" are, to a large extent, in their genesis, European phenomena ... I do not think that [the attempt to relate the Portuguese pidgin to Sabir] is necessary for explaining the genesis of "creole" dialects, nor do I think that a convincing case has been made for it.' However, he accepted relexification as the mechanism by which African substrate languages shaped the Atlantic creoles (1980:109).

Hall was perceived as the leading proponent of polygenesis via spontane-ous generation: 'A pidgin can arise . . . whenever an emergency situation calls for communication on a minimal level of comprehension' and then be 'creolized, i.e. [it] becomes the first language of a speech community' (1962:152–5). DeCamp (1971a:20) argued against monogenesis as the vehicle of African substrate influence: 'No one African language can account for all or even a majority of the "African" elements in Caribbean creole, nor is any significant "African" feature in creole shared by all or even a majority of the native languages of the slaves . . . Thus there could not have been any significant sys-tematic African "substratum".' He considered that the theory of monogenesis rested on a number of assumptions without documentary evidence, but still had points to recommend it:

> Even if we were to assume that the lexicon and the structure of a
> language were equally susceptible to change, relexification would still
> be a better explanation than restructuralization for the development
> of pidgins and creoles; for the influences which could bring about
> a whole-sale adoption of French vocabulary in French territories,
> English vocabulary in British territories, etc., are clear and obvious,
> whereas there is no known sociolinguistic influence which could explain
> why the structures of five different European languages should have
> been modified in precisely the same direction . . . The weaknesses in the
> monogenetic theory are first a very sketchy historical documentation,
> second the controversial status of Far Eastern pidgin English (which
> lacks many of the features shared by other pidgins and creoles), and
> third the problem of certain pidgins and creoles which clearly
> developed without any direct Portuguese influence.
>
> (DeCamp 1971a:23–4)

Voorhoeve (1973) proposed that the high percentage of Portuguese-derived words in Saramaccan CE provided evidence in favour of the theory of relexifica-tion, still closely associated with monogenesis. He rejected the traditional explanation that the Saramaccans' ancestors had fled from the plantations of Portuguese-speaking Jews who had immigrated to Suriname from Brazil, suggesting instead that slaves arriving directly from Africa spoke a pidgin Portuguese that began relexifying toward English when the colony was held by Britain. He believed that the Saramaccans' ancestors escaped from the coastal plantations before this process had been completed, so that their language retained a considerable amount of lexicon derived from Portuguese, but that the process of relexification continued on the coast so that Sranan, the creole spoken there today, has a much higher proportion of English-derived lexicon. However, Goodman (1987) later rejected Voorhoeve's interpretation in light of historical documentation supporting the traditional explanation.

48

The monogenetic theory has left its mark on creole linguistics, although few creolists today would claim, for example, that Tok Pisin is directly descended from the Lingua Franca via relexification. The concept of relexification itself has a considerable number of adherents in the more restricted sense of calquing on the level of the phrase, frequently accepted as the mechanism by which at least the Atlantic creoles of different lexical bases are related to a common substratum. Many still consider massive relexification plausible in the case of closely related lexicons such as a shift from creole Portuguese to creole Spanish. Robertson (1979) considers the replacement of Berbice Creole Dutch lexical items by words from (Guyanese Creole) English to be a form of decreolization with relexification, and Dalphinis (1985) explains a similar shift from St Lucian Creole French to (Creole) English lexical items as relexification. Koopman (1986) redefined relexification in generativist terms as 'the transfer of lexical properties from the native language into the target language' (p. 251). Indeed, the concept of relexification was a guiding principle in a research programme comparing the structure of Haitian CF and Fon-Gbe (Lefebvre 1993).

By definition, all theories besides monogenesis imply polygenesis, and many believe that pidginization and creolization occurred in different places at different times but under parallel circumstances that produced parallel results. Yet there are still creolists who describe the interrelationship of varieties (at least within Atlantic lexical base groups) in monogenetic terms, i.e. a family tree of creoles with a common origin, a proto variety that spread via normal linguistic diffusion (e.g. Hancock 1987). Although polygenesis and diffusion are often thought of as alternative explanations for the same phenomena – features common to widely separated creoles – they are by no means mutually exclusive.

Finally, there are still frequent references to a possible common West African origin of similar phenomena in Atlantic creoles of different lexical bases. For example, McWhorter (1995) has claimed a monogenetic origin for the English-based Atlantic creoles because there is no straightforward source in their substrate, superstrate or universals for six of their shared grammatical features: the copulas *de* and *da* (6.2), the pronoun *unu* (6.4.5), the anterior marker *bin* (6.1.2), the obligative verb *fu* (6.1.8) and the adverbial *self* 'even' – although the last may in fact be derived from an archaic English usage (Holm 1988–9:181).

2.11 The creole continuum

Just as the theory of monogenesis could not have evolved without the concept of relexification as a key mechanism, so too the historical connection between creoles and post-creole varieties such as African American Vernacular English required the concept of a continuum with decreolization as a mechanism of change. A creole continuum can evolve in situations in which a creole coexists with its lexical source language and there is social motivation for creole speakers to acquire the standard so that the speech of individuals takes on features of the latter – or avoids features of the former – to varying degrees. These varieties can be seen as forming a continuum from those farthest from the standard to those closest to it. Such a synchronic continuum can also serve as a conceptual model for a diachronic continuum of varieties resulting from a creole progressively dropping its nonstandard features and adding standard ones, or decreolizing.

Decreolization is an areal contact phenomenon, but the diffusion of linguistic features can result not only in creoles acquiring non-creole features, but also in non-creoles acquiring creole features. The fact that diffusion can work in both directions presents a serious problem in historical reconstruction: purely synchronic data might not provide enough evidence to determine whether a particular variety that is mixed (i.e. with both creole and non-creole features) resulted from a creole acquiring non-creole features or vice versa. It is only when seen in a broader historical context that the folk speech of Jamaica, for example, has been identified as a creole that has acquired non-creole features, whereas the folk speech of the Cayman Islands appears to be a non-creole that has acquired creole features (cf. Washabaugh 1983:174–8). The morphology of the verbal system usually provides a reliable guide as to whether the variety is a creole (with preverbal markers and no inflectional endings for tense) or a non-creole (with such inflections – at least in the case of the Atlantic varieties) – but sometimes even this indication has been obscured by the homogenizing effect of shared geographical (if not social) space of white and black speech varieties, as in Barbados, the Bay Islands of Honduras, and the southern United States.

For a long time linguists were unsure of how to classify varieties with both creole and non-creole features, particularly the English-based varieties of the West Indies. In 1869–70 Van Name said: 'We find in Surinam . . . the only English creole which deserves the name' (p. 125). In the 1890s Schuchardt (in Gilbert 1985:42) recognized the effect of what Bloomfield later dubbed 'de-creolizing' (1933:474), but later linguists were unsure of the direction of the change. Reinecke (1937:274–5) wrote that:

> The Surinam dialects, like West African Pidgin English, are
> unmistakably creole dialects in the sense of being simplified to a purely
> analytic structure. The other West Indian English dialects are not,
> however, so completely pruned down [. . . and] may be regarded as

what Schuchardt called creolizing languages – dialects on the way to
complete analytic simplification, but which have for various reasons
stopped a little short of it.

Reinecke's point is not as naive as it may at first seem. Although simplification is now associated with pidginization rather than creolization, it is also
recognized that inflections, for example, can be lost in contact situations that
do not involve full restructuring (1.3). There is still disagreement about the
nature and sequence of the linguistic forces that shaped such semi-creoles as
Afrikaans, Réunionnais and some varieties of Caribbean Spanish and Brazilian
Portuguese – or even Barbadian and AAVE. There is no consensus on what
role pidgins or creoles played in the development of these varieties, although
there is growing agreement that they played some role (Neumann-Holzschuh
and Schneider, fc.).

As recently as 1962, Stewart restricted the New World English-based creoles
to Sranan and Saramaccan (p. 36), noting that in the Caribbean proper
'varieties of English are best treated as dialects of English. That such dialects
are often referred to locally as *creolese* . . . should not be allowed to obscure
their basic difference from real Creoles' (1962:50–1). Stewart (p.c.) has
explained that at the time it seemed more prudent to exclude these varieties
from the discussion of creoles since it was unclear whether they were creoles
that had acquired non-creole features or vice versa. By 1967, however, he felt
confident that additional historical sociolinguistic information could clarify
this point regarding what had come to be widely recognized as post-creole
varieties in both the Caribbean area and the United States. Citing eighteenth-
century examples of restructured English used by American blacks, Stewart
concluded that 'After the Civil War, with the abolition of slavery, the breakdown of the plantation system, and the steady increase in education for poor
as well as affluent Negroes, the older field-hand creole English began to lose
many of its creole characteristics' (1967:54). Later, Alleyne (1980:194) agreed
that something similar had happened in the West Indies. In 1965 Stewart
applied the idea of the continuum to African American Vernacular English
and introduced the terms *acrolect* for the variety closest to the standard and
basilect for the variety farthest from it, with *mesolect* for those between. In
an article published the same year, B. L. Bailey (1965) also asserted that 'The
American Negro, like the Jamaican, operates in a linguistic continuum' and
suggested that the American black dialect be approached from a creolist
perspective: 'I would like to suggest that the Southern Negro "dialect" differs
from other Southern speech because its deep structure is different, having its
origin as it undoubtedly does in some Proto-Creole grammatical structure'
(p. 43).

Schuchardt had been the first but not the only linguist to suggest that AAVE had evolved from the interaction of a creole and local English. The American George Krapp (1925:253) suggested that it developed out of a pidgin, and Bloomfield (1933:474) speculated that a jargon had become nativized

> among Negro slaves in many parts of America. When the jargon has become the only language of the subject group, it is a *creolized language*. The creolized language has the status of an inferior dialect of the masters' speech. It is subject to constant levelling-out and improvement in the direction of the latter. The various types of 'Negro dialect' which we observe in the United States show us some of the last stages of this levelling. With the improvement of social conditions, this levelling is accelerated; the result is a caste-dialect . . . It is a question whether during this period the dialect that is being de-creolized may not influence the speech of the community – whether the creolized English of the southern slaves, for instance, may not have influenced local types of sub-standard or even of standard English.

Apparently these analyses, well ahead of their time, fell on largely deaf ears and it was not until the 1960s, with the surge of interest in the culture and history of African Americans that came along with the civil rights movement, that a significant number of people were ready to accept such a reading of American sociolinguistic history. The study of AAVE was encouraged not only by the Zeitgeist but also by government grants aimed at improving language-related educational difficulties of AAVE speakers. The growing acceptance of the historical relationship of AAVE to pidgin and creole English stimulated greater interest in creole linguistics in the United States, fostering more research and publications aimed at a broader readership than just linguists and educators (e.g. Dillard 1972). In 1966 Hall published the first undergraduate-level textbook on pidgins and creoles, helping to secure a place for the discipline in academia.

Although DeCamp (1961:82) was the first linguist to apply the word 'continuum' to the gradation of varieties between creole and standard English in the Caribbean, the notion (if not the word) had been current among dialectologists of Romance and Germanic languages for at least a century, although they were dealing with a basically different situation in which the gradation was between two varieties that were closely related structurally rather than two quite distinct linguistic systems. The notion of coexisting creole varieties at different distances from the standard goes back to the eighteenth century: Oldendorp (quoted by Gilbert 1986b) first discussed the various creoles and then added, 'Blacks generally corrupt the European language still more', implying that another variety, spoken by whites, was closer to the standard. This was also the implication of the 1869 Larousse definition of *creole*: 'This language, often unintelligible in the mouth of an old African, is extremely sweet in the mouth of white creole speakers' (quoted by Meijer and Muysken 1977:22). This is interpreted as suggesting that Europeans knew that 'there existed a gradation of speech varieties between a creole and its base language' (p. 23). Actually it suggests awareness of no more than two varieties, one used by blacks and another by whites. This would seem to reflect the historical origin of the varieties at each end of the continuum. Cassidy (1964:267) remarked on 'the linguistic spectrum following the social spectrum'. M. G. Smith (1972:258) described Jamaican society as 'divided into three social sections . . . the white, the brown, and the black . . . Although these color coefficients are primarily heuristic, they indicate the racial majority and cultural ancestry of each section accurately.' While making no claim about the correlation of an individual's race and social group today, this does suggest the historical origin of the various segments of the society, with African and European poles on a continuum of cultural traits that include language.

As early as 1934 Reinecke and Tokimasa referred to a 'dialect continuum' between Hawaiian Creole English and the standard (p. 48). In 1961 DeCamp proposed the continuum model for studying Jamaican:

> Nearly all speakers of English in Jamaica could be arranged in a sort of linguistic continuum, ranging from the speech of the most backward peasant or labourer all the way to that of the well-educated urban professional. Each speaker represents not a single point but a span on this continuum, for he is usually able to adjust his speech upward or downward for some distance on it. (1961:82)

DeCamp emphasized that despite the apparent social correlates, the continuum should first be described in purely linguistic terms to avoid the circularity of saying that 'words characteristic of high-school graduates are commonly used by high-school graduates' (p. 82). His strategy is clearer in his 1964 article proposing a theoretical model for converting the structures of standard English into those of the creole:

> Complex as such a set of conversion rules would be, they would be considerably simpler than an entire new grammar developed from scratch. And the result could be a grammar not of one but of all varieties of Jamaican Creole. For it is a characteristic of creoles that the proportions of the component of ingredients never remain constant. One might arrange all the speakers of a given creole in a row, in an order ranging from those whose creole most resembles

> the relevant standard to those whose variety is the most deviant. In
> Jamaica, by the way, these extremes are so different as to be mutually
> unintelligible. Yet our grammar will serve for all of them. As one
> moves down the row of speakers, one applies more and more of the
> conversion rules appended to our grammar. (1964:231)

In a later article (DeCamp 1971b), many more of the actual mechanisms of
the continuum model have been worked out. Illustrating it with data from 7
informants selected from his survey of 142 Jamaican communities, DeCamp
arranged these speakers in a continuum according to their use or non-use of
6 linguistic features, including lexicon (e.g. English *child* versus Creole *pikni*),
phonology (e.g. E /θ/ versus Creole /t/) and syntax (E *didn't* versus Creole *no
ben*). These features are numbered and arranged in a hierarchy on the continuum so that 'a redundancy convention could be formulated whereby the
presence of any index feature implied the presence of all other index features
of lower number' (1971b:353). For example, a speaker who says *nyam* 'eat'
(which is very far down the social scale) will also say *pikni* 'child' (which is
used much higher up the scale). After these lects were arranged by linguistic
criteria only, their speakers were found to fall into a corresponding social
hierarchy: the speaker of the variety most like English was a young, well-
educated business owner from an urban centre, whereas the most creole-like
variety was used bv an elderly and illiterate peasant farmer in an isolated
mountain village. DeCamp emphasized that the linear structure of the continuum is adequate because it is based solely on linguistic features: 'Of course
the sociological correlates of the linguistic variation are multidimensional:
age, education, income bracket, occupation, etc. But the linguistic variation
itself is linear if described in linguistic terms rather than in terms of those
sociological correlates' (1971b:354). However, Le Page and Tabouret-Keller
(1985) later objected that linguistic variation could also be multidimensional,
particularly in multilingual speech communities like Belize and St Lucia.

DeCamp's efforts to work out a theoretical model that could deal with
variation with sufficient rigour was also a reaction to the transformational
generative grammar that was coming to dominate American linguistics
(DeCamp 1977:14). Noam Chomsky had stated explicitly that his theory was
'concerned primarily with an ideal speaker–listener, in a completely homogeneous speech-community' (1965:3). William Labov (1969) tried to make
this framework more suitable for real speech communities, which are not
completely homogeneous, by adding variables to grammatical rules to indicate
the likelihood of a variant occurring in a given context. It is relevant that
Labov was working with African American Vernacular English; although all
natural speech has variable features, variation is particularly salient in creole

and post-creole continua. Indeed, this variation was what made these varieties so difficult to work with. B. L. Bailey tried to overcome this difficulty in writing a transformational grammar of Jamaican creole by 'abstracting a hypothetical dialect which could reasonably be regarded as featuring the main elements of the deep structure [of the creole]' (1965:43). Although few if any Jamaicans actually speak such pure creole, her construct fitted the static theoretical model of transformational grammar. Bailey tried to provide some suggestion of variation by appending a list of morpheme variants such as *de waak, da waak, waakin* or *iz waakin* – all 'is/are walking' (1966:139). However, Hellinger (1985:10) contends that the main impact of Bailey's 1966 book was to demonstrate the limited usefulness of the transformational generative model in dealing with creole languages. Yet DeCamp found Bailey's abstraction of 'pure creole' very useful: 'It is precisely the idealized extreme variety which had to be accurately described before we could begin on the many varieties intermediate between it and the standard' (1971b:351).

One of the most fruitful ideas that DeCamp brought to bear on his continuum model was that of the implicational scale, a device first used in psychology (Guttman 1944) and later linguistics (Elliott *et al.* 1969), although DeCamp developed it independently in the late 1950s while working on his Jamaican data (1971b:369). As noted above, he arranged variable linguistic features along a continuum so that the presence of a particular feature also implied the presence of other variables with lower numbers on the scale (1971b:353). Derek Bickerton, an English linguist working with data from Guyanese Creole English, devised grids of variable features arranged to show that if a rule was in the process of change, a hierarchy of environments could be established, ranging from least to most favourable, so that 'deviances apart, the presence of a basilect index alone in a given column implies the presence of similar indices in all columns to the left; while the presence of a non-basilectal index alone or otherwise implies the presence of similar indices, alone or otherwise in all columns to the right' (Bickerton 1973b:646). Bickerton's work tended to confirm the wave theory of the American C. J. N. Bailey: 'We have seen that, in the history of one rule-change, behavior followed the sequence categorical–variable–categorical, i.e. that inherent variability may be best regarded as a developmental phase coming between two categorical phases' (Bickerton 1971:487). His work with variation in complementizers (1971), the copula (1973a) and pronouns (1973b) indicated that such polylectal grids could be measured for well-formedness by scalability indices (percentages representing the sum of non-deviant cells divided by the sum of cells filled, with 100% indicating a deviance-free grid). The scalability of his tables ranged from 87.9% (mesolect copula) to 100% (basilect singular pronouns), well above the chance scalability of 66.6% for a three-place table. However, Bickerton's book-length discussion of the Guyanese continuum (1975a) was criticized for manipulating data to maximize scalability. Baker (1976) noted that although Bickerton was dealing with outputs (i.e. the speech of individuals which could vary according to circumstances), he labelled these as 'speakers' on his tables and graphs. Thus the same individual could be presented as both a basilect speaker (e.g. 'speaker' 186 on pages 25 and 64) and a mesolect speaker (p. 115). Baker concluded that such manipulations 'cast very serious doubt on Bickerton's methodology' and that the 'implicational relations do not hold' (1976a:22, 31).

Some scholars are still publishing quantitative analyses of variation along creole continua (e.g. Rickford 1992), and some sociolinguists still use associated devices such as implicational scales (e.g. Nagy, Moisset and Sankoff 1996). In general, however, interest in this area has waned, in part because of the excessive claims as to what such studies could reveal about a wide range of phenomena from language change to the psychological reality of grammars. Other scholars, particularly Le Page and Tabouret-Keller (1985), have, as noted above, objected that the unidimensional model that the continuum offers is too simplistic to convey the real complexity of actual creole speech communities, particularly those that are multilingual. Rickford (1987) has responded that it is the very simplicity of the unidimensional model that makes it usable, unlike multidimensional models, although the latter 'may be decomposable into combinations of two, three or four unidimensional continua'. Whatever the future of continuum studies, they have helped creole linguistics gain some very solid ground (as well as some rather boggy terrain), so that many of the aspects of dealing with decreolizing varieties are much less daunting today than they were until the 1970s.

Many would disagree that decreolization is only 'ordinary contact-induced language change, akin (for both social and linguistic reasons) to dialect borrowing from a standard to a nonstandard dialect' (Thomason and Kaufman 1988). Unlike the contact between two dialects that are in essence two variants of the same linguistic system, the contact between a creole and its lexical source language represents the collision of two very different linguistic systems, and the strategies for reconciling such irreconcilable differences are a quite extraordinary linguistic phenomenon.

In the 1970s the study of AAVE peaked and then began to decline. Labov, the leading scholar in this field and sociolinguistics in general, had long rejected the connection between AAVE and the Caribbean creoles: 'We must recognize that youth growing up in the inner cities today is not in contact with that Creole continuum' (1972:66). Yet he also encouraged research by young black linguists who often saw that connection as the source of the separate identity of AAVE (e.g. Rickford 1977). By 1982 Labov had also come to accept what he called 'the creolist hypothesis' of the origin of Black English, in part because of the parallel patterns of copula deletion in AAVE, Gullah and Jamaican Creole (Holm 1976, Baugh 1980).

A number of white American linguists who had come to feel unwelcome in Black English studies turned their energies to creole linguistics, and that field entered a phase of accelerated growth. In 1972 the Society for Caribbean Linguistics was organized at a conference in Trinidad. During the biennial meetings over the next decade at various universities in the West Indies, leadership shifted from North American and British linguists to largely anglophone West Indians, yet tensions within this organization remained largely those between first-world and third-world scholars (e.g. unfair distribution of access to publications and publishing, funding, and the machinery of academic advancement in general) rather than those between blacks and whites. However, there was a definite emphasis on English-based creoles as the focus of common interest. In 1976 the first Colloque International des Créolistes met in France to organize the Comité International des Etudes Créoles, leading to the publication of the journal *Etudes Créoles*, focusing largely on French-based varieties. Meanwhile a newsletter, the *Carrier Pidgin*, had been established in 1973 and work began on *A bibliography of pidgin and creole languages* (Reinecke *et al.* 1975), both becoming major mainstays of the discipline. A *Journal of Creole Studies* began and ended in 1977, but in 1986 a new *Journal of Pidgin and Creole Languages* emerged to become the organ of a new Society for Pidgin and Creole Linguistics. As the field became more central to general linguistics, series of books devoted exclusively to the study of creoles were organized, such as the Creole Language Library (John Benjamins in Amsterdam and Philadelphia) and the Kreolische Bibliothek (Helmut Buske Verlag, Hamburg).

A 1973 conference at the University of Papua New Guinea helped focus attention on Pacific pidgins and creoles, a focus that was maintained at the 1975 conference on pidgins and creoles at Honolulu, Hawaii. In 1989 the Society on Pidgins and Creoles in Melanesia was established in Papua New Guinea, and in Australia a newsletter on the use of Pidgins and Creoles in Education began. Atlantic creolists and Pacific pidginists publishing in English seemed to be growing more aware of the need to overcome their mutual isolation (Byrne and Holm 1993b). Meanwhile, the first Colóquio sobre Crioulos de base lexical Portuguesa was held in Lisbon in 1991 (D'Andrade and Kihm 1992), leading to the journal *Papia: Revista de Crioulos de Base Ibérica*, published in Brazil in Portuguese and Spanish, which encouraged further research in this area (Bartens 1995, 1996; Couto 1996; Perl and Schwegler 1998).

2.12 Universalists again

Although the general usefulness of the continuum model had gained wide acceptance by the mid 1970s, this model had nothing to do with the origin of the creoles, and thus cast no light on the perennial question of why the Atlantic creoles in particular should share so many structural features not found in their different lexical source languages. The position of the monogeneticists – particularly regarding the genealogical link between pidgin Portuguese and Sabir – remained unprovable and finally came to be seen as a matter of faith among a dwindling number of faithful. However, that part of the monogenetic theory linking the creoles to West African languages via substrate influence (whether or not this involved the intermediate stage of a pidgin based on Portuguese or another European language) was not disputed by the competing polygenetic theories and, as Hall (1968:365) noted in his summary of the state of creole linguistics at the end of the 1960s: 'At present, the existence of a considerable African element in the various Caribbean creoles, on all levels of linguistic structure, is recognized by all scholars.' Even Bickerton, who was later to deny the significance of any such influence, repeatedly referred to it in his 1975 book.

As before, language acquisition played a central role in the updated universalist theory. Chomsky (1965:27) had proposed that children were born with a predisposition to recognize certain universal properties of language that facilitated their acquisition of the language of their particular speech community. These universals were seen as the general parameters of language, unmarked for the specific characteristics of particular languages. Ferguson (1971) suggested that language universals also shaped the simplified registers 'that many, perhaps all, speech communities have . . . for use with people who are regarded for one reason or another as unable to readily understand the normal speech of the community (e.g. babies, foreigners, deaf people)' (143). He noted that baby talk and foreigner talk resembled the simplified register used in telegrams in omitting the copula, definite article and prepositions. He cited an early study of child language acquisition (Brown and Bellugi 1964) which noted that, without being fully aware of it, parents tend to simplify their language when speaking to very young children by avoiding subordination, using simple sentences and repeating new words. Ferguson suggested that:

the notion of simplicity in language is important in several ways, since it may be related to theories of language universals, language acquisition, and language loss . . . it is possible to hazard some universal hypotheses. For example, 'If a language has an inflectional system, this will tend to be replaced in simplified speech such as baby talk and foreigner talk by uninflected forms (e.g. simple nominative for the noun; infinitive, imperatives or third person singular for the verb).' Several such hypotheses might even be subsumed under a more general hypothesis of the form: 'If a language has a grammatical category which clearly involves an unmarked–marked opposition [cf. Greenberg 1966b] the unmarked term tends to be used for both in simplified speech.' (1971:145–6)

Ferguson concluded that language universals of simplification must play a role in the formation of pidgins since native speakers of the lexical source language followed them in the foreigner talk they used with non-native speakers. Although they did not refer to Ferguson (1971), Kay and Sankoff (1974) added to the list of possible universal features of pidgins. In addition to the replacement of inflectional morphology by free lexemes (1974:68), they suggested that pidgins seemed to be universally characterized by a shallowness of phonology or restricted morphophonemics and lack of allophony (p. 62) as well as the occurrence of 'propositional qualifiers . . . in surface structure exterior to the propositions they qualify' (p. 64). For example, sentential qualifiers of time, aspect and manner could be expected to occur outside the predicate, as well as negatives and yes–no question indicators. They concluded that: 'contact vernaculars may possibly reveal in a more direct way than do most natural languages the universals of cognitive structure and process that underlie all human language ability and language use' (1974:64). Todd (1974:42) made the connection between universals in simplification and universals in all languages:

> there are universal patterns of linguistic behavior appropriate
> to contact situations . . . pidgins and creoles are alike because,
> fundamentally, languages are alike and simplification processes are
> alike . . . human beings are biologically programmed to acquire
> *Language* rather than any particular language, and . . . the
> programming includes an innate ability to dredge one's linguistic
> behaviour of superficial redundancies.

Todd went on to note possible parallels in child language acquisition and the formation of pidgins:

> Lamso, in Cameroon, has a vocabulary set, containing several
> reduplicated forms, which is employed to and by children with whom
> also tonal contrasts are kept to a minimum. It is a stimulating thought

that pidgins may result from such 'simple' exchanges. Babies soon discard the simple 'idealized dialect' because social pressures put a premium on their acquiring the language of the adult community. But such pressure did not, in the past, prevail in pidgin situations and so the urge to modify towards a more 'acceptable' norm was not a factor in the formation of pidgins. (1974:47)

Although he built on such ideas, Bickerton (1974, republished 1980) departed from them by claiming that it was creoles rather than pidgins that reveal such universals (unstable pidgins remaining essentially chaotic) and that these universals could be characterized not just by general parameters but specific structures: 'there is a natural tense-aspect system, rooted in specific neural properties of the brain' (1980:12). Bickerton claimed that this verbal system – with preverbal markers for tense, modality and aspect occurring in that order in various combinations (6.1.7) – is part of a natural semantax, neurally based, which guides first language acquisition in its early stages but then is systematically suppressed in natural languages, which have developed their own marked (i.e. non-universal) structures. However, in the earliest stages of creolization, he claimed, children use this natural semantax and it is not suppressed by older members of the speech community, who themselves use an unstable or even chaotic pidgin variety of the language without many norms. Thus Hawaiian Creole English, which he claimed arose without any contact with the Caribbean creoles, developed a verbal system identical to theirs. Since there is no historical link between these creoles, he claimed, the only other explanation is the innate predisposition to learn this specific structure.

Bickerton (1980:5) claimed that his predecessors had focused entirely on the pidgin stage in their discussions of universals, but Givón (1979, written in 1973) had referred to creoles as well. While their positions are similar in a number of respects, Bickerton rejects Givón's understanding of universals as 'a kind of lowest common denominator, what is left when everything that is marked in "natural languages" has been stripped off' (1980:15) – essentially the view of Greenberg (1966b) – in favour of universals as specific linguistic structures.

In 1976 Bickerton offered additional data to support the above position in a comparative study of the syntax and semantics of the verbal systems of Hawaiian CE, a number of Atlantic creoles and creolized Arabic (see section 3.14). The last seemed to strengthen his claim for universals considerably since the similarity could not be explained by a common substrate or diffusion, but Thomason and Elgibali (1986:428) later noted that 'preverbal particles in the modern [Arabic-based] pidgins and Ki-Nubi cannot be used as evidence for a claim about universals of pidginization because all forms of Arabic

– C[lassical] A[rabic] as well as Coll[oquial] A[rabic] – have functionally and positionally similar tense/aspect markers in their verbal systems'.

In a later article (1977b), Bickerton distinguishes between pidgins and creoles whose speakers were displaced (which underwent early and rapid creolization) and those whose speakers remained in their original environment (often leading to extended pidgins) – cf. 2.8. He then shows that creoles spoken by displaced populations (which somehow include Hawaiians) have a number of features in common beyond their verbal systems: (1) a generic or nonspecific 0 article in addition to definite and indefinite articles; (2) fronting of noun phrases for focusing; (3) a distinction between attributive, locative–existential and sometimes equative copulas (cf. Holm 1976); (4) multiple negation.

In 1981 Bickerton published *Roots of language*, expanding what he now called his language bioprogram hypothesis (LBH). In addition to the four similarities among the creoles mentioned above, he added the following: (5) realized and unrealized complements (6.1.8); (6) relativization and subject copying; (7) the use of 'it has' to express both possession and existence (6.2.3); (8) bimorphemic question words (4.3.4); and (9) equivalents of passive constructions (4.3.2); as well as (10) an expanded discussion of the tense-mode-aspect system. To this and a chapter on pidgins (in which he concluded that Hawaiian Pidgin English was not the source of the structure of Hawaiian Creole English, nor are substrate structures in pidgins generally passed on to their ensuing creoles) were added chapters on first language acquisition and the origin of language itself in light of his bioprogram hypothesis. The book was widely read, not only by creolists, but also by those with a more general interest in linguistics and language acquisition, particularly psychologists. The controversy over his extreme universalist hypothesis heated up, leading to extended debates in a journal of psychology (Bickerton *et al.* 1984) and a special conference in Amsterdam on substrata and universals in creole genesis (Muysken and Smith 1986). Although the exchanges in both forums indicated that few creolists were willing to dismiss substrate influence and diffusion altogether in explaining the structural similarities among the Atlantic creoles, it was clear that Bickerton (1981) had had a considerable impact on creole studies.

2.13 Substratists again

As Hall (1968:365) noted, there was a consensus of opinion in the 1960s and early 1970s that the African substrate had had a considerable influence on the Atlantic creoles on all linguistic levels. Indeed, substrate influence was a key element in both the monogenetic and polygenetic theories that competed as explanations of these creoles' genesis. Douglas Taylor, whose publications

spanned three decades, became increasingly interested in the structural similarities of the Atlantic creoles (1971, 1977), which he attributed to substrate
influence: 'While African loanwords are relatively few in most West Indian
creoles . . . African loan constructions are both common and striking' (1977:7).
Taylor's comparison of ten linguistic features common to Yoruba and six
Atlantic creoles (many of which were later presented as universals in Bickerton
1981) led him to conclude that:

> Lesser Antillean Creole French in its formative period was in close
> contact with a language or languages very like Yoruba; and as
> French-based Haitian and Cayenne creoles and English-based Sranan
> and Saramaccan, and Iberian-based Papiamentu and Saotomense
> (Gulf of Guinea) show very much the same and other resemblances to
> Yoruba . . . we conclude that these creoles have diverged from what
> may well have been a common pidgin by lexical replacement from the
> languages of the slaves' European masters and overseers. (1977:9)

Bickerton (1981) objected that Yoruba was a particularly inappropriate language in which to look for substrate features since its speakers were largely
brought to the Caribbean area in the late eighteenth and early nineteenth
centuries, too late to have influenced the formation of the creoles. However,
Taylor's point had been that substrate influence had come from African languages 'very *like* Yoruba' and Yoruba is indeed typical of the Kwa group of
languages spoken by a significant proportion of the people brought from Africa
to the New World during the period in which the creoles emerged. This is demonstrated by a comparison of twenty structural features in seventeen African
and sixteen creole and post-creole languages (Holm 1976, 1987). Alleyne's
widely read *Comparative Afro-American* (1980) also supported a substratist
position, taking issue with Bickerton's bioprogram hypothesis. Some creolists
who acknowledged the influence of substrate languages (e.g. Baker in Baker
and Corne 1982:254) allowed that 'Innate rules as envisaged by Bickerton
could be the source of identical grammatical structures in any number of
creole languages which developed independently of one another', although
the logic of Bickerton's argument could not allow any significant substrate
influence on creoles (at least early-creolizing or 'radical' – i.e. 'true' – creoles),
since his original evidence for the bioprogram was that there was no other
explanation for the structural similarities of the creoles. Other creolists ignored
Bickerton's claim that structural parallels in substrate languages were irrelevant and continued their research in this area. A German linguist, Norbert
Boretzky (1983), provided what Bickerton (1984) claimed was lacking: a
'systematic and detailed comparison between substratum structures and
the creole structures supposed to have been derived from them'. However,

Boretzky did not provide a comprehensive theory for the influence of sub-strate languages in this work, nor did he provide the historical data needed to link the particular African languages he discussed with the particular creole languages he believed they had influenced. Instead, he let the linguistic data speak for itself, showing widespread parallels in the phonology and syntax of certain West African languages and the Atlantic creoles. He also examined a control group of what he considered non-Atlantic creoles with different substrata: Melanesian Pidgin English, Mauritian Creole French and the Spanish-based creoles of the Philippines. It spoke well for his method that only the Mauritian data yielded affinities with West African structures (particularly in the verb phrase) which he had not expected. This led him to speculate that there was some historical connection that was still not properly understood. This was in fact the thesis of Baker and Corne (1982), to which Boretzky did not have access: Mauritian CF may show 'a West-African substratal influence'; its features indicate 'typological identity with the Atlantic Creoles' (1982:122, 127).

Boretzky's later work (e.g. 1986) focuses on a more explicit explanation of substrate influence: why some features of substrate languages survive in creoles while others do not. From a comparison of the verbal systems of Fante (an Akan language of the Kwa group) and Jamaican Creole English, he concluded that a grammatical category from the substrate was more readily transferred to the creole if the superstrate had an available morpheme to express it which (a) could be easily isolated and identified, (b) had no allomorph that differed greatly, (c) was not homophonous with markers of other categories, and (d) was immediately translatable into the substrate language.

The Congolese linguist Salikoko Mufwene (1986a) pointed out that the substratist and universalist positions were irreconcilable only in their most extreme forms, i.e. when each excluded the possibility of the other. Most creolists agree that language universals played an important role in the selection of features that were ultimately retained in the creoles, such as the use of free rather than bound morphemes to convey grammatical information. Fewer find the bioprogram a convincing source of specific features, particularly because Bickerton's only proof of the bioprogram is his contention that there is no alternative explanation for the structural features common to the 'radical' creoles: 'neither substratum influence nor diffusion is adequate to account for the creation of creole languages. In the absence of further alternatives, the LBH or some variant thereof seems inescapable' (in Bickerton *et al.* 1984:184). However, serious doubts have been cast on the claimed irrelevance of both substrate influence and diffusion in the case of Hawaiian Creole English, which provides Bickerton's crucial evidence for the language bioprogram hypothesis. Goodman (1985a) provides evidence that Bickerton's data on Hawaiian Pidgin English, which supposedly led to modern Hawaiian Creole English, is from too late a period (1900 to 1920) to be relevant to the formation of the creole, which took place in the 1880s. While the later pidgin reflects substrate features from the languages spoken by later immigrants from Japan and the Philippines (features not found in the creole), Goodman asserts that the earlier pidgin that developed into Hawaiian Creole English grew out of an earlier English-based pidgin used between whalers and other seamen and Hawaiians, which spread from the ports to the plantations in the latter part of the nineteenth century (Reinecke 1969). If this pidgin served as the medium by which some of the substrate features of contact English in the Atlantic and Caribbean spread to Hawaii and the rest of the Pacific, there is no need to account for these features by means of a hypothetical bioprogram (Holm 1986).

Among the positive effects of Bickerton's criticism of substratist research was a renewed effort to sort out which African languages were most relevant to the formation of the various Atlantic creoles (e.g. Singler 1986). While considerably more research is needed in this area, including more comprehensive descriptions of the grammars and lexicons of the relevant African languages, a growing number of Africanists have begun working with creoles as well, and their research seems promising.

2.14   Other trends

Sociolinguistics continues to shape the theoretical perspectives of those working on pidgin and creole languages. Le Page and Tabouret-Keller (1985) proposed a multidimensional model to relate language and social identity in creole communities, viewing 'linguistic behaviour as a series of *acts of identity* in which people reveal both their personal identity and their search for social roles' (p. 14). They contrast communities that are socially and linguistically *focused* ('tightly-knit and closely-interactive communities . . . [in which] the sharing of rules, and the regularity of rules, can be considerable' – p. 5) as opposed to those that are *diffuse*, with great variation and seeming irregularity. Another important recent development in theory is the idea that the complexity of the structure of creole languages grew gradually over a number of generations, as suggested by the records of those creoles that have been documented since the eighteenth century (Arends 1986, 1993; Carden and Stewart 1988).

Since the mid 1990s international communication within the field has been both facilitated and accelerated by electronic mail and the Internet. The Creolist Archives website (http://www.ling.su.se/creole), set up at the

University of Stockholm in 1996 by Mikael Parkvall, provides pidgin and creole language samples, early texts, creolists' addresses, etc., along with an e-mail discussion group, the CreoLIST, which is conducted mainly in English but also in French, Spanish and Haitian.

Despite the growing body of creolist literature in German, Spanish and Portuguese, most continues to be published in English or French. This has tended to divide creolists into two camps, each of which is insufficiently aware of the work of the other. While the foregoing broad historical outline is relevant to the development of theory in both, it should be noted that theoretical debates in each camp have followed their own course. The literature on the French-based creoles, written largely in French, has tended to focus more on the influence of the superstrate. The idea of continuity between French and the French-based creoles was stressed in the theory that the creoles grew out of a variety of nautical French that represented a levelling of regional dialects and served as a kind of lingua franca among seamen and in ports (Hull 1968). Although it was later specified that this model included input from substrate languages via relexification (Hull 1979), Chaudenson (1974) minimized such input in his theory that the creoles evolved from a variety of colloquial French (*français avancé*) that was ahead of the standard language in following natural evolutionary tendencies such as the loss of inflections. It should be noted that Chaudenson was drawn to these conclusions while working with Réunionnais, whose status as a creole rather than a regional variety has been disputed. However, his theoretical model has been applied to the genesis of all the French-based creoles despite convincing counterevidence (Baker and Corne 1982) that the genesis of creoles such as Mauritian involved a clear structural break with French due to restructuring under the influence of other languages and universals of creolization. It should be noted that natural evolutionary tendencies of the source language have long been invoked to explain the origin of such semi-creoles as Brazilian Vernacular Portuguese (Révah 1963) and Afrikaans (Raidt 1983).

Determining the precise origin and development of such varieties with both creole and non-creole features poses one of the greatest challenges to creole linguistics in the twenty-first century (Holm 1998a, 1998b, fc.). The study of restructured languages in general and partially restructured varieties in particular has been strengthened by the contribution of an increasing number of historical linguists such as Thomason and Kaufman (1988), who have discussed theoretical questions regarding pidginization and creolization within the broader context of language contact and genetic linguistics. The greater degree of restructuring that they claim can take place in language shift has suggested a new scenario for the genesis of partially restructured languages such as Brazilian Vernacular Portuguese (Mello 1997a) and nonstandard Dominican Spanish (Green 1997, Holm, Lorenzino, and Mello 1999). Afrikaans studies have been further liberated politically by the coming of majority rule to South Africa in 1994, so that linguists who trace the language's origins to contact and partial restructuring no longer risk being ostracized. A poignant moment in the history of creolistics came during the Amsterdam meeting of the Society for Pidgin and Creole Linguistics when white and black South African linguists sat down together at a round table to discuss the origins of Afrikaans (Makhudu 1993, van der Merwe 1993, Waher 1993). The study of African American Vernacular English has undergone converse liberation, whereby it is now possible to discuss its non-creolization (Schneider 1993, Winford 1997–8).

However, there has also been serious opposition to the idea that creolization is a gradient phenomenon. Building on Chaudenson's (1992) view of creoles as simply varieties of their superstrate languages – approximations of approximations of the earlier regional dialects spoken by European colonists – Mufwene (1994, 1996, 1997) concluded that 'creole' is not a valid term for classifying languages, and therefore one language cannot be said to be more or less 'creole' than another. McWhorter (1998) countered that creoles are indeed synchronically distinguishable from non-creole languages in that they combine all three of the following traits: they have little or no inflectional affixation; they make little or no use of tone to contrast monosyllables lexically or to encode syntax; and they have semantically regular derivational affixation. This creole prototype, graded like most phenomena, is 'the direct result of severely interrupted transmission of a lexifier, at too recent a date for the traits to have been undone by diachronic change' (1998:812). This reaffirmation of such key concepts in the English-language creolistic tradition as 'pidgin', 'creole', and 'semi-creole' led to a lively encounter at the first joint meeting of the Society for Pidgin and Creole Linguistics and the Comité International des Etudes Créoles in Aix-en-Provence (1999).

While pidgin and creole linguistics has traditionally included partially restructured varieties (e.g. Reinecke 1937), there has been a recent movement to broaden the discipline's scope as contact linguistics (Thomason 1997c), including languages that have resulted not from pidginization and creolization (to whatever degree) but rather from other processes such as 'language intertwining' (Bakker and Muysken 1994), e.g. languages like Michif, which mix entire structures from both their source languages, largely intact. Such studies increase our understanding of the range of possible outcomes of language contact, and this understanding may well shed new light on the genesis and development of pidgins and creoles. Siegel (1997) examined immigrant koines (e.g. overseas Hindi), indigenized varieties (such as Singapore English) and even renativized Hebrew to conclude that the adoption of features in levelling is affected by certain factors: frequency, regularity, salience and transparency. This suggests a solution for the long search for principles that guide the selection of substrate features into pidgins and creoles.

Perhaps the most basic challenge for creolists in the twenty-first century is to write exhaustive linguistic and sociohistorical descriptions of all the known pidgin and creole languages and their various dialects. Full accounts of such previously undescribed or underdescribed languages as Angolar Creole Portuguese (Maurer 1995, Lorenzino 1998) and more complete collections of texts (such as those in Negerhollands in van Rossem and van der Voort 1996) are needed so that debates over theoretical models (and their implications for general linguistics) can be based on a more adequate and accurate body of knowledge. However, as we strive to improve our theoretical models and the concepts they are built on, we should bear in mind the wisdom of one of our discipline's modern founders:

> technical terms can be traps. They do sometimes serve to clarify insights, theories, discoveries – terms like *basilect, mesolect, acrolect, continuum* – but these convenient terms have a way of jelling or solidifying. We tend to accept them uncritically, forgetting that good science is never static, that there are no absolutes in science, no permanent conclusions: everything is potentially challengeable.
>
> (Cassidy 1994)

Having examined the theories attempting to explain the nature and origin of pidgins and creoles, we will now look at some actual examples of such languages, paying particular attention to the social circumstances that led to their emergence.

3
Social factors

3.0 Introduction

Pidgin and creole languages cannot be defined, nor can their genesis and development be understood, without taking into account the social factors that shaped them. Pidgins, for example, are defined in part by such sociolinguistic factors as their being no one's first language, their arising in a particular social context such as trade, and their evolving as the result of non-intimate social contact between groups of unequal power. Some aspects of the definition of a pidgin are purely linguistic (e.g. reduction and simplification), but even the crucial quality of stability is claimed to depend on the sociolinguistic factor of tertiary hybridization.

The crucial element in the definition of a creole is also sociolinguistic: that it grew out of a pidgin (or possibly an unstable pre-pidgin) that had become nativized in a particular speech community. The purely linguistic elements in the definition of creoles (e.g. structural complexity) do not distinguish them from other natural languages. While one could draw up a list of structural features shared by most of the Atlantic creoles (cf. chapters 5 and 6), there is little agreement that these could be used to determine whether a language is a creole without reference to its sociolinguistic history.

The validity of the theories put forward to explain the genesis and development of pidgin and creole languages crucially depends on whether these theories can satisfactorily take into account the many, various and complex sociolinguistic circumstances under which the known pidgin and creole languages came into being and developed. Considering the social histories of the speakers of the approximately 100 restructured languages surveyed in Holm (1988–9, vol. II) casts light on some (but not all) of the issues. For example, regarding the major definitional difference between pidgins and creoles, it remains unclear whether the key factor determining their structure is in fact nativization, if only because the effects of nativization cannot be isolated for observation in the real world. Creolists have never been able to observe cases of abrupt creolization, and, in the gradual creolization of expanded pidgins, competent adult non-native speakers always co-exist with the children growing up as native speakers, making it impossible to determine with any certainty which group is contributing what to the structure of the emerging creole.

A primary factor in defining pidgins has been their stability, but it now appears that this is irrelevant to the likelihood of a pidgin becoming a creole. While stability enables us to distinguish pidgins from jargons or pre-pidgin continua, creolization appears to depend instead on social factors, with either pidgins or jargons providing adequate input. Tertiary hybridization was thought to be crucial to a pidgin's stabilization, but some varieties such as Chinese Pidgin English appear to have stabilized without it.

The power and prestige relationships between the speakers of the languages involved in pidginization and creolization appear to be relevant in a number of respects. Pidgins like Russenorsk that evolved between two groups that were roughly equal in power seem to be quite rare, although the Amerindian-based pidgins may belong to this category if they evolved before there was contact with Europeans, or if the first Europeans who used them were less powerful than those who followed. Certain of the pidgins and creoles based on African languages may have arisen among groups of approximately equal power – e.g. Kituba, Lingala and Sango (3.13) – but it is by no means certain that these languages are not more like koines.

There is considerable evidence that relative social power and the consequent prestige are important factors in determining which language becomes the source of a pidgin's lexicon. Even the fact that in Russenorsk the lexicon is derived from the languages of both Russians and Norwegians in roughly equal proportion bears out this argument, since both had roughly equal power. However, the fact that Europeans have used pidgins based on indigenous languages in colonial situations in which the balance of power was quite clearly in their favour – e.g. Fanakalo, Bazaar Malay and Kisetla Swahili (3.13) – indicates that relative power is not the only deciding factor.

It has been suggested that colonialism or slavery might be key factors in the sociolinguistics of pidginization and creolization. While there are a number of counterexamples, the correlation is frequent enough to bear closer examination. The relevant factor would seem to be the degree of power of one group over another, since very powerful social forces are usually needed to counter the momentum of normal language transmission. However, given the right conditions in a social microcosm, the necessary power might be no greater than that of teachers over children in a boarding school or orphanage – cf. Philippine Creole Spanish in Cotabato (Riego de Dios 1979:276), Aboriginal Creole English at the Fitzroy Crossing mission school in Australia (Hudson 1983:10–14) or Unserdeutsch in New Guinea (Volker 1982).

Of course both colonialism and slavery represented a degree of power over others that permitted social engineering on a scale that could affect the genesis and development of a great number of pidgins and creoles from the fifteenth century onwards. Examples range from the Portuguese policy of fostering the growth of mixed communities in their holdings in Africa and Asia (Holm 1988–9:259–98), to the policies of the British that determined the social and linguistic history of Sierra Leone (412–17).

The political and cultural currents of the 1960s and 1970s encouraged a positive re-evaluation of the role of speakers of substrate languages in the development of creoles. It may now be time for a reassessment of the contribution of speakers of superstrate languages. There is considerable evidence that at the time of the creoles' early development Europeans often spoke them more fluently than has generally been assumed. Europeans' continued role in the development of Papiamentu (3.4) and Negerhollands (3.6) is now fairly clear. The work of Hull (1983) indicates that the Creole French spoken by Europeans was an important factor in the spread of that language to Louisiana and probably other colonies as well. The work of Williams (1983) demonstrates that the speech of Caribbean whites cannot be ignored in sorting out the development of Creole English in the West Indies.

A better understanding of the linguistic repertoires of colonial whites is surely needed to advance research in an area that may long remain one of the biggest challenges to creolists: reconstructing the development of semi-creoles like Afrikaans (Slomanson fc.), African American Vernacular English (Winford 1997–8), certain lects of nonstandard Dominican Spanish (Green 1997), Brazilian Vernacular Portuguese (Mello 1997a) and Réunionnais (Chapuis fc.).

Some very basic questions have yet to be satisfactorily answered: is creolization an all-or-nothing kind of process? There is mounting evidence that it can occur to varying degrees, as Hancock (1986:95) suggested. If different degrees of creolization can occur, is this simply the result of the ratio of superstrate to substrate speakers during the first generations of the speech community's existence, or are other factors of equal or greater importance, such as the social relationships between these groups? It is hard to imagine any progress being made in this crucial area of research unless data from the relevant languages are evaluated within the context of the social history of their speakers, and to do this we need to understand better the relationship between the two.

A number of these general issues will be illustrated in the rest of this chapter with specific case studies of the social history of the speakers of seven pidgin or creole languages, each preceded by an overview of its lexical base group: the Portuguese-based creoles (3.1), Angolar CP (3.2); the Spanish-based creoles (3.3), Papiamentu CS (3.4); the Dutch-based creoles (3.5), Negerhollands CD (3.6); the French-based creoles (3.7), Haitian CF (3.8); the English-based Atlantic creoles (3.9), Jamaican CE (3.10); the English-based Pacific pidgins and creoles (3.11), Tok Pisin PE (3.12); pidgins and creoles based on other languages (3.13), and Nubi Creole Arabic (3.14).

This will set the scene for the rest of the book, particularly the chapter on syntax, in which linguistic points will be illustrated mainly by data from these seven languages. This plan allows a broad overview of the structure of the Atlantic creoles (showing how their grammars often coincide with one another while differing from that of their lexical source languages). It also shows that the non-Atlantic varieties (Tok Pisin and Nubi) lack many of the features shared by the Atlantic creoles and their substrates.

The section on each restructured language begins with a summary of the sociohistorical events that shaped its development, followed by a description of its current sociolinguistic situation. After a discussion of some of the language's distinguishing linguistic features, there is a brief text with a morpheme-by-morpheme translation. These texts are taken from connected discourse phonemically represented in the International Phonetic Alphabet.

3.1 The Portuguese-based creoles

Portugal was the first European colonial power in the modern sense, exploring and extending its control over great parts of the coastlines of Africa, Asia and South America to build an overseas empire that made Portugal a great power during the sixteenth and seventeenth centuries. Because the Portuguese set many of the social and linguistic patterns of colonialism that were later taken up by other Europeans, the history of the outposts and colonies that evolved restructured varieties of Portuguese are of particular interest in creole studies.

One of the primary forces that led to this overseas expansion was the Christians' reconquest of Portugal from the Arabs, which had its impetus from the north; once completed, the Portuguese extended their campaign southward into North Africa in the early 1400s. Exploration of the Atlantic coast of Africa was fostered by Prince Henry the Navigator, who supported the development of better sailing vessels and instruments that made navigation out of sight of land safe for the first time. The Portuguese discovered Madeira in 1419 and the Azores in 1427, then reached Cape Verde in 1444 and what is now Sierra Leone in 1460. By the early 1470s they had explored the northern coast of the Gulf of Guinea and discovered its islands. In the 1480s they reached the Congo, Angola and the Cape of Good Hope, which they rounded in 1488.

Trading outposts for slaves led to the establishment of Pidgin Portuguese along much of the Guinea Coast over the following years. An outpost for supplying ships on the previously uninhabited Cape Verde Islands led to the development of creole Portuguese there from the 1460s onwards, making it the oldest known creole language today. The source of slaves on the mainland (today Guiné-Bissau) developed a mutually intelligible creole, which with Cape Verdean makes up the Upper Guinea varieties of CP. The Gulf of Guinea islands, with different substrate languages, developed several creoles quite distinct from those of Upper Guinea (3.2).

Da Gama reached India in 1498 with the help of an Arab pilot, and in 1500 Cabral discovered Brazil. Through military daring and political alliances with local rulers, the Portuguese wrested control over Asian trade routes from the Arabs and Malays, and established coastal outposts for trade throughout the sixteenth century from India and Ceylon (where Indo-Portuguese developed), to Malacca (Papia Kristang CP) and Macao (Makista CP). The wealth from this trading empire was offset by the fact that it depleted Portugal of manpower and led the Portuguese to neglect their domestic agriculture and industry in the hope of gaining riches quickly abroad. In 1580 a dynastic crisis led to the union of the thrones of Spain and Portugal; drawn into Spain's wars with the English and the Dutch, Portugal began to lose its overseas possessions to the latter. By 1640, when Portugal needed all its forces to extricate itself from this union against the wishes of Spain, the dissolution of its overseas empire was well under way. The Portuguese chose to abandon most of Asia, where their forces had been spread too thinly, in favour of Brazil and those parts of Africa needed as a source of slaves. In Brazil the pattern of settlement differed from that of both Africa and Asia, where Portuguese men often married local women, forming a mixed, creole-speaking community loyal to Portugal. A much higher proportion of Portuguese-speaking whites – especially women – settled in Brazil, establishing the vernacular language of Portugal. Still, Brazil received 38% of all Africans brought to the New World (compared to less than 5% who went to North America) and today Brazilian Vernacular Portuguese – the informal speech of most Brazilians – shows even clearer evidence of partial restructuring than does African American Vernacular English.

3.2 Angolar Creole Portuguese

Angolar, called *ngola* by its speakers, is a Portuguese-based creole spoken by the Angolares on the island of São Tomé. They constitute an ethnolinguistic minority group making up under 10% of the island's population. They have remained distinct from the general population of Forros (literally 'freedmen'), i.e. the creoles of the same island who speak São Tomense.

Angolar is one of the four varieties of creole Portuguese spoken on three small islands in Africa's Gulf of Guinea, several hundred miles south of Nigeria and west of Gabon (see map 1): São Tomé and Príncipe (forming a single country, which gained its independence from Portugal in 1975) and Annobón (part of Equatorial Guinea, which has been independent from Spain since 1968). The latter two islands each have their own creoles based on Portuguese: Principense (4,000 speakers), and Annobonese – also called fá d'Ambo – (2,500), while São Tomé has the two creoles mentioned above: São Tomense (85,000) and Angolar (9,000). All four are part of the same linguistic system, Gulf of Guinea CP, and there is some mutual comprehension between speakers of different varieties.

All three islands were uninhabited when the Portuguese first reached them around 1471. São Tomé, the largest, was the first to be settled in 1485, with colonists from Portugal and slaves from Benin (now southern Nigeria) and the Congo–Angola region. In 1493 some 2,000 Jewish children in Portugal were taken from their parents and sent to São Tomé so that, kept from 'the law of Moses, they should be good Christians, and . . . populate the said island' (quoted by Ivens Ferraz 1979:16). In 1506 it was reported that 600 had survived and intermarried with the Africans. Portuguese convicts were also sent to São Tomé and given slave women, who were then granted freedom along with their children. Marques (1976:242) notes that a 'native aristocracy of half breeds rapidly emerged and took control of the islands'. Ivens Ferraz (1979:17) comments that 'the free African population became wealthy, and took over the culture of the Portuguese. One may assume that these Africans and the Portuguese who married into the African population were instrumental in the development of the creole, providing the Portuguese model on which it was based.'

São Tomé became very prosperous in the first half of the sixteenth century as a way-station for the transshipment of slaves from the mainland to the Americas. The cultivation of sugar cane was introduced along with the system of large plantations, some with several hundred slaves. However, the island's economy began to decline during the second half of the sixteenth century due to raids by the French and Dutch, as well as attacks by the Angolar maroons. After a slave revolt in 1586, the Portuguese planters began abandoning the island in large numbers, most of them going to Brazil. By 1640, when the Dutch seized São Tomé for four years, the island was in ruins. The departure of almost all the Portuguese left the creole that had developed virtually cut off from its lexical source language.

Until recently the Angolares were thought to be a Bantu-speaking group whose ancestors had survived the wreck of a slave ship in the 1540s and established a community on the southern tip of the island, opposite and virtually isolated from the main Portuguese settlement. Valkhoff (1966:114) stated that 'their original vernacular is a Bantu language in process of being lusitanized and creolized . . . The Angolares are very reluctant to use the old language in public and they ordinarily express themselves in St Thomas Creole.' Ferraz (1974) rejected this theory, suggesting instead that the Angolares are the descendants of slaves who escaped from the Portuguese plantations on São Tomé in the sixteenth century, citing records of slaves who mutinied and fled from 1517 onwards. By the 1530s they had gained enough strength in numbers to pose a threat to the colony. In 1574 they mounted their heaviest attack, destroying plantations, sugar mills and much of the main settlement. In 1586 there was a general slave revolt and the leader, named Amador, proclaimed himself the king of São Tomé (Ivens Ferraz 1979:19). After most of the Portuguese had fled, the Angolares settled down to a peaceful coexistence with the rest of the island's population.

São Tomé continued to serve as a way-station for provisioning ships, and its creole-speaking inhabitants survived through subsistence farming and fishing: 'The Portuguese blood which ran in their veins was gradually lost in the constant crossings with the races of the mainland opposite because Portugal no longer even sent her convicts there' (quoted by Ivens Ferraz 1979:19). São Tomé's economy did not improve until the end of the nineteenth century with the introduction of coffee and cacao. Since the local creoles remained aloof, these plantations were manned by contract labourers brought in from Angola, Mozambique and the Cape Verde Islands. In 1963 São Tomé's population was made up of 45% creoles, 5% Europeans, 10% mixed, 11% Angolares, 4% Mozambicans, 20% Cape Verdeans and 5% Tongas, the descendants of indentured labourers born on the island (Valkhoff 1966:79).

The theory of the Angolares' origin as maroons explains the predominant Portuguese element of their language as stemming from the original São Tomé pidgin or creole to which their ancestors had been exposed before escaping (Ferraz 1974:181); this element makes up the 67% of the Angolar lexicon which is shared with São Tomense today. The unshared portion, consisting largely of Bantu words, probably also dates from the early pidgin or creole, but in São Tomense it is likely that these words were eventually relexified into words of Portuguese origin. Angolar is a tone language (Maurer 1995); its words of Bantu origin seem to correspond most closely to kiMbundu, widely spoken in Angola not only as a first language but also as a lingua franca. While the Angolar numbers from one to three are from Portuguese, those from four to ten are clearly from kiMbundu (Ferraz 1974:185). Angolar is also unusual among creoles in having the sounds /θ/ and /ð/, corresponding to São Tomense /s/ and /z/ respectively. Although not common in African languages, /θ/ and /ð/ do occur in Mbundu and Ndingi, both Bantu languages. Angolar also has words of Kongo, Bini and Yoruba origin that are also found in São Tomense (182–3).

The official language of the independent nation of São Tomé and Príncipe remains Portuguese, in which there is a literacy rate of 50%. Although younger speakers are taking on some Portuguese features into their native creole, it remains a completely distinct linguistic system. Most Angolares are also bidialectal in São Tomense; in fact, there is an increasing tendency for the Angolares to be absorbed into the Forros (Lorenzino 1998).

Angolar CP text (Lorenzino, p.c.)

Turu nge	ka	meθe	kɔpwa	vĩ	-ši	-ɛ	punda	vĩ
all person	HAB	want	buy	palmwine	DEM	DEM	because	wine

re	θa	maši	bwaru	punda	kwai	θuba	na	leča	n'	ɛ	wa...
his	COP	more	good	because	which	rain	not	enter	LOC	it	not...

Nge	ki	θe	ka	ngɔlɔ	kwa	si	θɛru	paθa	p'	e	te	maši
person	who	FUT	search	thing	DEM	soon	INT	for him	have	more

mɔčiru	ke	turu nge	θuba	θe	ka	lɛčia	n'	ɛ	e	na	ka	te
much	than	all person	rain	FUT	enter	LOC	it	it	not	FUT	have

valoru	wa.
value	not

'Everybody wants to buy that palmwine because his wine is better because the rain doesn't get into it. The person who tries to do it [make palmwine] too soon in order to earn more than everybody else – the rain will get into his palmwine and it will have no value.'

3.3 The Spanish-based creoles

Unlike the Portuguese-based creoles, the story of the Spanish-based varieties is much less the story of an entire colonial empire. The linguistic history of most of Spain's holdings in the New World was much like that of British North America or French Canada: shift to a European language effected through widespread immigration of Europeans, who controlled the wealth, government and cultural institutions of the colonies. Indigenous languages and the cultures they represented generally retreated to the hinterlands or disappeared, often leaving relatively few traces in the European languages which replaced them. Although the initial contact between speakers of the European languages and indigenous languages must have often been via pidgins, evidence of the very existence of these pidgins is frequently lacking. Among the indigenous populations, shift to the European languages usually took place via a continuum of unstable interlanguages or learners' varieties rather than creoles. The sociolinguistic conditions that led to the Portuguese plantation creoles in Africa or fort creoles in Asia were largely lacking in Spain's colonies.

However, Spanish-based creoles did develop in several atypical situations: among run-away slaves in northern Colombia (Palenquero CS); on some Caribbean islands that the Dutch took from the Spanish (Papiamentu CS – see section 3.4); and among a displaced group of Eurasians in the Philippines (Chabacano or Zamboangueño CS). Several varieties of restructured Spanish also arose and disappeared among Africans in sixteenth- and seventeenth-century Spain, and later in nineteenth-century Cuba. Today the nonstandard Spanish of the Caribbean shows some evidence of partial restructuring, but much less than Brazilian Vernacular Portuguese.

3.4 Papiamentu Creole Spanish

Papiamentu is actually based on both Spanish and Portuguese; it is spoken on the leeward islands of the Netherlands Antilles just north of Venezuela; these include Curaçao (population 141,000), Aruba (59,000) and Bonaire (7,800). Of the total population of approximately 208,000, about one-sixth are native speakers of other languages (mainly Dutch, Sranan CE, English or Spanish). Papiamentu enjoys unusually high prestige for a creole language; it is spoken by all social classes in many settings and is widely used in the media.

Although some persist in considering Papiamentu a dialect of Spanish (Todd Dandaré 1979), it was identified as a creole language over a century ago (Van Name 1869–70). Schuchardt (1882a:895) recognized its Portuguese element, which Lenz (1928) identified with the Portuguese-based creoles of the Cape Verde and Gulf of Guinea islands, suggesting that Papiamentu had evolved from an Afro-Portuguese pidgin used in the slave trade that had later shifted toward Spanish. An alternative view was suggested by Valkhoff (1966) and elaborated by Goodman (1987), who maintained that creole Portuguese was brought to Curaçao by seventeenth-century immigrants from Brazil.

The three islands were originally inhabited by Amerindians who spoke an Arawakan language. Curaçao was settled in 1527 by some 25 Spaniards, who set about raising cattle. Over the next century the several hundred Indians on Curaçao probably learned Spanish from them and missionaries from the mainland, but the use of this language was disrupted in 1634 when the Dutch seized Curaçao and Bonaire. The Spanish retreated to the mainland, leaving all but 75 of their Indian allies on Curaçao (Goodman 1987). The 400 Dutchmen who settled the island kept some 23 of these Indians as servants, and other Indians remained on Bonaire and Aruba after the latter was taken by the Dutch in 1638. It is unclear what language the Dutch used for contact with the Indians during this early period; having broken away from the Spanish empire (recently united with that of Portugal) in 1581, the Dutch often understood Spanish and Portuguese and used creoles based on the latter as the lingua franca in the Asian colonies they seized from Portugal in the early seventeenth century, reserving Dutch for use among themselves (see 3.5). They probably also used restructured Portuguese for contact in the part of northeastern Brazil that they seized in 1630. There they found allies in the Sephardic Jews who had fled the Inquisition in Spain and Portugal; the Dutch, more tolerant than the Portuguese, allowed them to revert openly to Judaism. When the Portuguese regained this part of Brazil in 1654, the Dutch and their Jewish allies had to leave along with their families and slaves. Some resettled in Dutch Curaçao, where they began arriving in 1659 – some ten years after the Dutch had started using the island as an *entrepôt* for their trade in African slaves. Although it is unclear what the contact language of this trade was in the 1650s, it is clear that the Iberian languages of the Sephardim (whether Portuguese or Spanish or Judeo-Portuguese or Judeo-Spanish or Galician or other regional varieties – all of which were largely mutually intelligible) played an increasingly important role in the slave trade on Curaçao during the second half of the seventeenth century. Since the Dutch had captured many of the Portuguese trading posts in West Africa, the Spanish granted them an *asiento* or monopoly in supplying their American colonies with slaves, which lasted until 1713. The Brazilian Jews, joined by other Sephardim from Amsterdam who also spoke Iberian languages, played a major role in the administration of the slave camps on Curaçao (Goodman 1987). The slave trade was economically much more important than plantation agriculture, which was carried out mainly to provision the camps since the dry soil was unsuitable for raising sugar.

The restructured Portuguese that the Jews had probably used with their slaves in Brazil seems likely to have been extended to use in contact with the new slaves arriving from Africa (Maurer 1998), some of whom probably knew pidgin Portuguese from its use as a lingua franca there. However, as Spanish-speaking mainlanders came to Curaçao in increasing numbers to purchase slaves, there probably arose a makeshift trade koine based largely on common Iberian lexicon, not unlike what Brazilians often use today in dealing with Spanish Americans. This seems likely to have drawn the language of Curaçao in the direction of Spanish from this early period onwards. In 1704 a Spanish-speaking priest described the language of the island's slaves as 'un español chapurreado' or 'bad Spanish' (Van Wijk 1958:169).

Although most of the slaves arriving from Africa were sent on to Spanish colonies, those remaining on Curaçao came to equal the white population in number by the 1680s (Maurer 1986); of the 2,400 slaves, only a quarter worked on plantations while the rest did domestic work (apparently including work in the camps). The whites apparently learned the emerging creole for contact, beginning a long tradition of bilingualism; about half were from the Netherlands and maintained Dutch as their home language, while the other half of the white population consisted of Jews. It is unclear what the latter's home language was, but their congregation used Portuguese until they changed to Spanish in the nineteenth century. The creole spoken on Curaçao apparently stabilized by around 1700, when it spread to Bonaire and then to Aruba. The unusually high degree of European influence on the creole, which is evident in the modern grammar (see below), probably stems in part from the long tradition of bilingualism in the creole among Europeans (leading to the transfer of language features) and closer contact between them and slaves than on the sugar islands of the English and French.

Maurer (1986) notes that increased contact with Spanish resulted not only from commercial links with the mainland but also from the missionary work of Spanish Americans and an increasing number of mixed marriages dating from the eighteenth century in which free people of colour married speakers of both Spanish and Dutch. The oldest surviving document in Papiamentu is a 1776 letter written by a Curaçao Jew to his mistress (published and discussed by Wood 1972a); the language is very similar to the modern creole. The 1790 census reveals that nearly 60% of Curaçao's population of 19,500 lived in the capital of Willemstad; African slaves made up only 47% of this urban population (with 30% whites and 23% free coloured) but 91% of the rural population (with 7% whites and 2% free coloured). Maurer (1986:16) speculates that this may have led to a more European-influenced urban dialect, although there have not yet been any dialect studies to confirm this. During the course of the nineteenth century the white population decreased from 20% to 10%, apparently through intermarriage (Reinecke 1937:370, 384). Although all groups speak Papiamentu today, there is still a significant correlation between ethnic group, religion and prestige language: Protestant whites attend services in Dutch, Jews tend to prefer Spanish, while the black and mixed population belong largely to the Catholic church, which uses Papiamentu.

Papiamentu's historical movement toward Spanish has included its early relexification and lexical expansion as well as later structural borrowing (the term 'decreolization' is inappropriate because of the creole's long autonomy and the lack of a continuum of lects). Van Name (1869–70:158) noted the existence of a passive construction over a century ago. Today many features of Papiamentu are more like those of a European language than an Atlantic creole; these include the semantics of preverbal markers, the behaviour of the plural marker -*nan* (Jeuda 1982) and the copula *ta* (Holm 1976). However, Maurer (p.c.) points out that creole and European structures often coexist in Papiamentu, e.g. the serial verb construction in 'Mi a bai Punda *bai kumpra* kos' versus the prepositional construction in 'Mi a bai Punda *pa* kumpra kos' – both 'I went to Punda to go shopping.' Still, Wood (1972b) points out the importation of Spanish morphology: 'e tábata papy*ando*' 'he was talking' is encroaching on 'e tábata papya', which has both the progressive meaning and the habitual meaning of 'he used to talk'. The new inflection is being used to mark the progressive meaning overtly, creating a semantic split. Such Hispanicization is more pronounced on Aruba, lying just fifteen miles off the Venezuelan coast, than it is on Curaçao, a factor that contributes to regional variation. This is both phonological (Todd Dandaré 1979) and lexical: Curaçoan Papiamentu is more likely to borrow from Dutch,while the Aruban variety borrows from Spanish or English (Reinecke 1937:384). Moreover, since Papiamentu is spoken by all social classes, there have evolved sociolects associated with prestige or stigma (Muller 1980). Such factors have led to many problems that are still unresolved in Papiamentu lexicography (Labadie Solano 1982) and grammatical description (Instituto Lingwístiko Antiano 1984). As the language moves toward standardization, strong cases have been made for replacing Dutch (which younger Antillean children usually cannot speak) with Papiamentu, at least in the primary schools (Muller 1975). The current use of Dutch, which is of limited usefulness in the region, has been blamed for an unnecessarily high failure rate among schoolchildren (Richardson 1979). However, Dutch Antilleans enjoy the highest level of literacy in the region (nearly 100%), which is probably not unconnected to the fact that they also enjoy the highest standard of living, resulting from the establishment of oil refineries early in the twentieth century. These factors, coupled with widespread multilingualism in Dutch, Spanish and English, have contributed to Papiamentu's unusual linguistic development and high social prestige. The current debates on its standardization and future role in education are manifestations of its growing importance as a symbol of national cultural identity. However, the political separation of Aruba may result in two different standardized varieties of Papiamentu.

A study based on some 2,500 words (Maduro 1971, analysed in Joubert 1976, Richardson 1972) indicates that about two-thirds of Papiamentu words are derived from Iberian languages, a quarter from Dutch, and the rest from other sources (English, French and African languages). Of the 66% Iberian,

28% could be either Spanish or Portuguese, 25% could only be Spanish, 4% could only be Portuguese, 3.5% could only be Galician, and 5.5% could be any of these. However, a definitive study based on a complete etymological dictionary with adequate data on Judeo-Spanish and Judeo-Portuguese sources remains to be done. The most complete dictionary to date is Joubert (1991) with some 23,000 Papiamentu entries.

In phonology, Papiamentu includes all the American Spanish phonemes, except that flapped [r] and trilled [r̃] are allophones (Peters 1982) and the voiced stops /b/, /d/ and /g/ do not have fricative allophones. Papiamentu has borrowed a number of vowels from Dutch, including front rounded /y/ and /œ/, as well as nasal vowels and a nasal glide, tonal oppositions and /ǰ, š, ž, h/ from various sources. Its sandhi phenomena – the merger of sounds in rapid speech – are similar to those in Yoruba and certain other African languages (Bendix 1983).

Beyond the syntactic features mentioned above, Papiamentu has certain features with counterparts in creole Portuguese. Those that could have been brought either directly from West Africa or via Brazil include certain preverbal markers (Michel 1992, Muller 1989). Those shared not with African but with Asian varieties of creole Portuguese are less readily explained. These include the future marker *lo* from P *logo* 'immediately' and the possessive morpheme *su* as in 'mi tata *su* buki' 'my father's book', although the latter has a Dutch equivalent (6.4.4).

Papiamentu text (from Hoyer 1948:87, rewritten in the official orthography by Maurer p.c.)

Laga nos drenta e   pakus di sombré i   despachá nos mas lihé ku
Let us enter the store of hat   and hurry   (us) most fast that

por, pasobra ya   ta   bira lat. 'Sea asina bon di mustra e
can because already PRES get late be so   good to show the

kabayero akí e   sombrénan ku   bo a   mustrami otro dia.'
gentleman here the hat PLUR which you PAST show me other day

3.5 The Dutch-based creoles

There is direct evidence to support the existence of only three varieties of fully creolized Dutch that resulted from the presence of Dutch traders and settlers in the New World in the seventeenth and eighteenth centuries. One arose in the Virgin Islands (Negerhollands CD – see 3.6); the other two (Skepi and Berbice CD) arose in what was originally Dutch Guiana, but then became British Guiana and later independent Guyana. All three creoles are now extinct or nearly so. Certain features of the variety of Dutch spoken by blacks in New York and New Jersey until around 1900 caused some to suspect creolization (Dillard 1976:32), but it remains unclear whether these features were those of a semi-creole or of a variety that had long been in contact with another language (English) and was approaching death. The case for semi-creolization is much clearer regarding the Dutch that became Afrikaans in South Africa, particularly in the nonstandard varieties spoken by some whites and people of mixed race with little education. Finally, a pidginized variety of Afrikaans (Fly Taal) has recently arisen among speakers of Bantu languages.

It is remarkable that there are so few linguistic remnants of the vast empire of the Dutch, which at its height in the middle of the seventeenth century circled the planet with outposts in what is today New York, the Caribbean, Brazil, Africa, India, Malaysia and Indonesia. The Netherlands Antilles (where Dutch is largely an official language only) are all that remain politically. In fact, except for the Dutch colonies in the Caribbean area and the East Indies, most of this empire was lost by the early nineteenth century – largely to Britain. Yet the Portuguese empire, on which the Dutch built their own, left a distinctly greater impact in the form of creole languages which have survived until today, despite its earlier dissolution. The lesser impact of the Dutch is largely attributable to the fact that they were usually neither the first nor the only Europeans to arrive in the areas they colonized, and in most cases they did not remain as long as the British and French. Moreover, their own attitudes may have undermined the spread of their language. It has been claimed that 'till the middle of the 19th century the Hollanders regarded their language as a sort of caste-language and heard unwillingly its employment by their inferiors' (quoted by Reinecke 1937:443). Their traditional proficiency in more widely spoken languages (which once included the Creole Portuguese of Asia) was probably also a contributing factor. Dutch took hold as a vernacular language only in those areas where the Dutch were the first European settlers (New York, Guiana, South Africa) and predominated numerically over other Europeans (the Virgin Islands).

3.6 Negerhollands Creole Dutch

Negerhollands (D 'Negro Dutch') was a creole language once widely spoken in what became the United States Virgin Islands (map 2); it recently became extinct. Although these islands were long ruled by Denmark, Danish never became established as anything except an official language. The European settlers and their African slaves brought a number of languages to these islands; English and Dutch predominated, and each evolved a creole variety spoken by the islanders, but English spread at the expense of Dutch over the past two centuries.

The interest of the Dutch in the Virgin Islands grew after they established bases on the nearby islands of St Martin (1631), St Eustatius (1636) and Saba (1640). A creolized variety of Dutch may have arisen on these islands during this early period and been taken to the Virgin Islands by those Dutch settlers and their slaves who later moved to St Thomas (Goodman 1985b), but evidence for this remains circumstantial. The Dutch made an unsuccessful attempt to colonize St Thomas, as did the English and the Danes in the 1660s. The Anglo-Dutch wars during this period frequently led to the dispersal of an island's entire population of a particular nationality. Meanwhile, other Protestant nations in northern Europe were trying to gain a portion of the lucrative trade in African slaves to the Caribbean. Like Sweden and Brandenburg-Prussia, Denmark established forts on West Africa's Gold Coast (modern Ghana) and needed an *entrepôt* in the West Indies for selling slaves. The Danes were less interested in St Thomas's limited agricultural potential than in its fine natural harbour; believing it to be unoccupied, they sent a shipload of settlers to the island in 1672. They found 'a considerable number of colonists . . . from the neighboring islands who were mainly Dutch' (Hesseling 1905:13). The Danish settlers suffered such a high mortality that by the following year they made up only 28 of the 98 whites on the island (Larsen 1950:19), so they permitted colonists of various North European nationalities to settle among them. By 1688 Dutch-speakers made up nearly half the whites, followed by speakers of English (22%) and Scandinavian languages (13%) (Reinecke 1937:395). Of the 64 white women on the island, 42 were Dutch creoles (Sonesson 1977:49). Although they married Danes and men of other nationalities, they raised their children as Dutch-speaking Calvinists. At this time blacks constituted some 57% of the population, but by 1754 their proportion had increased to 94% (Reinecke 1937:418). Stolz and Stein (1986:118) calculate that 'the bulk of the early slaves were Asante [e.g. Twi] speakers'.

Of the two other principal Virgin Islands, St John was settled from St Thomas in 1717 and St Croix was settled from both after 1735. St Croix had been held by the French but was wholly abandoned when purchased by the Danes. While Dutch Creole was taken to St John, English Creole predominated on St Croix, which had a much larger proportion of English settlers than the other two islands. The English seldom learned Dutch, and their slaves were obliged to accommodate themselves to their owners' language. The general use of Dutch on St Thomas and St John during the early period of settlement is confirmed both by the remarks of historians and by present geographical names, but there is no direct reference to the creole until 1732, when Moravian missionaries arrived and began to learn Negerhollands in order to preach the Gospel to the slaves (2.3). However, as Hesseling notes (1905:20), the creole had clearly originated at the beginning of the Danish colonization and may have even existed before that time among the slaves of the Dutch settlers.

The German-speaking Moravians and later Danish-speaking Lutheran missionaries translated the Bible into Negerhollands; in 1770 Jochum Magens, a Danish West Indian, published an eighty-page description of the language with texts – the first grammar of a creole. Some eighteenth-century authors may have taken liberties in 'repairing' what they considered to be deficiencies in the creole by borrowing Dutch liturgical lexicon and perhaps adding a passive voice (Oldendorp 1777:433). However, the literary dialect was in any case based on the less restructured speech of whites (Magens 1770:8; Oldendorp 1777 quoted by Stein 1984:92), who may have actually used many of the European features that are characteristic of this variety. Magens' observation that blacks did not produce the guttural sounds (probably the velar fricative, with its uvular variant in regional Dutch) or consonant clusters of European Dutch implies that the whites did in fact do so when speaking the creole. Oldendorp noted that all whites except the English spoke the creole (quoted by Sprauve 1981:90), suggesting that it came into use as a lingua franca among the whites because of their linguistic heterogeneity. The sociolinguistic situation seems to have been similar to that on Curaçao (3.4), where whites became proficient in the creole for the same reason but retained their European language for use among their own group – and apparently transferred features from it to their variety of the creole.

By the time books for teaching literacy in Negerhollands were published in the early nineteenth century, the language was already losing ground to English Creole. The warfare carried out in the Caribbean by the European powers in the late eighteenth century made the neutral Danish island of St Thomas one of the few safe havens for commerce, bringing a great influx of foreigners who usually knew English rather than Dutch. The British occupied the island from 1807 to 1815, and the presence of their 1,500 soldiers also promoted the spread of English. After the abolition of slavery in 1848, there was a general movement of population from the plantation (the stronghold of Negerhollands) to the towns (the stronghold of English). By the second half of the century uncreolized Dutch had dropped out of use and the Danish schools shifted to English as the medium of instruction. Negerhollands survived in isolated rural areas a while longer, but by the time the United States purchased the islands in 1917 nearly everyone's first language was local English. The last speaker with any real competence in the language was Mrs Alice Stevens, who was born on St John in 1898 and raised by her grandparents as a bilingual. She cooperated in making tape-recordings of Negerhollands to preserve samples of the language (Sprauve 1985, Sabino 1986); with her death in 1987, the language became extinct.

Hesseling (1905:21) described Negerhollands as having 'een zuiver Kreools karakter' 'a purely creole character'; this was confirmed by Stolz (1984), who demonstrated that it was similar to the other Caribbean creoles in most respects except its lexicon. Stolz (1984:46) found that of the 1,300 words recorded by De Josselin de Jong (1926), 84% were derived from Dutch, 7.5% from English, 5% from African languages, 2% from Iberian languages and 1.4% from Danish. The African component seems to be largely shared with other languages in the region, e.g. *bukrá* 'white man' or *funtji* 'cornmeal dish'. Words of Iberian origin (e.g. *mata* 'kill') may have been borrowed from the sizeable Papiamentu-speaking colony on St Thomas in the early nineteenth century (Hesseling 1933a). However, others are found in eighteenth-century literature and constitute core vocabulary (e.g. *kabae* 'to finish'), suggesting that they may be traceable to seventeenth-century Brazilian refugees speaking restructured Portuguese (Goodman 1987) or possibly the pidgin Portuguese used in the slave trade that was later largely relexified (see 2.10, 4.4.1).

Negerhollands phonotactic rules are like those of the most conservative creoles, such as those of Suriname and the Gulf of Guinea. There was a strong tendency toward CV syllabic structure (5.2), resulting in paragogic vowels (e.g. *grōtō-* 'great' from D *groot*, or *houtu* 'wood' from D *hout*), consonant-cluster simplification (e.g. *tom* 'stump' from D *stomp*) and epenthetic vowels (e.g. *kini* 'knee' from D *knie*).

In syntax, Sprauve (1976) showed that Negerhollands shared more features with such conservative creoles than had previously been recognized (Taylor 1971). These features include phrasal interrogatives like *a'pe* 'where' (4.3.4), and the use of the same verbal marker (*lo*) to indicate progressive, habitual and irrealis (6.1.6). Negerhollands also had another future marker *sa* found not only in Berbice and Skepi CD, but also in Sranan, Saramaccan and Guyanese CE (cf. D *zal* 'will' or E *shall*). As in many other Atlantic creoles, the third person plural pronoun (*sende* 'they') could be added to nouns to form a definite plural (6.4.2), e.g. *die boom sende* 'the trees' (Van Name 1869–70:160), in addition to several other functions (Hinskens 1995). Like the possessive particles in Papiamentu (*su*), Indo-Portuguese (*sa*) and Afrikaans (*se*), Negerhollands *shi* was used to construct possessive noun phrases, e.g. 'Jan *shi* boek' 'John's book' (6.4.4). The best book in English on Negerhollands is van Rossem and van der Voort (1996).

Negerhollands text (Magens 1770:66)

Maer wanneer ons sa   krieg Tee van Dag? Die Waeter no ka
but   when   we will get   tea today?   the water   not COMP

kook nogal. Die Boterham   sender no ka   snie? Ja, maer die
boil yet.   the bread and butter PLUR not COMP cut? yes, but   there

no hab Kaes, en Tata   no keer voor Botterham   soso.
not exists cheese, and Father not care for   bread and butter plain.

Lastaen sender braen van   die rook   Karang sender. Kassavie sa wees
let   them bake some the smoked rockfish PLUR. cassava will be

meer suet mit die Karang as   Broot. Ju bin een Creol waer-waer.
more sweet with the rockfish than bread. You are a   creole true true.

3.7   The French-based creoles

The French colonization of various overseas territories from the seventeenth
to the nineteenth century led to the establishment of a number of pidginized
and creolized varieties of French. One of the pidgins survives as a continuum
of restructured varieties in former French West Africa; in Vietnam and New
Caledonia earlier French-based pidgins have disappeared, but a creole called
Tayo (Corne 1995) was recently discovered in the latter. The division of the
remaining creoles into subgroups presents various problems, but it is widely
agreed that they fall into two major divisions.

Historically the first, the New World group includes those spoken in the
Caribbean area, primarily on islands (the Lesser Antilles and Haiti) but also
on the bordering mainland of South America (French Guiana, with Karipuna
CF spoken nearby in Brazil) and North America (Louisiana). Most of these
areas were settled in the seventeenth and early eighteenth centuries as plantation colonies that drew a large part of their slave population from West
Africa. The creoles of the French Antilles (Guadeloupe and Martinique) and
Guyane remain in close contact with French, but those of the Commonwealth
Antilles (Dominica, St Lucia, Grenada and Trinidad) coexist with English, and
the last two are disappearing. There is a good deal of mutual intelligibility
among the French-based creoles in the Caribbean area.

Historically the second, the Isle de France group includes those varieties of
creole French spoken on the islands in the Indian Ocean that were settled
from the Isle de France (today called Mauritius) in the eighteenth century.
These include the varieties spoken on Mauritius itself and its dependency
Rodrigues, and the Seychelles. The settlement of these islands resembles that
of the New World colonies mentioned above, except that their work force
was drawn not only from West Africa, but also East Africa, Madagascar and

– on Mauritius – India. Although there is a debate as to why, there is general agreement that Isle de France creoles are structurally quite similar to those of the New World – much more so, for example, than the Asian varieties of creole Portuguese are to the African varieties. This has led to the suggestion that the Isle de France varieties should be included among the Atlantic creoles.

Creolists take a special interest in several varieties of colonial French that have important historical and linguistic connections with neighbouring creole varieties. These include the vernacular French of St Barts (or Saint-Barthélemy) and St Thomas in the Lesser Antilles; the Cajun French of Louisiana; and Réunionnais, spoken on the island of Réunion southwest of Mauritius in the Indian Ocean. Only the last has clearly borrowed enough creole features on all linguistic levels to be considered a semi-creole, although in some respects (e.g. gender agreement in the NP) a case could be made for the St Barts variety to be considered partially (if weakly) restructured also (Denis 1998).

3.8 Haitian Creole French

Haiti occupies the western third of the island of Hispaniola, which it shares with the Dominican Republic (map 2). With well over twice the area and population of Jamaica, Haiti is the country with the largest number of creole speakers (6,611,000 in 1998).

The precise origins of Haiti's creole are unclear, but they probably lie at least in part in the speech of the seventeenth-century buccaneers, a mixed crew of French, English and Africans who established their headquarters in this area. During the previous century the Spanish had used Hispaniola as a base for conquering the mainland; the gold they found there led to the island's depopulation, drawing both the Spanish settlers and the native Arawaks they had enslaved. The Spaniards who remained were mainly in the eastern part of the island. Tortuga (or Ile de la Tortue), a small island lying a few miles off the northwest coast of Hispaniola, was first settled in 1631 by Englishmen from St Christopher, who gathered dye-wood and traded guns to the buccaneers living along the northwest coast of Hispaniola. The buccaneers hunted down wild cattle and swine and smoked the meat on a rack called the *boucan* (whence F *boucanier*) for sale to passing ships. By 1634 Tortuga's population had grown to 600, including a number of Frenchmen and African slaves (Crouse 1940:82). They were driven out by the Spanish the following year, but many simply joined the buccaneers on Hispaniola, which the French called Saint-Domingue.

In 1642 some 50 Huguenots from the French settlement on St Christopher left their Catholic countrymen to reestablish the settlement on Tortuga, where they were joined by 50 Protestant buccaneers from Saint-Domingue. This settlement, which came to include women and children, was routed in 1654 by the Spanish, but this again just increased the number of Frenchmen in buccaneer hideouts on Saint-Domingue. In 1664 these Frenchmen came under the protection of the French West India Company when Louis XIV laid claim to the western coasts of the island. The English, who had captured Jamaica from Spain in 1655, had their own plans: in 1662 an expedition from Jamaica temporarily captured a buccaneer settlement at Petit-Goâve in the south.

To encourage the French buccaneers to settle down, women (often orphans or prostitutes) were brought for them from France. The families they formed became *habitans* or settlers; the indigo and sugarcane they planted in the fertile soil grew well, but their need for labour increased the demand for African slaves. The French trading posts established in West Africa in the 1670s were intended to meet this need, but the French in Saint-Domingue also raided Spanish and English colonies for slaves. Jamaica came to be called the 'Little Guinea' of Haiti because of the number of slaves it furnished. After one such expedition the French returned to Petit-Goâve with a booty of 3,000 slaves (Reinecke 1937:326; Heinl and Heinl 1978:17), which represented a considerable proportion of the total number of slaves in Saint-Domingue during this period. Reinecke notes that 'Many of the women so taken became the concubines of the early settlers. Consequently the Creole of the South and West contains more English words than that of the North, which did not share in these expeditions to the same extent' (1937:297). This early contact with Jamaican pidgin or creole English may also account for some of the structural affinities between the creoles of Haiti and Jamaica, despite their differing lexical bases.

In 1697 Spain recognized the French claim to Saint-Domingue, which was becoming a classical sugar colony. Its slave population increased from 2,000 in 1681 (a third of the total) to 50,000 in 1728; by 1753 there were 165,000 slaves (91% of the total population – Reinecke 1937:298). While most of Saint-Domingue's slaves were drawn from other European colonies in the Caribbean during the early period of settlement (297), the French West India Company became an increasingly important supplier of slaves direct from Africa by the end of the seventeenth century – although by law these had to come by way of Martinique. Working from figures in Curtin (1969), Singler (1986a) concludes that 'The evidence for the period from 1711 through 1740 suggests that the two most important African language groups for the formation of Haitian Creole are Mande and Kwa, particularly Bambara-Malinke-Dyula and Ewe-Fon.'

Saint-Domingue came to produce more wealth from sugar than any other Caribbean colony in the eighteenth century, although at great human cost considering the high death rate among slaves in that colony. On the eve of the French revolution in 1789, there were nearly half a million slaves in Saint-Domingue while the white and free coloured population each constituted only about 5% of the total. It is clear from Ducoeurjoly (1802) that the white colonists also used the creole, not only in addressing slaves but also for relaxed conversations among themselves (Hull 1983). When the new French Republic abolished slavery in 1794 despite the resistance of the colonists, each of the three groups – black, white and mixed – was pitted against the others in a bitter and bloody struggle that led to mass emigration and finally to the independence of Haiti in 1804.

Haiti's linguistic and cultural isolation from France became almost complete for the mass of its peasantry, the 90% of the population that still speaks Creole as its only language (Reinecke *et al.* 1975:224). An elite adopted Creole-influenced French as the mark of its social identity, and this became the country's official language of government, education, etc., serving to help maintain the elite's power. The children of the bilingual minority group acquire both French and Creole at home and then perfect their control of the official language at school (Valdman 1984:79). This tradition of language transmission among the bilinguals maintained French despite Haiti's long lack of contact with French speakers. In the 1860s missionaries from France began coming to Haiti as teachers, followed by French Canadians (Pompilus 1969:38). During the United States' occupation of Haiti from 1915 to 1934, the constitution of 1918 specified for the first time that French was the country's official language and its use was 'obligatoire dans les services publics'. In 1964 this was attenuated to allow Haitians not knowing French to use Creole in such situations (38–9). The 1983 constitution declared both French and Creole to be Haiti's 'national' languages – with French serving as the 'official' language (Valdman 1984:79) – but the 1987 constitution declared Creole to be 'official' as well.

Ferguson (1959) used the current sociolinguistic situation in Haiti to define diglossia: among the bilingual minority, French is used in public or formal domains, while Creole is used in private or informal domains. However, Dejean (1983) challenged the appropriateness of the term diglossia to describe the situation in Haiti, where the great majority of the population is in fact monolingual and less than 5% can actually speak French fluently. Valdman (1984:79) further points out that among the bilingual minority the high language is not acquired solely in school, as in a classical diglossic situation. Moreover, 'true functional complementation no longer obtains between French and Creole. On the one hand, for the bilingual elite, French serves all vernacular functions. On the other hand, no domain of use and no communicative situation is exempt from the encroachment of Creole. In rural Haiti and among the urban masses, all intellectual, psychological, and social needs are served by Creole.' Rejecting diglossia as a model, Valdman sees Haiti as a nation composed of two linguistic communities: the bilingual elite and the monolingual rural and urban masses. There is little linguistic interaction between the two communities and the masses have few opportunities to use or even hear French since most receive no education.

Recently the relative prestige of the creole has been rising as it has been used increasingly in religious and political publications and even in a president's speech at the United Nations. In the early 1940s Ormonde McConnell, a Northern Irish Methodist pastor, and Frank Laubach, an American literacy specialist, devised a phonemic orthographic system for writing the creole as used in rural areas. C. F. Pressoir, a Haitian journalist, proposed an alternative system that was closer to French orthography (e.g. using *oun* for /ũn/ rather than McConnell–Laubach's *ûn*) and that was based on a more educated urban norm. A long debate ensued as to which system would be preferable for teaching literacy in Creole, which some saw as a bridge to literacy in French while others saw the goal as being for Creole itself to be more widely used in writing. Finally a team of linguists from the University of Paris worked out a compromise, and their system was adopted in 1980 by the Haitian Ministry of Education as the official orthography. Hoping to combat the country's staggeringly low rate of literacy (20% in 1984), the Haitian government adopted Creole in 1979 as the medium of instruction for the first four years of schooling and began teaching literacy in the creole. It has one of the richest literatures of any creole language, dating back to the early nineteenth century, but further enrichment will be needed as Creole takes on new functions in education. Unresolved problems in standardization include deciding not only which sociolect but also which allomorphic alternatives should become the norm. While full forms might be preferable in beginning literacy (e.g. '*Li* ale *avè ou*' 'He goes with you'), truncated and fused forms are often more natural and sometimes the only normal usage (e.g. '*L* ale *avòw*'): 'The most important tasks in the modernization of Creole are lexical enrichment, the elaboration of rhetorical devices appropriate for the new . . . domains that the vernacular is acquiring, and the expansion and diversification of the types of materials available to new literates' (Valdman 1984:94). Lexical studies include those by Bentolila *et al.* (1976) and Valdman *et al.* (1981), while the principal syntactic studies include those of Sylvain (1936), Hall *et al.* (1953), Lefebvre (1998) and DeGraff (1992). A course in Creole for English speakers is available in Valdman *et al.* (1988).

The continuing advance of Creole into new domains has cast doubt on the future role of French in Haiti. Valdman (1978:32) sees the desirability of more widespread bilingualism in which the urban Creole of Port-au-Prince, enriched by its contact with French, coexists with the latter without replacing it as the dominant language. However, Valdman (1984:94) also believes that English is replacing French as Haiti's 'window on the outside world', not only because of economic and cultural forces in the Caribbean but also because of increased contact with English among Haitians who live abroad for political or economic reasons but maintain strong links with their homeland and frequently return. Emigration over the past decades has been greatest to the Bahamas, Miami (which has a Creole radio station) and New York (now the city with the second largest Creole-speaking population after Port-au-Prince according to Chaudenson 1979:25), as well as Montreal. There is also a Haitian-Creole-speaking community on the Dominican Republic's Samaná Peninsula, made up of several thousand descendants of Haitians who migrated to this area when it was under the control of Haiti between 1822 and 1844. Their Creole could be expected to be more conservative than that spoken in Haiti today, but it has never been studied (J. Vigo, p.c.).

The urban speech of the capital is referred to as 'Central' Creole, one of three major regional varieties, the others being those of the north and the south. All have French-influenced sociolects, but such features are especially characteristic of the urban variety. They include front rounded vowels (urban *deu* 'two' versus rural *dè*; cf. F *deux* /dø/) and post-vocalic /r/ (e.g. urban *frèr* versus rural *frè*; cf. F *frère* /frɛr/) as well as the preservation of certain consonant clusters (e.g. urban *vyand* 'meat' versus rural *vyann*; cf. F *viande* /vyãd/ – Valdman 1984:87). While the difference between sociolects is largely phonological, the difference between regional varieties is largely lexical, e.g. northerners say *chandèl* for 'candle' (cf. F *chandelle*) while other Haitians say *bouji* (cf. F *bougie*), or southerners say *badinen* for 'to banter' (cf. F *badiner*) while others say *jwe* (cf. F *jouer* 'play') (86). However, there are also some regional differences in syntax: northerners use *a* as a connective before possessives (e.g. 'papa *a* m' 'my father') and have a distinctive form for the possessive pronoun (*'kin* a m' 'mine'), whereas other Haitians say *papa m* 'my father' and *pa m* 'mine' (85; Goodman 1964:55). Moreover, southerners often use *pe* or *ape* for the preverbal progressive marker instead of *ap*. There are also 'peripheral' usages that are usually farther than the corresponding 'Central' forms from standard French and therefore carry less prestige. These include forms that preserve archaic or regional French usages such as *swèf* 'thirst' instead of *swaf* (cf. F *soif*), or forms that reflect Creole sound change away from French (e.g. *say* 'well behaved'; cf. F *sage*) when the Central form preserves or returns to the French sound (*saj*). As might be expected, peripheral forms are often hypercorrections, such as *laj* 'garlic' versus Central *lay* (cf. F *l'ail* /lay/ 'the garlic': Valdman 1984:86).

> **Haitian CF text** (Valdman 1970:260, rewritten in the new orthography by H. St Fort p.c.)
> Te gen you tan zannimo te gen you wa ki te you nonm
> ANT have a time animals ANT have a king who ANT a man
>
> trè entèlijan epi trè malen. Li te toujou ap di konseye
> very clever and very cunning. he ANT always PROG tell advisers
>
> li yo, 'se mèt kò ki konnen kò.
> his PLUR, it's owner (of) body who knows body (i.e. himself).

> **New York Haitian CF text** (H. St Fort p.c.)
> Genyen ou seri Ayisyen lan Nouyòk k ap pwomennen
> there are a number Haitians in New York who PROG go about
>
> di ou bann betiz kòm kwa Kwins se kote gwo moun rete,
> say a lot foolishness like Queens is place big shots live,
>
> alóske Bwouklin se kote vakabon, wangatè, moun
> whereas Brooklyn is place rascals, voodoo practitioners, people
>
> pòv rete.
> poor live.

3.9 English-based Atlantic creoles

Britain was more successful than any other nation in implanting its language around the globe, both in terms of sheer numbers of speakers and in the proliferation of overseas varieties. Britain's 350 years of empire spread not only standard English and regional varieties overseas, but also more pidgins and creoles than any other language. There are two major groups according to historical, geographical and linguistic factors: the Atlantic group, spoken in West Africa and the Caribbean area, which was established in the seventeenth and eighteenth centuries (described in this section); and the Pacific group, established largely during the nineteenth century (described in section 3.11). The Atlantic group consists mostly of plantation creoles which are structurally similar to the other Atlantic creoles based on Portuguese, Spanish, Dutch and French, and they share many of the features described in chapters 4 to 6 because of the typological similarity of the Niger–Congo languages that formed their substrata – as well as other factors, such as universal features of adult second language acquisition and cultural contact phenomena, that affect the formation of pidgins and subsequent creoles. The Pacific group consists largely of pidgins that are structurally quite different from the Atlantic creoles because of the different typology of their substrate languages; however, there are also several Pacific creoles. The creoles spoken in Australia may prove to form a third major group.

While the subdivision of the Pacific group of English-based pidgins and creoles is still a matter of some controversy, those in the Atlantic area fall more naturally into subgroups because of settlement patterns. Pidgin and creole English developed during the seventeenth century on both sides of the Atlantic, i.e. in the Caribbean where the British were establishing plantation colonies, and in West Africa around the outposts where they were obtaining slaves for their New World colonies, among both the slavers and the slaves who crossed the Ocean. The two-way nature of this traffic, which helps explain some of the striking similarities among the different varieties of Atlantic Creole English, is underlined by the fact that the West African varieties were also shaped by the migrations of African Americans to Africa throughout the first half of the nineteenth century, resulting in Sierra Leone's Krio (which in turn shaped the Pidgin English of Nigeria and Cameroon) and Liberian English.

In the New World, the creoles of Suriname stand apart. This central part of the Guianas was first settled by the English in 1650 but then traded to the Dutch in 1667, isolating the creoles from English. The coastal variety, Sranan, was then influenced by Dutch; Ndyuka, spoken by the descendants of runaway slaves in the interior, suggests an earlier stage of Sranan (see text, section 1.2). Saramaccan, another maroon language, was heavily influenced by the Portuguese spoken by Jewish refugees from Dutch Brazil. Because of their long isolation from English, these creoles are largely unintelligible to English speakers.

The Creole English of the Lesser Antilles dates from the first half of the seventeenth century; the Eastern Caribbean varieties also include those of Trinidad and Tobago as well as Guyana. The Western Caribbean varieties include the CE of Jamaica (section 3.10) as well as the Caribbean coast of Central America and some off-shore islands. Although some of the latter coexist with Spanish, most varieties of Caribbean CE have long coexisted with standard English and are much closer to it than are the Surinamese creoles.

The North American varieties of CE include the closely related creoles of the Bahamas and Gullah (spoken in coastal South Carolina and Georgia) with the latter's off-shoot, Afro-Seminole. African American Vernacular English is debated to be either a post-creole or a semi-creole, as is its off-shoot spoken on the Samaná Peninsula of the Dominican Republic. Probably because of demographic factors affecting the genesis of all the North American varieties (e.g. a higher proportion of native speakers of English), their basilects are closer to English than are those of the Caribbean varieties. Finally, two varieties stand apart because of social and linguistic factors: the restructured English spoken by North American Indians, and the Caribbean Creole spoken in Britain.

3.10 Jamaican Creole English

Jamaica, with 2,616,000 inhabitants in 1998, is the most populous Creole-English-speaking country. Long the economic heart of the British West Indies, Jamaica remains the cultural centre of the anglophone Western Caribbean and beyond, a source of innovation in everything from music to turns of phrase (Pollard 1986). Given the country's importance, it is not surprising that its speech was the object of the first analysis of West Indian Creole English (Russell 1868) and of the first modern linguistic studies of the same (e.g. Le Page and DeCamp 1960, Cassidy 1961, Bailey 1966, Cassidy and Le Page 1980), the sources of much of the following section. The ethnic origin of the population in the 1960 census was 76% African, 15% Afro-European, 3.5% East Indian, 1% European, 1% Chinese and 3% other.

Jamaica was originally inhabited by Arawak Indians, who gave the island its name, 'Xaymaca'. The Spanish settlement which began in 1509 never prospered. Some 300 slaves were brought to the island in 1523; by the end of the sixteenth century the Indian population had almost disappeared and the Spanish, who raised livestock, had begun leaving the island for more prosperous areas. In 1655 the British, under Cromwell, intended to attack Spain by capturing Santo Domingo. A fleet of ships left England to recruit 4,000 more men in Barbados and 1,200 in the Leeward Islands before attacking Santo Domingo, where they were thoroughly routed. In an attempt to retrieve the expedition from total disgrace, the English attacked Jamaica, where the island's 1,500 Spaniards could mount little resistance. Their slaves, about equal in number, retreated into the mountains with them and most were eventually evacuated to Cuba, except for some 250 Maroons. In 1656 settlers from Nevis arrived to begin farming eastern Jamaica under the protection of British soldiers. Of the original 1,600 settlers (including 1,000 slaves), about one third were dead within a year from disease, but with further immigration Jamaica's population rose to 4,500 whites and 1,400 blacks by 1658. In 1664 about 1,000 more settlers arrived from Barbados. Western Jamaica was settled in 1671 by 500 refugees from Suriname, followed by another 1,200 in 1675, at least 980 of whom were slaves (Bilby 1983:60). The 7,700 white settlers were already outnumbered by 9,500 slaves, at least 10% of whom were from Suriname at this linguistically critical time. That there was some impact of proto-Sranan on the emerging creole of Jamaica is supported by Sranan-like features in the special ritual language that has been preserved among the Maroons (1983).

Sugar was the main crop and plantations were large almost from the very beginning, requiring the massive importation of slaves. While the white population remained constant over the next half century, the slave population increased to 86,000 in 1734, about 92% of the total (Reinecke 1937:288). Evidence that the slaves' Creole English had emerged by this time can be found in the complaint of an Englishman in 1739 that a white 'Boy till the Age of Seven or Eight diverts himself with the Negroes, acquires their broken Way of Talking, and their Manner of Behaviour' (quoted by Cassidy 1961:21). A contemporary remarked that 'the Creole language is not confined to the negroes. Many of the ladies, who have not been educated in England, speak a sort of broken English, with an indolent drawling out of their words' (22).

On the eve of emancipation in 1833, whites numbered 35,000 (7% of the total population) while blacks – including 1,200 Maroons – numbered 450,000 (93%). After abolition many former slaves settled in the more inaccessible mountainous areas and became smallholders, thereby preserving their Creole from much external influence. Such communities helped preserve archaic forms and words which have disappeared in most of the smaller Creole-English-speaking islands (Le Page and DeCamp 1960:93). The importation of indentured labour never reached the proportions it did in Trinidad and British Guiana. While the latter imported 144,000 and 239,000 East Indians respectively between 1844 and 1917, Jamaica brought in only 36,400, one-third of whom returned to India (95). In Jamaica the East Indians have to a large extent been assimilated culturally, though not racially (96).

Akers (1981) asserts that today some 94% of the Jamaican population are Creole-dominant bilinguals. Among monolingual Creole speakers, comprehension of English (e.g. as used by Jamaican newscasters) may be as low as 50% (Devonish 1986:33). Independence in 1962 did little to change the relationship between English and Creole in Jamaica, although literacy has increased to 85% (Famighetti 1997:787). Rickford (1987) notes that 'The only significant endorsement of linguistic norms different from those of standard English in the post-independence Caribbean occurs among the Rastafarian groups and their admirers.' Pollard (1983, 1984) has traced the linguistic impact of this Jamaican cultural movement on other parts of the Caribbean.

The text below is from a recording of a basilectal variety of Jamaican Creole used by a Maroon. Many of the linguistic features it illustrates are also found in other varieties of Atlantic Creole English. English *th* corresponds to Creole /d/ when voiced (*di* 'the') or /t/ when unvoiced (*truot* 'throat'). English diphthong off-glides correspond to Creole on-glides: /uol/ 'old', /liedi/ 'lady'. Question words are preceded by highlighters (/*a* wa/ 'what') and there are different words for 'be' before nouns (*a* or *iz*), locative phrases (*de*) and adjectives (zero copula): see 6.2. Verbs are uninflected (*sie* 'says' or 'said'), indicating tense, etc., with preverbal markers: *'de go* hapm' 'is going to happen'; *'ben* de' 'had been' (Patrick 1992). The third person pronoun is usually unmarked for gender or case: *hin* or *in* or *im* can mean 'he, she, it; him, her; his, its'.

> **Jamaican Creole English text** (Le Page and DeCamp 1960:141)
> di uol liedi sie, tan! a wa de   go hapm? wilyam sie, wa
> the old lady said, wait what PROG go happen? William said, what
>
> de   go hapm yu wi fain out. wiet a wail! hin sie, wel, aa
> PROG go happen you will find out. wait a while! she said, well, all
>
> rait! hin lit   doun wan a in eg so, wam! an di wata
> right! she smashed down one of her eggs so, wham! and the water
>
> mount di gyal siem plies we   im ben de,   anda in truot ya.
> rose to the girl's same place where it had been, under her throat here.

3.11 English-based Pacific pidgins and creoles

There is general agreement that the restructured varieties of English of the Pacific are quite different from those of the Atlantic, in terms of both their linguistic structure and the social history of their speakers. First, they were influenced by substrate languages belonging to completely different families, e.g. Austronesian languages (Keesing 1988). Secondly, most of the Pacific varieties developed into expanded pidgins (1.1), some of which became nativized as creoles, whereas the Atlantic varieties are almost all creoles that appear to have developed within a brief period out of pre-pidgin continua (1.2). Thirdly, most of the Pacific varieties evolved in the nineteenth century, while nearly all of the Atlantic varieties came into being during the seventeenth and eighteenth centuries.

Chinese Pidgin English developed around the city of Canton by 1700; by the end of the century mutineers from the *Bounty* founded what became a creole-speaking community on Pitcairn Island, which later led to an off-shoot on Norfolk Island. This same period saw the beginning of Pidgin English in both Australia and Hawaii (leading to later creoles and post-creoles) and the South Seas Jargon that developed among the mixed crews on British and American whalers in Polynesia and Micronesia. The latter evolved into the pidgin used in various kinds of Pacific trade, i.e. Sandalwood English or Beach-la-Mar (from the name of an edible sea-slug prized in China). During the second half of the nineteenth century, Pacific islanders were brought as indentured labourers to work on plantations in Queensland in northeastern Australia and elsewhere. There sociolinguistic conditions led to the development of a stable variety called Melanesian Pidgin English, with three modern branches: Tok Pisin in Papua New Guinea (section 3.12), Bislama in Vanuatu (formerly the New Hebrides) and Pijin in the Solomon Islands. Melanesian Pidgin English also influenced a local pidgin spoken off Australia's Cape York, resulting in Torres Strait Broken, now a creole.

Despite their diverse origins, the Pacific varieties share a number of features with the Atlantic creoles. Some of these, e.g. words for 'child' related to *pickaninny* (cf. Portuguese *pequenino*), can be explained by diffusion, which probably also explains some Pacific grammatical features which appear to come from the Atlantic substrate (Holm 1986, 1992b).

3.12   Tok Pisin

Tok Pisin (cf. *talk pidgin*) is also known as New Guinea Pidgin or Neo-Melanesian. It is by far the most widely spoken variety of Melanesian PE, used by over 2 million people in Papua New Guinea (Faraclas p.c.). This country, which gained its independence in 1975, consists of the eastern half of the island of New Guinea along with the Bismarck Archipelago (with the main islands of New Britain and New Ireland) and Bougainville, the northernmost of the Solomon Islands (map 1).

Tok Pisin serves as a lingua franca in an area with some 860 indigenous languages, but it is also the home language of an estimated 90,000 people (Mühlhäusler 1982:441). Like West African Pidgin English, it is an expanded pidgin (1.1) that is creolizing gradually at a late stage in its development. It has been claimed that different speakers use varieties representative of earlier stages (e.g. as a contact jargon or reduced pidgin in remote areas), so that its entire history can still be studied, but this is probably an oversimplification (Holm and Kepiou 1993).

Tok Pisin is not intelligible to English speakers who have not learned it. Although the same could be said of basilectal varieties elsewhere, this is especially true of the Surinamese creoles (3.9). A common factor in their development and that of Tok Pisin is that there was significant isolation from the lexifier language at an early stage, when colonizers speaking a different European language assumed control of the area where the pidgin or creole was used. Up to the late nineteenth century, eastern New Guinea had been claimed but not colonized by various European powers: Portugal, Spain, the Netherlands, Britain and France. Its availability attracted the German Empire, which did not become a colonial power until after unification in 1871. European interest in the New Guinea area had been growing since the 1840s, which saw the arrival of explorers, missionaries and traders in beach-la-mar (3.11), sandalwood, pearls and copra. New Ireland was on the shipping route from Australia to China, and it seems likely that early visitors made contact via the Pacific jargon, which was probably influenced by Chinese Pidgin English. However, Pidgin English did not become firmly established in the area until after 1884, when Britain declared a protectorate over south-eastern New Guinea (later called Papua) and Germany over the northeastern part (rechristened Kaiser Wilhelmsland) and the nearby islands. Western New Guinea had already been colonized by the Dutch as part of their East Indies.

German influence in the Pacific had been growing since a German com-pany established copra plantations in Samoa in the 1860s. Ironically, these Samoan plantations played an important role in establishing Pidgin English in German New Guinea – particularly the Bismarck Archipelago – as a lingua franca among labourers returning to New Guinea in the 1880s and later (Mühlhäusler 1976, 1979). The first German plantations in New Guinea used these returning labourers, who established the model for the contact language that was later used by other recruits. Although the Germans did not particularly like using Pidgin English (which they associated with their rivals, the British) and actively promoted the use of German in New Guinea after 1900, the early establishment of the pidgin solved their most pressing problems in communicating with the inhabitants of the Bismarck Archipelago, where their first plantations and trading centres were located. Unlike English speakers, the Germans regarded the pidgin as a totally for-eign language and learned it as such, giving it much more autonomy during the period in which it stabilized than pidgins developing in areas controlled by the British.

In the 1890s copra plantations in Kaiser Wilhelmsland imported indentured Chinese and Malay labourers from Singapore and the Dutch East Indies. Most spoke Coastal Malay (3.13), which became established as the lingua franca on the New Guinea mainland during this period, when imported labourers greatly outnumbered indigenous ones. However, their importation dropped sharply after 1900, and with it the importance of Coastal Malay, which was eventually replaced by Pidgin English. During this period, free Chinese speak-ing Chinese PE came as shop keepers to Rabaul, the German colony's administrative capital on New Britain, and their Pidgin English may have influenced the developing local variety.

Since most of the labourers first employed in Samoa had originated from the area around the tiny Duke of York island in the channel between New Britain and New Ireland, Kuanua (earlier called Tolai) and other closely related languages spoken in this area were of great importance in shaping the pidgins of both Samoa and New Guinea. Because Duke of York became a staging post in the recruitment of labourers from elsewhere and because the Pidgin English spoken there and in the nearby capital of Rabaul enjoyed relative prestige, it influenced varieties spoken elsewhere, thus spreading substrate features from Kuanua far beyond the area where the language is spoken.

On the whole, the lexical influence of local languages on the pidgin was considerable. Hall (1966:94) estimated that such words made up some 20% of the total, a portion much higher than that of most other European-based pidgins. Mühlhäusler (1979:199ff.) has identified some 15 words from Coastal Malay and nearly 150 from German. Perhaps because most of the latter are now archaic, the figure had been grossly underestimated by previous linguists.

Although there had already been considerable contact among the people of New Guinea and even indigenous pidgins, under the 'pax Germanica' that resulted from the gradual extension of government control over wide areas of the colony, peaceful contact between members of the area's diverse linguistic groups increased, and with it the use of Tok Pisin as a lingua franca. This use spread to domains beyond the plantation, e.g. with domestic servants and with police and other government agents. This was the beginning of what Mühlhäusler (1982:447) calls the pidgin's 'nativization', i.e. its use primarily as a lingua franca among indigenous people rather than as a language of communication with colonizers. However, there were also many Germans, especially on outstations and recruiting or trading vessels, who became proficient in speaking the pidgin.

The linguistic situation changed after the outbreak of the First World War; the Australians occupied German New Guinea in 1914 and then received it as a mandate under the League of Nations in 1921. Until 1942 the mandated territory remained administratively distinct from southeastern New Guinea, which had been changed from a British protectorate to the Australian Territory of Papua in 1906. A distinct variety of Pidgin English had become established in the Papuan islands just southeast of the mainland after labourers were recruited from there for Queensland in the 1880s (Mühlhäusler and Dutton 1977). It was used there and along parts of the Papuan coast until the 1920s, especially in multilingual settings such as plantations, prisons, gold mining areas and in the pearling industry (where it was heavily influenced by Torres Straits PE, section 3.11). After 1906, however, the Australian administration pursued a policy of eradicating this 'vile gibberish' (220) and replacing it with simple English or, failing that, Hiri Motu (3.13). The latter filled the gap and eventually prevailed; although this was remarkable as one of the few known instances of an official language policy that actually worked (mainly because sociolinguistic conditions were right for the spread of Hiri Motu), this policy eventually proved to be to the detriment of the political and cultural unity of independent Papua New Guinea: Tok Pisin and Hiri Motu now compete as lingua francas in Papua, where Hiri Motu became the focus of a 'Papua for the Papuans' movement in the 1970s (Mühlhäusler and Dutton 1977:219). Today Hiri Motu is just maintaining its status while Tok Pisin seems to be spreading, even outside the capital (Dutton p.c., Crowley p.c.).

The advent of the Australian administration also changed the sociolinguistic situation in the mandated territory. Although the Australians would have liked to see the use of Pidgin English discontinued there also, it was much too firmly entrenched. Mühlhäusler (1979) notes that, as English speakers, the Australians tended to repidginize Tok Pisin in an ad hoc fashion; accommodation to such speech by indigenous people (often domestic servants) led to a distinct variety which he calls Tok Masta. Although this vertical use between superiors and subordinates maintained Tok Pisin's status as a caste language (and indigenous people were sometimes actually discouraged from learning English as used by native speakers), the spread of Tok Pisin for horizontal communication with social peers was accelerated by its growing prestige as it entered the new domains of higher-status employment in mines, commerce, industry, shipping and lower-level government administration. It became the vehicle of what Mead (1931:144) recognized as a new culture that had resulted from contact, particularly in the growing urban centres. She noted that the pidgin was being acquired by small children, a fact which Mühlhäusler (1979:88) considers of greater importance for the development of more stable and grammatically more complex varieties than the occasional instances of creolization that were beginning to occur in this period. Another major factor in Tok Pisin's social and linguistic expansion was its use by certain missions, which studied and standardized the language for use in Bible translation. Moreover, the spread of government control to parts of the New Guinea highlands led to a new regional variety influenced by the anglicized pidgin spoken by patrol officers.

The Japanese occupation of much of New Guinea during the Second World War also changed the status of the pidgin and its indigenous speakers. The language was used in the millions of propaganda pamphlets dropped by Australian, American and Japanese airplanes all over New Guinea. The

Australians realized that the defence of their own country depended on the good will of the people in Papua and New Guinea, which helped break down the pre-war racial caste system as they fought together against the Japanese. The sense of equality continued to grow after the war as the indigenous people began to see more of the self-government that they had been promised. As social mobility increased, the teaching of English and its wider use were promoted. This coincided with a 1953 United Nations pronouncement calling for the discontinuation of the pidgin because of its association with colonialism. However, this was sociolinguistically naive since Tok Pisin could simply not be replaced in a number of domains, e.g. the media, government, and the urban centres in which Tok Pisin had become the primary language of tens of thousands of people.

Urban Tok Pisin has been drawing ever more heavily on English for new words, especially in the speech of the educated elite who enjoy the most prestige. This variety has now become distinct from the more conservative rural variety of Tok Pisin, whose speakers often have difficulty in understanding urban speech. Bickerton (1975b:25) predicted the eventual emergence of a continuum between Tok Pisin and English, but the practice of code-switching indicates that this has not yet occurred (Mühlhäusler 1982:455).

Tok Pisin has Austronesian language features that make its systems distinct from those of both English and the Atlantic creoles on all linguistic levels. In phonology, the phonetic qualities of the consonant allophones are largely unlike English and are reminiscent of those of local languages (Wurm 1977a:513), e.g. /r/ can be realized as an alveolar or retroflex flap, some stops have fricative allophones, and labial fricatives are mostly bilabial rather than labio-dental. There are also pre-nasalized stops (5.6.2) as in *ndai* 'die'. As in German, no voiced stops occur word-finally, e.g. *rot* 'road', or *dok* 'dog'. Todd (1984:163) has suggested that 'The devoicing of consonants in word final position may have become regularized when T[ok] P[isin] was being used as a lingua franca between New Guineans and Germans.' The only other variety of restructured English in which this is known to occur is Cameroonian (3.9), also spoken in what was once a German colony.

As in Austronesian languages, the personal pronouns indicate not only singular (e.g. *mi* 'I') and plural (*yumi* 'we'), but also dual (*yumitupela*) and trial (*yumitripela*). A further distinction is made between the preceding forms, which include the person spoken to as part of the meaning of 'we', and the exclusive forms *mitupela* 'we two', *mitripela* 'we three' and *mipela* 'we all'. There are several categories of adjectives, which may or may not take the suffix *-pela*, and verbs, which may or may not take the transitive suffix *-im*, e.g. *kuk* or *kukim* 'cook'.

Tok Pisin markers of tense and aspect seem to function much more like adverbs or serial verbs than such markers in the Atlantic creoles. To indicate an action in progress, *i stap* 'stay' or *i go* are used after the verb: 'Meri i kuk i stap' 'The woman is cooking.' Reduplication of the main verb or *i go* indicates durative action. Although the optional past tense marker *bin* immediately precedes the verb, the future marker *bai* (cf. *by and by*) can either precede or follow the subject: '*Bai* ol i wokim house' '(Sometime in the future) they will build a house' (Wurm 1977:524). Aitchison (1987) notes that the verb *save* 'know (how to)' is becoming a preverbal marker of habitual aspect (which usually takes the shorter form *sa*) for some younger speakers who use Tok Pisin as their primary language. She notes that whether such speakers distinguish between habituality and durativity depends on their social network, as does their use of fully developed relative clauses introduced by *we*. Sankoff (1980) has documented the rise of *ia* as a relative clause marker (which appears to be rare according to Aitchison), as well as the development of *(baim)bai* from an adverb to a tense marker.

Mühlhäusler (1982:449) summarizes the most important structural innovations of Tok Pisin's expanded pidgin and creole stage as embedding, compulsory marking of grammatical categories such as tense and number, productive word-formation rules, mechanisms for structuring discourse and stylistic differentiation.

Tok Pisin text (Mühlhäusler 1982:462)
Ol i kamap long hapsaid   bilong raunwara, long graun   long ol
they came to   other side of   lake,   to   country of PLUR

Gerasa.   Em i lusim bot pinis   na kwiktaim wanpela man i
Gerasenes. he   got off boat COMPL and quickly   a   man who

gat spirit doti   i stap   long en, em i kam painim Jisas. Dispela
had spirit unclean* stopped by him he   came to find Jesus. this

man . . . i save   slip long ples matmat.
man   HABITUAL slept in   cemetery.
*(i.e. was possessed)

3.13 Pidgins and creoles based on other languages

There are (or have been) restructured languages spoken around the world that are not based on Portuguese, Spanish, Dutch, French or English, the languages of the western European colonial empires. As indicated on map 1, African varieties include Fanakalo (pidginized Zulu in South Africa), Kituba (simplified Kikongo in the Democratic Republic of the Congo (D. R. C.) and Congo-Brazzaville), Lingala (spoken mainly in the D. R. C.), Sango (spoken mainly in the Central African Republic), restructured Swahili (spoken in the eastern D. R. C. and to the east) and restructured Arabic (see section 3.14).

Asian varieties include Nagamese (creolized Assamese in northeastern India), Coastal or restructured Malay (spoken in Malacca and in Indonesia east of Sumatra), Hiri Motu (pidginized Motu, spoken in southern Papua New Guinea), Pidgin Fijian and Pidgin Hindustani (both spoken in Fiji) and Pidgin Japanese (once spoken in Yokohama).

American varieties include Eskimo Trade Jargon (once spoken in northern Alaska and Canada), Chinook Jargon (pidginized Chinook and Nootka, once spoken in the northwestern United States), Mobilian Jargon (pidginized Choctaw and Chickasaw, once spoken in Louisiana), Delaware Jargon (pidginized Lenape, once spoken from Delaware to New England), Ndyuka-Trio Pidgin (a pidgin based on the creole Ndyuka (3.9) and Amerindian languages in Suriname) and Língua Geral (restructured Tupi, once spoken in Brazil).

Restructured European languages include Lingua Franca (restructured Romance languages, once spoken on the southern and eastern shores of the Mediterranean), pidginized Italian (spoken in Eritrea), restructured German (still spoken by foreign workers in Germany and once spoken in the Baltic area, Bosnia and German New Guinea), Russian-based pidgins (Russenorsk, once spoken in northern Norway, and Chinese Pidgin Russian, once spoken in Mongolia and Manchuria) and Pidgin Basque (once spoken from Labrador to Iceland).

It should be emphasized that the above list, completing this chapter's survey of the known pidgins and creoles, includes only languages which are documented and is almost certainly incomplete.

3.14 Nubi Creole Arabic

Nubi Arabic, a creole spoken today in Uganda and Kenya, grew out of a pidginized variety of Arabic which evolved in the nineteenth century in the country now called Sudan. Although Arabic is spoken natively in the northern two-thirds of that country, the black populations in the southern third speak languages variously classified as Sudanic (Greenberg 1966a) or Nilotic. Arabic seems likely to have long been important in the southern Sudan as a trade language, at least since the time of the Arabic slave traders who antedated the arrival of the Turco-Egyptian government, which extended its control into the Sudan from 1820 to 1870. Many of the 'recruits' in the Egyptian army were black slaves captured in the Nuba mountains south of Khartoum, the likely source of the term 'Nubian' or 'Nubi' for this military force of diverse ethnic and linguistic origins (Heine 1982:11). Although Arabic was the principal native language of the officers, who were mainly Egyptian, it was a foreign language for the local men, who came to make up 90% of the army. These soldiers evolved a pidginized variety of Arabic called Juba after the region's principal town, located some hundred miles north of the modern border with Uganda. Although the administrators of the later Anglo-Egyptian Sudan attempted to replace Juba Arabic with English as a lingua franca, the pidginized Arabic survived because of its usefulness throughout the southern Sudan.

Today this pidginized Arabic is widely spoken in and around Juba, and Owens (1980) notes that it is beginning to gain native speakers. Heine (1982:17) suggests that it drew its lexicon from a variety of Arabic closely related to the modern dialects of Egypt and Khartoum, but Owens (1985) demonstrates that many of its phonological features come from the dialects of the western Sudan. If Juba and Nubi Arabic are compared to these rather than other modern dialects of Arabic, they are much less divergent than originally assumed.

The local men recruited into the Turco-Egyptian army in southern Sudan in the second half of the nineteenth century formed the nucleus of a new ethnolinguistic group, the Nubi. Heine (1982:11–12) notes that the pidginized Arabic used as a lingua franca in the army eventually became this group's mother tongue. The recruits converted to Islam and married largely within the community that grew up around the army. Group cohesion was strengthened by their feeling of cultural separateness from surrounding groups, which were felt to be more backward.

In 1881 the Mahdists, following the Sudanese Muhammad Ahmad, began a revolt against the Turco-Egyptian colonization of the Sudan. In 1884 the Mahdists invaded Equatoria, the colony established by Egypt in 1871 in what is now the southern Sudan. The Egyptian governor had to flee south, accompanied by the Nubi, who remained loyal to him. By the end of the decade the British had managed to make the area part of an Anglo-Egyptian condominium, and Uganda was made a British protectorate in 1890. One group of Nubi troops had met up with Stanley on his 1888 expedition up the Congo River to Lake Victoria and agreed to follow him to the East African coast and from there to Cairo. However, the British decided to use the Sudanese mercenaries to help establish their rule in Uganda, where they eventually formed the backbone of the King's African Rifles. This group of Nubi consisted of 9,132 men, women and children, of whom 932 were soldiers (Heine 1982:12). Another group of some 11,000 Nubi (1,000 soldiers and 10,000 dependants) who had been separated from the first group reached Lake Albert, and in 1894 they also joined the British forces in Uganda.

Some of the Nubi were taken to western Uganda to guard British forts, while others were taken to what is now Kampala, the capital. Still others were brought to Nairobi in what is now Kenya, where the suburb of Kibera was set aside for them and their dependants. Today some 3,000 to 6,000 Nubi live in Kibera, and around 10,000 in Kenya as a whole (Heine 1982:15). The total number of Nubi in East Africa is estimated to be somewhere between 30,000 and 50,000. The largest concentration is at Bombo, some 30 miles north of Kampala.

As town dwellers and Muslims, the Nubi all use Swahili for out-group communication, and Nubi for in-group communication in a pattern of stable bilingualism. Some 30% also speak English, and they are often fluent in the local language as well, speaking an average of 3.5 languages well (16). They are known for their loyalty to their language and ethnic group; although Nubi men may marry Muslim women from other groups, their wives are expected to learn and use the Nubi language.

Owens (1977, 1980) describes Nubi and Juba Arabic as mutually intelligible dialects of the same language. Both indicate tense and aspect with preverbal markers parallel to those of the Atlantic creoles (Bickerton 1976, Owens 1980). This seems to strengthen Bickerton's claim for universals considerably since the similarity cannot be explained by a common substrate or diffusion, but Thomason and Elgibali (1986:428) note that 'preverbal particles in the [Arabic-based] pidgins and Ki-Nubi cannot be used as evidence for a claim about universals of pidginization, because all forms of Arabic . . . have functionally and positionally similar tense/aspect markers in their verbal systems'. Inflections have been eliminated, e.g. while Classical Arabic has root inflections to distinguish between the masculine singular and plural as well as the feminine in the word for 'who?' (*minu, minum, mini, minim* respectively), Nubi has the single form *munú* (Heine 1982:19). Although 90% of Nubi's vocabulary is from Arabic, these words can combine in compounds unknown in the lexical source language, e.g. *nyereku-bágara* or 'child of cow' for 'calf', *badna-iída* 'belly of hand' for 'palm', or *moy-ééna* 'water of eye' for 'tears' (20). Such compounds may have resulted from a universal strategy for expanding a pidgin vocabulary to fill lexical gaps, or they could represent calques on compounds in substrate languages (4.3.4). The examples cited happen to correspond to compounds in the Atlantic creoles. Finally, Owens (1980) notes that Nubi has syntactic features such as passive constructions, certain locative markers and reduplication, which are found not in Arabic but in Swahili.

Nubi Arabic text (J. Owens p.c.)
'ina 'kan 'g-agara,   ba'kan lisa 'kan 'ana 'g-agara   fu
we PAST CONT-study when still PAST I   CONT-study at

'bombo 'sudanis, 'ina 'kan 'endi 'din   te min 'subu, 'asede
Bombo Sudanese, we PAST have religion of morning, now

'din   te min 'subu 'de, 'ana 'agara 'owo, ke na 'kelem ja   fu
religion of morning this, I studied it, let us say came in

'wik 'way je'de,   'ana 'g-agara   'wwo 'mara tinen, 'yom
week one like that, I CONT-study it times two, day

'tan 'de.
some that.

'We used to study, and when I was still studying at Bombo Sudanese
School, we had religion class in the morning, and this religion class,
I was studying it. Every week I would attend say two times or so.'

Having examined the social circumstances that led to the development of a
number of pidgin and creole languages, we will now turn to some of the
striking similarities that these languages share with one another – features
that are often not found in the languages from which they drew their lexicons.

4
Lexicosemantics

4.0 Introduction

This and the following chapters on phonology (5) and syntax (6) compare a number of creoles of various lexical bases by linguistic level. These creoles share many features on all three levels which are not found in their lexical source languages. These similarities are discussed at some length because of their importance as evidence for various theories purporting to explain their origins, principally the monogenetic versus polygenetic theories (2.10), and universalist (2.12) versus substratist theories (2.13). Although some of the evidence used in these debates has been from phonology (e.g. Boretzky 1983), the most obvious linguistic level on which to seek features common to creoles of differing lexical bases has been syntax. The level of lexicon, which can be used to establish the similarity of languages in more traditional groupings, is not an obvious area in which to seek similarities among languages which have different vocabularies. In the early contact situations, the original pidgins and then the creoles that grew out of them had to use vocabulary that came primarily from the lexical source languages in order to serve their first function as bridges for communication. In the Atlantic colonies the Europeans spoke the language of political, economic and social power and the Africans, who had no such power in their state of slavery, had to do most of the linguistic accommodating. The influence of the European languages was further reinforced during the centuries when most of the creoles were used in colonies whose official language of administration was the same as their lexical source. For these reasons the creoles retained relatively few words (usually less than 10% of the lexicon) that were not from the lexical source language and therefore there are very few words shared by the Atlantic creoles based on Portuguese, Spanish, Dutch, French and English which might form the basis of a comparison (except, of course, the Romance or Germanic cognates also found in the European source languages). However, while vocabularies differ from one lexical group to another in *form*, they do share certain traits in the *kinds* of words they retain (e.g. words that are today archaic or regional in Europe) and the *kinds of changes* these words underwent. Some of these changes are at least partly attributable to a common African substratum (e.g. calques, certain semantic shifts and reduplication) and some to the wholesale restructuring which is characteristic of pidginization and creolization (e.g. the reanalysis of morpheme boundaries). However, all of the kinds of changes described below can be found in unrestructured languages as well. The only thing distinctive about pidgin and creole lexicons (for the following discussion is largely applicable to non-Atlantic varieties as well except for certain substrate features) is not the *kind* of changes that words have undergone but rather the extent to which the vocabulary has been affected by them. For example, while one might with luck find a dozen examples of the reanalysis of morpheme boundaries in English, e.g. *a napron* becoming *an apron*, hundreds of examples of this phenomenon can be found in any creole based on French.

In order to keep the discussion manageable, each point will normally be illustrated by only one example from each lexical base group: creole English, French, Portuguese, Spanish and sometimes Dutch or Arabic (respectively abbreviated CE, CF, CP, CS, CD and CA after names of particular varieties).

4.1 Pidginization and the lexicon

While there have been detailed studies of pidgin lexicons (e.g. Mühlhäusler 1979 or Schneider 1960), these have been the lexicons of extended pidgins such as Tok Pisin or West African Pidgin English. Regarding the lexicons of such pidgins *vis-à-vis* those of creoles, Hancock (1980) may well be right: 'I prefer not to acknowledge a distinction between *pidgin* and *creole* and to consider *stabilization* more significant than *nativization* in creole language formation' (p. 64; his emphasis). This seems particularly likely in the case of varieties that can be the primary (if not first) language of their speakers, such as Cameroonian English (usually called a pidgin) or Guiné-Bissau Portuguese (usually called a creole). The size, structure and development of the lexicons of such extended varieties contrast sharply with those of reduced pidgins, and even more with those of pre-pidgin jargons. Regarding the latter, estimates of a total lexicon of several hundred words or less have been given for nineteenth-century South Seas Jargon (Mühlhäusler 1979:182) and Russenorsk (Broch and Jahr 1984:47). Regarding pidgins, Bauer (1975:86) estimates that a knowledge of some 700 to 750 Chinese Pidgin English words was sufficient for most purposes in trade, the pidgin's only real domain. While one may object that such estimations of a pidgin's total lexicon on the basis of written records are as meaningless as saying that the vocabulary of the Beowulf poet was a particular number of words because those are all the words whose use was recorded, there is still every indication that the lexicons of early (i.e.

non-extended) pidgins are very much smaller than those of natural languages. However, certain characteristics of such lexicons partly compensate for their restricted size: multifunctionality (one word having many syntactic uses), polysemy (one word having many meanings) and circumlocution (lexical items consisting of phrases rather than single words).

Multifunctionality is discussed in more detail in section 4.7. Polysemy can be illustrated by the broad range of meanings usually found in pidgin prepositions such as Tok Pisin *bilong*, Cameroonian *fo*, Russenorsk *pa* or Chinese Pidgin Russian *za*, used to express nearly every locative relationship imaginable. However, this apparently universal tendency in pidgins may also be reinforced by substrate influence in some cases: like West African Pidgin English *fo*, Ibo *na* and Yoruba *ní* 'both refer . . . to location in a general way' (Welmers 1973:453). It seems likely that there is a relationship between polysemy in pidgins and the fairly frequent semantic broadening found in creole words (4.6.1), e.g. Krio CE *na*, which is also a general locative proposition. Stolz (1986:236) has pointed to the fact that Afrikaans *vir* can replace almost every other proposition as evidence of an earlier pidgin stage.

Polysemy in pidgins naturally leads to circumlocution with modifying phrases to specify the intended meaning, e.g. Tok Pisin *gras bilong fes* 'beard' as opposed to *gras bilong hed* 'hair' (Hall 1966:91).

4.2 Superstrate sources

Creole languages have typically drawn a considerable part of their lexicon from their source languages in forms virtually identical to those of the standard variety except for certain fairly regular sound changes (chapter 5). Even these often happened not to affect particular items, leaving words such as Jamaican CE *brij* or Haitian CF *põ* indistinguishable from English *bridge* or French *pont*. Moreover, those creoles that remained in contact with their lexical source languages, either through diglossia or a continuum, kept drawing on them for terms needed in modern life, such as French Antillean CF *òganizé*, *ékonomik*, *kapitalis*, etc. In a comparative lexical study, Bollée (1981) found that such parallels to contemporary standard French usage constitute over 60% of the Haitian CF lexicon; in Seychellois CF, which has coexisted with standard English rather than French since 1810, such parallels still constitute nearly 55% of the lexicon.

4.2.1 Survival of archaic usages

Bollée also found that over 16% of the Haitian CF lexicon and 9% of the Seychellois could be attributed to words that are today considered archaic or regional in France. There is no way to separate the two categories with any precision since the same word may fall into both. For example, *from* is found in a number of English-based Atlantic creoles as a conjunction with the temporal meaning of 'since', e.g. '*From* I was a child I do that.' This usage is part of both archaic and regional English. The last recorded use of *from* with this meaning in the *Oxford English Dictionary* was in 1602, suggesting that it was still current – if somewhat old-fashioned – in standard speech when English began spreading throughout the Caribbean in the seventeenth century. However, *from* with this meaning was still current in the regional English of Ireland and Scotland when Wright's *English Dialect Dictionary* was compiled around 1900. Thus there is no way of knowing whether *from* meaning 'since' was brought into Caribbean English creoles by speakers of standard (but archaic) English or by speakers of regional British dialects. Of course there are many other words that belong to only one of the two categories. Some examples are current Rama Cay CE *rench* and Sranan CE *wenke*, both 'young woman' from archaic English *wench*. Similarly Negerhollands CD *damsel*, still current around 1900, is from a Dutch (and ultimately French) word meaning 'young woman' which is now archaic in Holland. The word *bay* or *ba* meaning 'give' is current in many of the New World varieties of Creole French; it is from *bailler* 'give, deliver' (cf. E 'bail'), which was current in standard French until the seventeenth century but which is now archaic. The word for 'doctor' in Annobonese CP is *babélu* from Portuguese *barbeiro* 'barber', from days when members of that profession bled clients to cure their ailments.

Another kind of archaism found in creoles is the preservation of a pronunciation that is no longer current in the metropolitan variety. For example, Miskito Coast CE retains the /aɪ/ diphthong that was current in polite eighteenth-century British speech in words like *bail* 'boil' and *jain* 'join'; this sound became /ɔɪ/ in standard English after about 1800. This makes the creole word for 'lawyer' homophonous with standard English *liar* (but there is no confusion since the latter takes the dialectal form *liard* analogous to *criard* 'crier' and *stinkard* 'stinker' – cf. standard *drunkard*). The preservation of archaic pronunciations can be found in the creoles of other lexical bases as well, e.g. Haitian CF *chat* /šat/ 'cat', the earlier pronunciation of French *chat*, now /ša/. The São Tomé CP word for 'one' is *ũa* from older Portuguese *ũa* rather than modern *uma*.

Papiamentu CS appears to preserve a sixteenth-century Spanish pronunciation, although this may not be the whole story. Initial /f/ in Latin (e.g. *facere* 'do, make') became /h/ in earlier Spanish *hacer* and then Ø in the modern standard, although the /h/ pronunciation survives in Papiamentu *hasi* 'do, make' and in Caribbean Spanish dialects such as the one spoken in

Puerto Rico. However, the pronunciation *asi* with initial Ø is also quite current in Papiamentu, particularly on Curaçao. Moreover, initial /h/ alternates with Ø in a great number of Papiamentu words, including many that never had /h/ in Europe, such as Papiamentu *habri* 'to open' (cf. Spanish *abrir* from Latin *aperire*).

In fact, this alternation is found in a number of Caribbean creoles not based on Spanish, e.g. Miskito Coast CE *ej* and *hej* both mean 'edge' or 'hedge', while on the island of Abaco in the Bahamas *ear* is what you do with your *hear* (or vice versa). This alternation has often been blamed on Cockney in the Anglophone Caribbean, but this would not account for the same phenomenon in Negerhollands CD, in which *hō* can mean either 'hear' (cf. D *horen*) or 'ear' (cf. D *oor*). Stolz (1986:106) notes that Negerhollands /h/ seems to come not only from Dutch but also 'aus dem Nichts' ('out of nothingness'). Even aspirate French <h> springs back to life in Haitian CF *hey!* (cf. F *hé!* 'hey!'). Hesseling (1905:75–6) explained prosthetic /h/ as a general phenomenon in the creoles resulting from the lack of initial vowels in many West African languages, so that /h/ was carried over into this position to conform to substrate phonotactic rules. However, Singler (p.c.) notes that the preponderance of relevant West African languages, including most in the Kwa group, do in fact permit word-initial vowels. Thus Hesseling's hypothesis seems unlikely and we are left with yet another Caribbean mystery, although Cassidy and Le Page (1980:lxii) claim that 'initial [h] is frequently lost in unemphatic contexts and used as a hypercorrection in emphatic contexts', a pattern that is also found in Tok Pisin (Romaine 1992:203).

4.2.2 Survival of regional usages

Creoles also preserve forms, meanings and pronunciations that are now found only in regional dialects of their lexical source languages. In the case of the Atlantic creoles, this is a consequence of the fact that the great majority of Europeans who went to live in African or Caribbean colonies from the sixteenth to the eighteenth centuries were uneducated speakers of regional dialects. Studies of British regionalisms in Krio CE (Hancock 1971) and Miskito Coast CE (Holm 1981) suggest that there might be a relationship between the proportion of regionalisms from various districts in the creole and patterns of actual immigration from these districts to the colony where the creole developed. However, there are a number of factors that complicate such an inference. First, there is the often insoluble problem of determining whether a particular creole word preserves a regional rather than archaic usage, as discussed above. Secondly, the accuracy of European dialect studies in the nineteenth century (when many such words were already falling out of use) was often spotty regarding a word's actual geographic distribution; as Aub-Buscher (1970) remarked, 'le jeu de la localisation précise [dans la France] des formes créoles . . . est un jeu dangereux'. Finally, it is by no means clear where the particular mix of dialect forms occurred, i.e. whether it was in the colony itself or another colony from which there had been immigration to the colony in question. In the English-based creoles so studied (Krio, Miskito Coast and Bahamian) the similarity of the proportion of words from the North Country, Scotland and Ireland suggests that a general colonial variety of English may have formed before being creolized and spread by diffusion.

Examples of such regional forms include Miskito Coast CE *krabit* 'cruel' from Scots *crabbed* or *crabbit* 'ill-tempered'. Isle de France CF *mous* (*a myel*) and Caribbean CF *mouch a myel*, both 'bee', come from *mouche à miel* (literally 'honey fly') in the northwestern French dialects rather than standard French *abeille*. São Tomé CP *gumitá* 'to vomit' comes from regional and archaic Portuguese *gumitar* rather than standard *vomitar*. Negerhollands CD *kot* 'chicken coop' comes not from standard Dutch *hok* but Zeelandish *kot* (cf. English *dove-cot*). Papiamentu CS *wowo* 'eye' seems to come from Leonese *uollo* rather than Castilian *ojo*.

European pronunciations that appear to be regional have also been preserved in the creoles, but again it is often impossible to determine if these are in fact regional rather than archaic. Cassidy (1964:272) points out that Sranan words reveal the state of flux of certain vowels and diphthongs in the seventeenth-century English on which Sranan is based. For example, the shift from early Modern English /ʊ/ to /ʌ/ was apparently not yet complete; in some Sranan words, /u/ preserves the earlier pronunciation, as in *brudu* 'blood', while in others /o/ preserves the later pronunciation, as in *djogo* 'jug'. However, this shift has not taken place in many Midlands and North Country dialects of England, where these words are still pronounced /blʊd/ and /jʊg/. Therefore, there is no way of knowing whether Sranan *brudu* or even Bahamian *shoove* /šʊv/ 'shove' preserve an archaic or a regional British pronunciation. Other examples of regional pronunciation include Negerhollands *win* 'wine', preserving the pronunciation of Zeelandish *wien* /βi:n/ (also found in earlier standard Dutch) rather than modern standard *wijn* /βɛɪn/. Finally, the vowel in Haitian CF *mwen* 'I' or *bwè* 'drink' preserves the regional and archaic pronunciation of French *moi* or *boire*.

It should be noted that regional European dialects also appear to have contributed to the syntax of the creoles through specific lexical items. Examples include French *être après de* (*faire quelque chose*) 'to be (doing something)' (6.1.3) and Irish English habitual *be* (6.1.4). These are discussed in the chapter on syntax.

4.2.3 Nautical usages

Most creoles arose in maritime colonies in whose harbours docked slave ships, cargo ships, war ships and countless smaller craft. Because of the mixture of dialects and even languages found among ships' crews, nautical speech has always constituted a distinctive sociolect. A study of the English in log books kept by semi-literate captains and masters in the British navy from 1660 to 1700 (Matthews 1935) reveals that the sailors had a 'dialect . . . peculiar to themselves' which contemporaries described as 'all Heathen-Greek to a Cobler'. Hancock (1971:99–121) analysed both the phonological and the lexical data in Matthews, finding many similarities to Krio CE. This is not surprising, considering the important role that European seafarers played in the founding and maintenance of the colonies where the creoles developed. Today in eastern Nicaragua, kitchens or separate cooking huts are called *gyali* in Miskito Coast CE, from nautical English *galley*. In Haitian CF the normal word for 'pull' is *ralé* from nautical French *haler* 'haul' rather than French *tirer*, and 'lift' is *isé* from nautical French *hisser* 'hoist' rather than *lever*. On the Miskito Coast *haal* 'haul' and *hib* 'lift from below' (cf. *heave*) and *hais* 'lift from above' (cf. *hoist*) seem to be used much more frequently than in standard English. The Indo-Portuguese creole term for dismounting (a horse) is *disembarc* and a Bahamian term for returning home is *come 'shore*.

4.2.4 Slang and vulgar usages

Europeans brought the dialects of their social class as well as their region to the colonies. For the urban poor, soldiers and many others who made up the early settlers, slang was an important part of daily speech. Such words often became a part of the creole and often lost their European connotations in the process: if a creole's only word for 'urine' was *piss*, this word became as appropriate as *urine* in any domain, shedding the vulgarity of its etymon, e.g. Krio CE *switpis* 'diabetes', *pisbag* 'bladder', *pisol* 'urethra'.

The role of prostitutes in the building of empires has received scant comment from historians, but they were an important factor in settling the Caribbean colonies of Britain and France in the seventeenth century. Prostitutes were brought from France and given as wives to the buccaneers who had been using Haiti as their base, in order to encourage them to settle down and farm. An eighteenth-century observer commented that 'It is astonishing . . . that their manners, as dissolute as their language, are not perpetuated in their posterity to a greater degree than they appear to be' (quoted by Crouse 1943:133). In modern Haitian CF the term for 'nonchalant' is *fouben* from French (*je m'en*) *fous bien*, which today means 'I don't care' but in the seventeenth century was closer in strength to 'I don't give a fuck.'

In the Bahamas one of some twenty precise words for skin colour is *dingy* 'having the complexion of a dark-skinned person of mixed race', from the eighteenth- and nineteenth-century British slang term *dingy Christian* for a person of both European and African ancestry (note that *Christian man* could still be used for 'white man' in South Africa in the twentieth century). In Guiné-Bissau CP the normal word for 'breakfast' is *matabiiču*, from Portuguese *matar o bicho* (literally 'kill the bug') meaning 'morning alcoholic drink' reflecting the belief of early settlers that this protected their health. The term survives in Kikongo-Kituba and Lingala *matabisi* 'reward', in which *ma-* has been reanalysed as the mass prefix of noun class VI (S. Mufwene p.c.).

4.3 Substrate lexical influence

Niger-Congo languages were spoken natively by the generations of slaves who used the pidgins that developed into the Atlantic creoles, and they influenced the lexicons of these creoles in a number of ways discussed below. As mentioned above, the portion of non-European words in the pidgin could not exceed a certain level without impairing communication with the Europeans, which was the pidgin's initial function. The first generations of creole speakers were likely to have had some competence in the African languages of their parents. It seems likely that a pidgin-speaking mother often talked to her infant in her own language, but it also seems likely that she would use the pidgin as well, particularly if her spouse did not speak her ethnic language. Although it is difficult to reconstruct the sociolinguistic situation in Caribbean plantations in the seventeenth century with any certainty, it seems likely that the children of pidgin speakers – like the children of immigrants in other times and places – found their parents' first languages to be of limited usefulness with peers and with the larger community who used the pidgin or its creolized form as a lingua franca. Most children born in the New World probably never achieved full adult competence in an African language, particularly in those areas where slaves were purposely mixed linguistically. There is documentation that this was done in both Africa and the New World to make rebellions more difficult: Dillard (1972:73) cites the statement by the captain of a slave ship in William Smith's 1744 *A New Voyage to Guinea*: 'The safest Way is to trade with the different Nations, on either Side of the River [Gambia], and having some of every sort on board, there will be no more likelihood of their succeeding in a Plot, than of finishing the Tower of Babel.' However, there is disagreement as to how widespread or feasible the custom of mixing slaves by language actually was. In the Berbice colony of the Dutch in Guiana, a single African language, Eastern Ijo, appears to have predominated during the early period, judging from the ensuing Dutch creole, although this situation was unusual. Moreover, in Brazil 'linguistic homogeneity seems to have been valued as it enabled the older generations of slaves to teach the new arrivals' (Le Page and Tabouret-Keller 1985:33). Even in the West Indies, where mixing by language is claimed to have been widespread, its extent was limited by the planters' preference for certain ethnolinguistic groups that had come to be associated with various traits (Le Page and DeCamp 1960:79). Still, it seems likely that for most purposes competence in the African ancestral language was not transmitted beyond a generation or two in the West Indies, despite the continuing arrival of newly imported slaves.

However, under some circumstances African languages – or at least extensive parts of their lexicons – did survive. As might be expected, the African component of the lexicon of creoles spoken in maroon communities (i.e. those established by fugitive slaves) appears to be noticeably greater than that of other creoles, particularly in the domain of secret religious languages (e.g. Cassidy 1961, Daeleman 1972, Bilby 1983). Moreover, the particularly heavy importation of Yoruba speakers from what is today southwestern Nigeria in the nineteenth century led to the survival of their language until this century in Trinidad (Warner 1971) and Guyana (Cruickshank 1916) as well as Brazil and Cuba (Reinecke 1937).

4.3.1 Substrate lexical items

There is a terminological problem regarding words in the Atlantic creoles with etyma that have been traced to Niger-Congo languages. These have been called 'loans' or 'retentions', but neither term is always satisfactory. Some are retentions in that they were part of the original lexicon of the proto-pidgin reconstructed by Cassidy (1964) for the English-based creoles, suggesting that pidgins of other lexical bases had a similar category of words. Cassidy found that Sranan and Jamaican shared some twenty-seven words whose African source had been identified. This common vocabulary may be attributable to the migration of settlers and slaves from Suriname to Jamaica in the 1670s; only two of these words were also shared by Cameroonian. Nonetheless, it seems likely that some basic items that are today widespread in both African and Caribbean languages were indeed part of an early pidgin lexicon. Such items include *nyam* 'to eat', with cognates with related meanings in scores of Niger-Congo languages (Koelle 1854:80–1), and *fufu*, a dish made of boiled and mashed starchy vegetables like cassava, plantains, etc. If it is likely that such words were part of an early pidgin, they can hardly be called 'loans' into the creole any more than vocabulary derived from European languages. Moreover, while 'retentions' may be suitable for these words, it seems possible that other African-derived words were in fact loans, i.e. borrowed well after the establishment of the creoles. These may include the widespread words for Yoruba dishes such as *àkàrà* or cultural phenomena such as *èèsú* 'savings club'. Although it is difficult to date the adoption of such words, some inferences can be made. An *èèsú* presupposes a cash economy, suggesting that this was a nineteenth-century borrowing from Yoruba captives liberated by the British after 1808. On the other hand the variant pronunciation of Bahamian CE *moi-moi* or *mai-mai* from Yoruba *móin-móin* or Ibo *moimoi* (all referring to a dish consisting of mashed black-eyed peas boiled in a leaf) suggests a borrowing into Bahamian CE at a time when there was widespread variation between /oi/ and the earlier /ai/ in English-derived words such as *hais* 'hoist', although this might well have included the early nineteenth century as well as the eighteenth. Allsopp (1970) suggested an alternative term, 'apport', to avoid the problems connected with 'loan'; it also avoids those connected with 'retention'.

It is difficult to estimate the proportion of African-derived words in creole lexicons. Bollée (1981) found only 2.7% in her sampling of Haitian CF; later (1984:57) she noted that the dictionary she had used (Bentolila *et al.* 1976) was not very complete and that she had observed from her own lexicographical work that the proportion of non-French-derived vocabulary grew with the completeness of the lexicon. Cassidy (1961) estimated that general (i.e. non-Maroon) Jamaican CE preserves some 250 words of African origin, but it is difficult to establish a total number of words in the creole lexicon with which these 250 can be compared, since there is no way to determine where the creole lexicon ends and the standard lexicon begins in a continuum. Turner's (1949) study of the Gullah lexicon also lists some 250 words of African origin used in conversation, as opposed to the many more such words claimed to be preserved in personal names and some 90 expressions heard only in stories, songs and prayers.

Stewart (p.c.) has suggested that words of African origin were often felt to be stigmatized in the New World and were particularly subject to loss during decreolization if they had not already been adopted into the lexicon of the larger society (if the decreolizing speech community coexisted with one). If not replaced outright, such words may be 'masked' or reanalysed in terms of the European source language. For example, Caribbean CE *bákra* 'white person' has been traced to Ibibio and Efik *mbakara* (Turner 1949:191), which may in turn be related to *beké* 'white man' in Ijo dialects (Smith *et al.* 1987), a likely source of Berbice CD *bɛkɛ*, Lesser Antillean CF *beke* and the obsolescent Barbadian CE term *becky* with the same meaning. In Belizean CE *bakra* is explained as white people having their 'back raw' from sunburn

(Donahoe 1946), while in Guyanese CE it is thought to be 'a corruption of *back row*, where (in church, etc.) white prisoners and their descendants had to sit' (Yansen 1975). In Sranan the folk etymology is *ba kra*, literally 'brother soul', possibly influenced by *blue-eyed soul brother* in African American Vernacular English (Eersel p.c.). In Trinidadian CE it is believed to be a 'term originally used to refer to a Frenchman of low standing. From the French *bas courant*' (Ryan 1985).

Alleyne (1971:176) has suggested that those African words that did survive in the creoles 'belong to a semantic category that can be generally described as *private* in contrast with the broad semantic category of European-derived words that may be termed *public*'. In other words, African words often survived for intimate things, such as aspects of sexuality (e.g. Gullah CE *ɲini* 'female breast' from Mende *ɲini* – Turner 1949:199), religion (e.g. some 180 African-derived voodoo terms in Haitian CF; S. and J. Comhaire-Sylvain 1955) or other African cultural survivals with no equivalent in the European language (e.g. dishes such as Papiamentu CS *funchi*, Negerhollands CD *funtji* or Jamaican CE *fungee*, all 'cornmeal mush' from kiMbundu *funži* 'cassava mush') – exactly the kind of lexicon likely to survive among immigrants elsewhere.

4.3.2 Substrate semantic influence

While the proportion of actual words in creole lexicons that can be traced to substrate languages is usually small, the influence of these languages is much more extensive in the semantic range of creole words (Huttar 1975). Alleyne (1980:109) has suggested that this occurred via relexification (2.10): 'the historical development of the lexicon has been in terms of a substitution, massive and rapid in this case of West African lexemes by English (and Portuguese, Dutch, etc.) lexemes, leaving the former residual in . . . the semantic structures which underlie the lexicon'. For example, Twi *dùá*, Ibo *osisi* and Yoruba *igi* all have a semantic range including 'tree, wood, stick'. In Creole English the word *stick* can also mean 'tree' (e.g. Bahamian CE 'a stick name pine') or 'wood' (e.g. 'a piece o' stick'). The Spanish word *palo* (cf. Latin *pālus* 'stake') had its meaning extended to 'wood' and 'tree' after the sixteenth century, quite possibly under the influence of African languages in the New World. Portuguese *pau* has the meaning 'stick, wood' in Europe but also the meaning of 'tree' in its African-influenced cognates in São Tomé CP, Saramaccan CE and Brazilian Portuguese. Moreover, Twi *dùá* has the additional meaning of 'penis' (S. Obong p.c.); this is also an extended meaning of Jamaican CE *wood*, Haitian CF *bwa* (cf. French *bois* 'wood'), Papiamentu CS *palu* and Brazilian Portuguese *pau*, but not of the equivalent words in the European source languages (Holm 1987a).

African semantic influence had a far-reaching effect not only on the lexicon but also the syntax of the Atlantic creoles; it is particularly noticeable in the semantics of preverbal tense and aspect markers (6.1), which are fundamental to the structure of the creoles. The absence of a passive construction on a European model in the basilect of most Atlantic creoles could reflect a feature universally lost in creolization, but a case can also be made for substrate influence in semantics affecting syntax. While Bantu languages have a verbal suffix to mark the passive (generally used in impersonal, agentless sentences), almost all other Niger-Congo languages lack a special passive construction (Welmers 1973:344). Instead, they have two kinds of constructions that are also found in the Atlantic creoles: (1) like colloquial varieties of English and other Western European languages, they can have an active construction with an impersonal 'they' as its subject (cf. Miskito Coast CE '*Dem* bil dat hous laas yiir' 'They built that house last year'); or (2) transitive verbs can take on a passive meaning when their subject is not interpretable as the agent ('Dat hous *bil* laas yiir'). Syntactic parallels to both constructions can be found throughout the Atlantic creoles, e.g.:

> Haitian CF   Yo   rele li Mari.   Li rele   Mari.
> Papiamentu CS Nan ta yam' é María.   E yama María.
>   They call her Mary   She is-called Mary.

The effect of the second construction in the creoles based on Romance languages is the loss of the European reflexive pronoun (cf. F 'Elle *s*'appelle Marie', S '(Ella) *se* llama María'), with the reflexive (i.e. passive) meaning of the European verb becoming that of a creole stative. There appear to be two sources for this 'ergative' construction, sometimes referred to as 'passivization' of a transitive verb's meaning. First, like some European verbs (e.g. *sell* in 'He is selling balloons' and 'The balloons are selling well'), transitive verbs in many West African languages can have either an active or a passive meaning, e.g. Efik *ta* and Bambara *dùn* can both mean either 'to eat' or 'to be eaten':

> Bambara Tò   *dùn* Mali la.
>   Millet-porridge eat Mali in
>   'Millet porridge is eaten in Mali.'

Secondly, passive constructions in some European languages lent themselves to reanalysis: since past forms of 'be' could be reinterpreted as markers of tense only (6.1.2), the locus of passive meaning could be shifted to the verb itself as in many West African languages (Holm *et al.* 1997). For example, *was* could be interpreted as only a tense marker in 'This house *was* built last year', as could French *été* in 'Cette lettre lui a *été* envoyé' 'This letter was sent to him' (cf. Mauritian CF 'Sa lèt-la *ti* anvoy li').

4.3.3 Substrate syntactic influence on lexicon

Hancock (1980:78) quite rightly observes that 'Shift of formclass is extremely widespread in all the creoles, and in any language which has little surface morphology.' While this is evident in sentences like Nigerian Pidgin English 'Dì *bíg* wé yù dón *bíg* wélwél' 'You have really gotten big' (Rotimi and Faraclas ms.), it is also true that creoles are not syntactic free-for-alls in which any part of speech can become any other. As Hancock points out, Krio CE *ɔt* can function either as a preposition meaning 'out' or as a verb meaning 'put out; extinguish' (1980:78). However, not all Krio propositions are multifunctional, and it is worth asking what diachronic factors might have influenced apparent shifts from one syntactic category in the lexical source language to another in the creole. In this case, standard English *out* could be used as a verb meaning 'extinguish' until the seventeenth century, a usage that has survived in both British and American dialects. This suggests that the Krio 'shift' was actually the survival of an archaic or regional usage. Similarly, it is worthwhile asking why so many European adjectives became creole verbs – while relatively few European nouns, for example, underwent this syntactic shift. Examples include the following:

> Miskito Coast CE 'If yu wud *sief*, yu wud ron'
> 'If you want to be *safe*, you had better run'
> (Holm 1978:264)

> Haitian CF 'fãm té *blãš*' 'The woman *was white*'
> (Sylvain 1936:41)

> Angolar CP 'ɔmɛ ɛ *bwaru* fogawa' 'The man *is* really *good*'
> (Lorenzino 1998)

> Negerhollands CD 'Mie *doot* van Honger' 'I'*m dying* of hunger'
> (Hesseling 1905:261)

In the above examples, the creole words in italics derived from European adjectives do not need to follow the equivalent of 'to be' as in Western European languages (6.2.3). Moreover, to indicate past (or anterior) tense, these words take the same marker as the one used before verbs, e.g. *té* in 'fãm *té* blãš' above is also used to mark verbs as in 'li *té* mãšé' 'he had eaten'. In Miskito Coast CE, *did* is an anterior marker for words derived from English adjectives (e.g. 'evriting *did* chiip' 'everything was cheap') as well as those derived from verbs ('die did gat chilren' 'they had children'). While it is true that adjectives are universally more similar to verbs than nouns are, it is also true that the above pattern is parallel to that in most West African languages. For example in Kru, spoken in Liberia, adjectives are a type of verb and require no copula: 'ɔ kpákà', literally 'he *old*' (Singler 1981:20). Similarly in Yoruba, adjectives function like verbs in that they require no copula: 'ó *tóbi*' 'he *is-big*'). They also take a preverbal marker to indicate past or anterior tense: 'ó *ti* tóbi' 'he has become big' (Rowlands 1969). The case for European adjectives having become a type of creole verb under the influence of the African substrate is discussed further in section 6.2.3.

It is possible that in the case of some lexical items the general tendency of the Atlantic creoles to reinterpret European adjectives as verbs may have converged with other factors. In archaic English, *sick* was used as a verb meaning 'to become ill' until the end of the sixteenth century, a usage possibly preserved in Bahamian CE 'I thought Papa couldn't *sick*.' On the other hand, while *red* could be used as a verb meaning 'to redden' (cf. Bahamian 'Her eye started to *red*'), this usage was not recorded in standard English after the fifteenth century – well before English came into contact with African languages (although it could have survived in dialects).

4.3.4 Substrate calques

Calquing is a process whereby words or idioms in one language are translated word for word (or even morpheme by morpheme) into another. For example, the English word *foreword* is probably a nineteenth-century translation of the German term *Vorwort*, while German *Wolkenkratzer* (literally 'cloud-scraper') is a partial translation of English *skyscraper*. Whether or not the theory of relexification (2.10) is accurate in its entirety, there is considerable evidence that the calquing of African words and phrases was a major factor in the genesis of the Atlantic creoles. The semantic evidence for massive calquing is discussed above (4.3.2) and syntactic evidence can be found both above (4.3.3) and in chapter 5; this and the following section will deal with lexical evidence.

The calquing of a single morpheme can be traced only if this has affected its semantic range, as discussed above. Two-morpheme calques are more readily identified; in Bahamian CE *big-eye* means 'greedy; wanting the biggest and best for oneself', as do Haitian CF *gwo je* and Brazilian Portuguese *olho grande* (both literally 'big eye'). This metaphor is widespread in Africa, e.g. Twi *ani bre* or Ibo *aŋa uku*, both literally 'big eye' meaning 'greedy'. Calquing can also affect word-formation rules; in many creoles the sex of animate nouns can be indicated by juxtaposition of the word for 'male' or 'female', a pattern found in many West African languages:

	'child	'male'	'son'	'female'	'daughter'
Bahamian CE	chil'	boy	boy-chil'	gyal	gyal-chil'
Negerhollands CD	kin	jung	jung kin	menši	menši kin
Papiamentu CS	mucha	homber	mucha homber	muhe	mucha muhe
São Tomé CP	mina	mɔsu	mina mɔsu	mɔsa	mina mɔsa
Bambara	dén	ce	dén-ce	muso	dén-muso
Yoruba	ọmọ	okùnrin	ọmọ okùnrin	obìrin	ọmọ obìrin

It is possible that the English creole forms were influenced by the parallel Scots forms *lad-bairn* and *lass-bairn*, although it is also possible that these were themselves calques on Caribbean usages brought home by returning emigrants, much like the semantic extensions of Spanish *palo* and Portuguese *pau* discussed above (4.3.2). Boretzky (p.c.) has suggested that 'The repercussions of creole language phenomena on the respective metropolitan languages should be a new field of investigation.'

Taylor (1977:170) points out the two-morpheme parallels in question words in Ibo and a number of Atlantic creoles, corresponding to 'what thing?' (for 'what?'), 'what person?' ('who?'), 'what time?' ('when?'), and 'what place?' ('where?'). Bickerton (1981:71) completes this list by pointing out the parallel form 'what makes?' (for 'why?') in Guyanese CE *wa mek* and Seychellois CF *ki fer*. To these could be added Annobon CP *ja fé* (Schuchardt 1893:407) and Negerhollands CD *watmaak* (De Josselin de Jong 1926:106). Although Bickerton considers the influence of the African substratum on creoles to be insignificant, there are clear parallels in West African languages, e.g. Ibo 'gɛ nɛ merɛ' or Yoruba 'kíl 'ó ṣe', both literally 'what it makes?' meaning 'why?' – but no such parallels in the European lexical source languages.

A case might be made for creoles having arrived at such terms by a universally logical analysis in which units of meaning are lexicalized, e.g. 'what time?' (for 'when?') or 'male child' (for 'son'). Still others might be attributed to a straightforward description of a widespread culturally determined practice: the three stones used to support a pot above a fire have a parallel name in Bahamian CE *t'ree stone*, Haitian CF *twa pye*, Negerhollands CD *dri: ste:n* and Yoruba *ãrò mĕta* (Holm with Shilling 1982). However, many terms seem far too idiosyncratic to be universal. For example, if someone speaks ill of an effort that later fails, he is accused of 'putting the mouth on it' in Bahamian CE, i.e. cursing it. There are parallel phrases for this in Haitian CF ('mete bouch nan') and Papiamentu CS ('pone boka riba'). In Africa one simply points at such a person and says 'n'ano' in Twi or 'ẹnu rẹ' in Yoruba – both 'his mouth'.

Finally it should be noted that sometimes calques on turns of speech in substrate languages have not created new creole idioms but rather reinforced the choice of one of several possible phrases from the lexical source language. While it is possible if somewhat poetic to say 'rain is falling' rather than the more idiomatic 'it's raining' in Western European languages, the former is the normal phrase in a number of Atlantic creoles and African languages:

	Normal creole/African idiom			*European idiom*
	'rain'/'water'	PROG	'fall'	
Jamaican CE	ren	a	faal	E 'It's raining'
Haitian CF	lapli	ap	tonbe	F 'Il pleut'
Papiamentu CS	awa	ta	kai	S 'Está lloviendo'
Annobonese CP	awa	sa ka	se'be	P 'Chove'
Yoruba	òjò	n'-	rò	
Twi	nsuo	re-	tɔ	
Kongo	mvula	yi-	bwa	

Koopman (1986:246) notes that European 'weather verbs' (e.g. F *pleuvoir*) requiring a pleonastic subject pronoun (*il*) do not exist in creoles like Haitian CF or African languages like Vata and Abe. However, their absence cannot be attributed to the absence of pleonastic pronouns, which the latter languages have.

4.3.5 Reduplication

While iteration is simply the repetition of a word for emphasis ('a *long, long* walk'), reduplication is a mechanism for forming new words. It involves the repetition of a word (or part of a word) resulting in a distinct lexical item with a slightly different meaning. In European languages reduplication is often associated with hypocorism or baby talk (e.g. *wee-wee*, or French *bonbon*) but this is not the case in the Atlantic creoles and the Niger-Congo languages. It seems likely that reduplication became a productive mechanism for word formation in many creoles via calquing on substrate models. For example, the Yoruba word *ńlá* 'big' can be reduplicated to intensify its meaning, i.e. *ńláńlá* 'huge'; the same process can be seen not only in Kongo *múpátipáti*, also literally 'big-big', but also in CE *big-big*, Haitian CF *gran gran* and Guiné-Bissau CP *grãndi-grãndi*. Negerhollands CD *vroevroe* 'morning' (cf. Dutch *vroeg* 'early') indicates both intensification and shift of meaning. Cassidy (1961:69–73) noted some 200 reduplicated forms in Jamaican CE; he traced 16 of these directly to African sources, such as *putta-putta* 'mud' (cf. Papiamentu CS *pòtòpòtò* 'muddy') from Twi *pɔtɔpɔtɔ* 'muddy' or Yoruba *pòtòpòtò* or Baule *pòtopóto*, both 'mud'. The creole words represent retentions rather than calques. Another 10 of the Jamaican reduplications seemed to be

121

from African languages but no etyma could be found, while 6 seemed to be Jamaican onomatopoetic creations such as *pooka-pooka* 'sound of a kettle on the boil'. Similar emphatic 'phonaesthetic' reduplications are frequent in African languages, e.g. Mandinka *fitifiti* 'movement of a dog shaking itself' or Kongo *dunta-dunta* 'palpitate'. The largest category in Cassidy's study consisted of reduplications of English words. The productivity of this mechanism in creoles is attested by such forms as Miskito Coast CE *pokpok* 'slow passenger boat with an engine' or Liberian English *holiholi* 'bus', from 'Hold it! Hold it!' (Singler p.c.).

The following illustrate some of the kinds of semantic shifts achieved by reduplication; all CE examples are from Miskito Coast CE (Holm 1978). Related to the intensification of meaning discussed above is a superlative meaning, e.g. *las-las* 'the very last' (cf. Mandinka *lábang-labango* 'the very end'). Reduplication can also suggest the accumulation of many small things, e.g. *gravel-gravel* (cf. Kongo *lubwe-lubwe*). It can add the idea of distribution, e.g. *wan-wan* 'one by one, gradually'; cf. parallel Yoruba *ọkọkan*, Twi *baako-baako*, as well as Haitian CF *yun-yun* and São Tomé CP *ũa-ũa*, all literally 'one-one' with the same extended meaning. Sometimes the accumulation implied is that of parts into a mass, e.g. *mod-mod* 'a lot of mud' (cf. Twi *pɔtɔpɔtɔ*). Reduplication can also suggest reiteration, e.g. *krai-krai* 'constantly crying, fretful'; cf. Mandinka *ke* 'do' and *kée-kee* 'keep on doing'. It can also add the idea of familiarity, e.g. *fon-fon* 'done in fun or play' or *lafi-lafi* 'loving fun and laughter'. Such familiarity can also be connected to contempt, e.g. *priichi-priichi* 'continual harping and preaching'; cf. Kongo *bantu-bantu* 'ordinary folk' and Yoruba *hẹbẹhẹbẹ-hẹbẹhẹbẹ* 'waddle along'. Studies of reduplication in creoles (e.g. Ivens Ferraz 1979:58ff., Chaudenson 1974:1051ff.) and African languages (Rowlands 1959, Carter and Makoondekwa 1976) or both (Bartens 1998) reveal semantic categories more similar to each other than to those in European languages (Bollée 1978), although there are indeed parallels in all three, suggesting language universals also play a role.

4.4 Other lexical sources

The most important source of lexicon for any creole is, by definition, its superstrate, if only for the sheer proportion of words. The influence of substrate languages is relatively limited in terms of actual words, exceeded by adstrate borrowings in many cases (e.g. in Miskito Coast CE, which has borrowed hundreds of words from Miskito and Spanish), but the impact of the substrate may pervade the entire lexicon in its effect on semantics, as well as calques on compound words, idioms and reduplications – and quite likely subcategorizational rules (4.7), although little research has been done on the last. The remaining lexical sources are Portuguese, which appears to occupy a special position in the history of the Atlantic creoles, and adstrate languages. Since borrowings from the latter closely reflect language contact, which varied greatly from one creole to another, more precise information on any individual creole must be sought in its particular sociolinguistic history (e.g. Holm 1988–9, vol. II). The purpose here is simply to summarize.

4.4.1 *Portuguese influence on the Atlantic creoles*

Because of the early and prolonged role of the Portuguese in Africa, particularly in the slave trade that led to the formation of the Atlantic creoles, their language played a number of different roles in relation to these creoles. It served as the superstrate for the Portuguese-based pidgin and creoles of West Africa, as an adstrate for creoles of other lexical bases in the Guianas and the Caribbean, and possibly even as part of the substrate for Papiamentu.

The Portuguese-based pidgin that evolved in West Africa from the fifteenth century onwards was well established as the language of the slave trade in the seventeenth century when the Dutch, English and French began capturing Portuguese forts from the Gambia to the Congo to gain supplies of slaves for their colonies in the New World. It has been claimed that the Portuguese pidgin used around these forts (and possibly by the first generations of Africans brought to the Caribbean) was, according to the monogenetic theory (2.10), relexified or changed word for word toward the language of the Europeans currently in power. It is possible that the early Martinican contact French which Goodman (1964:104) quotes from Bouton (1640) and Chévillard (1659) contains words from an earlier Portuguese pidgin, although Goodman (1987) believes they were from Spanish. More convincing evidence of possible remnants of a Portuguese pidgin lies in core vocabulary like *sabi* 'know' (cf. P *saber*) or function words such as *ma* 'but' (cf. P *mas*) in creoles of non-Iberian lexical bases, e.g. Sranan and Saramaccan CE. Negerhollands CD also has *ma*, although in this case it might be converging with or derived solely from Dutch *maar* 'but' through the regular loss of a postvocalic /r/. There is also a general locative preposition *na* (cf. P *na* 'in the' before singular feminine nouns) in the same languages as well as Papiamentu CS (cf. S *en* 'in') and Krio CE, with possibly related forms in Haitian CF *nan* and Jamaican CE *ina*. Taylor (1971), who drew attention to these similarities, pointed out that the Ibo preposition *na* matched the semantics of the creole forms more closely than Portuguese *na* did, however (4.1). Hull (1974) pointed out that both the Portuguese-based creole of Príncipe and Lesser Antillean Creole French have the same preverbal markers for the progressive (*ka*) and future (*kɛ*). The future marker *lo* (cf. P *logo* 'immediately') is found not only in some of the Portuguese creoles of Asia but also in Papiamentu CS and Negerhollands CD. The completive marker *kaba* (cf. P *acabar* 'to complete, finish') is found in Portuguese creoles in Asia as well as Philippine CS, Papiamentu CS and the English-based creoles of Suriname; moreover, there is a possibly related completive marker *ka* in Sri Lankan CP and Negerhollands CD. The Portuguese source may have converged with an African form such as Bambara *ka ban* 'INF finish', which is also used after verbs to mark the completive aspect (Holm 1986).

Cassidy (1964) points out some fifty words apparently from Portuguese that are shared by Sranan and Jamaican CE. Aside from the uncertainty of some of the etymologies, there are problems in attributing these words to the remnants of an earlier Portuguese-based pidgin, as Voorhoeve (1973) did with the considerable Portuguese-derived vocabulary in Saramaccan CE (2.10). However, the traditional view attributed these words to the Portuguese of the Brazilian Jews and their slaves, who settled in Suriname in 1664 and 1665. Given their arrival during the crucial formative period of the English creole there, it seems plausible that they influenced its lexicon in the decade before most of the English settlers and their slaves left for Jamaica and other British islands after Suriname was transferred to the Dutch (Goodman 1987). Adstrate influence from the Portuguese of other Brazilian refugees during this period seems likely to account for loans in the creoles of French Guiana and the Antilles, e.g. *briga* 'to fight' (cf. P *brigar*) or *fala* 'to flirt' (cf. P *falar* 'to speak'). It would also seem to account for some of the basic vocabulary of Negerhollands CD, perhaps via Papiamentu CS, e.g. *kabae* 'to finish' (Goodman 1987). Still other Brazilian refugees during this period seem likely to have brought their contact-influenced variety of Portuguese to Curaçao, where it contributed to what became Papiamentu, although others attribute the Portuguese-derived lexicon in Papiamentu to the remnants of an earlier Portuguese-based pidgin brought directly by slaves from Africa (Megenney 1984).

There seems to be documentary evidence of such influence on Palenquero CS. Sandoval (1627) described the slaves coming to Cartagena in what is today Colombia as speaking 'un género de lenguaje muy corrupto y revesado de la portuguesa que llaman lengua de San Thomé' ('a very corrupt, entangled kind of Portuguese called the language of São Tomé'). Moreover, the Portuguese-derived elements in Palenquero cannot be attributed to any other historical source; lexical items include *bae* 'to go' (cf. P *vai* 'he goes' versus S *va*), *la* 'there' (cf. P *lá* versus S *allí*), *menino* 'child' (cf. P *menino* versus S *niño*) and others (Megenney 1982).

It should be noted that there is a quite different kind of influence from Portuguese in the adstrate borrowings of other creoles. Réunionnais, which may have contributed to the French-based creoles of the Indian Ocean, contains over seventy words from Indo-Portuguese, many apparently brought by women speaking that language who married seventeenth-century settlers (Chaudenson 1979). In the Pacific Ocean, Hawaiian CE apparently gained some loans from Portuguese via the Portuguese speakers from Madeira and the Azores who came first as crew members on New England whalers and then as plantation labourers (Carr 1972). Finally, Portuguese speakers from both island groups were also brought as indentured labourers to some British colonies in the Caribbean area after emancipation in the 1830s; they are the likely source of words like Guyanese CE *preyta* 'person of African descent' (cf. P *preto* 'black'; Yansen 1975:58).

4.4.2 Adstrate influence

Like all but unusually isolated languages, most creoles have been in contact with a number of neighbouring languages from which they have borrowed words. Quite apart from the linguistic restructuring that occurred as a result of contact between the indigenous languages that the colonizers encountered and the ones they brought in, the Europeans' efforts to impose their political, economic and social wills on their colonies were hardly likely to produce linguistic replicas of their mother countries. In the Caribbean, for example, islands are often within an easy sail of one another and thus anything but isolated. The realities of trade, war, fugitive slaves, and later labour markets, tourism and education have made the Caribbean an area of intense linguistic and cultural contact, like most of the other areas where creole languages have developed.

Amerindian languages have contributed a number of words for flora and fauna to the Caribbean creoles, often via Spanish and sometimes via Portuguese. At the time of contact, the two dominant language groups in the Caribbean proper were the Caribs in the Lesser Antilles and the Arawakans elsewhere. Examples of loans include Island Carib *mabi*, a species of tree (*Colubrina reclinata*) whose bitter bark is used in preparing a drink of the same name in Papiamentu CS as well as Puerto Rican and Dominican Spanish; it is called *mabi* in Haitian CF, and *maubi* in Eastern Caribbean CE. An Arawakan loan is *kenepo*, a tree (*Molicocca bijuga*) bearing small, tart green fruit with a large stone; cf. Caribbean Spanish *quenepo*, Papiamentu CS *kenepa*, Haitian CF *kenèp* and CE *kinép* or *ginép*. Many Arawakan words for flora and fauna were carried via Spanish to Central and South America, where terms from other languages made the return journey. One of the latter is

Nahuatl *ahuacatl* 'avocado' from *ahuaca-cuahuitl*, literally 'testicle tree' from the use of the fruit as an aphrodisiac or perhaps its shape. The standard Spanish form, *aguacate*, is quite close to the Nahuatl, but the local Guatemalan variant, *avocate*, suggests an older form that led to French *avocat* and Haitian CF *zaboka* (from the French plural *les avocats*; cf. 4.5.1 below) and Bahamian CE *avogado* and *alvakada*, leading to *alligator pear* by folk etymology. Miskito, a Macro-Chibchan language spoken in eastern Honduras and Nicaragua, has contributed many words to the English creoles of the Western Caribbean, including *tahpam*, a large sea fish (*Megalops atlanticus*), which was borrowed into standard English as *tarpon* but retains its Miskito form in English creoles from Nicaragua to the Bahamas. Other Miskito words have been calqued in creole English, e.g. *sanki dusa* (literally 'bat tree') for a shrub (*Saphrantus foetidus*) which is called *rat-bat bush* in CE and the equivalent *palo de murciélago* in local Spanish.

Spanish served not only as the vehicle of a number of Amerindian words borrowed into the creoles, but also as a source of loanwords in its own right. When North European explorers and privateers began coming to the Caribbean in the sixteenth century, Spanish was already well established in many areas and had acquired the vocabulary needed for local natural and cultural phenomena. Spanish words that became part of the creoles include Lesser Antillean CF (*y*) *iš* 'child' from Spanish *hijo* 'son' or *hija* 'daughter', in which *j* was pronounced /š/ until its shift to /x/ in the seventeenth century (Goodman 1987). Contact between Spanish and creoles based on other languages was prolonged in several areas: Creole English speakers along the Caribbean coast of Central America as far south as Panama live in officially Spanish-speaking countries, and this is reflected in their lexicons. In an incomplete survey (Holm 1978) of some 3,000 Central American CE words differing from those in current standard English, over 200 were found to be from Spanish.

The question of whether such borrowings are from an adstrate or a new superstrate language is not always clear. Where the language of administration differing from a creole's lexical source language remained distant from creole speakers and had little impact on their lexicon (e.g. Danish in the Virgin Islands, which has left only a few words in the Creole English like *gade* 'street'), the language can hardly be considered a superstrate. New languages of administration with a much greater and more intimate impact on creoles (i.e. on their phonology and syntax as well as lexicon) could well be considered new superstrates. Examples might include the relationship of Dutch to the English-based creoles of Suriname, and possibly of English to the French creoles of Trinidad and Louisiana.

4.5 Morphological changes

The above sections discussed external lexical influence on creoles from various languages. The remainder of this chapter will deal with internal linguistic processes that led to certain widespread types of changes in creole words vis-à-vis their superstrate etyma. As mentioned above, these processes affect the lexicon of all languages, but the extent to which they are evidenced in creoles suggests that they are accelerated by restructuring.

4.5.1 Morpheme boundary shift

Pidgins and creoles are sometimes claimed to be languages without any inflectional morphology whatsoever. While this seems to be true of most fully restructured varieties that are not decreolizing, there are some ambiguous cases. The Portuguese-based creoles of West Africa have what appear to be an inflectional marking of the past participle, e.g. Príncipe CP *fá* 'speak', *fádu* 'spoken', corresponding to P *falar* and *falado* respectively (Günther 1973). Forms ending in -*du* can be used actively (e.g. 'n táva *fádu*' 'I had spoken') but such constructions are rare; the -*du* form is primarily used to give the verb a passive meaning (e.g. 'ótu *samádu* pédu' 'The other was called Peter'). It is possible that this creole -*du* plays a semantic and syntactic role that is distinct from that of its Portuguese model. According to the analysis of Smith (1979b), etymologically related Sri Lankan CP '-*tu*, "perfect participle", is actually a post-clitic whose preferred position is attached to the verb'. In Guiné-Bissau CP, verbs with -*du* have a passive meaning similar to those of Príncipe CP (Kihm 1980), e.g. *skribi* 'write' versus *skribidu* 'written': 'kriol i ka ta *skribidu*' 'Creole is not written.' However, Kihm analyses -*du* as a derivational rather than an inflectional morpheme, analogous to the suffix -*tu* on intransitive verbs in Mandinka (both a substrate and adstrate language): e.g. *bàng* 'finish (transitive)' versus *bànta* 'finish (intransitive)'. The fact that both Guiné-Bissau and Sri Lankan CP coexist with languages with a similar morpheme may explain this as a later borrowing. Although this would not explain the Príncipe CP forms with -*du*, the latter may also be a derivational rather than an inflectional morpheme.

Papiamentu CS has a partially similar syntactic category of what appears to be a past participle. In verbs of Iberian origin this involves a shift of accent to the final syllable, e.g. *máta* 'kill' versus *matá* 'killed' (cf. S or P *máta* '[he] kills' versus *matádo* 'killed'). In verbs of Dutch origin the past participle is marked with a prefix, e.g. *fangu* 'catch' versus *difangu* 'caught' (cf. D *vangen* versus *gefangen*). The Papiamentu prefix has the allomorphs *gi-*, *ge-*, *he-*, *i-* and *e-*. Still other past participles take no marking: 'Su plannan a wordù *dòbelkròs*' 'His plans were stymied' (Maurer 1986:17). While the history of these forms is not known to the present writer, the inflections appear to be relatively recent borrowings akin to decreolization. Wood (1972b) points to the importation of Spanish morphology ('E tábata papya*ndo*' 'He was talking') encroaching on older, uninflected Papiamentu forms ('E tábata papya').

Perhaps the best case for the existence of inflectional morphology in basilectal Atlantic creole is that of Berbice Creole Dutch, which has what appear to be verbal endings. For example *draɪ* 'become' takes -*tɛ* to mark the past: 'a draɪ*tɛ* gu' 'It became big' (Robertson 1979:228). The superstrate source of this marker is clearly the Dutch past tense ending, e.g. 'ik hoop*tɛ*' 'I hop*ed*.' While this is unambiguously an inflectional ending in Dutch, the status of the Berbice CD morpheme is less certain. Historically the Dutch ending appears to have converged with the Eastern Ijo suffix -*tée*, which marks perfect aspect (Smith *et al.* 1987). Like other languages with subject-object-verb word order, Ijo has postpositions rather than prepositions and postverbal markers rather than preverbal markers (Robertson 1986). The closeness of the relationship of verbal markers to verbs is somewhat ambiguous in both West African and creole languages. Although verbal markers are often treated as free morphemes and written separately, in some African languages they are written together with the verb like bound morphemes. The Africanist/creolist Jan Voorhoeve (1970) suggested that the preverbal markers in Sranan CE should be treated as prefixes, i.e. bound morphemes. Except for the atypical Papiamentu future marker *lo* (6.1.6) and certain completive markers whose status as verbal markers rather than serial verbs is unclear (6.1.5), most Atlantic creole verbal markers cannot be separated from the verb to which they refer except by the other markers with which they combine (6.1). They may indeed occupy an intermediate status between bound and free morphemes, somewhat like clitics.

The above suggests that the status of morphemes transferred from European to creole lexicons could change from inflectional to derivational, and perhaps from bound to free. European morpheme boundaries also disappeared in the creoles: in Creole English one can speak of one *ants* or one *matches* or one *tools*, in which the English word and its plural inflection have become a single creole morpheme with either singular or plural meaning (6.4.2).

A similar morpheme boundary change occurred more frequently in the French-based creoles, e.g. Haitian CF *zié* 'eye' (from the French plural 'le*s* yeux' /lezyø/ rather than the singular 'oeil') or *zanj* 'angel' from 'le*s* anges'. In both cases the final sound of the plural definite article (pronounced /lez/ before a noun with an initial vowel, but /le/ elsewhere) has been agglutinated to the creole noun to form a single morpheme, e.g. 'youn *zanj*' 'one angel'. The same phenomenon occurs, although much less frequently, in creoles based on other Romance languages, e.g. São Tomé CP *zonda* 'wave' from P *as ondas*, or Papiamentu CS *sanka* 'buttocks' from S *las ancas* or P *as ancas* (Maurer 1986:8).

Other forms of the article have also become agglutinated, e.g. Haitian CF *legliz* 'church' (cf. F *l'église* 'the church') or *lalin* 'moon' (F *la lune*). In some cases two etymologically related forms both survive, each with a distinct meaning, e.g. Haitian CF *nonm* 'man (i.e. a male adult)' from F *un homme* 'a man' as opposed to *lezòm* 'man (i.e. mankind)' from F *les hommes*. Baker (1984) surveyed CF lexicons for count nouns having an initial syllable wholly derived from a French article; he found 112 in Haitian, 337 in Rodrigues, 444 in Seychellois and 471 in Mauritian – but only 12 in Réunionnais, providing further evidence that the last was not as extensively restructured. Such morpheme boundary reanalyses are much less frequent in creoles of other lexical bases, but they do occur, e.g. São Tomé CP *osé* 'sky' from P *o céu* 'the sky'. Papiamentu CS *lamá* 'sea' is from S *la mar* 'the sea', while *dehel* 'hepatitis' is from regional or archaic Dutch *de geel*, literally 'the yellow' (cf. standard D *geelzucht* 'hepatitis'). Sranan CE *didibri* 'devil' may come from English *the devil*. The agglutination of articles has also occurred in loans into non-creole languages, e.g. English *alligator* from Spanish *el lagarto* 'the lizard', or Spanish *algebra* from Arabic *al jabr*, literally 'the reduction'. Other function words can also be agglutinated, e.g. Jamaican CE *nej* 'to ache (of teeth)' comes from 'on edge' by reanalysis of /mi tiit an ej/ as /mi tiit a nej/, in which *a* is interpreted as the progressive marker (Cassidy and Le Page 1980). Similarly, some New Yorkers speak of 'a nurge' (e.g. to kill).

Agglutination of this kind in creoles usually reflects the frequency of the source form in the European language, e.g. some words are more likely to be heard in the plural like CE *shuuz* 'shoe' (made unambiguously singular with a quantifier: 'wan *fut* a shuuz') or *brienz* 'brain' (with the derived adjective *brienzi* 'intelligent'). Similarly, some verbs may be more likely to occur in their past or past participle form, which serves as the etymon for the creole verb, e.g. CE *marid* 'to marry'. However, CE *brok* 'break' seems to come from Scots and Irish English *bruck* 'break' rather than from standard *broke*. Similarly, CE *lef* 'leave' and *las* 'lose' appear to come from regional British *leff* and *loss*, although these could well have been reinforced by the standard past tense forms losing their final /t/ through a regular phonological rule (5.2.3). Evidence that *lose* may have been more likely to occur in its past form can be found in the parallel Berbice CD form *flɔrɔ* 'lose' (cf. D *verliezen* 'to lose' versus *verloren* 'lost'; Robertson 1979:263). Finally, English creole verbs sometimes agglutinated the *-ing* ending (e.g. Bahamian *to courtin, to loadin, to fishin*) and could then take the mesolectal progressive marker *-in*, e.g. *go fishinin*.

There is some question about the survival of European morphemes as separate entities when they have been borrowed into creoles in combinations, i.e. French *jugement* 'judgement' consists of two morphemes, but does Haitian CF *jijman*? Taylor (1953:295) suggested that Hall *et al.* (1953) created a false impression by treating certain morphemes under 'derivation' since the actual derivation had occurred in French but could not occur in Haitian CF, in which morphemes like *de-*, *pro-*, *tras-*, *-e*, *-te*, *-asyo*, etc., could not be used in forming new words, even though they might be recognizable as distinct elements. Similarly, Hancock (1980:83) claims that 'an English incoining such as *destaticize* could not occur in a creole (unless it were a monomorphemic lexical adoption from English)'. As a matter of fact, new morpheme combinations are indeed found in creoles, e.g. Haitian CF *sivéyé* 'watch' (cf. F *surveiller*) plus *-man* 'nominal suffix denoting action' yield *sivéyman* 'surveillance' (cf. F *surveillance*; Valdman 1978:139). Hancock (1980) himself mentions Trinidadian CE *brɔːtʌpsi* 'a state of being well brought up' from *brought up* plus *-cy*, and *makošǝs* 'prone to gossip' from *mako* 'gossip' plus *-tious*. An explanation for this apparent contradiction could be that in their early stages of development the creoles had lexicons consisting of almost entirely monomorphemic words and although these could combine as free morphemes (4.5.2), there were no productive derivational affixes. Later, through analogy (e.g. contrasting items like *jij* 'judge' and *jijman* 'judgement') and possibly further contact with the European lexical source language, some (but not all) creole words derived from European morpheme combinations became reanalysable along the lines of their etyma, and the derivational morphemes thus isolated became available for new combinations. Still, Valdman has remarked that 'in creole the productivity of the derivational process seems very weak, especially compared to that of . . . French' (1978:144). By contrast, Mühlhäusler (1979:vi) notes that in Tok Pisin, which is not an Atlantic creole, the 'powerful derivational lexicon distinguishes NGP from virtually all other pidgins and many creoles'.

4.5.2 New morpheme combinations

Although the number of new combinations of bound morphemes in creoles is quite limited, free morphemes have readily combined to create new compounds, particularly in the English-based creoles. Combinations that were influenced by the African substrate languages were discussed above (4.3.4). Many more seem to have been creole innovations to meet new communicative needs, some probably with the collaboration of the European colonists. In Miskito Coast CE, for example, two familiar words (*mountain*, *cow*) were combined to refer to the unfamiliar tapir. When the settlers and their slaves came across a fifty-pound rat with webbed feet (*Hydrochoerus capybara*), they christened it *water hog*. A parallel example in Guiné-Bissau CP is *piis-kabalu* 'hippopotamus' from Portuguese *peixe* 'fish' plus *cavalo* 'horse'. Some such terms impose a cultural redefinition on their etyma, such as Miskito Coast CE *fiéri bwai* (cf. *fairy boy*) 'ancestral spirit inhabiting the jungle'.

Some of the English-based creoles have created a number of new phrasal verbs such as Miskito Coast CE *apiir op* 'appear, show up', *daak op* 'turn dark', *dronk op* 'become intoxicated', *hog op* 'hug', *uol op* 'become old', *wet op* 'soak', *wind op* 'become flatulent'. However, caution is usually advisable before anything is labelled an innovation. Valdman (1978:131) points out the error of earlier lexicographers who labelled as such some creole morpheme combinations like Haitian CF *betize* 'to joke' (cf. F *bêtise* 'foolishness' plus *-er*, 'verb-forming suffix'). Although such combinations might seem new to speakers of standard French, they can be found in regional dialects and therefore may not represent innovations in the creoles. It is possible that some of the Miskito Coast CE phrasal verbs mentioned above actually represent survivals of archaic or regional British usages, but since lexicographers have largely ignored the status of phrasal verbs as separate lexical items until recently, such an origin for these terms is difficult to establish. However, when they include verbs based on English adjectives (e.g. *uol op* from *old* plus *up*), the case for their being true innovations is much stronger.

Some creole compounds seem redundant, for example Miskito Coast CE *hed skol* 'skull', *han elbuo* 'elbow' (*han* referring to both the arm and hand, like the corresponding term in many West African languages), *mout lip* 'lip', *rakstuon* 'stone', etc. These may be vestiges of an earlier stage of the lexicon's development, dating back to non-native-speaking parents (pidgin speakers) and their native-speaking children (creole speakers), and serving as a bridge between the two. Although they were members of the same speech community, their language was in a state of profound upheaval; it seems possible that teenagers and perhaps even older children had, as in other immigrant communities, English-derived vocabularies that far exceeded those of their parents, whose mother tongue was an African language. The precise English words, more likely to be unknown to the parent, may have come to be accompanied by a more general word of higher frequency of occurrence to serve as a mnemonic device. Similar examples in other creoles include Trinidadian CE *sɔu pɪg* 'sow', *gɔ:t kɪdi* 'kid', and Krio *blɛn-yai*, literally 'blind-eye', meaning 'blind' (Hancock 1980:72). As Hancock points out, it is also possible that some of these terms represent partial calques on African terms. For example, Yoruba *agbárí* 'skull' (from *igbá* 'calabash' plus *orí* 'head'; Abraham 1962) may have influenced the formation of CE *hed skol* via intermediate forms analogous to Ndyuka *kaabási fu éde* (Huttar p.c.) or Negerhollands CD *kalbas fan de kop* (Bradford 1986:93), both literally 'calabash of the head' meaning 'skull'; i.e. *skull* may have initially been interpreted as 'calabash', whence the combination *hed skol* to distinguish it from other kinds of calabashes.

4.5.3 Coining

Hancock (1980:68) notes that the spontaneous creation of words with no exterior model does not appear to be very common in any language. However, he lists some creole examples such as Trinidadian CE *bobolups* 'fat lady', Krio CE *flɛŋbɛnšis* 'smartly dressed' and Papiamentu CS *kɔŋkəl* 'to knock together' (although Dutch *konkel* has the regional meaning of 'box on the ears'; Den Besten p.c.). Bahamian CE examples might be *spokadocious* 'very attractive (of women)', or *pamolly* 'a swelling from a bump on the head' or *wumpers* 'sandals made from the rubber of a car tyre' (although this last might be onomatopoeic).

4.6 Semantic changes

In previous sections there were discussions of differences between the meanings of creole words and their superstrate etyma due to the influence of archaic usage (4.2.1), regional usage (4.2.2) and usage in substrate languages (4.3.2). This section deals with semantic changes resulting not from external influences but rather from internal developments that may have taken place some time after the pidginization of the lexical source language.

4.6.1 Semantic shifts

Like any language used in a new geographical setting, when the languages that provided the creoles' lexicons were first taken to the tropics, they lacked words to refer to local plants, animals, customs, objects, etc., that were unknown in Europe. While some of these gaps in the lexicon were filled by borrowing or creating new words, very often old words were simply used for new referents. On the Miskito Coast, *lion* came to be used for the local cougar, and *tiger* for the jaguar. Similarly, in Guiné-Bissau CP the hyena is called *luubu* from Portuguese *lobo* 'wolf'. Obviously such semantic shifts had to be made by Europeans who knew both referents. A further example is Negerhollands CD *pinapəl* 'pineapple' from Dutch *pijnappel* 'fir cone'. The relationship of English is unclear; until the eighteenth century, *pine-apple* had the latter meaning, which still survives in British dialects. A 1665 document cited by the *Oxford English Dictionary* in reference to the tropical fruit notes that 'To outward view it seems, when it is whole, to resemble our Pine-apple', while a contemporary source refers to 'The Ananas or Pine-Apple'. Another semantic shift occurred in the French term *l'hivernage*, which in Europe referred to the laying up of ships during winter (cf. F *hiver* 'winter'); in Lesser Antillean CF *livèrnaj* came to mean 'hurricane season'. Other shifts may have resulted from misunderstandings: Guiné-Bissau CP *kaloor* 'sweat' comes from Portuguese *calor* 'heat', often used in the phrase *faz calor* (literally 'it makes hot') meaning 'it is hot' in reference to the weather.

4.6.2 Semantic broadening
Semantic shift represents an extension of a word's meaning with the loss of its earlier meaning (e.g. *pineapple* no longer means 'fir cone' in standard English). Semantic broadening is such extension without the loss of the original meaning. For example, *tea* in most English creoles refers not only to the infusion made from various leaves, but also to any hot drink. A Bahamian CE speaker can say, 'I must have my tea before I go to bed – either coffee or cocoa.' *Coffee-tea* is used throughout the Anglophone Caribbean, including Guyana where Berbice CD speakers use the term *kofitei* (Robertson 1979:265); while this may have been influenced by the CE term, the final vowel suggests its lexical source was Dutch *koffie* and *thee*. In Lesser Antillean CF, 'hot cocoa' is *dite kako* (cf. F *du thé* 'some tea'). The semantic source of this extension of the meaning of 'tea' might be the calquing of monomorphemic words in West African languages meaning 'hot drink', a meaning apparently transferred to *ti* even as a loan in Twi. Another example of semantic broadening is Papiamentu CS *blat*; while Dutch *blad* can refer to a blade of grass, a leaf or a sheet of paper, Papiamentu *blat* can have the more general meaning of 'one of two sides or parts of an object', e.g. *blat di chanchan* 'buttock'.

As mentioned above (4.1), the extension of meaning is characteristic of pidgins, which in their reduced form must make do with a much smaller lexicon than creoles and other native languages. Such polysemy is seen in Cameroonian *bɛli*, which has not only the meaning of its English etymon *belly* but also 'appetite, hunger, pregnancy, internal parts, seat of emotions, secret place, secret' (Schneider 1960) – although some of these meanings may have been influenced by African substrate languages. The many extended meanings of the word for 'belly' in a number of English-based creoles (Alleyne 1980:117) suggest that some of the polysemy of pidgin lexicons may be retained in certain items of their creole descendants.

4.6.3   Semantic narrowing

The restriction of a word's meaning seems to be less frequent than its extension in creole languages. One example in Miskito Coast CE is that *stew* has acquired the specialized meaning of 'boiling meat and vegetables in coconut milk', while boiling them in plain water is to *run them down*. In Haitian CF, which makes no gender distinctions in adjectives as French does, *vè* (from the French masculine form of *vert* 'green') means only the colour while *vèt* (from the feminine *verte*) means 'unripe'.

4.6.4   Other kinds of semantic change

Hancock (1980) classifies several other kinds of semantic shifts. One is metaphor. Bahamians call a machete whose blade is sharp on both sides a *French knife*, which is also a term of abuse for a two-faced person. Haitian CF *kouto dè bò* and Papiamentu CS *kuchu di dos banda* also have both meanings. Hancock also identifies playforms such as phonological modifications, intentional puns and intentional etymologies. The last might include Bahamian *donkeyfy* 'not caring, especially about social norms'; there is a slightly different alternatire pronunciation, *don't-ca(re)-if-I* (do or don't), but the first form carries the extra idea of a donkey's stubbornness. The final category of semantic change is that caused by a word's use as a euphemism. In Bahamian *hip* is a euphemism for 'buttocks'; it is the only part of their anatomy that ladies ever fall on. The Krio euphemism is *wes* from *waist*.

4.7   Change of syntactic function

External (i.e. substrate) influence on creole words taking on a syntactic function different from that of their superstrate etymon (primarily adjectives becoming verbs) was discussed above in section 4.3.3. This section deals with language-internal factors causing such changes. In the pidgins there was a general lack of morphology to help maintain syntactic categories. In English, for example, words that can take an *-ed* inflection are usually verbs, while those that take *-ly* are usually adverbs. The absence of such bound morphemes makes it easier for words to change their syntactic function, e.g. *jump* can be either a verb or a noun in English but *jumped* can only be a verb (or verbal participle), and it is quite impossible to make a noun out of *easily*. Moreover, the first generations of pidgin speakers had to contend with notional equivalents that did not always correspond to the same syntactic categories in both their mother tongues and the target language. For example, *to be thirsty* and *avoir soif* refer to the same notion, but the English phrase consists of a copula and an adjective while the French phrase consists of a verb and a noun (literally 'have thirst'). Yet another language might use a single intransitive verb for the same idea, like archaic English *thirst*. If a native speaker of a substrate language which had the third construction encountered a Frenchman saying 'J'ai soif' and the meaning was clear, he might analyse the words as 'I thirst' or 'X thirst'. In fact Mauritian CF *mo swaf* is a subject and verb meaning literally 'I thirst', i.e. the French noun *soif* has become a verb in the creole. Given these factors, it is not surprising that multifunctionality is quite widespread in pidgins and creoles, and many words take on different or additional syntactic functions. It seems likely that many such changes were later reversed in the direction of the lexical source language during decreolization. Some evidence for this can be seen in a comparison of Miskito Coast CE with English borrowings into the Amerindian language of the Miskito, which appear to preserve usages in an English-based pidgin documented from the early eighteenth century onwards (Holm 1978). Miskito includes words like *tayad* 'fatigue' and *sari* 'sorrow' that are not found in the modern creole. Category changes found in Miskito Coast Creole include nouns from adjectives ('He catch *crazy*' 'He became psychotic'), from adverbs (*afterwards* 'leftovers') and from prepositions ('He come from out', i.e. 'from abroad'). Verbs can come from nouns ('He *advantage* her', i.e. 'took advantage of') as well as adjectives ('She *jealousing* him', i.e. 'making him jealous'). In Haitian CF the French noun *peur* 'fear' has become a verb *pè* 'to fear' – 'Li *pè* lamo' 'He *fears* death' – while the F verb *chanter* 'to sing' has become a noun *chanté* 'song' (cf. F *chanson*). The F adverb *là-haut* 'up there' has become a creole preposition *lò* 'above, on' (Stein 1984:40–2).

Changes in subcategorizational rules for specific lexical items represent another kind of syntactic change affecting the lexicon. For example, in Miskito Coast CE some mass nouns have become count nouns so that one can speak of *one bread* 'one loaf of bread'. Some count nouns have also become mass nouns, requiring a count noun for the measurement of units, e.g. 'one grain of *beans*' 'one bean'. This parallels the Italian plural count noun *spaghetti* becoming a singular mass noun in English ('a piece of spaghetti'). Changes in subcategorizational rules for verbs have resulted in new sequences of permissible objects and complements: 'Guess *me* this riddle'; 'I would never do *you* that'; 'He beg me *a piece of fish*'; 'She curse me *black*'; 'I will give *you*.' Koopman (1986:245) found that similar 'lexical properties of verbs [i.e. double object constructions, selection of complement type] in Haitian and West African languages are parallel to a great extent, and differ in general from those of French'.

While some of the above changes in syntactic function and in subcategorizational rules can be attributed to the influence of substrate languages, others preserve archaic or regional usages in the lexical source language, while still others seem to have resulted from the general restructuring that took place during pidginization and creolization.

Having examined the many kinds of turns that words can take in becoming part of a pidgin or creole lexicon, we will now look at what can happen to the sounds that form these words.

5
Phonology

5.0 Introduction

This chapter is a study of some of the phonological features found in a number of creoles but not their lexical source languages. The theoretical orientation of this study is that discussed in section 1.4: the position that creole languages resulted from a number of forces and that their features reflect the influence of both superstrate and substrate languages, universals of adult second-language acquisition, borrowing from adstrate languages, creole-internal innovations, and the convergence of all or some of these.

Sorting out which of these influences may have resulted in particular phonological features is by no means an easy task. It is especially difficult to determine the degree of continuity from the superstrate language ('internal' phonological development – if this concept is indeed applicable to creolized languages) as opposed to influence of the substrate languages (sound substitution conditioned by systems external to the language creolized). For the Atlantic creoles, one of the major difficulties is the lack of detailed information about the phonology of the sixteenth- and seventeenth-century varieties of the particular superstrate dialects involved, to say nothing of the nearly total lack of documentation of the relevant substrate languages of this period. Still, the challenge of reconstructing the phonological development of creole languages has led to some fascinating linguistic detective work, e.g. Smith (1987).

Superstrate influence is problematical because there is less continuity between the European languages and their creoles than there is between them and their overseas regional varieties that have not undergone creolization. The latter are the products of ordinary language change, and one can speak of their features in the usual terms of historical linguistics, describing New England vowels, for example, as the 'reflexes' of the early Modern English vowels that preceded them. If, however, basilectal Jamaican Creole is a different language from English (and most would agree that it is at least a different linguistic system), is it still meaningful to speak of 'reflexes'? The whole question of what became what is complicated by the fact that there was multiple input from a number of African languages and European dialects. Yet the term 'reflex' is convenient for indicating that the vowels in the Sranan CE words *ai*, *bai* and *tai* correspond to those in English *eye*, *buy* and *tie*, so long as it is borne in mind that such correspondence is often irregular in creoles: cf. Sranan *pai* 'pay' or *ten* 'time' (Smith 1987:450–1).

Substrate influence on creole phonology has been assumed since Van Name (1869–70:124). Schuchardt (1882a:895) explicitly states, 'In the phonological system of São Tomé [CP] the influence of African languages can be clearly seen; this explains its many correspondences with other creole languages [Negerpatois].' However, Schuchardt's views on African influence can hardly be called an assumption since he goes on to compare specific phonemes in São Tomé CP and Mbundu. Objections to the significance of substrate influence have come mainly from universalists who have focused on syntax (primarily Bickerton 1974ff.) and not denied substrate influence on creole phonology. The very mechanism of such influence requires some reference to universals, not in the Bickertonian sense of innate linguistic structures (2.12) but rather the universals of adult second language acquisition that played a role in pidginization. Valdman (1983), building on the work of Schumann (1978) and others, makes a strong case for the parallels between pidginization and second language learning, claiming that both processes involve cognitive and linguistic universals at play in the acquisition of another language. The crucial difference is that in the case of pidginization there is a restriction of information about the target language that is determined by the social situation (i.e. trade, slavery, etc.). In creolization, the pidgin-speaking community's restricted version of the target language (with considerable transfer of first-language features) is nativized, perpetuating many such features. Thus later monolingual creole speakers have features of substrate languages in their speech although they themselves have no knowledge of their forebears' languages.

The kinds of phonological changes that can result from language contact are outlined by Weinreich (1953). Transfer results from speakers identifying a phoneme in the second language with one in their first language and then subjecting it to the latter's phonetic rules. This can result in underdifferentiation (the merger of two sounds that are distinct in the second language but not in the first), overdifferentiation (the imposition of phonemic distinctions from the first language on allophones of a single phoneme in the second), or outright substitution (using a phoneme from the first language for a similar but distinct phoneme in the second). Moreover, there can be similar transfer in intonation and syllabic structure.

Universals can also be seen to play a role in the pidginization and creolization process in that sounds that are found throughout most of the world's languages (e.g. /d/ or /m/) are more likely to survive pidginization and creolization than sounds that are relatively rare (e.g. /θ/ in English and Greek, or /ð/ in English and Icelandic), if only because of the relative improbability of contact between languages which both have the same highly marked (i.e. non-universal) sounds. In general, contact languages are built on those features common to the languages in contact, so the phonemic inventory of a pidgin can be expected to be based on such sounds, although the phonetic realization of particular phonemes may vary to follow the rules of each speaker's first language. Creoles are likely to select those realizations of a pidgin's phonemes that are most common among the group whose children are beginning to speak the language natively – not those of superstrate speakers. However, creoles can also have phonemes (as well as phonetic realizations of phonemes) that are not found in their superstrate language, particularly if superstrate influence is removed at an early stage of the creole's development or contact is maintained with substrate languages (e.g. the co-articulated stops in Saramaccan and Krio; cf. 5.6.1). Language universals can also be seen as including the general patterns of phonological change that are found throughout the world's languages. For example, high front vowels are so often associated with the palatalization of preceding consonants that the change of Portuguese /ti/ to Príncipe CP /či/ (e.g. *čia* 'aunt') could be attributed to this universal tendency without reference to any substrate pressure in this direction. However, it is the position of the present study that the likelihood of such change is greater when both substrate influence and universal tendencies converge.

There is such strong evidence to support substrate influence on creole phonology that the validity of this interpretation has never been seriously challenged. Beyond the systematic correspondences discussed in this chapter, some creoles have phonological features found in their substrate but not their superstrate languages. In addition to the co-articulated stops /kp/ and /gb/ mentioned above, some creoles have word-initial pre-nasalized stops (/mb, nd, ɲdj, ŋg/; cf. 5.6.2), as well as phonemic tone (5.7). The importance of substrate influence is assumed in most studies of creole phonology, including those on which the present study draws.

Finally, the reader should bear in mind that authors do not always follow the same conventions in notation; some use /j/ for the palatal glide, others for the palatal affricate; some use /y/ for the former and others use it for the high front rounded vowel; some use /ɲ/ whereas others use /ñ/ for the nasal palatal; some use /ˊ/ and /ˋ/ to mark tones, others to mark stress or vowel quality. The present writer will try to use his own notational system consistently and clarify the potentially ambiguous usages of others where this is deemed necessary.

5.1 Continua

Before discussing creole phonology, it is necessary to consider the fact that the phonological systems of some creoles vary according to their speakers' socioeconomic status and education. As noted in sections 1.3 and 2.11, there is frequently a continuum of speech varieties ranging from the basilect (which diverges most from the standard) to the acrolect (distinguishable from the standard in only relatively minor ways). Intermediate varieties (the mesolect) share features with both the basilect and acrolect in various combinations. Speakers' phonologies can vary considerably depending on their position on this continuum of lects, as can the phonology of a single speaker who commands a range of lects for different social situations. Although there is a clear gap between many creoles and their superstrate languages for a number of sociohistorical reasons (e.g. São Tomé CP, Sranan CE, Haitian CF, Nubi CA), it is important to bear in mind the added complication of sociolinguistic continua in discussing the phonology (as well as the syntax and – to a lesser extent – the lexicosemantics) of certain varieties such as the post-creole English varieties of the Caribbean proper. To minimize this difficulty, it should be understood that, in the following discussion, it is always the phonology of the basilect that is being referred to unless otherwise specified.

5.2 Phonotactic rules

With relatively few exceptions (e.g. Ewe and Wolof), West African languages have a basic CV syllabic structure, i.e. a single consonant followed by a single vowel. In some cases the consonant can be a co-articulated stop, /kp/ or /gb/, which functions as a single phoneme (5.6.1). There can be nasalization of the vowel (5.4) and even the consonant (5.6.2), but the basic CV structure remains for all syllables except a limited number of function words consisting of a single vowel. There is abundant evidence that this phonotactic rule was carried over into a number of Atlantic creoles, particularly those whose structure was least influenced by that of their European lexical source language, such as the Portuguese-based creoles of the Gulf of Guinea or the English-based creoles of interior Suriname (often called the most 'conservative' creoles in reference to their African features, but also referred to as 'radical' creoles by Bickerton 1981). However, remnants of this phonotactic rule can also be found in decreolizing varieties. Since many words in the creoles' lexical source languages were incompatible with this rule, they had to undergo the phonological changes discussed below. These often had the effect of breaking up consonant clusters in the European words so that the corresponding creole word conformed to the CV syllabic structure rule.

5.2.1 Aphesis

Aphesis is the omission of one or more sounds at the beginning of a word. The omission of the initial member of a consonant cluster can achieve the CV pattern, as in Sranan CE *tan* (from E *stand*) or Negerhollands CD *tomp* 'stump' (D *stomp*). This is stigmatized in decreolizing varieties and leads to hypercorrections in which there is a 'replacement' of an initial consonant (usually /s/) which is thought to be missing, e.g. Bahamian CE *scrumbs* 'crumbs' or Papiamentu CS *strena* 'thunder' (cf. S *trueno* idem). The omission of an initial (usually unaccented) vowel can also achieve a CV pattern, e.g. Príncipe CP *bí* 'to open' (P *abrir*), *kupa* 'occupy' (P *ocupar*) or *géza* 'church' (P *igreja*). The fact that verbs never begin with a vowel in many West African languages may have reinforced the phonotactic rule in some cases, e.g. Trinidadian CF *vale* 'swallow' (F *avaler*), *rive* 'arrive' (F *arriver*) or *coche* 'to hook' (F *accrocher*) (Stein 1984:39). The widespread effect of aphesis can be seen in the word for 'American' in a number of creoles: Bahamian CE *Merican*, Haitian CF *meriken*, Papiamentu CS *Merikano* and Negerhollands CD *Merkin*; cf. AAVE 'M.B.B. . . .' Merican Black boy' (Labov 1972:210).

5.2.2 Syncope

Syncope is the omission of one or more sounds from the middle of a word. The omission of an internal consonant in a European word could also reduce a consonant cluster to achieve a CV pattern, e.g. Príncipe CP *gani* 'big' (P *grande*) or *buká* 'to seek' (P *buscar*). Examples from Sranan CE include *kosi* 'curtsy' and *sisa* 'sister'.

5.2.3 Apocope

Apocope is the omission of one or more sounds from the end of a word. While early creoles tended to add a vowel to a word to prevent a final consonant or consonant cluster (5.2.6), decreolizing varieties that have developed a phonotactic rule tolerating a single final consonant still omit the second element of a final consonant cluster in the lexical source language, particularly when the consonants are both voiced or both unvoiced. In the English-based varieties this represents an extension of the colloquial English rule permitting the dropping of a final stop in a cluster before a word beginning with another stop (e.g. *roun' table*) in that creoles and post-creoles also allow final stops to be dropped before a vowel (e.g. *roun' apple*) or Ø (*it's roun'*). Examples in African American Vernacular English include *roun* 'round' and *des* 'desk' (note like voicing of the elements in the final consonant clusters of the etyma). Parallels in Haitian CF include *wonn* 'round (e.g. of surveillance)' (cf. F *ronde*) and *ris* 'risk' (F *risque*). A Negerhollands CD example is *tan* 'tooth' (D *tand*). Since this loss of a final consonant can also be stigmatized, decreolizing varieties sometimes develop hypercorrect forms that 'replace' a consonant thought to be missing, e.g. Miskito Coast CE *sinimint* 'cinnamon'.

5.2.4 Prothesis

Prothesis is the addition of a sound at the beginning of a word; the addition of a vowel can give each consonant of a word-initial cluster its own vowel. Prothesis is frequently found in Spanish and Portuguese (e.g. *estado* 'state' from Latin *status*), but it is unusual in the Atlantic creoles, in which the tendency is toward a CV rather than a VCV pattern. However, it is found in the creole of French Guiana: *estatü* 'statue' (F *statue*), *espor* 'sport' (F *sport*), – perhaps under the influence of Portuguese (cf. P *estátua* and *esporte* versus Spanish *estatua* but *deporte*).

5.2.5 Epenthesis

Epenthesis is the insertion of a sound in the middle of a word; a vowel so inserted can serve to break up a consonant cluster. Such epenthesis is quite widespread in the Atlantic creoles; examples include Príncipe CP *álima* 'soul' (P *alma*), Negerhollands CD *kini* 'knee' (D *knie*) and Cameroonian *sitón* 'stone'. However, other factors besides phonotactic rules can also lead to such vowels. Bahamian CE *worrum* 'worm', like the corresponding word in most other English-based creoles, has a second vowel that does not correspond to the standard form but does correspond to archaic English *wurem* and the regional British form *worom*. Adam (1883:51) noted epenthetic vowels in Mauritian CF, e.g. *carabe* 'crab' (F *crabe*) and *pilime* 'feather' (F *plume*). His observation that this pronunciation was characteristic of 'most old people' suggests that it was already dying out. Epenthetic vowels in Papiamentu CS, like those in other creoles, tend toward vowel harmony (5.5), e.g. *sukú* 'dark' (S *oscuro*, P *escuro*), *delegá* 'thin' (S, P *delgado*) or *konofló* 'garlic' (D *knoflook*).

5.2.6 Paragogue

Paragogue is the addition of a sound to the end of a word; words in the most conservative Atlantic creoles often have such a vowel after what was the word-final consonant of their etymon: e.g. Príncipe CP *dósu* 'two' (P *dois*) or *méze* 'month' (P *mês*); Saramaccan CE *láfu* 'laugh' or *dagu* 'dog'; Negerhollands CD *grōtō* 'great' (D *groot*) or *ribi* 'rib' (D *rib*). There are remnants of paragogic vowels (probably once more widespread) in Caribbean CE and Krio; the latter has examples such as *gladi* 'glad' and *dede* 'dead'. The loss of final *-i* in two Krio words (*les* 'lazy' and *fambul* 'family') suggests hypercorrection. A similar pattern of addition and subtraction of paragogic (and a few other) vowels may have taken place in Papiamentu CS as well. Paragogic vowels were added to a number of loanwords from Dutch such as *boto* 'boat' (D *boot*) and *buki* 'book' (D *boek*). Although most Spanish words already end in a vowel, Papiamentu may have gone through an earlier stage of adding vowels to those that did not, followed by a later stage of decreolization in which such vowels were dropped. Hypercorrection could then have led to such modern Papiamentu forms as *kabes* 'head' (S *cabeza*) or *kas* 'house' (S *casa*) (Boretzky 1983:74). It should be noted that Nigerian PE has a kind of optional paragogue between words ending and beginning with consonants, which can be seen as a kind of epenthesis: *snék dé* ('There is a snake there') can be pronounced *sìnékì dê* (Faraclas 1996). Finally, both epenthetic and paragogic vowels are particularly susceptible to vowel harmony (5.5).

5.2.7 Metathesis

Metathesis is a change in the order in which two sounds occur in a word. In some cases metathesis served to break up consonant clusters, e.g. the Portuguese word *criar* 'to raise, bring up' became Príncipe CP *kiryá*, breaking up the initial Portuguese cluster and leaving each consonant with an adjacent vowel (*kir-ya*). The Virgin Islands CE word *pistarckle* 'person acting in a boisterous manner and otherwise making a spectacle of himself' (Valls 1981:96) comes from Negerhollands CD *pistárkəl* from Dutch *spektakel* via metathesis (Stolz 1986:98). Some cases of apparent metathesis like Sranan CE *wroko* 'work' may have resulted from epenthesis (*wóroko*) followed by a shift of stress to the epenthetic vowel (*woróko*) and then the elision of the original vowel (*wroko*). Evidence supporting this interpretation can be found in the double vowel of the related Saramaccan equivalent, *wooko*, which followed another course of development in which both the epenthetic and the original vowel were retained and the /r/ was lost through a later rule deleting intervocalic liquids (Alleyne 1980:47, Boretzky 1983:76). The development of Sranan *wroko* may explain the metathesis in other creole words such as French Guiana and older Haitian CF *dromi* and Papiamentu CS *drumi*, both 'to sleep' (cf. French, Spanish and Portuguese *dormir*). However, other cases of apparent metathesis may actually represent the survival of archaic or regional forms, e.g. Bahamian CE *aks* 'ask' or *cripsy* 'crispy'.

5.2.8 Elision of vowels

Elision is a sandhi rule involving the omission of sounds between syllables or words in connected speech. The loss of one of two vowels at a word boundary (e.g. XV##VX becoming XVX) is found in all the lexical source languages of the Atlantic creoles, e.g. English *there's*, French *c'est* (cf. *ce* 'this', *est* 'is'), Spanish *del* (cf. *de* 'from', *el* 'the [masculine singular]'), Portuguese *dos* (cf. *de* 'from', *os* 'the [masculine plural]'), Dutch *thuis* (cf. *te* 'at', *huis* 'home'). It is also found in many African languages (e.g. Yoruba *n'ilé* from *ní* 'at', *ilé* 'home') and Atlantic creoles, e.g. Príncipe CP *déli* from *da* 'for' and *éli* 'him'; Papiamentu CS *m'a bai* from *mi* 'I', *a* PAST, *bai* 'go'; Haitian CF *l ap vini* from *li* 'he, she', *ap* PROG, *vini* 'come'; Sranan CE *j e fgiti* from *ju* 'you', *e* HABITUAL, *fɔgiti* 'forget'. The loss of the vowel in *fgiti* is an example of syncope (5.2.2), or word-internal vowel elision. Unlike the elision of one of two vowels between words, the elision of a single vowel between two consonants in a word will lead to a consonant cluster (e.g. CVC at the beginning of *fɔgiti* becomes CC in *fgiti*). Eersel (1976) believes that an earlier CV syllable pattern in Sranan was disturbed by borrowing words from Dutch without making them conform to the CV pattern, e.g. *skrifi* 'write' (with an initial consonant cluster) from D *schrijven*. This development of a phonotactic rule permitting consonant clusters (which may have carried prestige through association with the official language) led to the creation of new consonant clusters through the elision of earlier epenthetic vowels, e.g. *sikóro* 'school' (now only heard in poems and in Ndyuka) became *skoro*.

To conclude this section on phonotactic rules, it should be noted that there are entire groups within the Atlantic creoles which do not share the tendency toward a CV syllabic pattern. As Ivens Ferraz (1987) notes, the Upper Guinea varieties of Creole Portuguese do not follow the same phonotactic rules as those spoken on the Gulf of Guinea islands. The Upper Guinea varieties have no constraint against words ending in a consonant, e.g. Cape Verdean *rapaž* or Guiné-Bissau CP *rapas*, both 'boy' (P *rapaz*). This can be attributed to the fact that the two groups of Portuguese creoles have different substrate languages within the Niger-Congo family: the Gulf of Guinea creoles were most influenced by Kwa and Bantu languages, while the Upper Guinea Creoles were influenced by Mande and West Atlantic languages. The latter permit final nasal consonants and final consonants respectively, and vowel elision in Mande languages results in consonant sequences not permitted in many other West African languages (Boretzky 1983:75). The French-based creoles show very few of the phonotactic constraints discussed above; except for the absence of word-final consonant clusters, there are few if any such constraints in the French-based creoles that are not found in standard French. Except for those spoken in colonies that later became officially anglophone, the French creoles remained in closer contact with their lexical source language than did the 'conservative' creoles of the Gulf of Guinea and Suriname. A further explanation might be that seventeenth-century pidgin French was more influenced by the West Atlantic languages (spoken in Senegal, where the French established their first trading post early in the century) than by the Kwa languages (spoken around Whydah, where they established another post in the late seventeenth century).

5.3   Oral vowels

The predominating vowel pattern in West African languages is the following:

	front	central	back
high	i		u
high mid	e		o
low mid		ε ɔ	
low		a	

This seven-vowel system is found not only in Kwa languages like Yoruba, Bini and Ewe, but also in Mande languages like Bambara and Susu. However, it should be noted that there are a number of languages with eight to ten vowels, ranging from Ibo to Dyola. In many of these [ε] and [ɔ] are sub-phonemic, conditioned by vowel harmony, etc. Moreover, Kongo and a number of north-western Bantu languages have a five-vowel system in which [ε] and [ɔ] are allophones of /e/ and /o/ respectively. Given these facts, it might be expected that the original vowel systems of the Atlantic creoles consisted of either seven vowels as above or five vowels with [ε] and [ɔ] as allophones. This does in fact appear to be the case.

The vowel systems of the European base languages range from five vowels with phonemic status in Spanish to nine in Portuguese to the twelve or thirteen vowels of French, Dutch and English. Thus it is noteworthy that the seven-vowel system found throughout much of West Africa is also the basic system of many of the Atlantic creoles, from the Gulf of Guinea varieties of creole Portuguese to the New World creoles based on French and English. Divergences from this pattern seem to lie largely in decreolizing varieties that have borrowed vowels from their superstrates. For example, Papiamentu's core vocabulary has the five-vowel system of Spanish, in which [ε] and [ɔ] are allophones of /e/ and /o/ respectively, but later lexical borrowings from Dutch (perhaps reinforced by African words like *flεngεflεngε* 'skinny' and *pɔtɔpɔtɔ* 'muddy') have resulted in the establishment of nine distinct vowel phonemes, including /ε/, /ɔ/ and two front rounded vowels.

The seven-vowel system was probably characteristic of many varieties of creolized English in the eighteenth century. Lalla (1986) postulates a more reduced five-vowel system for early Jamaican CE, but counterevidence lies in the fact that Sierra Leone Krio, which was probably influenced by the speech of Jamaican Maroons and North American blacks at the end of the eighteenth century, has seven oral vowels, as does West African Pidgin English.

In any discussion of the development of European vowels into their corresponding forms in the creoles, it should be recalled that the starting point was not necessarily the same as the modern vowel of the standard European language, but rather the corresponding vowel of the speech of the fifteenth to seventeenth centuries (for Portuguese and Spanish) or seventeenth to eighteenth centuries (for French, Dutch and English) (cf. 4.2.1). Moreover, this speech often represented social or regional dialects (cf. 4.2.2). However, since the purpose of this section is only to outline general sound shifts rather than to present a detailed study of each creole, some of these complicating factors will not be dealt with in order to present a clearer overview.

5.3.1 *Vowel length*

In some European languages vowel length is significant, e.g. Dutch *stal* 'stall' versus *staal* 'steel' (although here there are other differences besides quantity; the quality of the first is closer to /a/ and that of the second to /ɑ/). Boretzky (1983:52) has suggested that Negerhollands CD was the only Atlantic creole with phonologically relevant long vowels 'if one can trust the notation' (i.e. of De Josselin de Jong 1926). The latter's glossary lists pairs like *stal* 'stall' and *stāl* 'steel', but in each case of opposition (i.e. a, ā; e, ē; i, ī; o, ō) the shorter or unbarred vowel is indicated as 'variable' in the guide to the notation (1926), indicating that such minimal pairs could also be homophones. Boretzky notes that in the other European base languages vowel length does not carry a high functional load; it is conditioned by stress in Portuguese and Spanish, and is becoming nondistinctive in French (e.g. the difference between *mettre* 'put' /mɛtr/ and *maître* 'master' /mɛːtr/) is not being maintained). In English, earlier long and short vowels have been kept distinctive not by quantity but by quality, i.e. differences in height (and off-glides).

A great number of West African languages have what at first seem to be long vowels, i.e. two identical vowels in succession as in Yoruba *maa* 'preverbal marker of habitual aspect' as opposed to *ma* 'indeed'. However, while the effect of rearticulation is indeed one of length, it is clear that such double vowels actually represent two distinct syllables in that each can take a different tone, e.g. Yoruba *oore* 'kindness' as opposed to *òóré* 'vista'. As Boretzky notes, Saramaccan double vowels can also take different tones, e.g. *dóò* 'door' or *doón* 'drum'.

Alleyne (1980) postulates an absence of distinctive vowel length in all New World English creoles as the first stage in the reinterpretation of English vowels, accompanied by the earliest changes in the quality of corresponding vowels. Each vowel of the output, /i e a o u/, later acquired a long counterpart in some creoles in the second stage. This may have been a simple doubling of vowels as in substrate languages with no English difference in vowel quality judging from modern opposing pairs like Jamaican /i/ versus /ii/, /a/ versus /aa/, and /u/ versus /uu/. Finally, Alleyne postulates a third stage in which Jamaican /e:/ and /o:/ developed on-glides as /ie/ and /uo/ respectively, although these could also be the results of northern English and Scots dialect influence.

5.3.2 The unrounding of front vowels

With very few exceptions (e.g. the Bantu language Yansi), Niger-Congo languages do not have front rounded vowels. Although these are also absent in English, Spanish and Portuguese, they are found in French and Dutch, i.e. /y/ as in F *rue* 'street' or D *u* 'you (polite)'; /ø/ as in F *feu* 'fire' or D *sleuren* 'to drag'; and /œ/ as in F *sœur* 'sister' or D *fust* 'cask'. Regarding Negerhollands CD, De Josselin de Jong (1926:9, 10) lists the notational symbols *y* (/y/) and *ö* (/œ/), but no words with these are found in his glossary, suggesting that their status in Negerhollands was marginal. Stolz (1986:61) considers them to have belonged solely to the acrolect, but Den Besten (p.c.) interprets them as optional allophones conditioned by the phonetic environment, e.g. *bök* 'stoop', although related to D *bukken*, is probably /bek/ with some lip rounding conditioned by the preceding /b/. Papiamentu CS has borrowed two front rounded vowels from Dutch along with lexical loans, i.e. /y/ in Papiamentu *hür* 'hire' (D *huren* /hyrə/) and /œ/ in Papiamentu *drùk* 'press' (D *drukken* /drœkə/). Maurer (p.c.) has raised the question as to whether these borrowings are recent or possibly much older, long used by bilingual Papiamentu speakers of Dutch origin.

In the French creoles, Hall (1966:28) claims that two stages of borrowing from French can be distinguished in Haitian CF according to the way in which front rounded vowels were made to conform to the seven-vowel pattern. In the earlier stage, the vowels remained round but lost their front quality, i.e. /y/ became /u/, a back rounded vowel, e.g. F *brûler* 'burn' became Haitian *bule*. Likewise, the mid front rounded vowel /ø/ became the mid back rounded vowel /o/, e.g. French dialect *yeux* 'they' became *yo*. At a later stage the French vowels remained fronted but lost their rounding, i.e. /y/ became /i/ (e.g. F *coutûme* 'custom' became Haitian *kutim*) and /ø/ became /ɛ/ (e.g. F *l'heure* 'the hour' became Haitian *lè* 'hour, time'). Goodman (p.c.) rejects this interpretation, suggesting that the different equivalents were determined by phonetic factors (e.g. adjacency to /r/ or a palatal).

Valdman (1978:59) notes that the French front rounded vowels have been reborrowed into the Frenchified varieties of creole French often used by the urban elite. In such speech the French rounded vowel often varies with the creole unrounded equivalents, e.g. /žy/ varies with /ži/ for 'juice' (F *jus*), /zø/ with /zɛ/ for 'egg' (cf. F *les œufs* /lez ø/), and /kœ/ with /kɛ/ for 'heart' (F *cœur*). This *refrancisation* or 're-Frenchification' is a sociolinguistic marker in the francophone Caribbean, much as the use of the interdentals /ð/ and /θ/ is in the anglophone Caribbean.

5.3.3 Diphthongs

As noted in 5.3.1, vowel sequences in many West African substrate languages should be treated as two elements rather than one since they can carry different tones and thus represent distinct syllables. This is also the case in Saramaccan, e.g. *léi* 'teach' or *láu* 'wilted', in which each vowel constitutes a separate syllable rather than the vowel and glide of a diphthong. European diphthongs were often replaced by single vowels without glides in the early creoles. Some examples from São Tomé CP include the change of Portuguese /ai/ to CP /a/ (e.g. *basu* 'under' from P *debaixo*) or P /oi/ to CP /o/ (e.g. *dodo* 'crazy' from P *doido*, or possibly the older form *doudo*).

Burling (1973:33) notes monophthongization in African American Vernacular English and the more general dialect of the southern United States, in which the glide is reduced or lost in words like *pride* (/ai/ becoming /a:/) and *proud* (/au/ becoming /a:/), especially before voiced consonants; /oi/ also tends to become /o:/ before /l/ and in certain other positions. It is possible that there is a historical connection between this and the parallel reduction of diphthongs in some Atlantic creoles. Evidence supporting such an interpretation can be found in the fact that there 'is some difference between the way blacks and whites pronounce stressed vowels in that blacks tend to have more monophthongal pronunciations' (Schneider 1989:17).

5.4 Nasal vowels

Normally the air stream producing oral vowels is released through the mouth, but in most languages an oral vowel preceding a nasal consonant (such as the [ɪ] in [ɪ̃n]) is slightly nasalized: the air stream is partly released through the nose in anticipation of the nasal consonant. This weak nasalization is phonetic since it is conditioned by the environment and does not occur in minimal pairs; thus the phonetic realization of /ɪn/ is [ɪ̃n] in English. However, a great number of West African languages have nasal vowels with the status of phonemes, i.e. ones that contrast with oral vowels in minimal pairs such as Yoruba *dá* 'to be rare' versus *dá̃* 'to polish'. Such nasalization is much more noticeable than the assimilation of nasality on the phonetic level, which is also a feature of many West African languages. Thus Yoruba /ɔmɔ/ 'child' is phonetically realized as [ɔ̃mɔ̃] with nasalization that is both regressive (occurring before a nasal phoneme) and progressive (occurring after it). The nasal phoneme triggering the assimilation of the nasality of adjacent sounds can be a nasal vowel as well as a consonant, and the sounds assimilated can be consonants as well as vowels, as in the regressive nasalization in Ijo /sɔrɔ̃/, which is phonetically [sɔ̃r̃ɔ̃] (Boretzky 1983:56). Assimilation of nasality over word boundaries is also found in African languages such as Yoruba, in which /wɔ̃ á wá/ 'they will come' is phonetically [wɔ̃ ã̃ wã́] (A. Oyedeji p.c.).

Boretzky (1983) claims that the influence of substrate languages affected the assimilation rules of nasal vowels in creoles derived from European languages that already had such vowels (i.e. Portuguese and French) and led to nasal vowels with phonemic status in creoles derived from languages that did not have them (i.e. English, Dutch and Spanish). Portuguese has five nasal vowels with phonemic status, /ĩ, ẽ, ã, õ, ũ/; these can combine to form nasal diphthongs. Historically these are derived from the regressive nasalization of a vowel preceding a nasal consonant followed by a stop or word boundary. Even today, the phonetic realization of the nasal in *entro* 'I enter' can vary from [entru] to [ẽntru] to [ẽtru]. Speakers of European Portuguese are struck by the strength of nasalization of vowels preceding a single intervocalic nasal consonant in Brazilian Portuguese, so that *Copacabana* seems to be pronounced *Copacabãna* (Ivens Ferraz p.c.); this may reflect the substrate influence of African languages on Brazilian Portuguese. However, while the assimilation of nasalization is only regressive in Portuguese, it is also progressive in the Portuguese-based creoles, e.g. São Tomé CP *kamĩza* 'shirt' (P *camisa* [kamiza]).

French has four nasal vowels with phonemic status, /ɛ̃, œ̃, ɔ̃, ã/, although the contrast between /ɛ̃/ and /œ̃/ is not maintained by all speakers. Like the Portuguese nasal vowels, they are historically derived from the regressive nasalization of a vowel preceding a nasal consonant followed by a stop or word boundary. This is reflected in the orthographic use of nasal consonants to indicate the nasalization of preceding vowels, and in the usual generative treatment positing an underlying nasal consonant (e.g. /bɔn/ for [bɔ̃] 'good'), justified by the pronunciation of the nasal consonant as such when followed by words beginning with a vowel, e.g. [bɔn ami] 'good friend'. Until the seventeenth century, vowels could also be nasalized before a single nasal consonant belonging to the next syllable e.g. *jamais* 'never' could be pronounced [žãmɛ]

(Stein 1984:29). Today the French creoles have nasal vowels resulting not only from the latter kind of regressive nasalization but also from progressive nasalization, e.g. Haitian and Lesser Antillean CF *žãmẽ* 'never'. This suggests that African substrate languages had a similar effect on nasalization in creoles based on both Portuguese and French; whereas nasalization is only regressive in the two European languages, it is also progressive in their creoles. African influence is especially clear in the case of Haitian CF, which has two nasal vowels not found in French, i.e. [ĩ] in [kašĩmbo] 'clay pipe' (cf. kiMbundu *kišima* 'perforated shaft') and [ũ] in [bũnda] 'buttocks' (cf. kiMbundu *mbunda*). These two nasal vowels only occur in words of African origin, but their phonemic status is unclear since there are no minimal pairs: they have resulted from assimilation on a phonetic level. Valdman (1978:65) points out that Haitian has two kinds of nasal vowels, which are apparently phonemic and phonetic respectively. The first kind, which produces quite noticeable nasality and is the only kind found in French, is that which occurs before non-nasal consonants (e.g. *dimãš* 'Sunday' from F *dimanche*) and in word-final position (e.g. *šẽ* 'dog' from F *chien*). The second kind of nasality, which is weaker, characterizes nasal vowels near a nasal consonant, e.g. in *mẽnẽ* 'to lead' (F *amener*).

The contrast of oral and nasal vowels adjacent to a nasal consonant is rare among the world's languages (Singler p.c.) but it can be found in Haitian in minimal pairs like /šam/ 'charm' (F *charme*) and /šãm/ 'room' (F *chambre*). This kind of phonemic contrast is also found in Twi (Fromkin and Rodman 1993:77). However, there are often serious problems in determining the phonetic or phonemic status of nasal vowels adjacent to nasal consonants in creole languages; Boretzky (1983:55) posits an earlier stage in which progressive nasalization was much more widespread, so that the formulation of a synchronic rule is not possible. Regressive nasalization remains much more frequent in the Atlantic creoles; vowels before the nasal consonants /m, n, ɲ, ŋ/ are often nasalized even over word boundaries, as in some West African languages. For example, in Haitian CF /li mẽm/ 'he himself' is phonetically realized as [lĩ mẽm].

Although European varieties of English, Dutch and Spanish have no nasal vowels with phonemic status, nasal vowels of uncertain status are found in the creoles derived from all three. De Josselin de Jong (1926:13) indicates nasal vowels in Negerhollands CD words corresponding to an oral vowel before a nasal consonant in Dutch, e.g. *dãs* 'dance' (D *dans*); others correspond to oral vowels before non-nasal consonants in Dutch, e.g. *mẽši* 'girl' (D *meisje*). Stolz (1986:61) considers Negerhollands' nasalized vowels [ẽ, õ, ã] to be subphonemic variants of the corresponding oral vowels. Nasalized vowels also occur in Papiamentu CS /kamĩnda/ 'road' (S *camino*) and *nẽnga* 'deny' (S *negar*) (Tinelli 1981:8ff.).

The nasalization of vowels is found throughout the English-based creoles and post- or semi-creoles; indeed, it is one of the features that speakers of British English find most noticeable about African American Vernacular English and more general regional varieties that have been in contact with it. However, there is disagreement as to whether nasal vowels have phonemic status in any English-based creole. There would seem to be minimal pairs, e.g. Sranan [brõ] 'to burn' and [bro] 'to breathe'. However, Alleyne (1980:35) points out that this contrast does not exist before nasal consonants, e.g. Ndyuka [santi] or [sãnti] 'sand'. Huttar (p.c.) points out the further variant [sãti] but *not* *[sati]; in other words the phonetic realization of /VN/ is [VN], [ṼN] or [Ṽ] – as in Portuguese *entro* discussed above. This suggests that there *is* a nasal phoneme that is realized phonetically as a nasal vowel, a nasal consonant or both. These may be in free variation as in Ndyuka *santi*, or they may be allophones conditioned by the phonetic environment, like African American Vernacular English /don/ 'don't', which is [don] before a vowel ([don ai] 'don't I?') and [dõ] elsewhere, like French *bon*. Both would seem to be the synchronic result of a similar diachrony: Alleyne (1980:37) postulates that in the earliest forms of the English-based creoles, English words with a vowel followed by a syllable-final nasal consonant (i.e. one before another consonant or a word boundary, e.g. *man*) were reinterpreted as ending with either a nasal vowel plus nasal consonant (*mãn*), or just a nasal vowel (*mã*) or an oral vowel (*ma*). Since /Vn/, /Vŋ/ and /Vm/ could all merge as /Ṽ/, the original form of the nasal consonant could not always be reconstructed later during decreolization. This could account for such hypercorrect forms as Miskito Coast CE *skriim waya* 'screen wire' and denasalized forms such as Bahamian CE /əbáras/ 'embarrassed'.

It should be noted that some Atlantic creoles have not only nasalized vowels but also a nasalized palatal glide. In Haitian CF the nasal palatal consonant /ɲ/ in /gẽnyẽ/ 'have' (cf. F *gagner* 'gain') can be replaced by a nasalized palatal glide [j̃]. This sound, found in a number of West African languages but not in European French or Portuguese, also occurs in Papiamentu CS and Príncipe CP, and regularly corresponds to European Portuguese /ɲ/ (written *nh*) in Brazilian Portuguese.

5.5 Vowel harmony

A number of West African languages have classic harmony systems, in which vowels are divided into two mutually exclusive harmonic sets (e.g. according to height or laxness) so that all the vowels in a word will belong to either one set or the other. For example in Ijo all the vowels will be either tense (i, e, u, o) or lax (ɪ, ɛ, ʊ, ɔ) (Williamson 1965). This and other kinds of vowel harmony are found in other Kwa languages like Ewe, Fante and Ibo, as well as in Bantu languages like Kongo (Boretzky 1983, Ivens Ferraz 1979). A more restricted kind of vowel harmony is found in Yoruba, in which words can contain either the high mid vowels /e/ and /o/ or else the low mid vowels /ɛ/ and /o/, but not members of both sets. Yoruba also has a related but distinct phenomenon called vowel copying; for example, the third person singular object pronoun is simply a repetition of the vowel of the preceding verb, e.g. 'mo ra *a*' 'I bought it' versus 'mo yí *í*' 'I turned it.' Vowel copying can be seen as the assimilation of adjacent sounds on the phonetic level, while classic harmony systems are something quite different: morpheme structure rules restricting possible sequences of vowels.

Vowel harmony or copying appears to have played a role in determining the paragogic vowel (5.2.6) in the Surinamese creoles, e.g. Sranan *bigi* 'big', *dede* 'dead', *ala* 'all', *mofo* 'mouth', *brudu* 'blood' (Alleyne 1980:67). Epenthetic vowels (5.2.5) also seem likely to have been affected, e.g. Ndyuka *somóko* 'smoke' or *sutuún* 'lemon' (cf. D *citroon* /sitrú:n/) (Huttar p.c.). There may be remnants of vowel harmony or copying in Krio (e.g. *pɛtɛtɛ* 'potato') and Jamaican, particularly in the epenthetic vowels in *simít* 'Smith' and *wɔrɔm* 'worm' (although the latter may actually be a British regionalism).

In the Gulf of Guinea varieties of creole Portuguese, paragogic vowels are also usually the same as the stressed vowel of the etymon, e.g. São Tomé CP *dotolo* 'doctor' (P *doutor*), *mɛlɛ* 'honey' (P *mel*), or *zulu* 'blue' (P *azul*). Harmony or copying may also have affected other vowels, e.g. *kɔdɔ* 'rope' (P *corda*) or *sebe* 'to know' (P *saber*). Such a rule was even applied to words borrowed from other African languages, e.g. São Tomé CP *oko* 'calabash' (cf. Bini *uko*) or *lɔlɔ* 'to lick' (Bini *lalo*).

In Haitian CF the harmony of vowels in particular lexical items is much less widespread, often involving only a tendency toward the same vowel height, e.g. *gwɔsɛ* 'size' from F *grosseur* (with both vowels low mid instead of the expected *gwose* (although Valdman (p.c.) has encountered the latter form as well). However, Haitian also has a synchronic rule of vowel harmony or assimilation involving the personal pronoun *ou* /u/ 'you, your', which can assimilate to the height of the vowel in the preceding word, e.g. /pje u/ 'your foot' becomes /pje o/ (both vowels high mid) while /avɛ u/ 'with you' becomes /avɛ ɔ/ (both low mid) (Valdman 1978:93).

Vowel harmony or copying in Papiamentu CS can be found not only in epenthetic vowels (5.2.5) but in other cases as well, e.g. *dede* 'finger' (S *dedo*), *kaya* 'street' (S *calle*), *rosponde* 'answer' (S *responde*), *bichi* 'insect' (S *bicho*).

In Negerhollands CD epenthetic vowels seem to have been similarly affected (e.g. *kini* 'knee' from D *knie* versus *konop* 'button' from D *knoop*) as do paragogic vowels (e.g. *bede* 'bed' from D *bed* versus *duku* 'cloth' from D *doek*) (Stolz 1986:56).

While it is difficult to find clear evidence for the survival of any Niger-Congo language's vowel harmony *system* in the Atlantic creoles, there is abundant evidence for at least a pattern of vowel copying in the earliest stages of some creoles, particularly in epenthetic and paragogic vowels. Although this suggests substrate influence, a case can also be made for a universal tendency here: such added vowels do not actually come out of nothingness since the mouth is already in the appropriate position to produce the original vowel. However, some specific rules (e.g. the assimilation of the Haitian CF pronoun *ou* from /u/ to /o/ or /ɔ/) seem likely to have resulted from substrate influence.

5.6 Consonants

In addition to the seven oral and nasal vowels discussed above, Alleyne (1980:76) has proposed the consonants in table 1 as part of the earliest creole English phonological system. This table suggests a more general picture of the consonants of the earliest Atlantic creoles of other lexical bases as well: if we disregard for the moment certain African consonants found mainly in the Surinamese creoles (i.e. the co-articulated and pre-nasalized stops), the system that is left (adjusting the palatal stops to the affricates /tš/ and /dž/, and /sj/ to /š/) is approximately that of the other Atlantic creoles before their acquisition of certain consonants peculiar to their superstrates (e.g. the Portuguese

Table 1. *Consonants in the earliest Creole English phonological system*

Manner of articulation	bilabial	labiodental	alveolar	palatal-alveolar	palatal	velar	labiovelar	glottal
				Point of articulation				
Stop	p b		t d		tj dj	k g		
Co-articulated stop							kp gb	
Nasal	m		n		ɲ	ŋ		
Pre-nasalized stop	mb		nd		ɲdj	ŋg		
Liquid			l~r					
Fricative		f		s~sj				
Glide/ continuant	w				j			h

palatal lateral /λ/ or the French rounded palatal glide /ɥ/) – consonants that today can be found in the acrolect but are marginal to the creole's basic system. Like modern Yoruba, many of the early creoles apparently had only voiceless fricatives, but most now include the voiced fricatives /v, z, ž/. Symmetry (and Alleyne 1980:51) suggest the inclusion of /ŋ/; although this sound lacks phonemic status in such creoles as Ndyuka (Huttar p.c.) and Negerhollands (Stolz 1986:64), it is a phoneme in Haitian and some other French creoles despite its absence in French (Valdman 1978:51).

5.6.1 Co-articulated stops

A number of Niger-Congo languages (largely West African) have voiceless and voiced labio-velar co-articulated stops, represented as /kp/ and /gb/ respectively although each represents a single phoneme. They are articulated with the back of the tongue against the velum and the lips closed; the tongue is lowered and the lips open simultaneously while air is expelled (or drawn in in the case of the labio-velar implosives /kɓ/ and /gɓ/). Each contrasts with the corresponding labial or velar stop (e.g. Yoruba *gbọ́* 'to hear' versus *bọ́* 'to nourish' versus *gọ́* 'to embarrass') and acts as a single consonant in the CV syllabic pattern. They are found in the eastern West Atlantic languages as well as in Mande, Kru, Gur and Kwa languages and some northern Bantu languages. The creole Portuguese of Príncipe (but not São Tomé) has /gb/, which Günther (1973:41, 45) describes as a labio-velar plosive and treats as an integral part of the creole's phonological system. However, Ferraz (1975:155) treats it as an implosive which 'is not a productive unit in the incorporation of borrowings and is only found in archaic borrowings from African languages', e.g. *igbegbé* 'snail' or *igbé* 'testicles'. Saramaccan CE has both /kp/ and /gb/, often in words of African origin for flora and fauna, e.g. *kpasí* 'vulture' or *gbono-gbono* 'moss' (Alleyne 1980:50, who refers to them as implosives). Donicie and Voorhoeve (1963:v) note that Saramaccan /kp/ and /gb/ have the allophones [kw] and [gw] respectively; indeed, [kp] has replaced [kw] in some words of European origin such as *kpéi* 'slobber' (cf. Dutch *kwijlen*). Boretzky (1983:62) notes that in some dialects of Ewe /kp/ and /gb/ correspond to /kw/ and /gw/ in other dialects of the same language.

Saramaccan /kp/ and /gb/ often correspond to Sranan /kw/ and /gw/, e.g. *kpini* versus *kwinsi* 'squeeze' (cf. British dialect *squinch*) or *dagbe* versus *dagwe* 'type of snake'. Ndyuka also generally has /kw/ and /gw/ like Sranan, but while Sranan lacks the co-articulated stops, some Ndyuka speakers have variants of certain words with them, e.g. *kwo-kwo* or *kpo-kpo* 'type of fish soup', or *gwé* varying with *gbé* 'leave' (cf. E *go away*) (Huttar p.c.). Alleyne speculates that such pairs resulted from allophones in the earliest Surinamese creole(s), as well as in some of the African languages which were the mother tongues of some pidgin speakers. Boretzky's data on Ewe dialects would support this hypothesis. Alleyne further surmises that the [kw] allophone came to predominate and eventually to replace [kp] in those varieties that remained in contact with Dutch, which lacked the co-articulated stops.

Although Bickerton (1981:122) claims that these stops are found in no creole besides Saramaccan, both /kp/ and /gb/ are part of the phonological systems of Krio (Fyle and Jones 1980:xix), Liberian CE (Singler 1981:25) and Nigerian Pidgin (Faraclas 1996). Boretzky (1983:60) suggests that these may represent more recent (i.e. nineteenth-century) borrowings from neighbouring African languages; indeed, most words with these phonemes do occur in loan words such as Liberian *gbasa jamba* 'cassava leaf' from Vai, or *kpiti* 'fists' from Klao (Kru). Turner (1949:241) mentions the occasional use of co-articulated stops in Gullah CE but, of the four words he mentions, only one (*wulisãkpakpa* 'woodpecker' from Mende) is among words listed as used in conversation rather than as used only in stories, songs and prayers. The status of the co-articulated stops would therefore appear to be quite marginal in Gullah.

5.6.2   *Pre-nasalized stops*
Among the Niger-Congo languages, Alexandre (1967:48) notes 'la fréquence très grande (presque universelle, en fait) des consonnes prénasalisées', although Singler (p.c.) notes that they are not found in many Mande or Kru languages. Pre-nasalized stops consist of stops preceded by homorganic nasals (e.g. /mb/, /nd/, /ŋk/) functioning as a single phoneme – e.g. as C in languages permitting only CV syllabic structure. Such monophonemic pre-nasalized stops (in which the nasal is part of the segment) are not to be confused with homorganic nasals (in which the nasal is a separate segment which takes on the place of articulation of the following segment). The separate status of homorganic nasals in Yoruba is made clear by the fact that they can take a tone distinct from that of the following segment. For example, a homorganic nasal indicating progressive aspect can precede a verb: *dé* 'arrive', *ńdé* 'is arriving'; *bọ̀* 'come', *ḿbọ̀* 'is coming'; *gbọ̀* 'hear', *ńgbọ̀* 'is hearing' (phonetically [ŋ̃m̃gbɔ̃] with a co-articulated nasal) (Ogunbọwale 1970:197).

Although a number of Atlantic creoles have nasal consonants that are homorganic with a following stop occurring at the beginning of a word or syllable, it is often difficult to determine whether these are monophonemic prenasalized stops or biphonemic sequences. In the absence of tones that might distinguish syllabic nasals from a following segment, only the strictness of

CV syllabic structure rules can indicate whether it is a case of one consonant or two, but often the phonotactic rules of the original creole have been disturbed by those of the superstrate language so that no solution is possible. That said, both analyses indicate substrate influence on the creoles since neither pre-nasalized stops nor phonotactic rules permitting syllable-initial nasals plus stops can be attributed to the superstrate languages or language universals.

The Gulf of Guinea creoles have word-initial nasals that are homorganic with following stops, e.g. São Tomé CP *nda* 'to walk' (P *andar*), *ŋgana* 'fowl' (P *galinha*), *njanja* 'quickly' (cf. P *já já!* 'immediately'). Ivens Ferraz (1979:26) analyses these as sequences of two consonants, although the language has a predominant CV syllabic structure. His analysis also requires a special rule for CVC syllables ending in a nasal followed by a homorganic consonant beginning another syllable, e.g. *sum-bu* 'lead' (P *chumbo*), *tam-pa* 'lid' (P *tampa*), *ziŋ-ga* 'to move' (P *gingar*). Treating the nasal-plus-stop sequence as a single phoneme, on the other hand, yields a consistent CV-CV syllabic structure: *su-mbu, ta-mpa, zi-ŋga*.

Palenquero CS, which may be closely related to the Gulf of Guinea creoles, also appears to have pre-nasalized stops. Bickerton and Escalante (1970:256) noted these in words of African origin such as [ŋguba] 'ground-nut', but Patiño also found a number of words of Spanish origin with this feature, e.g. *ngatá* 'spill, waste' (S *gastar*), *nda* 'give' (S *dar*), *mbosa* 'purse' (S *bolsa*) (Friedemann and Patiño 1983:99ff.). Because such forms with initial nasals vary with others without them, minimal pairs cannot be obtained to establish the phonemic status of the initial segment; for this reason, Patiño chooses to analyse the difference between the two sets as subphonemic.

Stolz (1986:76) identifies some nasals plus stops in Negerhollands CD where Dutch has only nasals, e.g. *haːmbu* 'hammer' (D *hamer*) or *skandu* 'entirely' (Stolz derives this from *schoon* 'beautiful, clean' in its comparative form *schoner*, but a more likely source semantically is the idiom *schoon op* 'all gone'). Although he calls the nasal clusters 'pränasalierte Okklusive', he analyses them as biphonemic.

In Haitian CF the elision of vowels can yield sequences such as *mpil* 'a lot' (F *en pile*) or *ntirɛlmã* 'naturally' (F *naturellement*) according to Tinelli (1981) – although Valdman (p.c.) claims that the forms are *ãpil* and *natirèlmã* respectively. The Haitian personal pronouns *mwẽ* 'I' and *nũ* 'we, you' can lose their vowels before verbs, but instead of becoming part of pre-nasalized stops they become syllabic nasals, e.g. *n tunẽ* 'we return' is phonetically [n̩tunẽ] (Valdman 1978:88). However, in St Lucian CF when *mwẽ* occurs before certain preverbal particles, it fuses with the following stops producing a homorganic nasal: *mwẽ* 'I' and *ka* PROG become [ŋa], while *mwẽ* and *pa* NEG yield [ma] (1978:93).

Rountree (1972:22ff.) assigns phonemic status to the four pre-nasalized stops in Saramaccan, i.e. /mb/, /nd/, /ndj/ (i.e. /ɲɟ/) and /ng/ (i.e. /ŋg/). She justifies this on the grounds that the allophone [i], which occurs only in non-nasal syllables, occurs before pre-nasalized stops (e.g. [vinde] 'throw'), indicating that the division of syllables must be [vi-nde] rather than [vin-de]. Moreover, native speakers indicate a syllable break *before* a pre-nasalized stop but *after* a nasal followed by other consonants (e.g. [vi-ndel 'throw' but [vin-tu] 'wind'). Ndyuka has word-initial nasals that are homorganic with following stops, mostly in words of African origin, e.g. *mboma* 'boa constrictor', *ndiká* 'fishtrap', *ŋkólá* 'snail'. However, Huttar (p.c.) analyses these nasals as syllabic rather than part of pre-nasalized stops. Sranan has simple nasals where Saramaccan has nasals with stops, e.g. *metí* instead of *mbéti* 'meat', *neti* instead of *ndéti* 'night', etc. There is similar variation within Saramaccan which, according to Alleyne, suggests that pre-nasalized stops may once have been more widespread, replacing not only simple nasals but also nasals followed by voiceless stops, as in Saramaccan *kandá* 'sing' (cf. P *cantar*), *diíɲi* 'drink', *djómbo* 'jump', *piɲdja* 'pinch'. They also preserved (while transmuting) sequences of a nasal plus a voiced consonant that were simplified in Sranan, e.g. Saramaccan *béndi* versus Sranan *beni*, both 'bend'.

Turner (1949) indicates several Gullah words with initial nasals homorganic with following stops that were used in conversation, e.g. *ndo* 'to know' (cf. Mende *ndɔ* 'to find out') or *mpuku* 'rat' (cf. Kongo, Tshiluba *mpuku*). However, these seem to be marginal, as do those in Krio found in loans from local languages, such as *nkɔdɔ* 'my friend' (Temne) or *mbolo* 'long dust maggot'. However, Wilson (1962:14) notes that while Krio's three nasal phonemes are distinct before a pause, they are identical before a following sound, i.e. homorganic with stops and nasals but nasalizing the preceding vowel before all other sounds. Final nasals behave similarly in Mandinka and Guiné-Bissau CP (Rowlands 1959:10–11, Wilson 1962:13).

5.6.3 Palatalization

Palatalization is the raising of the tongue toward the hard palate, often as a secondary feature of articulation, as in the initial sound of the standard British pronunciation of *dew* as opposed to *do*. Such palatalization affects several sounds in a number of the Atlantic creoles. Since the symbols used to indicate palatalization are not always consistent, table 2 is provided to make clear the notation used in the discussion below.

Table 2. *Palatalization*

		alveolar	alveo-palatal	palatalized alveolar	palatalized velar	velar
Plosive:	voiceless	t	tš	ty	ky	k
	voiced	d	dž	dy	gy	g
Fricative:	voiceless	s	š	sy		
	voiced	z	ž			

In many languages there tends to be palatalization of consonants articulated before front vowels, especially high ones that bring the tongue near the palate. For example, the Latin phoneme /k/ developed the allophone [tš] before the higher front vowels /i/ and /e/. In Italian /tš/ is now a phoneme, with contrasting pairs such as *ciarpa* /tšarpa/ 'scarf' versus *carpa* 'carp'. Similarly Latin /g/ became palatalized in Italian to /dž/ (originally only before higher front vowels), but retained its velar position elsewhere; today there is a phonemic contrast between the two in *giusto* /džusto/ 'just' and *gusto* 'taste'.

Palatalization is also a feature of many African languages. For example in a southern variety of Kongo the alveolar phonemes /t/, /s/ and /z/ all palatalize before the high front vowel /i/ to their respective alveo-palatal allophones [tš] (in the present notational system), [š] and [ž]; e.g. /tobola/ 'to bore a hole' is phonetically [tobola], but /tina/ 'to cut' is phonetically [tšina] (Ivens Ferraz 1979:51ff.). It should be noted that the alveo-palatal affricate /tš/ can result from the palatalization of either the alveolar /t/ (as in Kongo above) or the velar /k/ (as in Italian), just as its voiced counterpart /dž/ can result from the palatalization of either alveolar /d/ or velar /g/ (as in the CF examples below). There can also be correspondences between palatals and palatalized alveolars; for example, in some Twi dialects [ky] corresponds to [ty] in other dialects, and there is a similar correspondence between their voiced counterparts [gy] and [dy] (Westermann and Bryan 1952:90). In general, African languages with palatal consonants fall into two broad categories: in the first, palatal and the corresponding non-palatal sounds are allophones of the same phoneme (like late Latin [k] and [tš], or southern Kongo [t] and [tš]); in the second, they constitute separate phonemes (like Italian /k/ and /tš/).

In Portuguese, as in Italian, palatals are distinct phonemes that contrast with their non-palatal counterparts, e.g. *chapa* 'metal plate' (/šapa/, earlier /tšapa/) versus *tapa* 'slap'. However, the Creole Portuguese of São Tomé has developed a system in which its alveo-palatals are in complementary distribution with their non-palatal counterparts, apparently under the influence of substrate languages like southern Kongo discussed above. According to Ivens Ferraz (1979:41ff.), São Tomé CP alveo-palatals [tš], [dž], [š] and [ž] occur only before high front vowels, while the corresponding non-palatals [t], [d], [s] and [z] occur elsewhere. In words of Portuguese origin, non-palatalized alveolars have been palatalized before the high front vowels, e.g. *kẽci* [kẽtši] 'hot' (P *quente*), *daji* [dadži] 'age' (P *idade*), *kwaži* 'almost' (P *quase* /kwazi/) – while Portuguese palatals in this position have remained palatals. Elsewhere, however, Portuguese palatals have been depalatalized – e.g. *bisu* 'animal' (P *bicho* /bišu/), *zɛmɛ* 'moan' (P *gemer* /žɛmer/) while non-palatal alveolars have remained the same. There are relatively few exceptions to these rules, although some can be found in words recently borrowed from Portuguese, e.g. *dozi* 'twelve' (P *doze*) replacing the older São Tomé *dɛš ku dusu*, literally 'ten and two'. The parallels between palatals and non-palatals in São Tomé CP and southern Kongo are striking, particularly in comparison to Portuguese; it seems clear that substrate languages like southern Kongo imposed this part of their phonological system on São Tomé CP, which in turn affected the phonology of Portuguese in Brazil. There *tia* 'aunt' is /tšia/ (versus /tia/ in Portugal) and *dia* 'day' is /džia/ (versus /dia/ in Portugal).

In Papiamentu CS, some Spanish consonants followed by a palatal glide have been reinterpreted as alveo-palatals, e.g. *džente* 'tooth' (S *diente*) or *šete* 'seven' (S *siete*). There has also been palatalization before /i/, as in *kušina* 'kitchen' (S *cocina*) or *duši* 'sweet' (S *dulce*). In Negerhollands CD, [s] and [š] appear to have merged into a single phoneme tending to have the allophone [š] before /i/, and [s] elsewhere, e.g. [ši] or [si] 'his' (D *zijn*) but [pus] 'push' (from the English) (Stolz 1986:72). Moreover, [t] varies with [ty] and [tš] before /i/, e.g. *biti*, *bitji* (i.e. /bityi/) and *bitši*, all 'a little bit' (D *beetje*) (Bradford 1986:86).

Caribbean varieties of CF tend to palatalize French /t/ and /d/ before /y/, as well as /k/ and /g/ before any front vowel (all of which are high or mid in French, whether rounded or not). This can be seen in Goodman (1964) and in the examples below from Stein (1984:24–5), given in the notation discussed above. The forms are from the creoles of the Lesser Antilles, French Guiana and Haiti; some are variants within the same dialect.

tiens bien	'hold [on] well'	tšẽbe		kyẽbe	kẽbe
cœur	'heart'	tšɛ	tyɔ	kyɛ	kɛ
diable	'devil'	džab	dyab	gyab	
gueule	'muzzle'	džɔl		gyɔl	

This pattern is partially parallel to Twi dialect variation between /ky/ and /ty/ on the one hand and /gy/ and /dy/ on the other, as discussed above. Lesser

Antillean CF alveo-palatals can be followed by /w/, e.g. *tšwizin* or *twizin* 'kitchen' (F *cuisine* /kɥizin/), and *zedžwi* or *zedwi* 'needle' (F *les aiguilles* /lez egɥiy/). Although /w/ is back and non-palatal, its lip-rounding preserves a features in the French high front rounded semivowel /ɥ/ and may correspond to similar labialization of certain monophonemic segments in Twi dialects represented as /kw/ (or /tw/) and /gw/ (or /dw/). Before /i/ these palatalize to [tšw] and [džw] respectively, whence the pronunciation of the language's name, [tšwi] (Boretzky 1983:64, Westermann and Bryan 1952:90). It should be noted that in Haitian CF /t/ and /d/ become palatalized to [ts] and [dz] before /i/, another feature of Akan/Fanti (or Fantsi) dialects. While New World varieties of creole French have /s/ and /š/ as two distinct phonemes that generally correspond to their French counterparts, there is occasionally some variation, as in Haitian [šošɛ] or [sosyɛ] 'witch' (F *sorcière*).

Certainly palatalization, like other aspects of the phonology of the creoles based on French and other languages, has been subject to many influences besides that of substrate languages. In a comparative study of the phonology of French dialects, Canadian French and the French creoles, Hull (1968, 1979) points to the importance of maritime French in the spread of a number of features. Canadian French has palatalized forms like /tšur/ 'heart' (cf. F *cœur*) and *quienbin* 'catch, hold' (cf. CF *kyɛ̃be*). Moreover, 'palatalized /k/ and /g/ are found throughout northern France, and were virtually standard in the 17th century, so obviously would have occurred in Mar[itime]F' (1968:258). Of course phonological features, like sailors, could travel in all directions, which makes it difficult to establish that any single source of a feature is the only true one.

Alleyne (1980:56ff.) deals with palatalization in a number of English creoles (his use of /j/ corresponds to English <y>). He traces the palatal plosives in the Surinamese creoles to two different sources. First, /k/ and /g/ developed palatal allophones before front vowels, e.g. *géi* 'to resemble' varied with *djéi*. Secondly, the alveo-palatals /tš/ and /dž/ in English and earlier Portuguese were also reinterpreted as palatalized alveolars, e.g. *djombo* 'jump' and *tjuba* 'rain' (P *chuva*). Since these also occurred before back (i.e. non-palatalizing) vowels, a phonemic split took place because the palatalized alveolars now contrasted with velar stops, e.g. Saramaccan *tjubi* 'hide' versus *kúbi* 'kind of fish'. Later influence from English and Dutch established velar [k] before front vowels, particularly in Sranan, leading to variants such as [kina] and [tjina] for 'leprosy'. It also led to forms such as *waki* 'watch' (via *watji*) and *wegi* 'wedge' (via *wedji*). The Surinamese creoles generally have /s/ where English has /š/ (e.g. Sranan *sípi* 'ship') but Ndyuka has the allophone [š] before /i/ and /y/ (e.g. [šipi] 'ship', [šyɛ̃ŋ] 'shame') and even before /wi/ (e.g.

[švíti] 'pleasant' from E *sweet*) (Huttar p.c.), suggesting a connection to the palatalization of labialized consonants in Twi and CF discussed above.

Alleyne (1980:58) points out that while the decreolizing shift from palatalized stops to English alveo-palatal affricates is virtually complete in Jamaican CE and other varieties in the Caribbean proper, there are lexical remnants of an earlier variation between velars and palatals, e.g. *kitibu* or *tšitšibu* 'firefly' and *gaagl* or *džaagl* 'gargle'. As Cassidy and Le Page (1980:238) point out, the intermediate form for the last was probably /gyaagl/. The palatals /ky/ and /gy/ occur in a number of Jamaican CE words (e.g. /kyaad/ 'card', /gyaadn/ 'garden') in which they would not be expected because of proximity to any high front vowel. In seventeenth-century British usage [k] and [g] occurred before back vowels like /ɔ:/ (preserved in Jamaican CE /kaad/ 'cord' and /gaadn/ 'Gordon') while the palatals [ky] and [gy] occurred 'before low-front [a] and [a:]' (1980:lviii). While [a] is a low back vowel in American usage, it is indeed low front in IPA terms. Middle English /a/ had varying reflexes in early Modern English, including low front [æ] and mid front [ɛ], which led to the palatalization of adjacent velars. Despite the later backing of the vowel itself, this palatalization is preserved in an on-glide after the velar (e.g. *kyat* 'cat', *gyas* 'gas') and an off-glide before it (e.g. *bayg* 'bag'). The latter is lexically selective in the Caribbean – e.g. *hayg* 'hag' or *blayk* 'black' (Warantz 1983:84) – but regular in Ireland, as is the former.

A number of Surinamese CE words seem likely to have been based on palatalized British forms (now archaic or regional) such as *kyabbage* (cf. Saramaccan *tjábisi* 'cabbage'). Jamaican has the word *john-crow* /džangkra/ 'buzzard', which Cassidy and Le Page (1980:250) derive from *carrion crow* via a shift of the initial sound from /ky/ to /ty/ to /dy/ to /dž/. Part of this process may have occurred in Suriname (cf. Sranan *djankro* and Ndyuka and Saramaccan *djankoo*), after which the form with the palatalized alveolar spread to Jamaica and elsewhere via diffusion.

5.6.4 Apicals

Apical consonants are produced with the tip of the tongue against the upper teeth or the alveolar ridge; they can be a stop (e.g. [d]), a nasal [n], a lateral [l] or a flap [r]. These sounds are related in a number of African languages, either as allophones or as the distinctive parts of allomorphs or as corresponding sounds in different dialects of the same language. For example, in Bambara the perfective marker has the allomorphs *-ra, -la* and *-na*. In Yoruba the contraction of *ní* 'say' is *l*: 'nwọn *l'*ó kú' 'they say he died' is the equivalent of 'nwọn *ní* ó kú'. Twi /r/ corresponds to /l/ in other Akan/Fanti dialects, and in Ewe [l] and [r] are in partial complementary distribution. Klao (Kru) and some related Liberian languages have various kinds of alternation between [l], [d] and [n], which can all vary with [r] in Liberian English.

In the Portuguese creole of São Tomé, /l/ replaces both Portuguese flapped /r/ (e.g. *ali* 'air' from P *ar*) and trilled /r̃/ (e.g. *latu* 'rat' from P *rato*). A number of Papiamentu CS words have apical consonants differing from those of their etyma, e.g. *nanisi* 'nose' (S *narices*), *karson* 'pants' (S *calzón*), *mitar* 'half' (S *mitad*). Alternation of apical consonants is also widespread in Palenquero CS, e.g. *merio* 'half' (S *medio*), *lemedio* 'medicine' (S *remedio*), *selá* 'to close' (S *cerrar*) and *kumina* 'food' (S *comida*) (Friedemann and Patiño 1983:94ff.). Some such alternation can be found in Negerhollands CD *wolter* 'root' (D *wortel*) or *re:l* 'to bring up' from English *rear* (Stolz 1986:65).

In Haitian CF /l/ and /n/ can alternate in certain allomorphs as in Yoruba (above); the definite article is *la* after a nonnasal consonant (e.g. *jurnalis la* 'the journalist') but *nã* after a nasal consonant (e.g. *bòn nã* 'the maid'). There is a similar variation of *li* 'his/her/its': *papa li* 'his father' but *manman ni* 'his mother'.

In the Surinamese varieties of creole English, /l/ and /r/ merged as /l/ in word-initial position, e.g. *lobi* 'love; rub'. Sranan frequently has /r/ between vowels (e.g. *kaseri* 'kosher'), even when the etymon had /l/ in English (e.g. *furu* 'full') or Dutch (e.g. *eri* 'whole' from D *heel*). The English creoles of the Caribbean retain only a few remnants of earlier alternation between /r/ and /l/, e.g. Miskito Coast CE *flitaz* 'fritter' or Bahamian CE *ling* 'ring for playing marbles'.

5.6.5 Labials

Voiced labials include the bilabial stop [b], the bilabial continuant [w] and the labiodental fricative [v]. The last sound is not found in some Atlantic creoles; it is also absent from the phonemic inventory of a number of West African languages from Mandinka to Yoruba, although it is found in other Niger-Congo languages. In Bambara and Malinke, which do not have [v], intervocalic /b/ sometimes becomes the bilabial fricative [β], as does intervocalic /w/.

Contrasting /b/, /v/ and /w/ are found in the Gulf of Guinea varieties of Creole Portuguese, but Ivens Ferraz (1979:35) notes that in standard Portuguese there was alternation between /b/ and /v/ until the end of the fifteenth century, when the African colonies were founded. Thus there are cases in which Portuguese /v/ (possibly /b/ at the time of first contact) corresponds to São Tomé CP /b/, e.g. *bo* 'you' from archaic P *vós*. In other cases there is no change (e.g. *vede* 'green' from P *verde*). However, in the Upper Guinea varieties of CP in Guiné-Bissau and Cape Verde (whose substrate languages differ from those of the Gulf of Guinea), /v/ is only found in recent loans from Portuguese and in most cases P /v/ corresponds to CP /b/, e.g. Cape Verdean CP *baka* 'cow' (P *vaca*, with an initial /v/ in the standard, but /b/ in rural dialects of central Portugal).

There are few lexical remnants of a lack of contrast between /b, v, w/ in the French-based creoles, but in a small area of Guadeloupe one finds the forms *bini* for *vini* 'comes', *bje* for *vje* 'old', etc. (Goodman 1964:61). Word-initial /v/ sporadically becomes /w/ in CF, e.g. French Guiana CF *wa* is an archaic future marker corresponding to Haitian CF *va* (1964:87). In Negerhollands CD there are also some examples, e.g. *bobo* (cf. D *boven*), and *o:bn* varying with *o:vn* 'oven' (D *oven*) (Stolz 1986:69). Moreover, [v] can function as an allophone of /w/, e.g. *huwe:l* or *huve:l* 'how much?' (D *hoeveel*) or *wɛstə* or *vɛnstə* 'window' (D *venster*). However, it should be noted that Dutch orthographic *w* represents a labiodental continuant with less friction than /v/ rather than English /w/ (except in Flanders), and it is no longer possible to know the exact value of the symbols used to represent sounds in this extinct creole. Although there is no contrast between orthographic *b* and *v* in American Spanish (both /b/ with the allophone [β] between vowels), /b/ and /v/ are separate phonemes in Papiamentu CS, apparently from Dutch influence, e.g. *biaha* 'travel' (S *viajar* /byaxár/) and *vibora* 'snake' (S *vibora* /bibora/).

Alleyne (1980:60) postulates that there was no /v/ in the earliest English creoles. In Sranan, /b/ regularly corresponds to English /v/, e.g. *libi* 'live', but Saramaccan has acquired /v/ in loans from Portuguese and other languages, e.g. *vivo* 'alive' (P *vivo*). Ndyuka has /v/ in some words of African origin, e.g. *vongo-vongo* 'biting fly' (cf. Moore *vounouvougou* 'black mud wasp') (Huttar p.c.). There are remnants of /b/ for English /v/ in the CE of the Caribbean proper, in which there is variation in a few words such as *beks* 'to be annoyed' (cf. E *vexed*) or *nabel* 'navel'. In Gullah and Bahamian, /v/ and /w/ have fallen together as a single phoneme /β/ with [v] and [w] as allophones in apparently free variation. This feature is also found in the speech of whites in coastal South Carolina and the Bahamas (Holm 1980) as well as in the Caribbean proper, e.g. the Bay Islands of Honduras (Warantz 1983). It may also be related to the alternation of /v/ and /w/ in some varieties of eighteenth- and nineteenth-century London speech. Singler (p.c.) notes that /b/ and /v/ frequently become [β] in Liberian English.

5.7 Suprasegmentals

It has long been noted that the intonation of Atlantic creole and post-creole languages differs markedly from that of their European lexical source languages. Herskovits (1941:291) speculated about a possible explanation: 'That the peculiarly "musical" quality of Negro English as spoken in the United

163

States and the same trait found in the speech of white Southerners represent a non-functioning survival of this characteristic of African languages is entirely possible, especially since the same "musical" quality is prominent in Negro-English and Negro-French everywhere.' Megenney (1978:160) notes that this feature is shared by the Portuguese spoken in the predominantly black areas of Brazil and by the variety of creolized Spanish called Palenquero. However, he adds that 'no definite conclusions can be drawn from present data concerning the influence of African tonal languages on Indo-European languages since these data are highly subjective in nature. Only careful studies carried out with the aid of the good ear of a linguist acquainted with a variety of African tone languages will be able to yield positive results in helping to solve this most intriguing problem.'

Indeed, little progress was made in this difficult area until it attracted the interest of Africanists – particularly Berry (1959), Voorhoeve (1961), Dwyer (n.d.) and Carter (1979ff.) – and native speakers of creoles such as Lawton (1963), Allsopp (1972) and Holder (1982). One of the fundamental problems is the difficulty experienced by most speakers of non-tonal languages (e.g. most Indo-European languages) in dealing with tone in tonal languages (e.g. all the Niger-Congo languages except Fula, Wolof and Swahili), particularly in practice – i.e. recognizing and producing the tone patterns that are crucial to meaning. On an abstract level, however, the basic difference between intonational and tonal languages is easily explained; Maurer (1995) offers a very helpful treatment of tone in a creole language.

Three interrelated features in intonational languages like English are (1) pitch – i.e. high versus low notes, comparable to those on a musical scale; (2) stress – i.e. loudness or intensity; (3) length – i.e. how long the articulation of a syllable is drawn out. These are linked in English in that syllables that receive primary stress also receive greater length and more prominent pitch (usually higher, but sometimes noticeably lower, than surrounding syllables) as in the word 'uni*ver*sity' or the sentence 'I want to *walk.*' However, the association of these features is not constant; pitch can vary in English according to factors such as utterance type, attitude, position in the sentence, etc. (Carter 1983). Moreover, English is stress-timed, i.e. there is approximately the same amount of time between syllables receiving primary stress regardless of the number of intervening syllables (although this feature is not linked with English being an intonational language).

Most tone languages are syllable-timed, so there are no reduced syllables with reduced vowels (although there are also intonational languages like Spanish that are syllable-timed – i.e. this feature is not linked with tone). The distinguishing feature of tone languages is that each syllable has its own tone or relative pitch, which is not related to stress. In tone languages the relevant pitch pattern is that of each word or segment, while in intonational languages the relevant pitch and stress pattern is that of the whole sentence (e.g. to convey emphasis, a question, an attitude, etc.).

There is also an intermediate type of language which is neither a tone nor an intonational language; this is the pitch-accent language, in which 'there cannot be more than one syllable per word which receives the tonal accent' (Hyman 1975:231).

Yoruba is a tone language with three tones: high (´), low (`) and mid (no mark). Low tone could be thought of as the musical note do, mid as re, and high as mi (although the important thing is their pitch relative to one another). The word for 'school' is *ilé-ìwé* (literally 'house of books'), which basically has the tone pattern mid-high/low-high, or re-mi/do-mi (although this is something of a simplification ignoring low-level phonetic rules of tone sandhi). The word must have this same little tune every time it is said or it may not be understood. Many words are distinguishable only by their tone, e.g. *kí* 'to greet' versus *kì* 'to arrest'. Tone is therefore phonemic; it may seem partly analogous to stress in English, which is the distinguishing feature between the noun *súbject* and the verb *to subjéct*. Here, however, besides the slight difference of vowels, there is a difference in the loudness and length of the syllables as well as the difference of pitch, and all three of these features are variable, as pointed out above.

Besides its function in the lexicon, tone can also play an important role in grammar. For example, in Kongo the difference between *engudi* 'mother' (pre-verbal subject) and *éngudi* 'mother' (post-verbal object) is signalled not only by word order but also by tone (Carter 1979:3). Of course stress can also disambiguate syntactic relationships in intonational languages, e.g. *Énglish teacher* (noun adjunct: a teacher of English) versus *English téacher* (adjective plus noun: a teacher from England). The point is that tone is an integral part of the *system* of tone languages, just as stress is an integral part of the entire system of English. This point is an important one, because in attempting to demonstrate whether certain Atlantic creoles are tone languages – as were most of their substrate languages – researchers have sometimes focused on ambiguous surface phenomena rather than the system as a whole (Carter 1979).

Finally, it should be pointed out that tone systems can vary considerably from one language to another. For example, one Niger-Congo language may have two tones while another has four; in one, tone may carry a heavy load in distinguishing otherwise identical lexical items, while in another this load may be very light. Tone may play an important role in the tense system of one language but not in another. Carter (1979:3) notes that 'It seems a priori unlikely that speakers of such diverse systems would take over into English a coherent and consistent structuring of tonal signalling – though aprioristic reasoning is notoriously subject to error – but in the sense of persistence of surface features, whether or not they retain their original values, I think there is strong evidence for African survivals.'

Günther (1973:48–51) claims that Príncipe CP is a tone language with high tones (´) corresponding to stressed syllables in Portuguese and low tones (unmarked) corresponding to unstressed syllables, e.g. *tóši* 'a cough' (P *tosse*, stressed on the first syllable) versus *toší* 'to cough' (P *tossir*, stressed on the second syllable). In addition there is a third tone that is rising (ˇ), representing a development from Portuguese words whose final stressed syllable was lost in the creole, e.g. *kwê* 'run' (P *correr* /kuʀér/) versus *kwě* 'rabbit' (P *coelho* /kwéʎu/. As can be seen from the above examples and monosyllables such as *fá* 'speak' (P *falar*) and *fa* 'negative particle' (origin unknown), minimal pairs present opposition between high and low tones and between high and rising tones, but not between low and rising tones.

Ferraz and Traill (1981), working from recordings of Príncipe CP made by Ferraz, rejected Günther's assertion that the creole is a tone language, claiming instead that it is a 'free pitch-accent language'. Ferraz found that his informant also used a falling pitch (which they symbolize more conventionally as /ˆ/) in opposition to a rising pitch (/ˇ/ in their notation), e.g. *fŭːtà* (falling-low) 'steal' (P *furta* 'he steals') versus *fŭːtà* (rising-low) 'breadfruit' (P *fruta* 'fruit'). They deduce that the falling pitch resulted from the deletion of a sonorant after the stressed syllable in Portuguese, while the rising pitch resulted from its deletion before it. Their logic in concluding that the creole is a free pitch-accent language is based on the distribution of pitch: in polysyllabic words, there is only one 'tonal accent' (high, rising, or falling pitch) which must cooccur with a 'non-tonal accent' (the less prominent low pitch) on all other syllables. The term 'free' comes from the fact that any syllable can be the prominent one, undergoing 'increases in loudness, pitch and [vowel] length' (1981:208), although its prominence is primarily one of pitch.

In Papiamentu CS, tonal distinctions seem to be important mainly in the domain of verbs (Römer 1977, Marta Dijkhoff 1985). The verb *mata* 'kill' (cf. S *máta* 'he kills') has a low-high pattern with tonal accent on the first syllable, while the passive participle *matá* (cf. S *matádo*) has the same pattern except with the accent on the second syllable. Both are distinct from *mata* 'plant' (same in S), which has a high-low pattern with the tonal accent on the first syllable.

Very little has been done on the suprasegmental features of the French creoles aside from Ariza (1980), which focuses largely on pitch patterns on the level of the phrase rather than the word in Haitian CF and draws no conclusions regarding tonality. Sylvain (1936:42) remarked that there was a difference of tone in Haitian CF reduplications of adjectives: the first, the tone of whose syllables she indicated as '—__', conveys intensity of meaning, e.g. *ron-ron* 'very round'; the second, the tone of which is indicated as '/–', conveys attenuation, e.g. *ron-ron* 'rather round'. Goodman (1964:114) points out that Baissac (1880:89) noted that pronunciation indicated a similar difference of meaning in Mauritian CF reduplications, although he did not describe the pitch patterns.

In the English-based creoles, Carter (1987) distinguishes between the Guyanese tone patterns in iteration (conveying intensity) and reduplication (conveying attenuation). Iteration is the simple repetition of a word with no change in pattern, e.g. 'táll! táll'. In her notational system, this indicates that both syllables have high tone (′) but there is a downstep (!) at their juncture. (Downsteps are the result of an earlier high-low-high sequence of tones in which the low tone makes the following high tone phonetically lower than the first high, although it remains higher than the low; later the low is lost but the second high still remains lower than the first high.) Reduplication, on the other hand, shows the same tone pattern as compounding: the first element loses its high tone and is incorporated into the tone-group of the second element, whose first syllable has high tone no matter what its uncompounded pattern is, e.g. 'tall-táll' 'rather tall'. Carter notes that 'compounding and reduplication patterns such as those of Guyanese can certainly be found in Twi, and the dominant Guyanese pattern is very similar to the Twi one; however, both of these are paralleled in the other African languages here discussed' – i.e. Yoruba and Kongo (1987).

Voorhoeve's 1961 'Le ton et la grammaire dans le saramaccan' was among the first publications identifying a creole as a tone language. He isolated two tones, high (′) and non-high (no mark), in minimal pairs such as *dá* 'to give' and *da* 'to be'. Moreover, he demonstrated that tone plays an important role in Saramaccan not only on the lexical level but also on the grammatical level, marking compound words and other syntactic units. For example, the tones of the words *mí* 'my' and *tatá* 'father' are different in isolation from their tones when they occur as a noun phrase, *mí tata* (1961:148). Rountree (1972b) furthered research on tone in Saramaccan in relation not only to grammar but also to intonation conveying attitude. Saramaccan words normally have high tone on the syllable corresponding to the stressed syllable in their etyma, e.g. *fája tóngo* 'tongs for a fire' or *fáka* 'knife' (P *fáca*) or *dáka* 'day' (D *dag*). In Sranan, which is not a tone language, such syllables are marked by stress. Alleyne (1980:73) postulates that tone became distinctive in the earliest English

creoles, of which Saramaccan is the best preserved example, when it distinguished otherwise identical words from different sources, such as Saramaccan
kai (from English *call*, via the intermediate form *kali* plus deletion of the
intervocalic liquid) versus *kaí* (P *cair* /kaír/). Ndyuka, which is also a tone language (De Groot 1984:1), also has this minimal pair. It is relevant that such
creoles preserved a large number of African words with their tone pattern. In
most of the English-based creoles that remained in contact with English,
stress took over the role of tone in distinguishing lexical items. However,
earlier pitch patterns appear to have remained a characteristic feature of
larger segments such as phrases and sentences.

Cassidy (1961:26ff.) identified some of the features distinguishing Jamaican
intonation from that of English. He noted that 69% of the syllables in the
Jamaican speech he studied represented a change in pitch, whereas only
35% of the standard English syllables did. The frequent change of pitch in
Jamaican stopped only when a speaker became excited and went to his
highest pitch and stayed there. Moreover, declarative sentences in Jamaican
ended on rising pitch, making them sound like questions to speakers of standard North American and British English (although a pattern similar to that
of Jamaican is found in some regional varieties of the last two).

In her 1979 paper 'Evidence for the survival of African prosodies in West
Indian creoles' Carter concluded that her data provided 'insufficient evidence
to permit a judgement on whether or not the Creoles are systematically tonal,
in the sense of signalling distinctions of grammar and lexis by pitch differences.
The surface features however are entirely consistent with derivation from
African tonal systems.' She further noted that, despite superficial resemblances,
creole English pitch patterns did not seem to be derived from English. For
example, they did not include the tail, a primary feature of English prosody.
(The English pitch pattern for sentences has its nucleus on the last accented
words and its tail consists of all following syllables until the end of the
sentence.) Moreover, creole intonation patterns consistently conveyed unin-
tended connotations to speakers of British English; intonation patterns that
conveyed a pleasant attitude in creole English were almost without exception
interpreted as unpleasant (e.g. surly, judicial, detached, cold, hostile, etc.).
After surveying intonation patterns most common in creole speech, Carter
concluded that:

> Creoles have more patterns than does the typical African tone-
> language. Thus, only a portion of Creole features could in any case be
> directly derived from the latter. If the Africanisms are cases of survival,
> they have certainly acquired different values from those with which
> they arrived. The system (or systems) now obtaining have developed

into something which is neither African nor English nor French, nor anything else but distinctively Creole. (1979:14)

However, in 1982 Carter reversed her position after she and David Sutcliffe studied the speech of a Jamaican student who had moved to Britain at the age of nine; his normal speech was educated Jamaican English rather than British English and he could still speak Jamaican Creole to some extent. They found that his speech showed a pattern of pitch polarity: each syllable was opposite in tone to the preceding one, i.e. it started on a high tone, then low, then high, etc. In other words, tone depended on where a word happened to fall in this alternation, e.g. *Pául Nelsón* but *Kévin Nélson*. Since the classical definition of a tone language is one in which 'pitch patterns belong to segments' (Guthrie 1954), Carter concluded that the segment to which the tone-pattern of Jamaican Creole belongs is not the word but the phrase, which she calls the 'tone-group' (1987).

Carter (1987) agrees with Allsopp (1972) and Holder (1982) that tone does indeed distinguish lexis in Guyanese CE in the many minimal pairs displaying pitch-accent such as *turkéy* (the bird) versus *Túrkey* (the country), concluding that Holder 'rightly observes that this feature would make Guyanese qualify as a pitch accent language' (1987). Lawton (1963) had shown how pitch disambiguates various syntactic structures in Jamaican CE such as *di man háas* 'the man's horse' versus *di mán háas* 'the stallion', or *mieri bróng* 'Mary Brown' versus *miéri brong* 'Mary is brown.'

It is less surprising to find creole tone languages in Africa, where many speakers are bilingual or multilingual in other tone languages. Berry identified Sierra Leone's Krio as a tone language as early as 1959; Liberian CE, which has a partly parallel history, appears to be a pitch-accent language (Singler p.c.). In 1966 G. D. Schneider established that it was pitch rather than stress that was contrastive in the Cameroonian variety of West African Pidgin English. Dwyer (n.d. – *c.* 1967) and Mafeni (1971) confirmed this for the Nigerian variety also, in which the study of tone is now well advanced (Faraclas 1996). Clear minimal pairs are found, such as *tú* 'two' and *tù* 'too' (1996).

This chapter has compared a number of phonological features in creoles of various lexical sources and pointed to parallel features in languages that seem likely to have been part of the creoles' superstrate and substrate. While in a number of cases there seems to have been converging influence from the creoles' superstrates (e.g. the palatalization of velars) or language universals (e.g. the alternation of [l] and [r]), it can clearly be concluded that the influence of the substrate languages on the creoles' phonology was both systematic and fundamental.

Phonology

Having examined the varied sources of the sounds that make up the phonology of pidgin and creole languages, we will now look at what many consider the basic enigma of these languages: the syntactic similarities they share with one another but not with their lexical source languages.

6
Syntax

6.0 Introduction

This chapter is a study of some syntactic features that are shared by a number of creoles (both Atlantic and non-Atlantic) but not by the standard languages from which they draw their vocabularies. The number of such features is quite large, and they are so widespread that their existence can hardly be explained by mere coincidence. One of the most central issues in creole studies has been the development of a theory of genesis that satisfactorily accounts for these syntactic similarities. The grammatical features discussed in this chapter are generally considered to be of primary importance in evaluating the relative merits of these theories, which are discussed in some detail in chapter 2. The orientation of the present study is that these common features reflect the influence of both superstrate and substrate languages, as well as universals of adult second-language acquisition, creole-internal innovations, or the convergence of all or some of these sources.

6.0.1 Sources of creole syntax: universals

Language universals – in the Greenbergian or Chomskyan sense of general parameters on possible structures rather than the Bickertonian sense of specific, innate structures – seem likely to have played an important role as a filter in the selection of syntactic features in the pidgins and the creoles that grew out of them. With few exceptions, basilectal creoles rely on free rather than inflectional morphemes to convey grammatical information. This seems likely to have resulted from a universal tendency in adult second-language acquisition to isolate such information through lexicalization, i.e. using a word rather than an ending to convey such information as tense. However, this universal tendency was probably reinforced by a similar tendency in many substrate languages, such as those of the Kwa group spoken in West Africa, which typically isolate morphemes carrying grammatical information.

6.0.2   Sources of creole syntax: superstrate and substrate

The importance of the superstrate input is surely not restricted to lexicon; the European auxiliary verbs that provided the etyma of many of the preverbal markers found in the Atlantic creoles, for example, are related to the latter not only on the level of lexical form, but also on the level of syntax and semantics. However, the creole preverbal markers also bear a fundamental and systematic relationship to the preverbal markers in many substrate languages; indeed, this semantic and syntactic similarity is on the whole greater, and often cannot be explained solely by reference to the properties of superstrate auxiliaries.

Bickerton (1974ff.) claimed that the influence of substrate languages on creole syntax was insignificant. He argued against drawing any conclusions from the similarity of syntactic structures in the Atlantic creoles to those in African languages because of their diversity (1984:8). While the Niger-Congo languages are certainly not uniform, they do share a significant number of structural features, which is one of the reasons for their classification into a single language family. Languages within subgroupings (e.g. Mande, West Atlantic, Kwa or Benue-Congo) show a greater degree of similarity to one another.

Bickerton (1984:10) also claimed that 'No substratum argument has ever supplied . . . historical evidence that speakers of the relevant languages were in the right place at the right time in the right numbers to have had even the possibility of influencing the development of particular creoles.' However, the validity of this second objection presupposes the validity of his first objection, i.e. that there was insufficient typological similarity among the Niger-Congo languages to influence a particular creole in similar ways. When typological studies of African languages (e.g. Heine 1976) indicate that a syntactic feature is found in 80% to 95% of the 300 languages compared, it is illogical to insist that a parallel structure in a creole must be traced to only one of the hundreds of languages that may have influenced it.

Niger-Congo languages extend along the entire area from which Africans were taken in slavery to the New World, primarily the west coast from Senegal to Angola (Greenberg 1966a, Rawley 1981). Although there are often considerable problems in determining the precise origins of people brought to particular colonies during particular periods, great strides have been made over the past decades in interpreting the relevant historical documents. In some cases very precise assertions can now be made, e.g. 'The evidence for the period from 1711 through 1740 suggests that the two most important African language groups for the formation of Haitian Creole are Mande and Kwa, particularly Bambara-Malinke-Dyula and Ewe-Fon' (Singler 1986a). The value of linguistic data in discovering historical facts should not be underestimated; the African origin of the earliest speakers of Berbice Creole Dutch was identified as the Niger delta through the presence of many Eastern Ijo words in the creole (Smith, Robertson and Williamson 1987). This was confirmed by the rediscovery of the fact that the Dutch family running the colony in Guiana obtained its slaves from precisely this area during the relevant period.

Creolists looking for parallel structures in substrate languages have generally been guided by known historical patterns and common sense; southern and eastern Bantu languages have not been pursued, and widely spoken languages have been preferred to small, obscure ones. Lexical evidence (e.g. Twi words in Jamaican) has also tended to guide studies in comparative syntax. Moreover, structures from African languages presented for comparison with parallel structures in creole languages are understood to imply only the general claim that structures of this *type* exerted substrate influence, not that the structure in this particular language was the *source* of the creole structure.

Although there are many syntactic similarities between the Atlantic creoles and their substrate languages, it should also be borne in mind that there are some important similarities between the substrate African languages and the superstrate European languages. For example, in most Niger-Congo languages the usual word order is subject-verb-object (except the Mande and Gur languages which are SOV; Bantu languages are SVO with noun objects but SOV with object pronoun affixes; Welmers 1973:382). SVO is also the usual word order in the superstrate languages (except for SOV with object pronouns in the Romance languages, and in Dutch subordinate clauses). During the initial stages of contact it is likely to have been significant (although not crucial) that the Europeans as well as most of the Africans were looking for a basic SVO pattern in one another's attempts to communicate – the pattern now found throughout the Atlantic creoles.

Many of the creole syntactic features discussed below are viewed here as historically linked to similar features in substrate languages, rather than as constituting any kind of typology of creole languages in general. In other words, no claim is being made that languages with these features are likely to be creoles, or that all creole languages will have these particular features. On the contrary, a creole language with a different substrate would seem likely to have different features that could be traced to that substrate. These features might sometimes coincide with those of the Atlantic creoles; they may even represent features that have spread from the Atlantic area by diffusion. However, the identification of a language variety as a creole requires some knowledge of its sociolinguistic history rather than its having a particular set of 'features that define creoles as creoles' as Markey surmised (1982:170).

This chapter began as a comparative study of some 20 syntactic features in the Atlantic creoles and some 20 African languages, undertaken with the help of some faculty members of the University of London's School of Oriental and African Studies (Holm 1976; 1978:238ff.; 1987b). It was later expanded to include some 100 syntactic features in 16 Atlantic and non-Atlantic creoles (Holm ms.). To make the data more manageable, syntactic structures will be illustrated with just a few sentences from a number of possible languages, including one substrate language and one creole from each lexical-base group of the Atlantic creoles: Miskito Coast Creole English (Holm 1978), Haitian Creole French (DeGraff ms.), Papiamentu Creole Spanish (Michel ms.), Angolar Creole Portuguese (Lorenzino ms.) and Negerhollands Creole Dutch (De Kleine ms.), as well as two non-Atlantic creoles: Nubi Creole Arabic (Khamis and Owens ms.) and Tok Pisin Pidgin/Creole English (Faraclas ms.).

6.1 The verb phrase

The verb phrase has been of central importance in creole studies. While it is true that no particular set of syntactic features will identify a language as a creole without reference to its sociolinguistic history, it is also true that the structure of the verb phrase has been of primary importance in distinguishing creole varieties (e.g. Jamaican CE) from non-creole varieties (e.g. Caymanian English) of the same lexical base. In the Caribbean, the non-creoles have their European system of tense marking (e.g. auxiliary verbs and verbal in-flections) more or less intact, whereas the creoles have a radically different way of dealing with tense and aspect. With few exceptions, basilectal Atlantic creole verbs have no inflections, although they can include the fossilized remains of European inflections, as in CE *marid* 'to marry'. Instead, they are preceded by particles indicating tense (the time of an action's occurrence) or aspect (referring to its duration, recurrence, completion, etc.). These often have the outer form of auxiliary verbs from the lexical source language (which occupy a similar position and serve a similar function), but semantically and syntactically they are much more like the preverbal tense and aspect markers in many of their substrate languages.

Table 3 provides an introduction to the verbal system found in a number of conservative Atlantic creoles and an overview of what will be discussed in the following sections. It is partly parallel to Table 4, *Tense and aspect markers in various creole and African languages*, which shows many (but not all) of the preverbal markers (but omits subject pronouns and verbs) in Atlantic creoles based on Portuguese, Spanish, Dutch, French and English. These are com-pared with preverbal markers in Yoruba (a Kwa language) and Bambara (a Mande language, also of the Niger-Congo family). It should be borne in

Table 3. *Verbal markers in Sranan CE and Haitian CF*

	TMA	SRANAN CE	HAITIAN CF	
1	Unmarked	Mi ___ taki.	Mwen* ___ pale.	'I talk/ed.'
2	Anterior	Mi *ben* taki.	Mwen *te* pale.	'I (had) talked.'
3	Progressive	Mi *e* taki.	M *ap* pale.	'I am talking.'
4	Anterior + Prog.	Mi *ben e* taki.	Mwen *t ap* pale.	'I was talking.'
5	Habitual	Mi *sa e* taki.	Mwen *konn* pale.	'I talk.'
6	Completive	Mi taki *kaba*.	Mwen *fin* pale.	'I have talked.'
7	Irrealis	Mi *sa* taki.	Mwen *va* pale.	'I will talk.' (less certain)
		Mi *(g)o* taki.	M *ap* pale.	'I will talk.' (more certain)
8	Anterior + Irrealis	Mi *ben sa* taki.	Mwen *t a* pale.	'I would have talked.'
9	Irrealis + Prog.	Mi *sa e* taki.	M *av ap* pale.	'I will be talking.'
10	Anterior + Irrealis + Prog.	Mi *ben sa e* taki.	Mwen *t av ap* pale.	'I would have been talking.'

* Allomorphs: m = mwen; t = te; a = av = va

mind that given the number of languages, tenses and aspects involved, there are sure to be a substantial number of individual differences of varying importance. Still, the general similarities are indeed remarkable and merit the closer examination they are given below.

6.1.1 The unmarked verb

In most Atlantic creoles the simple form of the verb without any preverbal markers refers to whatever time is in focus, which is either clear from the context or specified at the beginning of the discourse. For example, in the following passage it is clear that the verbs refer to a permanent state of affairs, corresponding to the simple present tense in English. A speaker of Nicaragua's Miskito Coast CE is discussing how each jungle spirit guides the animals under his protection to hide them from hunters: 'Him a di uona. Him *tek* dem an *put* dem an dis wie . . . die *kom* an him *liiv* dem all hiia an *guo* de', i.e. 'He is their owner. He *takes* them and *puts* them on the right path . . . They *come* and he *leaves* them all in that place and *goes* off' (Holm 1978).

On the other hand, unmarked verbs can also refer to past actions which in English would be expressed in the simple past tense. In the following passages another speaker of the same creole is relating how he and his family moved to town so he could go to school: 'Wi *liiv* from der an *kom* doun hiir fo stodi. Ai *staat* to pas mai gried-dem' i.e. 'We *left* that place and *came* down here so I could study. I *started* to pass from one grade to the next' (1978).

Table 4. *Tense and aspect markers in various creole and African languages*

	Unmarked		Progressive		Habitual		Completive		Irrealis	
		Anterior		Anterior		Anterior		Anterior		Anterior
São Tomé CP	θ	ta(va) -	s(a)ka -	tava ka -	ka -	tava ka -	- za	a - kaba	ka -	ka
Cape Verde CP	θ	- ba	ta -	ta - ba	ta -	ta - ba	- ja	a - ba	ta -	ta - ba
Papiamentu CS	θ		ta -	tabata -	ta -	tabata -	- kaba	a - kaba	lo S -	lo S a -
Palenquero CS	θ		ta -	taba -	ase -	aseba -	a -	a - ba	tan -	tanba -
Negerhollands CD	θ	(h)a -	lo -	a lo -	lo ~ ka(n) -	a ka -	ka -	a ka -	lo ~ sa(l) -	a sa -
Lesser Antillean CF	θ	te -	ka -	te ka -	ka -	te ka -	- fin?		ke -	te ke -
Haitian CF	θ	t(e) -	ap -	t ap -	θ ~ ap -	t(e) -	fin -?	te fin -	(v)a -	t a -
Sranan CE	θ	(b)en -	(d)e -	ben e -	θ ~ (d)e -	(b)en -	- kaba		(g)o ~ sa -	ben o -
Jamaican CE	θ	ben -	(d)a ~ de -	(b)ena -	θ ~ a -	doz -	don - ~ - don	don - ~ - don	go ~ wi	wuda
Gullah CE	θ	bin -	(d)a - ~ - in	bina -	da ~ doz -	doz -	don -	don -	gwɒi	wuda
Yoruba	θ	ti -	ń	ti ń -	maa ń -	ti maa ń -	tán	ti - tán	á ~ yío	yío ti -
Bambara	θ		bɛ -	tun bɛ -	bɛ -	tun bɛ -	ye - ka ban	tun ye - ka ban	bena -	tun bena -

-, position of verb; S, subject.
(From Holm 1988–9:149)

This is similar to the way tense is handled in a number of languages without verbal inflections. Yoruba is typical of many such West African languages; Rowlands (1969:18) observes that the 'Yoruba verb does not contain any built-in distinction between past and present'. For example, *mo jẹun* could mean either 'I eat' or 'I ate', depending on the context (1969:76).

A good deal has been written about the importance of the creole distinction between stative and non-stative verbs regarding tense. However, this actually has more to do with the problem of translating unmarked creole verbs into the suitable European tense, rather than any overtly marked distinction made within the creole verbal systems. A stative verb refers to a state of affairs (e.g. 'I *have* a sister' or 'I *know* the way') rather than a single action ('We *put* it there'). When people talk about an action, it is simply more likely to have already occurred (and thus to correspond to the English past tense) than is a state, which by the very nature of its meaning is more likely to be open-ended and extend into the present. However, it is not the case that unmarked creole stative verbs always correspond to the English present tense and that unmarked creole non-stative verbs always correspond to the English past tense, although this is often the case because actions frequently occur at a single point in time whereas states occur over a span of time.

The following chart summarizes the findings of a survey of the syntax of the seven creole languages described in chapter 3: Angolar Creole Portuguese (A), Papiamentu Creole Spanish (P), Negerhollands Creole Dutch (N), Haitian Creole French (H), Jamaican Creole English (J) and two non-Atlantic varieties, Tok Pisin (T) and Nubi Creole Arabic (B). These data are part of the results of a broader research project on comparative creole syntax covering some ten additional creole languages in Holm *et al.* (1994, 1997, 1998, 1999, fc.), which present and analyse the actual data in a number of areas of syntax. The data on Jamaican Creole English is from Patrick (ms.) while the data on the other creoles is from the work of the linguists cited in section 6.0 above. Here, the focus is on the tense reference of unmarked verbs, i.e. those with no preverbal markers; + indicates that a structure is attested, 0 that its absence is attested, ? that its presence is unknown, and R that it is rare:

CHART 1. UNMARKED VERBS	AP	NHJ	TB
1.1 Statives with non-past reference	++	+++	++
1.2 Statives with past reference	+0	+0+	R+
1.3 Non-statives with past reference	+0	+++	++
1.4 Non-statives with non-past reference	00	+++	R+

These creoles are unlike European languages, in which all verbs, stative or non-stative, require marking to indicate past tense (the so-called 'historical present' is not really like the creole system discussed in 6.1.1 and 6.1.2). The above chart shows that it is not always the case that the unmarked creole verb 'signifies past with nonstatives and nonpast with statives' as claimed by Bickerton (1979:309). Although unmarked verbs in most of the creoles can have past reference, in Papiamentu they cannot, suggesting the influence of Dutch or Spanish, which require inflectional marking to indicate the past (Holm *et al.* fc.).

6.1.2 *Anterior tense*

Many Atlantic creoles have a verbal marker indicating anterior tense as opposed to the past tense found in Indo-European languages. In these creoles, anterior markers (table 4) indicate that the action of the following verb took place before the time in focus (i.e. the time reference of the unmarked verb). The anterior tense can correspond to the English past or past perfect; unlike these, however, the anterior is relative to the time in focus in the preceding discourse rather than to the time of the utterance. This parallels the use of anterior markers in a number of relevant Niger-Congo languages such as Yoruba (Rowlands 1969:76). For example, while the unmarked verb in *mo jęun* can be translated as either 'I eat' or 'I ate' depending on context, when the verb is preceded by the anterior marker *ti* in *mo ti jęun*, it can be translated as either 'I have (already) eaten' or 'I had (already) eaten', again depending on the context.

However, in creoles that coexist with a standard European language, the semantic import of the anterior marker may begin merging with that of the past tense. This seems likely in Papiamentu CS, which has long had native speakers who are bilingual in Dutch or Spanish.

While the function of creole anterior markers seems to follow that of parallel markers in West African languages, their lexical form is often derived from the past or past participle of the word for 'be' in the European superstrate. Largely lacking semantic content other than tense, these forms were apparently reinterpreted as markers of tense only, yielding São Tomé CP *tava* (cf. P *estava*), Papiamentu CS *tabata* (cf. S *estaba*), Haitian CF *te* (cf. F *était* or *été*) or Jamaican CE *ben* (cf. E *been*). Decreolizing varieties of CE often have alternate forms derived from *did, had* or *was*; these result in constructions that are frequently less deviant from standard usage and thus less stigmatized.

Each of the following sentences has a preverbal marker of anterior (or past) tense, which is italicized:

Haitian CF	Bouki *te* konn repons lan.
	'Bouki knew the answer.' (DeGraff ms.)
Papiamentu CS	Mi *tabata* ke kuminda.
	'I wanted food.' (Michel ms.)

Negerhollands CD Di hon *a* ne: si fripampi.
              'The dog took his leash.' (De Kleine ms.)

Nubi CA   Ana *kan* arufu uwo.
                  'I used to know him.' (Khamis and Owens ms.)

Tok Pisin P/CE   Mi *bin* save long yu.
                  'I knew you.' (Faraclas ms.)

Referring back to table 4, the overall pattern is fairly clear: most of the Atlantic creoles have a preverbal marker indicating anterior tense that can occur either independently or before another preverbal marker. This led Bickerton (1980:6) to claim that 'all markers are in preverbal position . . . [and] . . . can combine, but in an invariant ordering, which is: 1. anterior. 2. irrealis. 3. nonpunctual'. Muysken (1981) and others have noted that this is not always the case; there are some postverbal markers (e.g. Cape Verdean CP anterior -*ba*) and the Papiamentu CS irrealis marker *lo* can occur before the subject – quite outside the verb phrase. However, the overall similarity of the pattern from one creole to another – and to Yoruba and Bambara, representative of the substrate languages that influenced the creoles – is nonetheless remarkable.

It should be noted that in some creoles anterior markers can indicate the counterfactual ('If I *had gone* . . .', see section 6.1.6), or indicate the past reference of a predicate with no verb but only an adjective (6.2.3) or a locative copula (6.2.2).

CHART 2. ANTERIOR (OR PAST) TENSE MARKERS	AP	NHJ	TB
2.1 With statives, indicating past reference	0+	+++	++
2.2 With non-statives indicating (past-before-) past ref	0+	+++	++
2.3 Anterior = counterfactual	0+	+++	R+
2.4 Anterior with adjective	00	?++	++
2.5 Anterior with locative	0+	?++	++

This chart indicates that both stative and non-stative verbs in most of the creoles surveyed can take a preverbal marker to indicate a shift in focus to an earlier time. However, in Angolar CP stative verbs are always unmarked for tense, and non-stative verbs can only take an anterior marker co-occurring with a progressive marker. Among the other creoles, anterior markers can also indicate the counterfactual, and most can mark a predicate consisting of an adjective (or adjectival verb) or a locative copula.

6.1.3 *Progressive aspect*

While certain features of the creole verb phrase discussed above may seem unfamiliar to speakers of English, there is nothing alien to us about the notion of progressive aspect, the difference between our 'simple present' (actually habitual) 'She sings' and the present progressive 'She *is* sing*ing*.' When a Miskito Coast CE speaker says, 'Mi baan wen hi waz ruulin' 'I was born when he was ruling', the progressive construction would seem to be straight from English, but its history is probably more complicated.

The progressive in English is not a tense (referring to the time of an action's occurrence) but rather an aspect (referring to its duration, recurrence, completion, etc.). There has been some mystification of aspect in creoles, as if this made their verbal systems totally unlike those of their European source languages, but of course both tense and aspect are dimensions in the semantics of the verbal systems of both groups of languages. While there are some fundamental differences, there is also a fair amount of common ground, as in the case of the progressive aspect.

It is interesting to note that the progressive 'tenses' of those superstrate languages that have them (i.e. Portuguese, Spanish and English) did not develop into their present form until around the time of contact. While the progressive constructions in these European languages appear to have evolved from purely language-internal developments and there is no need to postulate their being borrowed from external sources, it is still possible that their development was reinforced through contact with similar constructions in the New World creoles. Latin had no verbal forms with progressive meanings but late Vulgar Latin developed a construction with an auxiliary verb and gerundive: *stat spargendo*, literally '(he) stands scattering'. This led to the Portuguese construction *está espargindo* with the same meaning (first recorded in the sixteenth century) and the equivalent Spanish *está esparciendo*, in which the auxiliary verb had evolved in meaning from 'stand' to 'be' (in reference to states and location) and was followed by the present participle of the main verb. Today the Spanish construction is in frequent use in both Spain and Spanish America; the Portuguese construction thrives in the received language of Brazil, but in Portugal it has largely been replaced since the early nineteenth century by an infinitival construction, *está a espargir*, literally '(he) is at scattering'.

English progressive constructions are rare before the sixteenth century (Baugh 1957:352). However, there is a Germanic infinitival construction, e.g. German *ich bin am Schreiben* or Dutch *ik ben aan 't schrijven*, both literally 'I am at writing.' Although these are in no way comparable in frequency to modern English *I am writing*, they are similar in structure to early modern English *I am on writing*, which developed into *I am a-writing* and the modern form.

The semantic connection of all of these progressive constructions with position or location is striking and suggests a language universal. Indeed, a semantically parallel progressive structure is found in a number of African languages such as Bambara 'A *bɛ* na tobi *la*', literally 'He *is* sauce cook *at*,' i.e. 'He is cooking sauce' (Singler p.c., Bird *et al.* 1977). The Bambara progressive marker *bɛ* is identical to the form of 'be' indicating location, e.g. 'A *bɛ* Bamakɔ' 'He is (in) Bamako.' Parallels are found in many other Niger-Congo languages, which have progressive constructions based on expressions of location: 'to be at (doing something)'.

In the English-based Atlantic creoles, the progressive marker *de* is the same as the word for 'be (somewhere)' (6.2.2), and to emphasize that an action is in progress, Jamaican can use the preposition *pan* 'at' (cf. E *upon*): 'Judy *deh pon* dyin' (Cassidy and Le Page 1980:147). Location is linked to the etymological source of most of the other progressive markers in table 4 as well. São Tomé CP *ka* may be related to P *cá* 'here' or *ficar* 'stay' as used in the construction *fica olhando* '(he) keeps looking'. This *ka* may have been transferred to Lesser Antillean CF, and through convergence it may be linked to the Mandinka *ka*, also used to indicate both progressive and habitual aspect (6.1.4). The marker *ta* in Cape Verdean CP, Papiamentu CS and Palenquero CS comes from Portuguese or Spanish *está* 'is (located)', often pronounced /ta/ in informal speech in both the Iberian Peninsula and Latin America.

Creole English *de* (with variant forms *da* and *a*) is thought to come from English *there* (6.2.2); it could also be related to Twi *da* 'lie, be situated' and the Twi progressive marker *re* (originally *de* 'to be'). The *a* form may have been influenced by archaic and dialectal English *a*, as in 'He's *a*-comin' and possibly by *are* as an auxiliary in the present progressive. In decreolizing varieties, *de* can alternate with or be replaced by a more English-like construction with no auxiliary before the verb plus *-in*, as in this Miskito Coast CE passage: 'Di gal no *de* briid, man. Di gal, shi did fiil laik shi *wa* briid*in*, bot shi no __ briid*in*' 'The girl wasn't pregnant. She felt as if she was pregnant, but she wasn't pregnant' (Holm 1978:258). The anterior marker takes the form *did* before *fiil*, but *wa* or zero before the *-in* verb *briidin*. Progressive *-in* is one of the first inflections found in decreolizing varieties of CE; it is also among the inflections acquired earliest by children (Fromkin and Rodman 1993:402), perhaps because its semantic content is comparatively easy to identify.

The Negerhollands CD progressive marker *lo* appears to come from the Dutch verb *lopen* 'run, walk, go', which can be used in durative constructions such as 'Ik heb een hele tijd *lopen* dubben', 'I have been worrying for some time.' Haitian CF *ap* is from the archaic and regional French construction 'je suis *après* chanter', literally 'I am after singing' used in the progressive sense of 'I am singing.' F *après* is usually temporal in meaning, but it can, like E *after*, also be spatial.

In the following sentences, the progressive marker is italicized:

Haitian CF	Bouki *ap* danse.
	'Bouki is dancing.' (DeGraff ms.)
Papiamentu CS	Wan *ta* kanta.
	'John is singing.' (Michel ms.)
Angolar CP	N *tha ka* lumba ki kuma.
	'I'm speaking with my comadre.' (Lorenzino ms.)
Negerhollands CD	Mie *lo* skrief.
	'I am writing.' (De Kleine ms.)
Nubi CA	Uwo *gi*-akulu memvu.
	'He is eating bananas.' (Khamis and Owens ms.)
Tok Pisin P/CE	Yu wokabaut *i stap.*
	'You are walking.' (Faraclas ms.)

Note that in the Angolar CP sentence above, the progressive aspect marker *ka* must follow the present form of 'be', *tha* (Lorenzino ms.). In the Tok Pisin sentence above, the optional progressive marker is derived from *i stap* 'it is (located)'. In many of Tok Pisin's Austronesian substrate languages, the progressive marker is also derived from the locative copula, also follows the verb and is also optional (Faraclas ms.).

It should be noted that the anterior marker can precede the progressive marker in all of the creole and African languages in table 4, resulting in a meaning corresponding to English 'he was doing' or 'he had been doing'. It should be further noted that in many creoles progressive aspect markers can refer to the immediate future (6.1.4 and 6.1.6) or precede adjectival verbs to indicate a state that is coming into being (6.2.3).

CHART 3. PROGRESSIVE ASPECT MARKERS	AP	NHJ	TB
3.1 Indicating progressive	++	+++	++
3.2 Indicating future	++	+++	00
3.3 Anterior plus progressive	++	+++	++
3.4 Progressive with adjective = inchoative	+0	?+0	+0

All of the creoles surveyed here have verbal markers indicating progressive aspect, and in the Atlantic creoles this marker can also indicate the immediate future. All can combine the anterior and progressive marker ('was doing') and several can combine the progressive marker with adjectival verbs for an inchoative meaning (6.2.3).

6.1.4 Habitual aspect

Many creoles have a marker of habitual or iterative aspect, which indicates that an action occurs or recurs over an extended period of time. For example, a speaker of Miskito Coast CE used the habitual marker *doz* to stress the fact that his seventy-year-old aunt was in the habit of paddling her canoe some forty miles to Bluefields to sell produce and buy supplies: 'Shi aluon *doz* guo doun to bluufiilz bai kanu.' The European superstrate languages have various ways of indicating that an action is habitual; English can use the simple present tense, e.g. *she goes*, or constructions like *she often goes* or *she used to go*. The basic idea of the habitual aspect is that the action occurs not at just one point in time (punctual) but rather is spread out over a span of time (non-punctual). In this respect habitual aspect is like progressive aspect; they are both non-punctual or durative, but habitual aspect indicates greater duration.

A number of African languages use the same durative or non-punctual marker to indicate both progressive and habitual actions. In Bambara, for example, the non-punctual marker *bɛ* (discussed in 6.1.3) can have either progressive or habitual meaning, e.g. 'A *bɛ* na tobi' can mean either 'He is cooking sauce (right now)' or 'He cooks sauce (regularly)' (Singler p.c.). If there is a possibility of confusion, the addition of sentence-final *la* 'at' unambiguously marks the progressive. Like Bambara, Yoruba also uses a non-punctual marker for both progressive and habitual aspect, but, unlike Bambara, Yoruba disambiguates by marking the habitual but leaving the progressive unmarked. Still other Niger-Congo languages have completely different verbal markers for progressive and habitual aspect.

As can be seen in table 4, a number of Atlantic creoles are like African languages that use the same non-punctual marker to indicate both the progressive and the habitual, e.g. *ta* in Cape Verde CP, *lo* in Negerhollands CD and *ka* in Lesser Antillean CF. In fact, where creole French has influenced creole English in the Lesser Antilles (e.g. in Grenada and Trinidad), not only the progressive but also the habitual meaning of CF *ka* has been calqued onto CE verb + *-in*, as in Grenada CE 'Gud childrin go-*in* tu hevn' 'Good children go to heaven' (Le Page and Tabouret-Keller 1985:163). Like other African languages, São Tomé CP uses the same non-punctual marker (*ka*) for both progressive and habitual aspect, but distinguishes progressive by adding a marker (*sa ka*). Still other creoles, e.g. Palenquero CS, have completely different markers for progressive and habitual. Finally, table 4 shows that habitual markers in most of the creole and both of the African languages discussed can also take an anterior marker to refer to a habitual action before the time in focus.

Taylor (1971, 1977) proposed that the Atlantic creoles should be grouped according to the similarity of their syntax rather than their lexicon; one of his major criteria was whether habitual aspect was indicated by the progressive marker (as in the creoles discussed above) or by the same marker as the future or irrealis (São Tomé CP *ka*, Cape Verde CP *ta* and Negerhollands *lo*), or by no marker at all (e.g. Haitian and Louisiana CF and Jamaican CE). These differences do exist, despite Bickerton's (1980:6) claim that in all 'true' creoles 'a marker of non-punctual aspect indicates durative [i.e. progressive] or iterative [i.e. habitual] aspect for action verbs'. In other words, Bickerton claims that habitual aspect is always expressed by the progressive marker, whereas Taylor claimed that some creoles express it with the future marker and others with no marker.

There is a plausible substrate explanation for the link between habitual, progressive and future markers. As noted above, habitual and progressive meaning are both indicated by the same non-punctual marker in a number of West African languages. Moreover, many such languages also use the non-punctual to indicate the immediate future, much like the English progressive in 'I'm leaving tomorrow' (6.1.6). Those creoles that Taylor indicated as using the future marker for the habitual (Negerhollands CD and the Portuguese-based creoles of Africa) do in fact use the same marker for the progressive (although preceded by *sa* in the Gulf of Guinea creoles). Thus both Taylor and Bickerton were right: the habitual marker may coincide with one, both or neither of the other two markers depending on the creole, but when there is an expressed habitual marker, it is usually the same as the progressive marker or at least related to it historically (Palenquero CS *ase* being a notable exception).

In the following sentences, the habitual marker is italicized:

Haitian CF	Bouki te *konn* vann liv.
	'Bouki used to sell books.' (DeGraff ms.)
Papiamentu CS	Maria *sa* bende piska.
	'Mary sells fish.' (Michel ms.)
Angolar CP	N tha ua ɔmɛ *ka* pixika mɔtxiru.
	'I am a man who fishes a lot.' (Lorenzino ms.)
Negerhollands CD	Mie *kan* verloor altiid.
	'I always lose.' (De Kleine ms.)
Nubi CA	Uwo *gu*-so kidima fileli.
	'S/he usually works at night.' (Khamis and Owens ms.)
Tok Pisin P/CE	Mi *save* wokabaut go wok.
	'I always walk to work.' (Faraclas ms.)

Note that Jamaican CE does not usually have a preverbal habitual marker, using instead the unmarked verb. The Eastern Caribbean CE habitual marker *da* is clearly related to the progressive marker of the same form, but it has apparently been influenced by the English auxiliary *does*. Like the simple present tense in general, this auxiliary conveys the idea of habitual action (e.g. 'He does drink') and in the seventeenth century it did not require emphasis as in the modern standard. Unstressed *does*, *do* and *da* survive in England's southern and western dialects with habitual force. Similar forms, perhaps influenced by Gaelic, also survive in Irish English with habitual meaning, e.g. 'He does write' or 'He does be writing.' Today habitual *doz* is found in mesolectal varieties of CE throughout the Caribbean, with the notable exception of Jamaica. This habitual *doz* has the reduced forms *iz* and *z*, e.g. Bahamian CE 'They *is* be in the ocean.' Rickford (1980) suggests that the complete loss of these reduced forms left *be* itself with habitual force in some varieties, e.g. Bahamian 'Sometime you *be* lucky' or 'They just *be* playing.' However, there is a good case for the convergence of multiple forces in the development of the latter forms, which are also found in African American Vernacular English. In addition to substrate influence on progressive/habitual *da* (6.1.3) and the creole-internal innovation reducing and deleting *doz*, there is good evidence for influence from regional varieties of the superstrate. Rickford (1986) suggests that northern (i.e. Ulster) Irish English habitual *be* influenced AAVE habitual *be* in North America (where the Scots–Irish predominated), whereas southern Irish English habitual *do be* influenced the development of *does be* in the Caribbean, where the southern Irish predominated in the seventeenth century.

Finally, there is a widespread semantic merger between a number of creole habitual markers and verbs ranging in meaning from 'know (how to do)' to 'be able (to do)'. These similarities may have resulted more from semantic universals linking these notions with habitual activity than from lexical diffusion. Portuguese *sabe* 'know' found its way into a number of pidgins and creoles, and some of them (e.g. Papiamentu CS, Sranan CE and Tok Pisin) have a habitual marker with the form *sa*.

The usual Negerhollands habitual marker is *kan*, which is also the creole and Dutch word for 'can'. The latter can merge with a habitual meaning, e.g. 'Hij *kan* heel aardig zijn' 'He can be very nice.' As in English, the meaning here seems to be less one of physical or mental ability than a habitual (if interrupted) trait. Gullah CE has a similar habitual use of *kin* 'can': 'In de wintertime 'e *kin* rain' 'In the winter it rains.'

CHART 4. HABITUAL ASPECT MARKERS	AP	NHJ	TB
4.1 Zero marker for habitual	0+	+++	0+
4.2 Progressive marker for habitual	++	+R+	0+
4.3 Marker for habitual only	++	++0	+0
4.4 Anterior plus habitual	++	+++	++

In other words, in most of the creoles surveyed habitual aspect can be indicated either by no marker, the progressive marker, or a special habitual marker. These can combine with the anterior marker in all of the creoles to indicate a previous habitual action.

6.1.5 Completive aspect

The completive aspect marker indicates that an action has been completed, as in Miskito Coast CE 'Ai *don* giv im a dairekshon' 'I have (already) given him an address' (Holm 1978). As the English translation suggests, there is considerable semantic overlap between the creole completive and the perfect tenses in English. However, the latter convey not only the idea of the completion of actions (corresponding to the completive) but also the idea that their completion occurred prior to another event (corresponding to the anterior tense in many creoles), so that English speakers sometimes confuse the meaning of completive and anterior markers. However, the two are not interchangeable. For example, the anterior marker *di* could not replace the completive marker *don* in Miskito Coast CE 'Wen i *don* skuor im, i salt im op' 'When he had scored him, he salted him up' (1978). In fact, the two markers can co-occur as in the following sentence, where the anterior marker *di* emphasizes the fact that the completion of the action marked by *don* occurred prior to the 'time-line' of the story: 'Nansi *di don* gaan an lef Taiga der' 'Anansi had already gone, leaving Tiger there' (1978). There is evidence from discourse studies of a number of creoles that completive markers are used primarily to preserve or reinforce the time-line, not to disrupt it.

The following creole sentences all contain completive markers, which are italicized:

Haitian CF	Mwen *fin* bati kay la.
	'I have finished building the house.' (DeGraff ms.)
Papiamentu CS	Mi a kome bonchi *kaba*.
	'I've already eaten beans.' (Michel ms.)
Angolar CP	N *kaba* taba.
	'I've finished working.' (Lorenzino ms.)
Negerhollands CD	Api ju *ka:* lo, di andə een ha fo loo daa oka.
	'Wherever you've gone the other one has to go too.' (De Kleine ms.)
Tok Pisin P/CE	Mi save *pinis* olsem yu kam.
	'I already know that you came.' (Faraclas ms.)

Note that the etymological sources of the creole completive markers often mean 'finish'. CE *don* was probably influenced not only by the meaning of standard English *done* but also by sixteenth-century Scottish English constructions like *done discus* 'discussed' (*Oxford English Dictionary*). French *finir* 'finish' provided the lexical model for CF *fin(i)*, while Portuguese *acabar* 'finish, complete' is the source of the completive marker *kaba*, found not only in Portuguese-based creoles and Papiamentu CS, but also in the English-based creoles of Suriname, Guyanais CF and even Negerhollands CD (in the form of *ka*). P *acabar* may have converged with an African completive construction: Bambara *ban* /bã/ 'finish' occurs with the infinitive marker *ka* after the main verb, as in 'A ye na tobi *ka ban*', literally 'He PAST sauce cook to finish', i.e. 'He has already cooked the sauce.'

While Nubi Creole Arabic has no completive marker, the Tok Pisin completive marker *pinis* follows the verb and is derived from the verb meaning 'finish', as in most of Tok Pisin's Austronesian substrate languages, which happen to parallel many West African languages in this respect. These have serial verb constructions (6.3) with a verb signalling completion at the end of the clause, e.g. Yoruba *tán* 'finish' in 'mo kà á *tán*', literally 'I read it finish' i.e. 'I finished reading it' (Rowlands 1969:134).

Welmers (1973:347) notes that in some Niger-Congo languages completive markers can be used with adjectival verbs that have an inceptive meaning (e.g. 'get sick') to produce what corresponds to an English present-tense meaning, e.g. Fante *ɔáfònáo* 'he has become tired' or 'he is tired'. This is also found in the Atlantic creoles, e.g. Negerhollands CD 'mi *ka* moe' 'I am tired' or Nigerian PE 'im *dón* sik' 'he is sick'. In some creoles completive markers can emphasize the meaning of adjectival verbs, e.g. Lesser Antillean CF 'i led *fini*' or Liberian CE 'hi *feni* ɔgli', both 'he is extremely ugly'.

CHART 5. COMPLETIVE ASPECT MARKERS	AP	NHJ	TB
5.1 Completive only (before or after verb)	++	+++	+0
5.2 Completive + adjective	00	+++	+0
5.3 Anterior (or other markers) + completive	0+	+++	+0

6.1.6 *Irrealis*

The irrealis marker indicates that the action of the following verb is not (yet) a part of reality. Used alone, it approximates in meaning the future tense of European languages, e.g. Guyanese CE 'Fraidi awi *go* mek' 'Friday we will make [some]' (Bickerton 1975a:42). Used in combination with the anterior marker, the irrealis marker can impart the idea of European conditional or subjunctive constructions, e.g. Guyanese CE 'awi *bin go* kom out seef' 'we would have come out all right' (1975a). Irrealis has been treated not as tense but as mode in a number of studies since Voorhoeve (1957:383), thus forming one part of a tripartite system of marking verbs for tense, mode and aspect (6.1.7).

Like Guyanese CE *go*, the irrealis marker in a number of other creoles is also modelled on superstrate forms of words meaning 'go' which can be used to form constructions with future meaning, such as English 'We are *going* to leave.' In fact, part of the English *-ing* ending is preserved in Gullah CE *gwõi*, although this may represent convergence with British dialect forms like *gwainin*; actual forms heard in Caribbean CE include *gwain*, *wan*, *an* and *a* (Aceto 1996). The Haitian CF irrealis marker *va* (with the alternate form *a*) is related to F *va* 'is going' used with future meaning in expressions like 'Il *va* parler' 'He is going to speak.'

However, the Haitian marker *va* or *a* may also be related to the Ewe future marker *á* from *vá* 'to come'. Future or irrealis markers are derived from verbs meaning 'to come' in a number of West African languages, such as Yoruba *á* from *wá*. As noted in table 4, Bambara *na* 'to come' is preceded by the progressive marker (and copula) *bɛ*, to form the irrealis marker *bɛna*. The choice of an etymon meaning 'go' rather than 'come' for the above creole irrealis markers suggests strong superstrate influence, although some substrate languages also mark the future with a verb meaning 'go', e.g. Ibo *gá* or Grebo *mu*.

In this context it is interesting that creole irrealis markers from superstrate 'go', like Haitian *va* or even Caribbean CE *gwain*, can be reduced to /a/. In both Sranan CE and Nigerian PE the irrealis marker *go* has an allomorph *a*, while in African American Vernacular English *go* becomes *a* in the expression 'I'm *a*na + V' or 'I'm-*a* + V' 'I'm going to V' (DeStefano 1973:134). The Jamaican CE progressive marker *a* can also be used with future meaning. While present progressive constructions can be used with future meaning in English as well (e.g. 'I'm leaving tomorrow'), similar usage in some West African languages suggests the converging influence of the substrate and/or universals. For example, Bini *ya* indicates progressive or habitual aspect as well as the immediate future. As noted above (6.1.4), this convergence of the progressive, habitual and irrealis in a single marker is found in a number of Atlantic creoles, e.g. Cape Verde CP *ta*, São Tomé CP *ka* and Negerhollands CD *lo*. The last may be related to D *lopen* 'walk, go' through its use as a progressive and habitual marker (6.1.3) or possibly through the use of *lopen* as 'go', perhaps converging with an irrealis marker in an African language, such as Mende *lo* (Migeod 1972:215). In Papiamentu CS the irrealis marker also happens to be *lo*, but this marker is thought to come from the Portuguese adverb *logo* 'immediately'. Like an adverb – and unlike all other creole verbal markers – it can occur outside the verb phrase, e.g. 'I will not go' is '*lo* mi no bai', 'mi *lo* no bai' or even 'mi no *lo* bai'. Bickerton (1981:80ff.) speculates that its anomalous position outside the verb phrase is the remnant of an earlier pidgin stage in which *lo* still functioned as an adverb.

A number of creoles distinguish between an immediate, certain future and a distant, less certain future. Ndyuka CE can use the progressive marker *e* (from *de*) to convey an immediate future that is certain: 'Mi *e* go wasi' 'I am going to wash (right now).' The use of *go* (or its alternant *o*) alone retains the idea of certainty without immediacy: 'Mi *o* wasi' 'I'll certainly wash (some time).' A different future marker *sa* (cf. E *shall* or D *zal*) conveys a lack of certainty: 'Mi *sa* wasi' 'I'll wash (as far as I know)' (Huttar p.c.). The Negerhollands CD irrealis marker *sa* also connotes less certainty than *lo*, used for an immediate future that is certain and seldom negated. A similar distinction of certain versus uncertain future is found between Krio CE *go* versus *fɔ* and Mauritian CF *pu* versus *a*. Some African languages make a similar distinction (Welmers 1973:355, Boretzky 1983:123–6), but further research is needed to clarify the relationship between these and creole usages.

Finally, as noted above, the anterior and irrealis markers can combine in many Atlantic creoles to produce a conditional meaning, as seen in the italicized markers in the following sentences:

Haitian CF   Mwen *t a* vini si m te kapab.
                'I would have come if I could have.' (DeGraff ms.)

Papiamentu CS   *Lo* mi *tabata* baña.
                'I would have been taking a bath.' (Michel ms.)

Negerhollands CD Ju *sa ka:* dra: di a ju han.
                'You should have carried it in your hand.'
                                                (Stolz 1986:173)

Nubi CA   Umwon *kan bi*-zuru sabi tomwon fi Nairobi.
                'They would have visited their friend in Nairobi.'
                                        (Khamis and Owens ms.)

Tok Pisin P/CE Mi *bin laik* kamap, tasol rot bagarap.
                'I almost made it, but the road was no good.'
                                                (Faraclas ms.)

It should be noticed that in the Negerhollands CD sentence above, the marker after irrealis *sa* is the completive *ka:* rather than the anterior *(h)a*. However, Magens (1770:15) offers evidence that a conditional structure with the latter marker did exist earlier: 'Mie *ha sa* wees' 'I would have been.' The presence of a parallel structure in Nubi Creole Arabic, with anterior *kan* and the irrealis prefix *bi-* combining to produce conditional meaning, suggests the influence of a universal tendency, which is also supported by the parallel construction with Tok Pisin anterior *bin* and proximal future *laik*, resulting in a meaning that is conditional insofar as it refers to an event that almost occurred.

A similar construction can be found in a Niger Congo language: in Bambara, anterior *tun* and irrealis *bɛna* combine to produce a conditional meaning: 'A *tun bɛna* na tobi' 'He would have cooked sauce.' However, this combination is not widely attested in West African languages, lending support to the interpretation that the creole construction reflects a semantic universal, also found in the 'past future' construction of the conditional in English *would* (the past of *will* in indirect discourse) or Spanish *sería* '(it) would be' (future *será* plus the imperfect).

CHART 6. IRREALIS MODE	AP	NHJ	TB
6.1 Future (= progressive marker?)	++	+++	00
6.2 Anterior + Irrealis = conditional	0+	++0	R+
6.3 Anterior + Irrealis = future in the past	0+	0++	+0
6.4 Anterior + Irrealis = future perfect	0+	0?0	+0

In most of the creoles surveyed, the progressive marker can indicate future or irrealis mode. In several creoles the irrealis marker can combine with the anterior marker to indicate the conditional ('I would have gone'); this combination can sometimes also convey the future in the past ('I said I would go') or the future perfect ('I will have gone').

6.1.7 *Other preverbal marker combinations*

From the above discussion of the verbal markers in table 4, several general patterns emerge. First, the creoles indicate tense, mode and aspect with verbal markers rather than inflections, and most of these markers occur before the verb. Secondly, there are striking semantic and syntactic similarities among the corresponding markers of each category that cannot be explained adequately by referring only to the creoles' lexical source languages. Although these have usually provided the lexical forms of the markers (derived from European auxiliary verbs with partially similar semantic and syntactic features), the creole markers are part of a verbal system that is quite different from that of the European lexical source language in many respects.

Regarding the ordering of the markers, at least one pattern is clear: each aspect or mode marker (including Ø) can be preceded by the anterior tense marker, although there are some exceptions apparently due to decreolization – e.g. Gullah progressive [verb + -*in*] replacing [*da* + verb], or the Jamaican conditional *wuda* instead of **ben go*. Further claims about the ordering of these verbal markers have been the subject of some debate. Bickerton's (1980, 1981) analysis of the creole verbal system, based largely on Voorhoeve (1957), is that there are three basic components – tense (± anterior), mode (± irrealis) and aspect (±non-punctual) – and their markers occur in that order only (see 6.1.2 for discussion). The category of [± non-punctual] is based on the conflation of progressive and habitual into a single aspect which does not include the completive, which Bickerton claims to be a later innovation. Given these alternatives, + or – choices yield the possible combinations of markers shown in figure 1.

ANTERIOR	IRREALIS	NON-PUNCTUAL	ant	irr	non	Verb
–	–	–				V
–	–	+			e	V
–	+	–		sa		V
–	+	+		sa	e	V
+	–	–	ben			V
+	–	+	ben		e	V
+	+	–	ben	sa		V
+	+	+	ben	sa	e	V

Figure 1. Possible combinations of Tense, Mode and Aspect markers (from Bickerton 1980:14, illustrated with Sranan CE markers from Voorhoeve 1957:383)

Not all these combinations can be found in decreolized varieties like Hawaiian and Guyanese CE, but they are all found in conservative varieties like Sranan and Saramaccan CE as well as Haitian and Lesser Antillean CF. These include two combinations not discussed in the previous sections. The first is the combination of the future and progressive marker (Sranan *sa e*, Saramaccan *o ta*, Haitian *av ap*, Lesser Antillean CF *ke ka*) corresponding in meaning to the English future progressive 'will be (do)ing'. The second is the sequence [+anterior +irrealis +progressive] (Sranan *ben sa e*, Saramaccan *bi o ta*, Haitian *t'av ap*, Lesser Antillean CF *te ke ka*) corresponding in meaning to the English conditional perfect progressive, 'would have been (do)-ing'. This tripartite system is clearly different from the verbal systems of Krio CE or Mauritian CF, both of which have two distinct irrealis markers for certain versus uncertain future, as well as two distinct aspect markers for non-punctual and completive. However, Bickerton suggests that such systems developed out of the tripartite one shown in figure 1. A number of linguists (e.g. Muysken 1981, Alleyne 1980, Gibson 1986) disagree with the universality of the creole TMA system posited by Bickerton (1980).

CHART 7. OTHER COMBINATIONS OF
VERBAL MARKERS   AP NHJ TB
7.1 Irrealis + progressive .... 0+   ++0   ++
7.2 Anterior + irrealis + progressive .... 0+   0+0   0+

6.1.8 Complementizers

Caribbean CE has several complementizers that correspond to the English infinitive marker *to*. Miskito Coast CE has *fo* ('A fried *fo* guo tek di tingz' 'I'm afraid to go take the things') and Ø ('Ai niid Ø tes mai ai' 'I need to have my eyes tested') in addition to *tu* ('Bai tingz *tu* iit' 'Buy things to eat'). Bickerton (1971) argued that the variability of the Guyanese CE complementizers *tu* and *fu* was evidence in favour of the wave model of language change. He used implicational ranking (2.11) to order individual speakers' use of these complementizers to chart a polylectal grammar of this feature, claiming that the change progressed regularly from favoured to less favoured environments, first as a variable and then as a categorical rule. The most favoured environment was after verbs whose meaning was 'inceptive' (e.g. *staat*, *bigin*), then verbs whose meaning was 'desiderative' (e.g. *want*) and finally 'purposive' and other verbs, which favoured *tu* least and *fu* most. Washabaugh (1977), using data from Providence Island CE, found that complementizer scalability was 91% on the basis of simple lexical items rather than any 'deep structural semantic constraints'.

There are historical reasons why CE *fu* (with variants *fo* and *fi*) may be most firmly entrenched after purposive verbs. In regional British dialects, *for* is used as a complementizer implying purpose (e.g. 'I came *for* see') in the West Country and Liverpool, while 'I came *for to* see' is found in both regional and archaic English. The choice of *fu* as a complementizer in creole English might have been further reinforced by similar constructions in substrate languages, such as the Mandinka particle *fó* expressing purpose, e.g. 'm bàtu ngá táa *fó* íte s'iíla dòokuo nyáa sòto' 'Let me go *so that* you may have a chance to do your work' (Rowlands 1959:82). There is syntactic evidence for such convergence in that CE *fu* introduces not only infinitives (like its regional and archaic English model) but also tensed verbs like Mandinka *fó*, e.g. Miskito Coast CE 'Dem sen dem *for ai* drink' 'They sent them for me to drink.' This construction could be attributed to the further development of the standard English construction in which the object of *for* is the subject of a following infinitive (as in the above translation), but there is evidence in creoles unrelated to English that points toward the English *for* construction converging with a creole construction influenced by the substrate. In a number of creoles not based on English there are particles that function similarly to CE *fu* which are homophonous with prepositions meaning 'for' derived from Portuguese or Spanish *para*, French *pour* or Dutch *voor*; unlike standard English *for*, these can be followed by tensed verbs:

Haitian CF	Mwen te mande *pou* l te vini.
	'I asked that s/he come.' (DeGraff ms.)

Papiamentu CS   Mi no ke *pa* bo grita.
                    'I don't want you to yell.' (Michel ms.)

Angolar CP   E ra nɔ kwine pata *pa* nɔ ba me.
                    'He gave us ten *"dobras"* to go and eat.'
                                          (Lorenzino ms.)

Negerhollands CD Am a lo: kuri *fo* pupa kri am fan.
                    'He was running so that his father would catch him.'
                                        (De Kleine ms.)

This construction seems to be confined to creoles found in the Atlantic area. In Nubi Creole Arabic, the complementizer *ke* which introduces such a tensed clause (e.g. 'Umwon aju *ke* ana ja', literally 'They want that I come') is not homophonous with the preposition meaning 'for'. In Tok Pisin, the complementizer *long* (e.g. 'Mi baim *long* ol pikinini bai ol kaikai' 'I bought it for the children to eat') is homophonous with a preposition, but one whose meaning is generally locative (see 6.5.2) rather than specifically 'for'.

Because the Atlantic creoles generally lack case and tense marking and it is not found in the structures after 'for' above, there was some debate whether these structures should be considered clauses with tensed verbs. However, by considering *wh*-extraction and the distribution of anaphors, Koopman determined that in Haitian CF 'complement clauses headed by *pu* are opaque tensed clauses containing a subject marked for nominative Case' (1986:238). The validity of this analysis for other creoles is supported by the work of Byrne (1984:102), who found actual tense marking in such a clause in Saramaccan CE:

Mi kê tsuba kai *fu* ma   *sa-* go a wosu.
1s want rain fall so 1s-NEG IRR go to house
'I want it to rain so I won't have to go home.'

Portuguese has a partly similar construction with a 'personal infinitive' (i.e. a non-tensed verb which nonetheless takes a subject pronoun): 'Eles pediram *para eu voltar*', literally 'They asked *for I to-return*', i.e. 'They asked me to return.' If this construction converged with a similar one in a substrate language (e.g. the Mandinka structure with *fó* discussed above), this may be evidence for relexification in the creoles based on languages other than Portuguese. Yet no substrate languages have been identified in which the subordinator meaning 'so that' is homophonous with the preposition meaning 'for'. While recent research has begun to cast light on the origin of the creole 'for' construction, much more work remains to be done.

In some creoles based on English and French, there is a choice of complementizers that conveys a semantic distinction. In Jamaican CE 'im gaan *go* bied' 'he went to wash', *go* cannot be used if the intended action was not actually carried out, in which case *fi* must be used: 'im gaan *fi* bied, bot im duon bied' (Bickerton 1981:59ff.). Similarly, in Mauritian CF the complementizer *al* (cf. F *aller* 'go') can be used with an action that is carried out, e.g. 'li desid *al* met posoh ladah', literally 'she decide *go* put fish in-it' (Baker 1972). However, if the action is not realized, the complementizer *pu* (also an irrealis marker) must be used. However, it is unclear how widespread this semantic distinction in creole complementizers is; in Belizean CE *go* can be used with an unrealized action, e.g. 'i no waan *go* chap planteej' 'he did not want to [go and?] clear the scrub' (Le Page and Tabouret-Keller 1985:104).

CHART 8. COMPLEMENTIZERS

	AP	NHJ	TB
8.1 Zero infinitive marker	++	+++	++
8.2 'For' as infinitive marker	++	+++	+0
8.3 'For' as a (quasi-) modal	0+	+++	+0
8.4 'For' introducing a tensed clause	++	++0	++
8.5 Subordinator from superstrate 'that'	0+	+++	00
8.6 Distinct subordinator after verb of speaking	++	+0+	+0
8.7 Zero subordinator	++	+++	++

All the creoles surveyed can use the simple verb in constructions corresponding to the English infinitive 'to go'. The word corresponding to 'for' can mark infinitives in all the Atlantic creoles surveyed here; nearly all can use the same word as a modal indicating an arranged future or to introduce a subordinate clause. While nearly all have borrowed a subordinator like 'that' from their superstrate, they can also have subordinate clauses without any complementizer at all (unlike Romance languages, for example). All but two have a special subordinator after verbs of speaking or thinking.

6.1.9 Negation

Regardless of the pattern of negation in their superstrate languages, most creoles negate verbs by placing a negative particle before the verb phrase (i.e. the verb preceded by any preverbal markers):

Miskito Coast CE Shi *no* kom op de.
'She doesn't come up there.' (Holm 1978)

Haitian CF Jan *pa* t av ale nan mache.
'Jan would not have gone to the market.'
(DeGraff ms.)

Papiamentu CS Ana *n'* ta studya tur dia.
'Ann does not study every day.' (Michel ms.)

Negerhollands CD Mi *no* we:t, wa ju gut fo.
'I don't know what you're good for.' (De Kleine ms.)

Nubi CA   Uwo *ma* bi-ja. 'S/he won't come.'

                                               (Khamis and Owens ms.)

Tok Pisin P/CE   Yu *no* laik go long ples?

                                   'Don't you want to go to the village?' (Faraclas ms.)

However, the verbal negator does not precede the verb phrase in all creoles. Although it does in the Nubi Creole Arabic sentence above (representing the variety spoken in Kenya), in Ugandan Nubi the negator *ma* or *mafi* occurs at the end of the sentence: 'Uwo bi-ja *mafi*' 'S/he won't come' (Khamis and Owens ms.).

The creole syntactic pattern for negation is parallel to that of Portuguese and Spanish; this pattern is also found in many West African languages, e.g. Yoruba 'a *kò* mò', literally 'we not know', i.e. 'we do not know' (Rowlands 1969:16). This pattern represents a basic restructuring of negation in English ('I *do not* know'), French ('je *ne* sais *pas*') and Dutch ('Ik weet *niet*'). In decreolizing varieties of English-based creoles the negator *no* is replaced by a less stigmatized form, *duon* (cf. *don't*), a single morpheme with the same distribution as *no*, e.g. Miskito Coast CE 'Di wata *duon* pulin it eni muor' 'The water isn't pulling it any more.' Through hypercorrection, this form can also replace English *not*, as in Bahamian CE 'Dancie say you better *don't* mess round with her nigger' 'Dancie said that you had better not fool around with her boyfriend' (Holm with Shilling 1982:142).

Bickerton (1981:65) claimed that 'in creoles generally, nondefinite subjects as well as nondefinite VP constituents must be negated, as well as the verb, in negative sentences'. He offered only a few examples in Guyanese CE ('*Non* dag *na* bait *non* kyat' 'No dog bit any cat') and Papia Kristang CP ('*Ngka ng'koza nte* mersimentu', literally 'Not no-thing no-have value' i.e. 'Nothing has any value'). This interesting claim regarding negative concord merits more substantiation. Labov (1972:130) noted such concord in African American Vernacular English 'It *ain't no* cat *can't* get in *no* coop', i.e. 'There isn't any cat that can get into any coop' – which leaves no nondefinite unnegated. However, Bahamian CE can extend negation to NPs as definite as proper nouns: 'They can't sell that in *no* Haiti' (Holm with Shilling 1982:143). Liberian CE can even negate adverbial particles: 'I not standing *no* up', an emphatic way of saying 'I refuse to stand up' (Singler 1981:91). Shilling (1976) notes negative concord in the French-based creoles and underscores the parallel structure of negation in Bahamian CE with a word-for-word translation into the latter, e.g. 'li *pa* repon *naye*' becoming 'he ain' answer nothin''. However, it must be remembered that French itself requires the negation of the verb before a negative indefinite, e.g. 'Il *n'*a *rien* répondu.'

Spanish and Portuguese have similar negative concord; although there are no studies comparing this phenomenon in creoles lexically based on them, isolated examples suggest a similar pattern, e.g. Papiamentu CS '*Nada no* ta pasa' 'Nothing is happening' (Marta Dijkhoff p.c.) – cf. Spanish '*No* pasa *nada*.' Negative concord can also be found in Negerhollands CD, e.g. 'Sender *no* leer *niet* een Gut', literally 'They don't learn nothing' (Hesseling 1905:170). However, double negation could also be found in seventeenth-century Dutch (Brachin 1985:22), as in archaic and nonstandard English.

Several Atlantic creoles have discontinuous double negators, i.e. one before the verb phrase and another at the end of the clause, as in Angolar CP 'Kikie *na* methe me *wa*', literally 'fish not want eat not', i.e. 'The fish aren't biting' (Lorenzino ms.). The sentence-final negator *wa* can be substituted by *fo*; this pattern of negation in Angolar suggests its close relationship to São Tomé CP (in which the discontinuous negators are *na . . . fa*) and the varieties of creole Portuguese spoken on the neighbouring Gulf of Guinea islands of Annobom (*na . . . -f*) and Príncipe (with a single utterance-final negator *fo*).

Across the Atlantic Ocean, Palenquero CS has a single negator *nu* which occurs at the end of the utterance but which can also occur before the verb for emphasis: '*Nu* ablá ma *nu*', literally 'Not say more not', i.e. 'Don't say any more' (Bickerton and Escalante 1970:259). This double negation is normal in imperative constructions (Friedemann and Patiño 1983:171) and can occur in nonemphatic sentences as well (De Granda p.c.). Discontinuous double negators are also found in Berbice Creole Dutch, e.g. 'ɛk *na* ni wat fi pam ju *ka*', literally 'I not know what to tell you not' i.e. 'I don't know what to tell you' (Robertson 1979:158). The clause-final negator *ka* has been traced to the Eastern Ijo negator *-ka* (Smith *et al.* 1987). Other African models for the creole discontinuous negators have also been proposed. Hancock (1979c:415) points out the parallel Kongo structure in 'Omuuntu *ke*-wàmmbi-*ko*' 'The man is not wicked', in which each emphasized particle is a negator. Boretzky (1983:102) notes that Ewe surrounds the verb with the disjunctive negators *me . . . o*, the first element of which can sometimes be omitted; the second comes at the end of the sentence. He points out that the discontinuous creole negators could be innovations as well as the result of substrate influences but they could hardly have resulted from a universal creole tendency toward simplification since they represent more complex structures than the single negators in their superstrates.

Discontinuous negators are also found in several non-creole language varieties that have other creole-like features. Nonstandard Brazilian Portuguese has an optional postverbal negator which is unusual in standard Portuguese:

'*Não* quero *não*', literally 'NEG I-want-to NEG', i.e. 'I don't want to' (Marroquim 1934:196). The first *não* can be omitted for emphasis, leaving a construction unknown in European Portuguese: 'Quero *não*.' A variety of Spanish spoken by blacks on the Pacific coast of Colombia also has both initial and sentence-final negators (De Granda 1978:515). Afrikaans has a postverbal negator (as does Dutch) which is followed by a second negator at the end of the sentence (not found in Dutch): 'Ek kom *nie* na jou toe *nie*', literally 'I come not to you not' (Markey 1982:198). Although this has been attributed to an apparently similar construction in dialectal Dutch, Den Besten (1986) finds the parallel faulty; there is a closer parallel to a Khoekhoe structure, lending support to the theory of substrate influence on the development of Afrikaans.

CHART 9. NEGATION	AP	NHJ	TB
9.1 Single negation (verbal)	++	+++	++
9.2 Discontinuous double negation	+0	000	00
9.3 Negative concord	++	+++	00

Of the creoles surveyed, all have a single negator before the verb; none but Angolar has discontinuous double negation. All the Atlantic creoles have negative concord like the Romance languages and archaic or nonstandard Dutch and English.

6.2 Forms of 'be'

While studies of the verb phrase made clear the Atlantic creoles' structural similarity to one another and autonomy *vis-à-vis* their superstrates, it was the first comparative studies of the various words for 'be' in creole and African languages that unequivocally demonstrated that the creoles were not merely simplified forms of European languages. These studies showed that the creoles were in some respects more complex than their lexical source languages in that they made certain grammatical and semantic distinctions not made in the European languages. This can be seen in table 5, which shows that these languages often use quite different words for 'be' depending on whether the following structure is a noun phrase, an adjective or an indication of location. A fourth category, the highlighter, is explained below (6.2.4).

From the perspective of these creole and African languages, these words are not necessarily related beyond the fact that they all occur in the position of the verb (except for the highlighter). Their link here is that they all happen to be translatable by English *be* or its equivalent in the other European superstrate languages. To this category could be added one of the preverbal markers discussed above (6.1.3): the progressive aspect marker also corresponds to a

Table 5. *Forms of 'be' in various creole and African languages*

	—NP	—LOC	—ADJ	HL
ATLANTIC CREOLES				
Jamaican CE	a/iz	de/Ø	Ø	a/iz
Guyanese CE	a	de	Ø	a
Krio CE	na	de	Ø	na
Sranan CE	(n)a/de	de	Ø	(d)a
Negerhollands CD	(n)a	bi(n)	mi	(n)a
Berbice CD	da	jɛndɛ	Ø	da
Haitian CF	se/Ø	Ø/ye	Ø	se
Dominican CF	sé/Ø	Ø	Ø	sé
Palenquero CS	é/hwe	(a)ta	hwe/ta	—
Papiamentu CS	ta	ta	ta	ta
Capeverdian CP	e	sta	e/sta	—
Guiné-Bissau CP	i/sedu	sta	Ø/sta/sedu	—
Angolar CP	tha	tha	tha/Ø	—
AFRICAN LANGUAGES				
Yoruba	ṣe/jẹ́	wà/sí	Ø (rí/yà)	ni
Mandinka	mu	be	Ø	le
NON-ATLANTIC CREOLES				
Seychellois CF	Ø	Ø	Ø	—
Nagamese CAs	ase/Ø	ase	ase/Ø	—
Tok Pisin P/CE	Ø	stap	Ø	em
Nubi CA	Ø	fi/Ø	Ø	—
Zamboangueño CS	Ø	t-alyá	Ø	—

Sources: see Holm 1988–9:175, Holm *et al.* 1999

use of *be* in English ('he *is* writing'). Loosely calling all of these forms of 'be' copulas, Labov (1969) found in a quantitative study that African American Vernacular English had a definite pattern for 'deleting the copula' (i.e. using Ø) depending on the following syntactic environment, i.e. a low rate of deletion before nouns, a higher one elsewhere, etc. Since Labov did not believe at that time that AAVE was historically linked to the English-based Caribbean Creoles, he could offer no explanation for their common, un-European pattern. However, Holm (1976, 1984) showed that a similar pattern prevailed in a number of Atlantic creoles as well as Yoruba, indicating that their copula system reflected that of their substrate. For variationists this constituted 'the first serious evidence for the Creole hypothesis' of the origin of AAVE (Labov 1982:198), although creolists had long been taking other evidence seriously as well.

6.2.1 Equative 'be'

Equative 'be' is a true copula in the Latin sense of a word joining two others, i.e. a subject and a complement as in 'Mary *is* my sister.' *Be* is equative before a noun phrase in that it means that the subject equals (i.e. is the same as) the complement – quite a different meaning from *be* before a locative ('Mary is home') or a participle ('Mary is gardening'). Equative 'be' is expressed by words that are different from those used to express other meanings of 'be' in a number of creole and African languages (table 5). While Mandinka has only one copula before noun phrases, Yoruba has two: '*jẹ́* is used when we are thinking of natural, in-born, permanent characteristics while *ṣe* is used of what is accidental, acquired or temporary' (Rowlands 1969:152). Sranan's two equative copulas also convey this distinction; *na* and *de* have contrasting meanings in two sentences equivalent to 'I am a boatman', i.e. 'mi *na* botoman' expresses general capability or qualifications while 'mi *de* botoman' expresses current occupation (Favery, Johns and Wouk 1976:89). However, Jamaican CE (which is closer to English) does not make this distinction: basilectal *da* and its variant *a* (which become *iz* in the mesolect) express both meanings.

Regarding the overall pattern of the equative copula in table 5, it should be noted that in the African languages as well as the Atlantic creoles based on English and Dutch there is an expressed (i.e. not Ø) form of the copula, although Ø forms begin to appear in the mesolect as the semantic and syntactic distinctions of the basilect become blurred. In the Atlantic creoles based on French, both expressed copulas and Ø can occur before nouns, but the expressed forms predominate, as in the other Atlantic creoles (Valdman 1978:233, Stein 1984:84).

6.2.2 Locative 'be'

A number of Atlantic creoles use a distinct word for 'be' when referring to location. The creole English form of this word, *de*, appears to be derived from the adverb *there*, perhaps converging with substrate forms for locative 'be' such as Twi *dé*. Although the semantic connection between *there* and locative 'be' is clear, the syntactic connection is less so. The link may lie in the fact that *de* can be omitted before locative phrases, e.g. Miskito Coast CE 'Ai no nuo if it [*de*] in di baibl' 'I don't know if it's [there] in the Bible' (Holm 1978:266). This makes *de* ambiguous as either locative 'be' or 'there' after a zero copula. The creole use of *de* may have left its mark on colloquial American English: CE 'We im *de*?' 'Where is he?' may have decreolized to 'Where['s] he *at*?', a usage that strikes British speakers as particularly American.

As previously noted (6.1.3), locative 'be' has the same form as the progressive aspect marker in a number of creole and African languages, probably due to the influence of a substrate feature that is itself the manifestation of a semantic universal. While Bambara *bɛ* has both the locative and the progressive meaning, the Yoruba form for locative 'be' (*wà*, with the negative form *sí*) is less directly related to the progressive marker (Welmers 1973:315). The semantic range of *wà* parallels CE *de* in that both can assert existence, e.g. Yoruba 'Olọ́rún *wà*' 'God exists' and CE 'a *de*' 'I (still) exist', in response to 'How are you?', paralleling Haitian CF 'M la'.

However, the usual creole equivalent of existential 'there is' is '(they/it) have', e.g. Guyanese CE *get*, Haitian CF *gen*, Papiamentu CS *tin*, São Tomé CP *te*, Negerhollands CD *die hab*, Ndyuka CE *a abi*. Bahamian CE uses *it have*, which may be a link to AAVE *it's* (via *it has*). In other partially restructured varieties, Caribbean Spanish uses *tiene* (versus S *hay*) and Brazilian Portuguese uses *tem* (versus P *há*). The creole expressions have been traced to 'Bantu languages where the existential verb is also the verb "to have"' (Ivens Ferraz 1985:111).

Haitian CF normally uses Ø before locative expressions (e.g. 'Li Ø isit' 'S/he is here') but it also has an expressed form (*ye* from F *est* /e/ 'is'), used only at the end of clauses, e.g. 'Kote li *ye*?' 'Where is s/he?' Guyanais CF has the optional use of *sa*: 'Nu (*sa*) ada lit-a' 'We (are) in bed', with *fika* (cf. P *ficar* 'stay') corresponding to clause-final Haitian *ye*: 'Kuma u fika?' 'How are you?' It should be noted that Haitian *ye* is used in clause-final position after nouns and adjectives as well as locatives, although only the latter is indicated on table 5.

6.2.3 *Adjectival verbs*

Creole words that correspond to European adjectives semantically seem to correspond syntactically to verbs of similar meaning in a number of Niger-Congo languages. Arguments for treating these as a subcategory of verbs, at least in basilectal varieties, are discussed in section 6.3.3 in connection with the comparison of such adjectives (or, more accurately, 'adjectival verbs'). As noted, in most Atlantic creoles adjectives do not follow a copula as in their European superstrates; instead they follow the tense and aspect markers that precede verbs, as in African languages like Mandinka and Yoruba. Thus when no such markers are needed, their absence (Ø) corresponds to the position of the word for 'be' in European languages. It is misleading to speak of the 'deletion of the copula' or even 'Ø copula' before adjectival verbs in such languages, since these terms imply that copulas occur (or should occur) in this position. While most Yoruba adjectives are verbs which take no copula, there are some phonaesthetic descriptive words unrelated to verbs which do follow a copula (*rí*), while another copula (*yà*) is followed by words 'denoting a type of person of whom Yoruba society disapproves' (e.g. *òle* 'lazy')

(Rowlands 1969:122, 155). While this latter category corresponds semantically to English adjectives, it is in fact made up of nouns. This distinction is not found in the creoles.

As noted above, adjectival verbs in the Atlantic creoles can take preverbal markers of anterior tense (6.1.2) and completive aspect (6.1.5). In some creoles they can also take the marker of progressive aspect (6.1.3), indicating that the quality is inchoative (i.e. coming into being) or is being intensified, e.g. Sranan CE 'a *e* dipi' 'it is getting deep' or Haitian CF 'l'*ap* malad' 'he is getting sick'. This is also a widespread feature in African languages, e.g. Yoruba 'ó *n*tutù' 'it is getting cold' (Rowlands 1969:61).

In table 5, no copula occurs before adjectival verbs in any creole based on English or French. Of those based on Dutch, Negerhollands has the expressed form *mi*; this alternates with *we:s*, which is the form that occurs in all environments (except the highlighter) if a preverbal marker co-occurs, much like *wa* in Berbice CD, which otherwise has no copula before adjectives. The Atlantic creoles based on Spanish and Portuguese do not follow this pattern, apparently because of superstrate influence. Palenquero CS and Cape Verdean CP both have two different expressed copulas before adjectives which preserve their superstrates' distinction between states that are permanent (from S, P *ser*) and those that are temporary (from S, P *estar*). In both creoles the former copula occurs before noun phrases and the latter before locative expressions, as in their superstrates.

6.2.4 Highlighter 'be'

The Atlantic creoles have a particle that highlights or emphasizes the following word to make it the focus of discourse. This emphasis could be translated into English by simply stressing the word – '*John* lives there' (not Jim) – or by using *it's* to introduce it: 'It's John who lives there.' Yoruba, like a number of other West African languages, has a highlighter, a morpheme that emphasizes the word it occurs next to, somewhat like English *it's* except that the Yoruba highlighter (*ni*) occurs after the word or clause that it emphasizes, which is brought to the front of the sentence. For example 'mo rà aṣọ' 'I bought cloth' becomes 'aṣọ *ni* mo rà' 'It was cloth I bought' (not paper). If a verb is to be emphasized, it is fronted and prefixed by its initial consonant plus *i* and then recopied in its original position, i.e. 'nwọn *pa* a' 'They killed it' becomes 'pí*pa* ni nwọn *pa* á' 'They *killed* it', literally 'Killing it-was they killed it' (Rowlands 1969:189). This process, which is called verb-fronting or predicate clefting, is unknown in the European superstrate languages but is found throughout the Caribbean creoles. It is discussed here since it provides a convenient way to identify the highlighter in these creoles (italicized below).

Note that adjectives can usually undergo the same kind of fronting with recopying as verbs, indicating that they are in fact a subcategory of verbs in these languages:

Jamaican CE	*Iz* tiif dem tiif it.
	'It was certainly stolen.' (Cassidy 1964:273)
Haitian CF	*Se* malad Bouki malad, li pa mouri.
	'Bouki is SICK, not dead.' (DeGraff ms.)
Papiamentu CS	*Ta* traha e *ta* traha.
	'S/he is really working.' (Michel ms.)
Negerhollands CD	*Da* breek sender ka breek.
	'They are BROKEN' (Hesseling 1905:155)

This construction seems to be confined to the Atlantic creoles. It does not occur in Nubi Creole Arabic (Owens and Khamis ms.) and a similar construction in Tok Pisin is only partially equivalent:

Em kros   ia   (we)   mi kros   long en.
HL be-angry DEM (REL) 1s be-angry LOC 3s
'It's that antagonism that I am angry about.' (Faraclas ms.)

Here the highlighter *em* (which also functions as the third person singular pronoun) precedes the fronted element, and a relative clause marker optionally follows. However, the structure is not uniform even among the Atlantic creoles. In the Papiamentu sentence above there is a second *ta*, which seems more likely to be a preverbal marker than another highlighter – this construction serves either to emphasize the meaning of the verb (as in the other creoles) or to emphasize the progressive aspect of the verb (Michel ms.); nor does Papiamentu recopy fronted adjectives: '*Ta* malu mes Hose ta' 'Joseph is really sick' – perhaps under the influence of Dutch or Spanish. On the other hand, in Angolar CP fronted verbs are not introduced by a highlighter: 'Vugu ma kɔmpa vugu' 'The *compadre* really had a fight' (Lorenzino ms.). Similar verb fronting without a highlighter is found in two semi-creoles: Afrikaans 'Kom sal hij kom' 'He will certainly come' (Stolz 1986:207), and nonstandard Brazilian Portuguese 'Falar ele falou' 'He certainly talked' (L. Cagliari p.c.).

The creole highlighters can introduce other elements besides verbs and adjectives, but these structures are less striking since, as in English, the element is merely fronted without being recopied in its original position. However, the creole highlighters do have another function without a European parallel; this is their use before question words, which are also fronted:

Jamaican CE	*A wa* du yu? 'What is bothering you?'
	HL what bother you (Patrick ms.)
Haitian CF	*Se kimoun* ou ye? 'Who are you?'
	HL who you be (DeGraff ms.)
Papiamentu CS	*Ta kiko* bo ta hasi? 'What are you doing?'
	HL what you PROG do (Michel ms.)
Negerhollands CD	*Da wie* bin daeso? 'Who is there?'
	HL who be there (De Kleine ms.)
Nubi CA	*Munú yá* gi- ja? 'Who is coming?'
	who HL PROG come (Owens and Khamis ms.)
Tok Pisin PE	*Em* olsem wanem [na] yu mek-im?
	HL how [and] you do -TR
	'How did you do it?' (Faraclas ms.)

Note that the structure for highlighting question words, with the emphasizer preceding, is more similar within the Atlantic group, although there are differences. Among the non-Atlantic creoles above, the Nubi emphasizer follows the question word, and although Tok Pisin *em* precedes it, the following clause can be conjoined.

In Yoruba, which is typical of the languages that form the Atlantic creoles' substrate, the highlighter *ni* must also be used with question words: '*ta* ['who?'] and *kí* ['what?'] . . . are always emphatic, i.e. followed by *ni*' (Rowlands 1969:26). Bailey (1966:88ff.) treats the Jamaican CE highlighter *a* as an integral part of question words like *a-wa* 'what?', noting that 'the introductory *a* is often omitted in questions, probably as the result of the competing English forms'.

The creole highlighters represent a syntactic category in the substrate languages that does not correspond very closely to anything in the superstrate languages. The variety of forms that the highlighter has taken in the creoles suggests a ghost-like syntactic function rummaging through the European lexicons in search of some suitable corporeal form. Its earliest form may well have been African: *na*, the highlighter in the Surinamese creoles and Krio as well as a variant of Negerhollands *da*, was traced to the Twi highlighter *na* by Schuchardt (1914b:132). Given the alternation of apical consonants in the creoles (5.6.4), *na* seems likely to have given rise to *da* (possibly influenced by E *that* or D *dat*) and the reduced form *a* found in creoles based on English, Dutch and even French. In Guyanais CF the highlighter *a* alternates with the more general copula *sa*, used before nouns and adjectives (e.g. '*sa* bo' 'it's good'), while *a* is used elsewhere (e.g. '*a* mo' 'it's me') (St Jacques-Fauquenoy 1972:228). The Haitian CF highlighter *se* seems likely to come from F *c'est*

/se/ 'it's'. It should be noted that the creoles based on French, Dutch and English have highlighters that are nearly identical in form to equative 'be', the link possibly being the frequency with which the highlighter also occurs before noun phrases.

In the mesolect, Jamaican CE uses *iz* as a highlighter instead of basilectal *a*, as does Miskito Coast CE: 'O laad, *iz* hou orl truo mi wie laik dat?' 'Oh Lord, how is it that Earl could have rejected me like that?' (Holm 1978:271). In both creoles *das* functions as a highlighter with somewhat more deictic force: '*Das* di smuok' 'That's the smoke' (270). While English *that's* was clearly the model for CE *das*, it should be noted that there are no rules within the creole for contracting *iz* to *z* or *s* as in English, suggesting that CE *das* functions as a single morpheme like the highlighter *da*, which is homophonous with a demonstrative pronoun meaning 'that'. This interpretation is borne out by the occurrence of *das* as 'that', e.g. '*Das* would be de bes' place.' Interestingly, African American Vernacular English has a parallel form /ðæs/ for 'that's', which differs from the contraction usually used by whites, /ðæts/ (Labov 1972:114ff.).

To conclude, table 5 reveals some clearly discernible patterns for the predominating form of 'be' in relation to the following syntactic environment: among the Atlantic creoles, with few exceptions, an expressed copula is required before noun phrases; a copula of a different form occurs before locative expressions, but this can sometimes be deleted; usually no copula occurs before adjectives; a highlighter of the same form as the equative copula often occurs before fronted constituents.

The principal exceptions are Papiamentu CS and Angolar CP (which have a uniform expressed copula) and Haitian and Dominican CF (which can have a zero form throughout, except for the highlighter). Two Atlantic creoles which have expressed copulas before adjectives, Palenquero CS and Cape Verdean CP, preserve their superstrates' distinction between permanent and temporary states.

The general Atlantic pattern is not found in the non-Atlantic creoles. Nubi can have zero copulas throughout and Nagamese can have expressed copulas throughout, and neither has a highlighter comparable to the kind generally found in the Atlantic creoles. Tok Pisin has the system of copulas most resembling the general pattern of the Atlantic creoles, but it has no expressed copula before predicate NPs. Zamboangueño, which has an Austronesian substrate like Tok Pisin, has a similar pattern of copulas but no highlighter, while Seychellois CF has no pre-predicate copulas at all.

Beyond the importance of substrate influence on the copula systems of the Atlantic creoles, this comparison makes clear that creoles are not merely simplified forms of their superstrate languages. As noted above, in some areas of syntax the creoles are more complex in that they make grammatical and semantic distinctions not made in their lexical source languages.

CHART 10. THE COPULA	AP	NHJ	TB
10.1 Expressed equative copula (with NP)................++		+++	00
10.2 Distinct locative copula ....++		+0+	++
10.3 Zero copula with adjective? ....+0		0++	++
10.4 Highlighter with question words ....?+		+++	++
10.5 Highlighter with other structures ....?+		+++	++
10.6 Existential ('have' = 'there is'?)...............++		+++	++

All of the Atlantic creoles surveyed here have an expressed copula before predicate noun phrases (this varies with zero in the case of Haitian). Most have a distinct copula before locative predicates. All treat adjectives as verbs requiring no copula (except Papiamentu, influenced by Dutch and Spanish). Except for Angolar, all use highlighters before question words and some other structures. All express existence by '(it) has'.

6.3 Serial verbs

Serial verbs are frequently found in the Atlantic creoles, e.g. the two verbs in Miskito Coast CE 'all di waari *ron kom* bai mi', literally 'all the wild-boars *ran came* by me', i.e. 'came running up to me'. As their name implies, they consist of a series of two (or more) verbs; they both have the same subject and are not joined by a conjunction ('and') or a complementizer ('to') as they would be in European languages. This working definition of serial verbs was proposed by Jansen, Koopman and Muysken (1978:125); they went on to exclude verb combinations with an auxiliary, modal or infinitive, but this part of their definition was rejected by Boretzky (1983:164) since these categories are not always appropriate for creole and African languages. While the closest models for creole serial verb constructions are to be found in the Kwa languages (see below), European languages have some partially analogous constructions with conjunctions or complementizers that can sometimes be omitted, e.g. French '*Viens prendre* ta lettre' and its English translation '*Come take* your letter' or '*Go get* your book.'

Serial verbs can be treated in the context of either lexicon or syntax. Valdman (1976:228) sees them as 'ensembles lexicalisés' in that the combined meaning of the verbs is not always immediately deducible from the sum of the parts, e.g. Haitian CF *mennen vini* 'to bring' (literally 'lead come'), requiring the combination to be treated in the lexicon. However, the combined meaning of the verbs can be seen as falling into several broad categories; one of these is directionality, as in the above examples in which 'come' conveys the idea of 'motion toward'. The opposite idea, 'motion away from', can be achieved by using the word equivalent to 'go', as in the following three-verb series meaning 'run away from him' (literally 'run go leave him') from Alleyne (1980:12):

> Jamaican CE   ron go lef im
> Papiamentu CS kore bay lagá e
> Haitian CF   kuri ale lese li
> Saramaccan CE kule go disa en

A similar use of 'go' for 'away' can be found in other creoles, e.g. Negerhollands CD 'Džak a *kuri lo* si pat', literally 'Jack ANT *run go* along path' i.e. 'Jack ran away' (Van Diggelen 1978). This parallels a structure in the Kwa languages, e.g. Ibo 'ọ gbàrà ọsọ́ gáa áhyà', literally 'he *ran go* market', i.e. 'he ran to the market' (Huttar 1974:58). In these languages, verbs in series often serve the semantic function of European adverbs or prepositions.

This kind of serial verb construction is also found in a non-Atlantic creole, Tok Pisin, as in most of its Austronesian substrate languages: '*kisim* plet i *go*', literally 'get plate he go', i.e. 'take the plate away' (Faraclas ms.). In Nubi, however, *ruwa* 'go' cannot be used in this way (Owens and Khamis ms.).

Another broad semantic category that serial verbs can fall into is the instrumental, e.g. Ndyuka 'a *teke* nefi *koti* a meti', literally 'he took knife cut the meat', i.e. 'he cut the meat with a knife' (Huttar 1981). An African parallel is Yoruba 'ó *fi* ọbẹ *gé* ẹran', also literally 'he *took* knife *cut* meat' (Huttar 1981, but in conventional Yoruba spelling). Jansen *et al.* (1978) note that the instrumental construction with 'take' is usually found in the Kwa languages rather than other members of the Niger-Congo family, but Boretzky (1983:177–8) points out parallel constructions in the West Atlantic, Mande and Gur groups. Still he concurs with their general conclusion that the presence of certain kinds of serial verb constructions in the Atlantic creoles points to the importance of the substrate influence of the Kwa group, where such constructions are widespread. They are largely absent in the Guiné CP of Senegal, with its non-Kwa substratum, which supports this conclusion. However, more general kinds of serial verb constructions (e.g. in which each verb represents part of a complex sequence of actions) are found in languages around the world and are by no means confined to the Atlantic creoles:

> Papiamentu CS El a   *bula kai lora para.*
> He PAST jump fall roll stop (Michel ms.)

Nubi CA	Umwon kan *agderi ruwa abidu jeribu so* kazi tomwon.
	3p ANT able go begin try do work their
	'They were able to go and begin to try to do their work.' (Owens and Khamis ms.)
ZM	*Nesesíta mandá ánda prúba saká* el kárt ditúyo ermána.
	Need tell go try get DET card of-your sister
	'It is necessary to tell [someone] to go try to get your sister's card.' (Santoro ms. citing Forman 1972:205)

The following subsections will discuss certain serial verbs that are part of some well-known creole constructions. In addition to these and the serial verb constructions discussed above indicating directionality and instrumentality, there are some syntactic features taken up elsewhere in the present chapter that may have evolved from serial verb constructions either in Africa or in the New World, e.g. the complementizer/modal/preposition *fu* or *pu* (6.1.8), the completive aspect markers *don*, *fini* and *kaba* (6.1.5) and perhaps the irrealis marker *go* (6.1.6).

6.3.1 Serial 'give' meaning 'to, for'
Most of the Atlantic creoles have a serial verb construction in which the verb meaning 'give' occurs as the second element with the meaning of the preposition 'to' or 'for':

Krio CE	Olu *fes* di buk *gi* mi.
	Olu fetch the book give me
	'Olu brought the book to me.' (Yillah ms.)
Haitian CF	Boukinèt te *pran* yon fle *bay* Bouki.
	Boukinèt ANT take a flower give Bouki
	'Boukinèt gave a flower to Bouki.' (DeGraff ms.)
Papiamentu CS	*Kumpra* pan *duna* e yu.
	buy bread give the baby
	'Buy bread for the baby.' (Michel ms.)
Angolar CP	Thange *bi* ki ɔtɔ mɛ *ra* nɔ.
	lady come with more food give 1p
	'The lady came with more food for us.' (Lorenzino ms.)
Negerhollands CD	Ju kan *fang* som fligi *gi* mi.
	you can catch some flies give me
	'You can catch some flies for me.' (De Kleine ms.)
Tok Pisin PE	*Kisim* plet *givim* mi. 'Give me the plate.'
	get plate give me (Faraclas ms.)

207

This structure seems to be largely confined to the Atlantic creoles; it does occur in Tok Pisin, but not in other non-Atlantic creoles such as Nubi (Owens and Khamis ms.). Schuchardt (1882a:913) was the first to note that the prepositional use of 'give' is found in both West African languages and creole Portuguese, English and French. Herskovits and Herskovits (1936:131) pointed out specific African constructions as plausible models, such as Ashanti *ma* or Ga *ha*, both 'for' as well as 'give', to which Goodman (1964:63) added the parallel Ewe *na*. Yoruba *fún* 'give' can also be used serially, e.g. 'rà á *fún* mi' 'buy it for me' (Rowlands 1969:83).

6.3.2 Serial 'say' meaning 'that'

In a number of creoles and post-creoles the verb meaning 'say' can be used to introduce a quotation, and in some varieties this word can also be used after verbs whose meaning involves thinking (e.g. 'know', 'believe') to introduce a sentence complement which would begin with *that* in English:

AAVE	They told me *say* they couldn't get it.
	(Rickford 1977:212)
Sranan CE	M sab *tak* a tru. 'I know *that* it's true.'
	(Voorhoeve 1962:26)
Krio CE	A yɛri *se* Olu de fes di buk kam. (Yillah ms.)
	'I heard *that* Olu is bringing the book along.'
Gullah CE	dɛ lɔ *se* wi tu ol. 'They admit *that* we're too old.'
	(Turner 1949:211)
Negerhollands CD	am noit sa prat *se* a Tekoma a mata di kui.
	'He will not say *that* it was Tekoma who killed the
	cow.' (Van Diggelen 1978:71)
Berbice CD	ɛkɛ pamtɛ ju *bi* fa las jer ɛk a motɛ mu kiki di
	dispɛnsa. 'I told you *that* (lit. 'say') last year I went
	to see the dispenser.' (Robertson 1979:148)

Herskovits and Herskovits (1936:133) pointed out that this creole construction corresponded to usage in West African languages such as Ewe, in which the verb *krɔipi* 'say' is repeated to introduce quotations. Turner (1949:201) pointed out the formal and syntactic similarity of Gullah *se* and Twi *sɛ* 'that, saying' and English *say*. Cassidy (1961:63) noted that the pronunciation of Jamaican *se* is /sɛ/ when it means 'that' rather than /sey/, leading him to support the connection with Akan *se*. Boretzky (1983:177) finds the lexical borrowing of *se* into the creoles an inadequate explanation in light of the fact that the Surinamese creoles have completely different forms, i.e. Sranan *tak(i)* and Saramaccan *táa*, leading him to believe that the substrate influence on this construction lay in the grammar rather than the lexicon. Frajzyngier (1984) takes the opposite position, claiming that the origin of CE *se* is more likely to be English *say* since none of the French-based creoles has a lexically and syntactically parallel complementizer. Frajzyngier was apparently unaware of the parallel forms in the Dutch-based creoles; while a case might be made for Negerhollands *se* being a borrowing from Virgin Islands CE, it could be derived from Dutch *zeggen* 'to say' via quite regular phonological rules. However, there is no possibility of such lexical borrowing in the case of the Berbice CD complementizer *bi* from *bifi* 'say'.

The evidence from creole French does not favour the lexical versus syntactic origin of the complementizer in CE as unambiguously as Frajzingier assumes. Pringle (1985) notes that in Seychellois CF verbs like *dir* 'say' and *uar* 'see' can take the complementizer *pur-dir* (cf. F *pour dire* 'to say'): 'i al dir li *pur-dir* sa pa ê dimun' 'He goes to tell him *that* it's not a person' (Corne 1977). The latter suggests a calque; Sebba (1984) notes a similar construction in the eastern Bantu languages likely to have influenced Seychellois CF.

The case for substrate syntactic influence on serial 'say' in the Atlantic creoles seems quite convincing, but such influence by no means precludes converging influence from language universals or lexical diffusion. Evidence supporting universals can be found in biblical Hebrew: *lé'môr* 'saying that' corresponds directly to the 'spake . . . saying' construction frequently encountered in translations of the Bible into English and even Tok Pisin PE, e.g. 'Em i tok *se*: Yupela kam . . .' 'He spoke saying: Come . . .' (Todd 1984:203). Todd notes that Tok Pisin *se* and serial *i spik* belong to 'mission-influenced speech . . . quite widely used by older speakers'. It is also conceivable that these constructions were reinforced by German or British missionaries who had learned Pidgin English in West Africa, which has the complementizer *sei* (140). Owens and Khamis (ms.) note that in Nubi CA the subordinator after verbs meaning 'say' or 'believe' can be *gali*, from Arabic *gaal* 's/he said', although they know of no Arabic dialect in which the latter is used as such a subordinator.

Sebba (1984a) finds support for the spread of *se* via lexical diffusion in that its similarity in form to *say* makes it acceptable in varieties quite close to standard English, e.g. upper mesolectal Caribbean CE, Black London English and African American Vernacular English. A parallel even exists in the nonstandard Dutch of Suriname, which has been influenced by Sranan CE: 'Want soms zeg ik hem ook *zeg* nee je moet niet zo koppig zijn', literally

'Because sometimes I say to him also *say* no, you shouldn't be so stubborn' (De Kleine 1999).

6.3.3 Serial 'pass' meaning 'than'

In a number of Atlantic creoles, a verb meaning 'pass', 'surpass' or 'exceed' is used after adjectives or adjectival verbs to indicate comparison:

> Krio CE   Olu big *pas* in padi.
> 'Olu is bigger than his friend' (Yillah ms.)

> Haitian CF   Boukinèt bèl *pase* Mari.
> 'Boukinèt is more beautiful than Mari' (DeGraff ms.)

> Principe CP   rimá mɛ mayš fɔrti *pasa* mi.
> 'My brother is stronger than I' (Valkhoff 1966:102)

> Nubi CA   Uwo kebir *futu* ana.
> 'S/he is bigger than I' (Owens and Khamis ms.)

Note that in Tok Pisin PE, the corresponding verb *winim* also means 'surpass', but it is not part of a serial verb construction: 'Kros bilong mi *winim* kros bilong yu' 'I'm angrier than you' (Faraclas ms.).

Arends (1986) notes that an exact parallel to the Atlantic creole structure is found in a serial verb construction that is widespread in Kwa and other West African languages, e.g. Ewe 'so lolo *wu* tedzi', literally 'horse big exceed donkey', i.e. 'the horse is bigger than the donkey'. As in the creoles, the first element of the serial verb is the adjectival verb (*lolo* 'be big') and the second is the verb meaning 'exceed' or 'surpass' (*wu*). Bantu languages like kiMbundu have a partly parallel construction: 'iu *uatundu* una mu kuuaba', literally 'this exceeds that in beauty', i.e. 'This one is more beautiful than that one.' This non-serial-verb construction is rare in creoles, but Arends provides an example in Sranan: 'a *moro* mi na koni' 'he exceeds me in cleverness', i.e. 'he is cleverer than I am'. Faraclas (ms.) notes an exact parallel in Tok Pisin: 'mi *winim* yu long kros' 'I'm angrier than you.'

Boretzky (1983:104–7) suggests that creole constructions closest to the model 'big pass me' are probably the most conservative and are likely to be in the process of being replaced by structures more similar to those of the superstrates. The Príncipe CP structure 'mayš fɔrti pasa mi', literally 'more strong pass me', contains the element *mayš* 'more' which is part of the corresponding superstrate structure (cf. P 'mais forte que'). This alternates with another structure in which CP *pasa* is replaced by *di* (cf. P 'mais de dez' 'more than ten'). Similarly, the CF construction with *pase* alone appears to be the oldest; it alternates with *pli . . . pase* and *pli . . . ki*, the last being closest to F 'il est *plus* grand *que* moi'.

CHART 11. SERIAL VERBS   AP   NHJ   TB
11.1 Directional with 'go' .... ++   +++   +0
11.2 Directional with 'come' .... ++   +++   +0
11.3 Serial 'give' meaning 'to, for' .... ++   +++   +0

11.4 Serial 'say' meaning 'that' .... +0   +0+   0+
11.5 Serial 'pass' meaning 'more than' .... 0R   ?+0   ++
11.6 Three serial verb constructions .... ++   +++   ++
11.7 Serial constructions with four or more verbs .... ?+   ?+0   ++

To summarize the occurrence of serial verb constructions, most are found in the Atlantic creoles and in Tok Pisin; some are even found in Nubi Creole Arabic. However, a broader survey reveals that they are largely absent in creoles such as Cape Verdean and Guiné-Bissau CP and Palenquero CS, which were less influenced by Kwa languages (Holm *et al.* 1998).

Regarding the syntactic status of creole adjectives as possible verbs, in Jamaican CE the equivalent of serial 'pass' is *muor an*, which is used with adjectival verbs in exactly the same way it is used with other verbs in the basilect, i.e. 'Mieri *big muor an* Jan' is parallel to 'Mieri *wok muor an* Jan' 'Mary works more than John' (Bailey 1966:128). Thus at this level of the continuum there is a good case for treating adjectives as a subcategory of stative verbs. As noted above (6.2.4), they are fronted in predicate clefting and recopied in their original position, like verbs but unlike words in other syntactic categories. Valdman (1978:245) notes the usefulness of this syntactic test for creole verbs. For example, Haitian CF *souèf* corresponds to the French noun *soif* 'thirst' but it can only be a verb since 'Bouki *souèf*' 'Bouki is thirsty' can undergo predicate clefting to become 'Sé *souèf* Bouki *souèf*,' 'Bouki is really thirsty.' The verbal status of *souèf* might be further supported by the fact that it can take preverbal markers such as anterior *te*: 'Bouki *te* souèf' 'Bouki was thirsty.' However, as DeGraff (ms.) points out, Haitian and other creole preverbal markers can often precede not only predicate adjectives but also predicate nouns and locative phrases, indicating that what these markers actually specify are predicates in general rather than verbs in particular.

While Valdman's (1978) argument remains convincing for accepting predicate clefting as a valid test for the verbal status of adjectives in certain creoles, there are some valid reasons for assigning separate syntactic status to adjectives and verbs on leaving the basilect in a creole English continuum. Bailey (1966:42) points out that only adjectives can take the mesolectal comparative ending *-a* (e.g. *biga* 'bigger') and occur before nouns; in addition, verbs cannot follow the intensifiers *so* and *tuu*. Moreover, the occurrence of preverbal markers before adjectives is not convincing proof of their verbal status since preverbal markers often occur directly before other syntactic categories; thus they do not specify verbs but rather predicates (Holm *et al.* 1999).

Historically many creoles represent the continuing merger of two systems: one with strong African traits (the most conservative creoles and the basilects of continua) and the other with strong European traits (the acrolects). Whether adjectives are verbs, like many other questions in creole syntax, depends on which system predominates in the variety under discussion.

CHART 12. ADJECTIVES: VERBS?	AP	NHJ	TB
12.1 Preverbal markers before adjectives	++	+++	+0
12.2 Preverbal markers before nouns	0+	?+0	+0
12.3 Preverbal markers before locatives	++	?+0	++
12.4 Predicate clefting: adjectives or adjectival verbs	0+	+++	+0
12.5 Predicate clefting: other verbs	++	+++	+0
12.6 Comparison with 'pass'	0R	0+0	++
12.7 Comparison as in superstrate	++	+++	++

6.4 The noun phrase

The various elements that make up the noun phrase in the creoles are so closely interrelated that none can be discussed meaningfully without reference to the others. Dealing with number (e.g. singular versus plural) requires reference to determiners (e.g. *the*) and word order, and word order is a key element in indicating possession or natural gender. The following discussion has been divided up somewhat arbitrarily for the sake of convenience, however. Table 6 provides an overview of several parts of this discussion, focusing on the

Table 6. *Determiners in various creole languages and Yoruba*

	the man	*this* man	*these* men
ATLANTIC			
Príncipe CP	ɔ́mi *sé*	ɔ́mi *šaki*	inɛ ɔ́mi sé
Haitian CF	nɔ̃m *la*	nɔ̃m *sa*-a	nɔ̃m sa-*yo*
Papiamentu CS	e hòmber	e hòmber *aki*	e hòmber-*nan* aki
Saramaccan CE	di ómi	di ómi *aki*	déé òmi aki
Sranan CE	*a* man	a man *disi*	den man disi
Jamaican CE	*di* man	dis man (*ya*)	dem man ya
Yoruba	ọkùnrin *náà*	ọkùnrin *yi*	àwọn ọkùnrin yǐ
NON-ATLANTIC			
Tok Pisin P/CE	man	man *ia*	ol man ia
Nubi CA	ragi	ragi *de*	rujál *dolde*
Seychellois CF	*sa* zonm	*sa* zonm	sa ban zonm

definite articles, demonstratives and ways of indicating plurality. This table is based on information in Chapuis (ms.), Faraclas (ms.), Günther (1973:55), Owens and Khamis (ms.), Rowlands (1966:195–7), and Taylor (1977:174).

6.4.1 Determiners

In the first two creoles examined in table 6 above, the definite article 'the' does not follow the word order of the superstrate language: while the article precedes the noun in Portuguese (*o homem*) and French (*l'homme*), as it does in English, it follows the noun in Príncipe CP (ɔ́mi *sé*) and Haitian CF (nɔ̃m *la*). The parallel to a number of relevant African languages such as Yoruba is especially clear when there is an intervening phrase or clause (indicated in parentheses below):

> Príncipe CP 'bášta (di óru) *sé*',
>> lit. 'cane (of gold) *the*' (Boretzky 1983:97)
>
> Haitian CF 'istwa (wu rakonté li) *a*',
>> lit. 'story (you told it) *the*'
>> i.e. 'the story you told' (Boretzky 1983:98)
>
> Yoruba   'owó (tí nwọ́n fún mi) *náà*',
>> lit. 'money (which they gave me) *the*' (Rowlands 1969:197)

In other words, it is not just that the definite articles come after the nouns to which they refer, but rather that they mark the end of the entire noun phrase (note that Haitian CF *a* is an allomorph of *la* in table 6). Except for the decreolized varieties, the creoles appear not to have borrowed definite articles from the superstrate languages but rather to have created them anew from demonstratives and other particles. Príncipe CP *sé* appears to come from P *esse* 'that', which is also the likely source (along with S *ese*) of Papiamentu CS *e* (note that the pronoun referring to 'e hòmber *aki*' is 'esaki' 'this one'). Haitian CF *la* appears not to come from the French feminine definite article of the same form but rather *là* 'there', which can add the idea of definiteness, e.g. F 'cet homme-*là*' 'that man (there)'. However, there may also have been convergence with Ewe *la* 'the', which not only has the same form but also occurs at the end of the noun phrase (Sylvain 1936:60). Saramaccan *di* and Sranan *a* appear to come from E *this* and *that* respectively; other restructured languages have definite articles more clearly derived from superstrate demonstratives, e.g. Seychellois CF *sa* (cf. F *ça* 'that') or Cape Verde CP *kel* and Malayo-Portuguese *akel* (cf. P *aquel* 'that [yonder]'). The Afrikaans article *die* (corresponding to Dutch *die* 'that' rather than *de* 'the') may be a relexification of the Malayo-Portuguese article *akel*, but may also represent a universal. It seems likely that deixis or pointing plays an important role during the early stages of pidginization, when terms like 'that' and 'there' may have replaced more abstract notions of definiteness like 'the'. Also, it is known that definite articles have evolved from demonstratives in a number of cases of language change, such as the transition from Latin to the Romance languages and from Proto-Germanic to German and English.

The use of articles in the creoles does not necessarily follow usage in their lexical source language. Bickerton (1981:56) claimed that 'virtually all creoles have . . . a definite article for presupposed-specific NP; an indefinite article for asserted-specific ambiguous NP; and zero for nonspecific NP'. While the first claim is true of the Atlantic creoles, it is not valid in non-Atlantic creoles such as Tok Pisin and Nubi, in which the bare noun can be interpreted as definite. Regarding the second claim about the universality of indefinite articles in creoles, Mufwene (1986b) claims that CE *wan* should be treated as a numeral, i.e. as corresponding to E *one* rather than the indefinite article *a*. However, this interpretation would not be suitable for cases like Miskito Coast CE 'i tai im ananiit *wan* trii' 'He tied him under *a* tree.' Like *a* in English, CE *wan* asserts a specific instance of the category *tree*, which is not presupposed; its relevance is not really to numbers since a person could hardly be under more than one tree at once. Many substrate languages do not have any article in such a case, e.g. Yoruba 'oun jóko ní abẹ́ igi Ø', literally 'he sat under tree'; *kan* 'a, one' would be added only for the unlikely emphasis that the person in question was sitting under only one tree rather than more. Thus the creole usage of the indefinite articles differs in some respects from both superstrate and substrate usages but combines some aspects of each. Bickerton's third claim seems valid: the Atlantic creoles use a singular noun without an article to refer to general categories, unlike their lexical source languages. This is found in Miskito Coast CE 'Ø rigl iz jos a shaat ting' 'A riddle is just a short thing.' A parallel is found in substrate languages like Yoruba: 'ewúrẹ́ Ø gọ̀ púpọ̀', literally 'goat is-stupid very', i.e. 'a goat is very stupid' or 'goats are very stupid' (Rowlands 1969:42).

It can be seen in table 6 that to form the demonstrative ('*this* man'), a number of creoles add a word originally meaning 'here' to the noun and definite article (cf. P *aqui*, S *aquí*). Saramaccan uses *aki* after the noun while Sranan uses *disi* (cf. *this*). Like its equivalent in Seychellois, Haitian CF *sa* is from F *ça* 'that (one)'. Valdman (1978:366) notes that the combination of CF articles and demonstratives results in semantic nuances that can be conveyed in French only periphrastically, e.g. Haitian CF *chat-la* 'the (previously mentioned) cat' versus *chat-la-a* 'the cat (in question)'. He cites this as evidence of the creoles' systematicity and complexity, which must be seen as quite independent of those of French.

6.4.2 Number

Unlike nouns in their European lexical source languages, creole nouns are not inflected to indicate number, e.g. CE 'aal di animal__' 'all the animals'. Although some creole words contain fossilized remnants of plural inflections from their lexical source languages (e.g. CE 'tuulz' 'tool' or CF 'zanj' 'angel' from F *les anges*), these no longer function as inflections (4.5.1). However, in most of the Atlantic creoles nouns can co-occur with a free morpheme which indicates plurality and is homophonous with the third person plural pronoun 'they'. In table 6 the Atlantic creole noun phrases in the last column (*these men*) include this morpheme, which is italicized. In this column the pluralizer co-occurs with the demonstrative, which can be omitted, e.g. Príncipe CP '*inɛ* ɔ́mi' 'the men' or Haitian CF 'nõm *yo*'. The pluralizer is most frequently used with animate nouns, but this is not always the case, e.g. Nigerian PE 'dì nyám *dɛ̀m*' 'the yams'. The plural marker also conveys the idea of definiteness, as does the use of 'they' as a pluralizer in substrate languages like Yoruba, e.g. '*àwɔn* ɔkùnrin' 'the men'. In some African languages the plural suffix is closely related in form to the pronoun, e.g. Vai *-nu* (cf. *anu* 'they') or Malinke *lu* (cf. *alu* 'they'). Parallel constructions are frequent not only in West African languages but also, coincidentally, in the Austronesian languages which form the substrate of Tok Pisin, in which *ol* (cf. E *all*) serves as both the pronoun 'they' and the pluralizer (Faraclas ms.). Note that Seychellois CF, which also has an Austronesian language in its substrate (Malagasy), has the pluralizer *ban* (cf. F *bande* 'band, group'), also used as a pronoun meaning 'those' or 'some'.

Even certain sociolects of nonstandard Afrikaans use *hulle* 'they' to form the definite plural, as in 'die skaap *hulle*' 'the sheep [plural]', although in standard Afrikaans *hulle* can be used only after nouns referring to persons to include associates, e.g. 'Oom Sarel *hulle*' 'Uncle Charles and his people'. While possible sources for this construction include Nama (Hottentot), Eastern Malay (via Malayo-Portuguese) and even Frisian, it is also found in a number of West African languages, e.g. Yoruba '*àwɔn* Táíwò' meaning 'Taiwo and his family, schoolmates, or friends' depending on the situation. This is paralleled in most Atlantic Creoles, e.g. Miskito Coast CE 'di sukya *dem*' 'the medicine man and his lot', and may be connected to nonstandard English 'Mary and them' with the same meaning. In the Bahamas, 'Mary-dem' is decreolized to 'Mary and those'.

There are also several Atlantic creoles which have no 'they' pluralizer. One is Palenquero CS, which marks plurals with the free morpheme *ma* (cf. the dissimilar *ané* 'they'), which combines the semantic properties of definiteness and plurality, e.g. '*ma* ombre' 'the men'. This creole pluralizer appears to be derived from the Bantu plural prefix *ma-*. Other Atlantic creoles lacking the 'they' pluralizer use morphemes derived from plural determiners in the lexical source language, e.g. Lesser Antillean CF '*se* nõm-la' 'the men' (cf. F *ces* 'these/those') or Cape Verdean CP '*keš* rapaz' 'the boys' (cf. P *aqueles* 'those').

In table 6, the Nubi CA singular form (*ragi* 'man') comes from the Cairene dialect of Arabic, while the plural (*rujál* 'men') comes from Sudanese or southern Egyptian.

6.4.3 Gender

Like distinctions of number, distinctions of grammatical gender in the European lexical source languages were not maintained by inflections on creole nouns or adjectives. For example, the gender agreement in the Spanish NP '*una* cas*a* más bonit*a*' 'a prettier house' is not found in Palenquero CS 'uñ kasa má bonit*o*', in which the article and adjective are derived from the Spanish masculine forms, although S *casa* is feminine. Of course the very concept of grammatical gender is as irrelevant to the creole NP as it is to the English NP or the NP in most substrate languages. Although some Niger-Congo languages have noun class systems that distinguish animates from inanimates, most have nothing comparable to the system of grammatical gender in many European languages. Although two genders exist in Hausa (belonging to the Chadic subgroup of the Afroasiatic family rather than the Niger-Congo family), it seems less likely to have been a significant substrate language for the Atlantic creoles than languages spoken nearer the African coast.

Sometimes the creoles have preserved natural gender oppositions in specific nouns, but this is on the level of the lexical item rather than inflectional morphology, e.g. Papiamentu CS *rei* 'king' (cf. S *rey*) versus *reina* 'queen' (S *reina*). Sometimes a natural gender distinction is maintained through the juxtaposition of a noun indicating sex, e.g. Papiamentu *mucha hòmber* 'boy' (cf. S *muchacho* 'boy' and *hombre* 'man') versus *mucha muhé* 'girl' (cf. S *mujer* 'woman'); these appear to be calques on African idioms (4.3.4). While most adjectives in the creoles based on European languages have been modelled on the masculine form, the feminine forms have sometimes been preserved with a distinction in meaning, e.g. Guyanais CF *gró* 'fat' (cf. F *gros*) versus *grós* 'pregnant' (cf. F *grosse*).

Like their substrate languages, basilectal varieties of the Atlantic creoles do not usually indicate gender distinctions in the third person singular pronoun, e.g. *she* versus *he* (6.4.5). However, Negerhollands CD appears to have distinguished between animate (*h*)*am* 'he, she' (cf. D *hem* 'him') and inanimate *di* 'it' (cf. D *dit* 'this [neuter gender]').

CHART 13. NOUN PHRASE	AP	NHJ	TB
13.1 Bare nouns (generic?)	++	+++	++
13.2 Indefinite article	++	+++	+0

		AP	NHJ	TB
13.3	Definite article (from superstrate deictic?)	0+	+++	++
13.4	Plural marker (= 'they'?)	++	+++	+0
13.5	Personal noun plus plural marker	0+	?++	+0
13.6	Demonstrative	++	+++	++
13.7	Demonstrative plus definite or plural	++	?++	++
13.8	Relative clause followed by def. or pl. marker	00	0+0	++
13.9	Prenominal adjective	++	+++	+R
13.10	Postnominal adjective	++	++0	++
13.11	Gender agreement?	00	000	00

The creoles surveyed all use the bare noun to convey generic meaning. All but one have an indefinite article (usually the word for 'one') and a definite article from the superstrate deictic. All but Nubi use the word for 'they' as a plural marker with common nouns, and some do this with personal names as well to indicate associates. All have demonstratives, and most can use these with definite articles or plural markers. The latter can mark relative clauses in Tok Pisin and Nubi, but among the Atlantic creoles surveyed only Haitian has this feature. All can have adjectives before nouns (although this is rare in Nubi) as well as after them (except Jamaican). None has gender agreement within the NP (although Negerhollands distinguishes between animates and inanimates in its third person singular pronoun).

6.4.4 Possession

Possession – and related ideas, such as association – can be expressed with a variety of structures in the creoles as well as their superstrate and substrate languages, with several alternatives sometimes occurring within the same language. While there is no uniformity in the creole patterns, they frequently reflect convergence and compromise between superstrate and substrate structures.

A widespread way of indicating possession is the simple juxtaposition of two nouns in the order [possessor + possessed]:

Saramaccan CE	konu bo 'the king's bow' (Voorhoeve 1961:148)
Miskito Coast CE	di uman biebi 'the woman's baby' (Holm 1978:286)
African American VE	that girl shoe (Burling 1973:50)
Negerhollands CD	meester kabaj 'the master's horse' (Hesseling 1905:91)
Berbice CD	mista bulin kuiara 'Mr. Bullen's boat' (Robertson 1979:91)

The creoles with this structure are based on English and Dutch, Germanic languages that have a possessive construction similar in word order but with a genitive inflection, e.g. 'Shakespeare*'s* works' or 'Vondel*s* werken'. A number of West African languages have a construction with this word order but – like the creoles – with no inflection, e.g. Mandinka 'Báakari fáa' 'Bakari's father'. Possessive adjectives like 'my' also precede the noun in these languages – as they do in the Atlantic creoles' superstrate languages: E '*my* mother', D '*mijn* moeder', F '*ma* mère', S '*mi* madre', P '*minha* mãe'. This is the order of the possessive adjective in creoles based on English (e.g. Sranan '*mi* mama') and Dutch (e.g. Negerhollands '*mi* muma' and Berbice CD '*ɛkɛ* mama') as well as Papiamentu CS ('*mi* mama') and two varieties of New World creole French: Guyanais and Louisiana CF, both '*mo* mama'.

In addition to the genitive construction in English and Dutch, all of the European superstrate languages can indicate possession with a propositional construction of the type [possessed *of* possessor]: E 'the mother *of* John' (more usual with inanimate nouns), D 'de moeder *van* Jan', F 'la mère *de* Jean', S 'la madre *de* Juan', P 'a mãe *do* João'. This is also found in the creoles, but the preposition can sometimes be omitted:

Guyanais CF	ròb *di* mo mama; ròb Ø mama-a '(my) mother's dress' (St Jacques-Fauquenoy 1972:98)
Palenquero CS	rrancho *di* tigre 'Tiger's ranch'; losa Ø Tigre 'Tiger's clearing' (Friedemann and Patiño 1983:149–50)
Papiamentu CS	historia *di* mi pais 'my country's history' (Goilo 1972)
Negerhollands CD	die boek *va* Jan 'John's book' (Van Name 1869–70:160)

Regarding the creole constructions without a preposition like *de* 'of', noun adjuncts are unusual in Romance languages, which almost always have a preposition to show possession, as in the name of the Portuguese mountains Serra *da* Estrela or 'Mountains of the Star'. Thus the name of the country Sierra Leone probably comes from *Serra Leoa* or 'Mountains of the Lioness' in Pidgin Portuguese, which was spoken there from the sixteenth to nineteenth century.

A construction without a preposition but with similar word order [possessed + possessor] is found in a number of West African languages largely to the east of those mentioned above, e.g. certain Kwa and Bantu languages. For example, in Yoruba the construction is 'oko Aìná' 'Aina's farm'. In these languages the possessive adjective also follows the noun, e.g. 'oko *mi*' 'my farm'. A number of Romance-based creoles have possessive adjectives in this position despite the word order of their lexical source languages, e.g. Príncipe CP 'myén *mɛ́*' 'my wife', Palenquero CS 'mamá *mi*', Haitian CF 'sè-*m*' 'my sister'. While substrate languages may have influenced this order, Goodman

(1964:54) points out that it may also be 'due to analogical extension that the pronominal possessive in Caribbean [French] Creole is postposed precisely as is the nominal, and is thus a linguistic innovation' or what Boretzky calls an *innerkreolische* or 'creole-internal' development (1983:96). Apparently by analogy with F 'c'est *à* moi' 'it's mine', there is also another CF construction, e.g. regional Haitian 'tab-*a*-ou' 'your table', in which the postposed possessive follows *a*; this may have constituted a transitional stage in the development of the postposed possessive without *a*.

Some non-Atlantic creoles also have the [possessed (of) possessor] construction, e.g. Nubi CA 'be *ta* ragi de', literally 'home *of* man the', i.e. 'the man's home' (Owens and Khamis ms.). However, for nouns whose relation is inalienable, the use of *ta* is optional, so that 'branch' (literally 'hand of tree') can be either 'ida *ta* seder' or 'ida seder'. Note that, in Nubi, possessive adjectives follow nouns, e.g. 'baba *tayi*' 'father my'.

In Tok Pisin when two nouns have no marker between them to indicate their relationship, the usual order is [head + modifier] as in *pikinini Sipik* 'a Sepik child' – i.e. [possessed + possessor] (e.g. *haus man* 'men's house') as in Tok Pisin's substrate languages (Faraclas ms.). However, possession is more often indicated with the preposition *bilong* 'of', e.g. *haus bilong Mapu* 'Mapu's house' with the same [possessed *of* possessor] word order found in English.

Finally, there is a creole construction in which the possessive adjective occurs between two nouns in the order [possessor *his* possessed]:

Sranan CE	konu ala *en* moni 'all the king's money'
	(Hall 1948:107)
Krio CE	di man *in* os 'the man's house' (Yillah ms.)
Mauritian CF	mo frer *so* madam 'my brother's wife' (Baker 1972:83)
Papiamentu CS	mi uman *su* kasá 'my sibling's spouse' (Michel ms.)
Indo-Portuguese	Salvador-*su* cruz 'the Savior's cross'
	(Dalgado 1900:37)
Afrikaans	ma *se* hoed 'mother's hat' (Valkhoff 1966:227)
Negerhollands CD	Jan *shi* boek 'John's book' (Van Name 1869–70:160)
Berbice CD	sami *ši* jɛrma 'Sammy's wife'(Robertson 1979:92)

The possibility of an English model for this construction seems remote. *His* (as well as *her* and *their*) was used after nouns (chiefly proper) instead of the genitive *'s* inflection only from the fifteenth to the eighteenth century, particularly after personal names ending in *-s*, e.g. 'Purchas *his* Pilgrimage' (*Oxford English Dictionary*). Today this is the only possessive construction in

Krio; neither the juxtaposition of nouns nor the use of a preposition is possible in that language (Yillah ms.), although both strategies are found in many other Atlantic creoles based on English.

There is also a construction with the possessive adjective in colloquial Dutch: 'vader *z'n* hoed' 'father's hat' (cf. *zijn* 'his') or 'moeder *haar* hoed' 'mother's hat'. The masculine form with *z'n* apparently developed into the Afrikaans possessive particle *se* (and Negerhollands CD *sji* or *shi* and Berbice CD *ši*) which was extended to feminine nouns in standard Afrikaans and to pronouns in Orange River Afrikaans, e.g. 'ek *se* vriende' 'my friends'. The fact that this possessive particle occurs in all varieties of overseas Dutch (Stolz 1986:128) strongly suggests that it originated in the colloquial Dutch construction discussed above, although its presence in Afrikaans may have been reinforced by similar constructions in the languages with which it was in contact, such as Khoi and Asian varieties of creole Portuguese. A similar particle is also found in likely substrate languages of Indo-Portuguese, i.e. Marathi and Kannada. However, this structure is found in so many different language families (Indo-European, Khoisan, Niger-Congo, Dravidian) that it is as likely to be a universal strategy for indication of possession as the other structures discussed above, so there is no need to look for a particular substrate source and plot the likely route of diffusion for each creole in which this construction occurs.

While the above discussion covers the relationship of possession between two nouns and between a noun and a possessive adjective, there remains to be discussed the structure of possessive pronouns (e.g. *mine*) as opposed to possessive adjectives (e.g. *my*). There is some relationship between these structures, since in those varieties of CF in which the possessive adjective precedes the noun (e.g. '*mo* mama' 'my mother') the possessive pronoun consists of the possessive adjective preceding a noun substitute, e.g. Guyanais CF *mo pa* 'mine'. This is apparently from F *ma part* 'my part'; although this does not represent any kind of pronominal structure in French, there is a parallel (possibly via substrate influence) in Liberian English 'Where my part?', i.e. 'Where is mine?'

In those varieties of CF with a postposed possessive adjective, there is a corresponding structure for the possessive pronoun, e.g. Haitian CF *pa-m* 'mine'. In both varieties of creole French, the possessive pronoun can replace the possessive adjective for emphasis, e.g. Guyanais '*mo pa* kaz' or Haitian 'kay *pa-m*', both 'my own house'. There is a parallel in Yoruba, in which a possessive adjective (e.g. *wọn* 'their') can be preceded by the preposition *ti* 'of, belonging to' to form a possessive pronoun ('*tiwọn*' 'theirs') which can then replace the possessive adjective for emphasis. For example, 'oko wọn' 'their farm' becomes 'oko *tiwọn*', literally 'farm theirs' – i.e. *'their* farm' in the contrasting sentence 'oko *tiwọn* kò tóbi tó *tiwa*' *'their* farm is not as big as *ours*' (Rowlands 1969:47).

The possessive pronoun is formed with the preposition meaning 'for' in a number of creoles. In the English-based creoles of Suriname 'mine' is *fu mi*, while in Caribbean CE it is *fi mi*. The English model may have been 'This is *for you*', which is nearly equivalent semantically to 'This is *yours*.' In Ndyuka the possessive adjective (e.g. *'mi* oso' 'my house') can be replaced by the possessive pronoun for emphasis ('a oso *fu mi*' *'my* house'). Caribbean CE has a similar construction which may originally have been emphatic, but it precedes the noun, e.g. Miskito Coast CE *'fo-him* jab' 'his job' (Holm 1978:286).

There is also a prepositional construction which functions as the possessive pronoun in Negerhollands CD, e.g. 'alle wat mie hab, bin *van jou*' 'all that I have is yours' (Hesseling 1905:261). However, this is also Dutch: 'het is *van jou*' 'it is yours'. Yet, unlike Dutch but like CE, Negerhollands can use this possessive pronoun as a possessive adjective: *'fa am* pat' 'her way'. A prepositional construction is also found in Seychellois CF, e.g. 'mô lakaz i *vo plis ki pur u*' 'my house is worth more than yours' (Corne 1977:49). Again, for emphasis the possessive pronoun can be used with a noun: 'u ser *pur u*' *'your* sister'. Although the creole Dutch construction might be accounted for by reference to the superstrate, this could hardly explain the presence of this construction in creoles based on English and French, since *for you* and *pour vous* do not function as possessive pronouns in these languages. The likelihood that the model was African, such as the Yoruba construction with *ti* discussed above, seems greater, particularly since the Atlantic creoles can use this possessive pronoun as an emphatic possessive adjective, quite unlike their European lexical source languages.

The above pattern appears to be confined to the Atlantic creoles. Tok Pisin indicates possession with personal pronouns as with nouns, using the preposition *bilong* ('haus *bilong mi*' 'my house'), having no special forms for either possessive adjectives or possessive pronouns (Faraclas ms.). In Nubi Creole Arabic, the two forms are identical (Owens and Khamis ms.).

CHART 14. POSSESSION	AP	NHJ	TB
14.1 Nouns: juxtaposition [possessor + possessed]	00	+0+	+0
14.2 Nouns: preposition [possessed (of) possessor]	++	+++	++
14.3 Nouns: poss. adj. [possessor HIS possessed]	0+	+00	00
14.4 Possessive adjectives: prenominal?	0+	+0+	00
14.5 Possessive pronouns: distinct?	?+	+++	00
14.6 Possessive pronouns as emphatic poss. adj.	0R	+++	00

In creoles based on Germanic languages, the possessing noun can precede the possessed. In all of the creoles surveyed, a noun can indicate possession with a preposition (which can sometimes be omitted). In two creoles, nouns use a possessive adjective to indicate possession. In only three creoles do possessive adjectives precede nouns, as in their superstrates. Most of the Atlantic creoles surveyed have distinct forms for the possessive adjective and the possessive pronoun and use the latter as an emphatic possessive adjective.

6.4.5 Pronouns

The pronouns of the superstrate languages indicate number (except E *you* and the partially equivalent F *vous* and D *u*). Moreover, they frequently indicate case (*I, me, mine*) and sometimes gender (S *nosotros, nosotras* 'we'; *vosotros, vosotras* 'you [plural]'; *ellos, ellas* 'they') and degree of intimacy (P *tu* 'you [familiar]' versus *você* 'you [polite]'). Except for number, most of these distinctions are not made in the pronouns of basilectal creoles – or their substrate languages.

Table 7. *Personal pronouns in three Atlantic creoles and Nubi*

Number	Person	CE	CF	Papiamentu	Nubi
Singular	1	mi	mouen	(a)mi	ana
	2	yu	ou	(a)bo	ita
	3	im	i	e	uwo
Plural	1	wi	nou	nos	ina
	2	unu	zòt	boso(nan)	itakum
	3	dem	yo	nan	umwon

Table 7 shows the original basilectal personal pronouns that were posited for Caribbean creoles based on English (Bailey 1966:22) and French (Valdman 1978:205). To these have been added the pronouns of Papiamentu Creole Spanish (Michel ms.) and Nubi Creole Arabic (Owens and Khamis ms.). These pronouns serve as both subjects and objects, and do not make distinctions of gender ('he' versus 'she' versus 'it'). Moreover, for the Atlantic creoles these forms also serve as possessive adjectives (except for Papiamentu *e* 'he, she, it; him, her' versus *su* 'his, her, its'). The Nubi pronouns form a somewhat different system: they do not serve as possessive adjectives, but they do serve as reflexive pronouns (which the Atlantic creole pronouns do not).

Pacific pidgins and creoles based on Austronesian languages have a distinct system of pronouns, which is discussed below. It should be noted that the above paradigms do not include variant forms (e.g. third person singular CE *i* or CF *li*) that may depend on morphophonemic rules, regional dialects or levels of the continuum; nor are they valid for every variety of New World CE or CF, e.g. Guyanese CE includes a basilectal third person object form *am*, and in northern Haiti *zòt* means not only 'you [plural]' but also 'they', while in the rest of the country *nou* is used for both 'we' and 'you [plural]'.

However, the above paradigms are suggestive of what the earliest CE and CF pronominal systems may have been like. There is certainly evidence of the radical morphological simplification that one might expect from the pidginization–creolization process. This was not the only force involved, however: possible substrate languages such as Bambara and Susu also have a single set of personal pronouns, each of which serves as subject, object and possessive. However, such a lack of morphological complexity is by no means rare among the world's languages, so this common characteristic of these creole and African languages is in itself no real proof of substrate influence.

Substrate influence is less open to question when the features shared by creole and African languages are unusual and idiosyncratic. Among their pronouns one such feature can be found in the special use of the Príncipe CP third person singular *éli* (cf. P *ele* 'he') to connect sentences in a narration in the sense of 'and then'. Boretzky (1983:110) has uncovered a similar use of Ewe *éyè*, which is not only similar in form but also has the highly unusual combination of uses as 'he' and as a conjunction meaning 'and then'. Moreover, there is a parallel double function of Yoruba *òun* and Saramaccan CE *hεn* as both 'he' and 'and'. A similar feature in unrelated languages of the world seems unlikely, and the existence of this feature on both sides of the Atlantic cannot be credibly attributed to coincidence rather than substrate influence.

Table 8 indicates the striking parallel between some Pacific pidgins and creoles and their Austronesian substrate languages in the existence of pronoun forms not only for singular and plural but also for dual (i.e. two) and trial (three) number. If this is not sufficiently convincing evidence of substrate influence, there is also a distinction between first person pronouns including and excluding the person spoken to, i.e. 'we [and you]' as opposed to 'we [not you]':

All distinctions, including trial number, are made in Tok Pisin by combining English-derived morphemes (Faraclas ms.). Zamboangueño CS uses Visayan-derived plural pronouns to distinguish between the exclusive and inclusive first person (Lorenzino 1993). Tayo CF combines French-derived morphemes to distinguish between dual (but not trial) and plural number; however, Tayo does not make the inclusive/exclusive distinction (Corne 1995). Pitcairnese CE, with its Austronesian substrate, also makes distinctions

Syntax

Table 8. *Personal pronouns in three Pacific pidgins/creoles*

	Tok Pisin PE	Zamboangueño CS	Tayo CF
Singular			
1	mi	yo	ma
2	yu	tu	ta
3	em	éle	la
Dual			
1 (excl.)	mitupela		} nude
1 (incl.)	yumitupela		
2	yutupela		ude
3	tupela		lede
Trial			
1 (excl.)	mitripela		
1 (incl.)	yumitripela		
2	yutripela		
3	tripela		
Plural			
1 (excl.)	mipela	kamé	} nu
1 (incl.)	yumi	kitá	
2	yupela	kamó	uso
3	ol	silá	lesot

between the dual and plural on the one hand and between inclusive and exclusive 'we' on the other (Holm 1988–9:550). Mauritian CF can distinguish between *nu-tu* 'we; us [including you]' and *nu-zot* 'we; us [excluding you]' (Baker 1972:72); this distinction is found in Malagasy, one of its primary substrate languages, which is also Austronesian (Boretzky 1983:250).

In many of the Atlantic creoles the second person plural pronoun has a non-European form that seems likely to be of African origin. This form is *unu* in the conservative English creoles, with the variants *un* in Saramaccan, *u* in Ndyuka, *una* in Krio, *wʊnə* in Barbados, *hənə* in Gullah and *yinə* in the Bahamas. This may be related to Haitian CF *nu* or *n*, which is used for both 'we' (cf. F *nous*) and 'you [plural]' (cf. Common Bantu **nu* and other possible African sources discussed below). Equally confusing, both Ndyuka and Sranan CE have *unu* (with the variants *un, u*) for both the first and second persons plural. Possibly related forms are found in the pronouns for 'you [plural]' in Palenquero CS (*enú*), São Tomé CP (*inase*) and Negerhollands CD (*yina*), although the last could come solely from West Flemish *gijnder* /yinder/. These seem to have resulted from the converging influence of similar forms for 'you [plural]' in a number of Niger-Congo languages; in addition to Common Bantu **nu* mentioned above, these include Ibo *unu*, Yoruba *nyín*, Wolof *yena*, Kongo

224

yeno and Mbundu *yenu* (Cassidy and Le Page 1980; Holm with Shilling 1982). In decreolizing varieties of CE, the distinction between singular and plural 'you' is largely maintained by replacing the *unu* form with *you-all* /yɔ(l)/, perhaps a calque on Twi *mó nyina*, literally 'you all' (Herskovits 1941:288). Related forms include *all you* in Eastern Caribbean CE (Hancock 1987) and possibly Berbice CD *jɛndɛ alma*, literally 'you all' (Robertson 1979:76).

Finally, a number of Atlantic creoles can convey the idea of reflexive pronouns by using a word for 'body' (usually with a possessive) to mean 'self':

> Nigerian PE   A kọm si (ma) *bọ̀di* fọ̀r glas.
> 'I saw myself in the mirror.' (Faraclas 1996:217)
>
> Haitian CF   Li koupe *kò* li. 'He cut himself.' (DeGraff ms.)
>
> Papiamentu CS El a horka su *kurpa*. 'He hanged himself.' (Michel ms.)
>
> Angolar CP   E ka mata *onge* re. 'He kills himself.' (Lorenzino ms.)

Sylvain (1936:65) noted the Old French use of *son cors* (literally 'his body') as 'himself', but she doubted whether it could have influenced the creoles since it had died out by the end of the fourteenth century, although Stein (1984:46) claims it was used in written French until the seventeenth century. Hall (1966:74) suggested that it survived in regional dialects, which Chaudenson (1974:734) documented. Still, the presence of this idiom in creoles of other lexical bases suggests that Sylvain was right to seek an African source. Yoruba *ara* 'body' is also used as 'self' and Akan *hõ* and Gurenne *inga* each have both meanings. However, the idiom is also present in Asian creoles, such as Papia Kristang CP 'eu lavá *corpo*' 'I wash myself' (Coelho 1880–6:177) and Zamboangueño CS 'Ya kulgá éle desuyo *kwérpo*' 'He hanged himself' (Santoro ms.), suggesting that it either spread by diffusion or arose independently through the influence of other substrate languages that also had the idiom, which may reflect a linguistic universal. Even English uses 'any*body*' in the sense of 'any person'.

Another widespread feature found in unrelated languages is synecdoche, the use of a part as a symbol of the whole, as in '$10 per head' meaning '$10 per person'. In fact, the word for 'head' is also used as a quasi-reflexive pronoun in some creoles, e.g. Haitian CF 'li tuyé *tèt*-li' (Sylvain 1936:66) and Cape Verde CP 'El máta *kabɛsa*' (Meintel 1975:232), both 'he killed himself'. Certain CE idioms also reflect this meaning, e.g. 'worry your head'. Wolof, a possible substrate language, uses the same word, *bob*, to mean both 'head' and 'self' (Sylvain 1936:66). Synecdoche is also connected to the use of the word for 'skin' as a reflexive in Sranan CE: 'A bron *en skin*' 'He burned himself' (Adamson ms.). There is a similar meaning in such expressions as 'bathe your skin' in Caribbean English, or 'sove po-ou' in Haitian CF, literally 'save skin your' i.e. 'save yourself'. Usage in African American English may have led to the phrase 'save your skin' (or 'save your hide') in more general English. The presence of this idiom in Dutch ('je huid redden') and German ('deine Haut retten') might be evidence for it being an Indo-European idiom – or for cowboy movies being a more important vehicle of lexical diffusion than hitherto recognized. Finally, synecdoche may have led to a similar use of the word for 'buttocks'. Achebe (1969:134) noted of an Ibo speaker that 'Many people laughed at his dialect and the way he used words strangely. Instead of saying "myself" he always said "my buttocks".' Haitian CF *bunda* can have both meanings (Carden and Stewart 1988:9), as can Bahamian CE *ass* as in 'watch your ass' (i.e. 'watch yourself; be careful') or 'carry your ass' ('get out') or even the emphatic 'my ass got stuck with it' (i.e. 'I got stuck with it myself'), sometimes made more *salonfähig* as 'my hip' (Holm with Shilling 1982:5).

Non-Atlantic creoles have various strategies for expressing reflexives. The use of the word for 'body' in Papia Kristang CP and Zamboangueño CS mentioned above is also found in Seychellois CF, e.g. 'I n êvit sô *lekor*' 'She had invited herself' (Chapuis ms. citing Bollée 1977:66). It was also noted that Nubi CA uses the same personal pronouns that serve as subjects and objects. Tok Pisin uses *yet* after pronouns to mark them as reflexive: 'Em lukim *em yet* long glas' 'He was looking at himself in the mirror' (Faraclas ms.).

CHART 15. Pronouns: basilect case distinctions?	AP	NHJ	TB
15.1 First person singular	00	000	0+
15.2 Second person singular	00	000	0+
15.3 Third person singular	++	000	++
15.4 First person plural	00	000	0+
15.5 Second person plural	00	000	0+
15.6 Third person plural	00	000	0+
15.7 Reflexive pronoun: distinct form?	++	+++	00
15.8 Interrogative pronouns: some bimorphemic?	++	+++	+0
15.9 Relative pronouns	++	+++	++

No basilectal creole surveyed has personal pronouns that mark a distinction between subject and object case. However, a distinction between these cases and the possessive is marked in Nubi and in the third person singular of some other creoles. All the Atlantic creoles have reflexive pronouns that are distinct from the corresponding personal pronoun, as well as some bimorphemic interrogative pronouns. All the creoles surveyed have pronouns that set off relative clauses.

6.5 Other function words

Various kinds of function words have been discussed so far in connection with particular areas of grammar, e.g. preverbal tense and aspect markers, copulas and negators in connection with the verb phrase, and determiners and pronouns in connection with the noun phrase. While a complete survey of the syntax of all the creoles is beyond the scope of this chapter, there are several other function words of a more miscellaneous nature which should also be discussed since they reveal syntactic similarities among the creoles across lexical boundaries.

6.5.1 Conjunctions

The foregoing included discussion of a subordinating conjunction homophonous with the word for 'say' (6.3.2) and a co-ordinating conjunction homophonous with the word for 'he' (6.4.5). In a number of Atlantic creoles there is also a co-ordinating conjunction that joins two noun phrases which is homophonous with the preposition 'with':

Sranan CE	Me weifi *nanga* mi pikin ɛ siki ɔgri ɔgri.
	'My wife and (lit. "with") my child are very sick.'
	(Herskovits and Herskovits 1936:150)
Haitian CF	Papa-m *ak* mama-m te vini. 'My father and
	(lit. "with") my mother came.' (Sylvain 1936:156)
Papiamentu CS	Papa *ku* mama a ba baila. 'Father and (lit. "with")
	mother went to a dance' (Richardson 1977:56)
Príncipe CP	Swá tetúga *ki* kõpwέ 'the story of the turtle and
	(lit. "with") the godfather' (Günther 1973:119)
Negerhollands CD	Di a ha ēn mēnši *mi* ēn juŋ man. 'Once there was a
	girl and (lit. "with") a young man.'
	(De Josselin de Jong 1926:47)

The usage in CF was traced by Sylvain (1936:164) to an African parallel. She noted that Haitian CF *ak* 'with, and' (cf. F *avec* 'with') was identical in form and function to Wolof *ak*. Homburger (1949:116) notes that 'In the majority of Negro African languages the conjunction "and" and the preposition "with" are rendered by the same particle (when "and" joins nouns).' Boretzky (1983:216) notes that a number of African languages (Yoruba, Ewe, Ashanti, Ibo and Bambara) use one word to join *parts* of a sentence (corresponding to both 'with' and 'and') and a distinct word or Ø to join entire sentences (corresponding to 'and then'). The latter would seem to correspond to Haitian CF *épi* (cf. F *et puis* 'and then'): 'Pòl acheté poul-la *épi* Mari kouit li' 'Paul bought the chicken *and* Mary cooked it' (Valdman 1978:266). On the other hand, Haitian *ak* 'with, and' appears to join sentence parts like nouns (as above) or verbs, e.g. 'yo montré nou lavé *ak* pasé' 'They taught us to wash and iron' (1978:267). However, usage varies in the French Antilles and French Guiana, where greater contact with French may have led to a blurring of the distinction between CF *ak* for sentence parts and *épi* for entire sentences, since no such distinction is found in French, which has the single conjunction *et* 'and' for both. A similar lack of distinction is found in the modern use of Sranan CE *èn* 'and' and *nanga* 'and, with' (probably from *along with*) (Adamson ms.).

In Papiamentu CS *ku* (cf. S *con* or P *com* 'with') can join both nouns and verbs, e.g. 'e muhé ta kanta *ku* baila' 'the woman sings and dances'. While *ku* could be replaced by *i* (cf. S *y* or P *e*, both /i/ 'and'), *i* would suggest a looser association than *ku*. For example, the above sentence with *ku* implies that the singing and dancing go together (as in an act), whereas *i* could imply that the woman sings on some occasions and dances on others (Richardson 1977).

Non-Atlantic creoles usually have a single word for 'and' joining both sentences and sentence parts, e.g. Tok Pisin *na* (Faraclas ms.), Nagamese *aru* (Bhattacharjya ms.) and Nubi *wu* or *ma* (Owens and Khamis ms.). However, it is worth noting that Nubi *ma* is also a preposition meaning 'with', so the current use of two different conjunctions to join both sentences and sentence parts may represent the levelling of an earlier distinction in their usage. Seychelles CF, which has a number of other features also found in the Atlantic creoles, maintains a distinction between *e(pi)* joining sentences and *(av)ek* joining sentence parts (Chapuis ms.).

CHART 16. Coordinating conjunctions	AP	NHJ	TB
16.1 'and' joining sentences	++	+++	++
16.2 'and' joining sentence parts: distinct?	++	+++	0+

All the Atlantic creoles surveyed have a conjunction to join sentence parts that is distinct from the conjunction joining full sentences, as does Nubi. Only Tok Pisin uses the same conjunction for both functions, as do the creoles' superstrates.

6.5.2 Prepositions

One of the most original contributions of Boretzky (1983:194–205) is his comparative study of prepositions in creole and African languages. Although this area of creole syntax is not yet well studied, the debate between Bickerton (1980, 1981) and Washabaugh (1980) regarding the status of CE *fu* or *fi* as a preposition or verb (6.1.8) has led to a growing number of studies in this area (e.g. Byrne 1985, Muysken 1985). The status of the second element of serial verb constructions (e.g. 'give' meaning 'to' or 'for', 6.3.1) as a verb or preposition is still a matter of some debate. However, in those creoles most influenced by their superstrate, there appears to be some evidence for evolution from verbal to prepositional status, so to some extent the answer may depend on the variety in question.

As mentioned above (4.4.1), a number of the Atlantic creoles have a general locative preposition *na* (with related forms *ina*, *nã*, *da*, *a*). This can be translated as 'in, at, to', etc., depending on context, a semantic range quite similar to that of Ibo *na* (Taylor 1971). However, Boretzky (1983:194) has observed that its meaning is closely tied to that of accompanying verbs, some of which can give *na* the meaning of 'from':

Sranan CE	M ben-kmop *a* pranasi. 'I had come from the plantation.' (Voorhoeve 1962:57)
Haitian CF	Paske li te-sɔti *nã* ras ak *nã* fãmi David. 'Because he came from the race and family of David.' (Hall *et al.* 1953:220)
Príncipe CP	E šyê *na* umátu. 'He went-out of the forest.' (Günther 1973:118)
Guiné-Bissau CP	Bó sai *na* matu. 'Come out of the bush!' (Peck 1988:442)
Seychellois CF	I sorti *dâ* lakaz. 'He comes out of the house.' (Chapuis ms. citing Corne 1977:186)
Zamboangueño CS	Kyére lé salé *na* água. 'He wants to get out of the water.' (Santoro ms. citing Forman 1972:196)

In other words, the accompanying verb specifies the meaning of *na* as 'location' or 'motion towards' or 'motion from'. While this might be seen as simply a problem of translation, it should be borne in mind that none of the possible European etyma of *na* such as P *na* 'in the [feminine]', F *dans* 'in' or D *naar* 'to' (earlier *na* 'near') has this semantic range, and one is hard put to think of any European preposition which does. However, there are parallel constructions in West African languages in which the meaning of a general locative preposition is specified as 'from' or 'out of' by a verb meaning 'exit from' or 'come out of', e.g. Yoruba 'ó jáde *nínú* ilé', literally 'he came-out LOC house', i.e. 'he came out of the house' (Rowlands 1969:141), or Fante 'o-fir ha *mu*' 'he came-out bush LOC', i.e. 'he came out of the bush' (Boretzky p.c.). Of course such substrate influence by no means excludes converging influence from the superstrate prepositions discussed above.

Unlike its European etyma, Atlantic creole *na* and its equivalents can often be omitted after verbs of motion, especially when used with the names of specific places:

<blockquote>

Miskito Coast CE I gaan Ø Manawa. 'He went (to) Managua.'
(Holm 1978:293)

Haitian CF   Mãmã-m al Ø lavil. 'My mother went (to) town.'
(Hall *et al.* 1953:75)

Papiamentu CS   E ta bai Ø Miami. 'He is going (to) Miami.' (Michel ms.)

Príncipe CP   E vɔtá Ø cyô. 'He returned (to) field.'
(Günther 1973:112)

Berbice CD   Ekɛ mua Ø kiriki. 'I'm going (to) church.'
(Robertson 1979:157)

Seychellois CF   I fek al Ø labutik. 'He has just gone (to the) store.'
(Chapuis ms. citing Corne 1977:111)

</blockquote>

This follows usage in such African languages as Mandinka: 'Names of countries, towns, etc. . . . generally follow verbs indicating movement towards or away from a place, or rest at a place, in which case they are used without postposition' (Rowlands 1959:117). Similarly, Welmers notes that 'in Niger-Congo languages generally, it must be emphasized that such verbs have meanings like "go to", "be from", "arrive at" and the like, and nothing like a preposition is used with them' (1973:454).

Welmers (1973:453) also discusses the hypothesis that certain prepositions such as Igbo *na* and Yoruba *ní*, which both refer to location in a general way, are derivable from verbs meaning 'to be located at'. While both appear to constitute true prepositions in the present structure of each language, each is often used with nouns to form more concise notions of location, corresponding to phrasal constructions like English *in the middle of*, which is composed of prepositions and a noun. For example, in Yoruba the preposition *ní* (with its allomorphs *n'* and *l'*) combines with *iwájú* 'face' to form *níwájú* 'in front of', and with *ábé* 'lower part, under side' to form *lábé* 'under', and with *órí* 'head, top' to form *lórí* 'on, on top of' (Ogunbọwale 1970:89–90, Abraham 1962).

Many of the most conservative creoles form phrasal prepositions in a similar manner. For example, 'under' is expressed by the general locative *na* plus a noun meaning 'under side' in Príncipe CP *na ubásu*, Sranan CE *na ɔndro*, Saramaccan CE *na basu* and Negerhollands CD *a mole* (Boretzky 1983:194–205). Tok Pisin, a non-Atlantic variety, has similar phrasal constructions with the general locative preposition *long* 'at, in, on, to', etc.: *antap long* 'on top of' (Faraclas ms.).

In Yoruba, phrasal prepositions act like nouns followed by possessives, e.g. 'ẹiyẹ náà wà *lórí igi*', literally 'bird the is-located on-head/top of-tree', i.e. 'the bird is on the tree' (Ogunbọwale 1970:89). The following noun is clearly a possessive (for which the position after the thing possessed is normal in Yoruba; cf. 'oko *Ainá*' 'Aina's farm', 6.4.4) rather than an object, since it is replaced not by an object pronoun but by a possessive adjective, e.g. 'lórí rẹ̀', literally 'on-top his', i.e. 'on him'. This corresponds to usage in some creoles, such as Sranan 'luk wan sani na *mi tapu*' 'look, something is on me' (Herskovits and Herskovits 1936:162). Other examples of creoles using possessives rather than object pronouns with phrasal prepositions include the following:

Saramaccan CE A dɛ a *mi* fesi. 'He is in front of me.' (Boretzky 1983:199)

Haitian CF   Li rete kote-*li* tut lãnwit. 'He stayed by his side the whole night.' (d'Ans 1968:139)

Papiamentu CS *mi* dilanti 'in front of me' (Goilo 1972)

Príncipe CP   ubasu *sé* 'under him' (Günther 1973:80)

In general, the French-based creoles do not follow the above pattern; it could be argued that Haitian CF *kote-li* is derived from F *à côté de lui*. Moreover, all the creoles have a number of non-phrasal prepositions that can be directly derived from etyma in their lexical source languages. However, there is convincing evidence that some creoles developed phrasal prepositions under the influence of parallel structures in substrate languages such as Yoruba, Ewe, Akan-Fante, Ibo and Mandinka (Boretzky 1983:201–4). It must be asked how else the phrasal prepositions could have developed in the creoles if, as claimed by Bickerton (1981, 1984), their substrates had no significant influence on their syntax. European prepositions were readily available for borrowing into the creoles since they were easily isolated units corresponding to a fairly clear meaning (however idiosyncratic at times) and required no complicated syntactic analysis. The fact that more complex phrasal prepositions were favoured over them in a number of creoles points squarely to substrate influence.

While most of the Atlantic creoles have *pre*positions, Berbice CD has *post*positions occurring after the noun, e.g. 'war *ben*' 'in the house' or 'wari *ɔndrə*' 'under the house', etc. (Robertson 1986). This creole has an unusually close relationship to one particular African language, Eastern Ijo, which as an SOV language has postpositions in the form of locative suffixes. Berbice CD has retained this structure although it is an SVO language, e.g. 'ɛk mua mu kop brɔt šap anga', literally 'I go-PROG go buy bread shop *in*', i.e. 'I'm going to go buy bread in the shop' (1986). This fact undermines Bickerton's thesis that creoles develop (rather than borrow) syntactic structures that fit their overall system: 'Languages, even creoles, are systems, systems have structure, and things incompatible with that structure cannot be borrowed; SVO languages cannot borrow a set of postpositions, to take an extreme and obvious case' (1981:50).

CHART 17. Prepositions	AP	NHJ	TB
17.1 General locative preposition (or postposition) ......++		+++	++
17.2 Zero preposition after motion verb + place ....++		?++	++

All of the creoles surveyed have a preposition with a general locative meaning. All (except Negerhollands, for which there is no conclusive data) can follow a verb of motion with an NP referring to a place without a preposition.

6.5.3   Sentence-final -o

A number of Atlantic creoles have a particle *o* which usually occurs at the end of a sentence to mark increased emotion or several other meanings discussed below:

Saramaccan CE   Mi ko *o*. 'I've come.' (response of an expected visitor to a greeting) (Rountree and Glock 1982:11)

Cameroonian CE Na palava dis *o*. 'There'll be trouble over this!' (Todd 1984 :122)

Liberian CE   A ná seti gɛ *o*! 'I am not a city girl.' (Singler 1984:283)

Haitian CF   Moun-sa-a menm, *o*! 'That's the guy!' (Valdman 1978:253)

Papiamentu CS   Mi a mir'e-*o*! 'I *did* see him!' (Michel ms.)

São Tomé CP   Bõ jáá-*o* 'Good day!' (Valkhoff 1966:135)

Príncipe CP   N fá fa *ó*. 'I didn't say that.' (Günther 1973:92)

Singler (1984, 1985) characterizes *o* in Liberian English as signalling personal involvement, so that a greeting with this tag is warmer and more heart-felt. Faraclas (1989:448) notes that the Nigerian PE equivalent 'lends a spirit of solidarity between speaker and hearer'. Moreover, *o* can imply that what has been said is of special interest and current relevance. For this reason, *o* is used when correcting someone's mistaken assumption as in the Príncipe CP and Liberian CE examples above.

Sentence-final *o* is used similarly in a number of West African languages. For example, in Yoruba 'mo rí i *o*' means 'I *did* see him (although you seem to think I didn't)' (Singler 1985). In Wobe, *o* added to a greeting implies that all is well between the speaker and hearer(s). Singler (1984:289) notes that 'Klao speakers say that those who would omit the *o* in leave-taking formulae . . . are either brusque to the point of rudeness or non-native speakers.' Singler (1985) notes the presence of this *o* in other Kru languages, Kwa languages (Twi, Yoruba), Mande languages (Mende, Kpelle, Mano), as well as in Kisi (West Atlantic) and Efik (Benue-Congo?). Beyond the Atlantic creoles mentioned above, it is also found in Krio CE, Ndyuka CE, Fernandino CE, Seychellois CF, and Sango. Singler concludes that in Liberian English it is 'an areal, hence substratal phenomenon' (1984:283). Tok Pisin, a non-Atlantic variety, shares with its substrate languages a sentence-final *o* with a more restricted vocative meaning: 'Bayang *o*. Yu kam *o*' 'Hey, Bayang. Come here!' (Faraclas ms.).

6.6 Word order

As noted above (6.0), the most frequent word order in both superstrate and substrate languages is SVO, which is also the normal order in all of the Atlantic creoles. However, SOV order is found in some Niger-Congo languages (6.0) and can occur in some of the relevant Indo-European languages as well. In Romance languages object pronouns normally precede the verb (e.g. S '[yo] *te* hablo' 'I'm speaking to you') but they always follow the verb in Romance-based creoles (e.g. Palenquero CS 'i ta ablá *bo*'; Bickerton and Escalante 1970:260). However, in Spanish and Portuguese, object pronouns follow infinitives as clitics (e.g. S 'quiero ver*te*' 'I want to see you'). It has been suggested that Iberian colonists addressing Africans and others may have spoken exclusively in infinitives, much as modern Spanish speakers sometimes do in addressing foreigners. Whether or not this was the case, it probably bears little relation to the use of postverbal object pronouns in the creoles; those based on French certainly did not get their word order from the exclusive use of infinitives in French, since in that language object pronouns precede infinitives (e.g. 'je veux *te* voir').

Like German, Dutch has SOV in dependent clauses; although SVO is found in independent clauses with one verb, the fact that the main verb occurs at the end of the clause whenever an auxiliary is used is taken as evidence of an underlying SOV order. Negerhollands CD, however, always follows the SVO pattern of the other Atlantic creoles, as does Berbice CD. However, Afrikaans generally follows Dutch word order, providing further evidence that it is not an Atlantic creole. Similarly, the occurrence of clause-final verbs in Indo-Portuguese and Nagamese reflects the SOV order of their substrate languages (Schuchardt 1883a:17, Bhattacharjya ms.) and is further evidence that they are not Atlantic creoles. Among other non-Atlantic creoles, Tok Pisin and

Nubi CA are SVO languages (Faraclas ms.; Owens and Khamis ms.), while Zamboangueño is VSO (Santoro ms.).

In the Atlantic creoles prominence can be given to the object and other elements normally occurring after the verb by fronting them, e.g. Miskito Coast CE 'an *kwéschon* dem di yúustu gi wi' 'And they used to ask us *questions.*' Such topicalization is also usual in relevant African languages such as Yoruba. As noted above (6.2.4), the object *aṣọ* in 'mo rà *aṣọ*' 'I bought cloth' can be fronted and followed by the highlighter *ni* to give it prominence: '*aṣọ* ni mo rà' 'It was cloth I bought.' Similarly, the Atlantic creoles often use a highlighter with fronted sentence elements, although the creole highlighter precedes such elements. For example, the Jamaican CE sentence 'wi a taak bout Jan' can become '*a Jan* wi a taak bout' 'It's John we're talking about' (Bailey 1966:86–9).

In addition to fronting verbs, which are then recopied in their original position (6.2.4), the Atlantic creoles front question words (like their superstrate and substrate languages) and often highlight them (unlike their superstrate but like some substrate languages). For example, Jamaican CE 'Boti lef ya den' can become '*a-wen* Boti lef ya?' 'When did Bertie leave here?' (1966). However, this is not always the case in non-Atlantic creoles. In Tok Pisin, as in its substrate languages, question words like *we* 'where' are not fronted: 'Yu go *we*?' 'Where did you go?' (Faraclas ms.).

As in the last example, there is nothing like *do* support in restructured varieties of English; the negator simply precedes the verb ('im *no* wier shuuz' 'He doesn't wear shoes') and there is no inversion of the subject and the auxiliary (or verb) to form questions ('im wier shuuz?' 'Does he wear shoes?'). Intonation alone can distinguish questions from statements in the creoles, but there are also question markers for emphasis, as in certain substrate languages like Yoruba, e.g. 'iṣu pọ̀ lónǐ *bí*', literally 'yams are-plentiful today QUESTION' (Rowlands 1969:37). Creole question markers are often indistinguishable from question tags in the superstrate language, but in the English creoles they have no syntactic relation with the main verb as in English, e.g. Miskito Coast CE 'das waz a swiit stuori, *duonit*?' 'That was a nice story, wasn't it?'

The creoles also have sentence-initial question markers, again with parallels in substrate languages such as Yoruba. In the French creoles the question marker *èské* is clearly from F 'Est-ce que . . . ?', e.g. Haitian '*èské* l ap chaché kostim-yo?' 'Is he looking for their suits?' (Valdman 1978:254). Haitian CF also has the decidedly un-French negative question marker *apa*: '*apa* ou kontan?' 'Aren't you happy?' (1978). In the English-based creoles the negative question marker is often derived from *ain't*, which frequently begins

questions in nonstandard English, e.g. Gullah 'ɛnti rɛbəl toim kʌmin bak?'
'Ain't slavery coming back?' (Turner 1949:262), or Liberian 'ɛ̃ your grandma
can speak Bassa?' (Singler p.c.).

To summarize, while the creoles' lexical source languages often require the
inversion of the subject and the verb (or auxiliary) to transform a statement
into a question, this is not a part of creole syntax:

Jamaican CE	We im de?, lit. 'Where he is?', i.e. 'Where is he?' (Hancock 1979b:9)
Haitian CF	Kote li ye? lit. 'Where he is?', i.e. 'Where is he?'; cf. F 'Où est-il?' (QW V S) or 'Où est-ce qu'il est?'
Palenquero CS	Bo ase kume kane? lit. 'you HAB eat meat?', i.e. 'Do you eat meat?' (Bickerton and Escalante 1970:258); cf. S '¿Come Vd. carne?' (VSO)
Príncipe CP	Kwaitu e sa kuštá â?, lit. 'How-much it ASP cost QUESTION', i.e. 'How much does it cost?' (Günther 1973:94); cf. P 'Quanto custa isso?' (QW V S)
Negerhollands CD	Am lo werək da? lit. 'He ASP work there?' i.e. 'Does he work there?' (van Diggelen 1978:91); cf. D 'Werkt hij daar?' (V S C)

Non-Atlantic creoles do not undergo subject-verb inversion in questions
either, but follow their normal word order for statements, whether SVO (e.g.
Tok Pisin), SOV (e.g. Nagamese) or VSO (Zamboangueño CS).

It should be noted that African American Vernacular English, usually considered either a post-creole or a semi-creole, has the usual English subject-
auxiliary inversion in questions that can be answered with 'yes' or 'no', e.g.
'Can I go?' (Burling 1973:68). However, with question words such inversion
is optional, i.e. both 'Where can I go?' and 'Where I can go?' occur. In embedded questions, which have no subject-auxiliary inversion in standard
English, inversion is again optional in Black English, i.e., 'I wonder where
can I go' occurs as well as 'I wonder where I can go.' In embedded 'yes'/'no'
questions AAVE may have no connecting *if* or *whether* but does have inversion: 'I wonder can I go' (1973:68). In this respect AAVE is unlike English-
based creoles which have no such inversion at all and therefore happen to
match standard English word order in embedded questions, e.g. Jamaican
CE 'dɛm a:ks mi if a want i' 'They asked me if I wanted it' (Hancock
1979b:14). A case might be made for AAVE being more similar to Irish
English, in which direct questions are also embedded, e.g. 'I don't know is
that right or not' (Barry 1982:108). While Irish English might well have

served as a model for AAVE at an earlier period (Rickford 1986), the AAVE pattern of subject-auxiliary inversion could also be the result of partial restructuring or decreolization. Bahamian English, which seems to be either more restructured or at an earlier stage of decreolization than AAVE, has no subject-auxiliary inversion in the basilect but frequent inversion in the upper mesolect, even in embedded questions. Thus one finds 'I can go?' varying with 'Can I go?', and 'I don't know where I can go' varying with 'I don't know where can I go.'

Most of the other differences in word order between the creoles and their lexical source languages are discussed in connection with specific morphosyntactic features in earlier sections of this chapter, such as those dealing with verbal markers. The remaining differences are largely limited in scope and depend on particular lexical items with subcategorizational rules differing from those of their superstrate etyma. In Miskito Coast CE, for example, the adverb *bak* 'back, again' often occurs sentence-finally after another adverb of place, e.g. 'an hiz wie huom bak' 'on his way back home'. Even at this level, though, one finds evidence suggesting more general forces such as substrate influence. For example, Negerhollands CD *werán* matches CE *bak* in both its semantic range and syntactic position: 'də džumbi-sini a dra:i *werán*', literally 'the ghost PLURAL ANTERIOR return back' (Stolz 1986:218). Sranan CE *baka* also occurs in this sentence-final position (1986); this may in fact be connected to its semantic range, which matches that of Ewe *megbe* (Herskovits 1941:290) and Yoruba *pada* (A. Oyedeji p.c.). Still, such lexically related syntactic differences are so numerous and miscellaneous that they are usually best treated in lexical studies of each creole.

CHART 18. Miscellaneous	AP	NHJ	TB
18.1 Word order: questions SVO?	++	+++	++
18.2 Sentence-final -o	++	0+?	R0

To summarize, none of the creoles surveyed has subject/verb inversion to indicate a question, and some employ a particle 'o' at the end of a sentence to signal heightened emotional involvement.

Having examined pidgin and creole languages from the perspective of theory, social factors and the structure of their lexicon, phonology and syntax, we will see what conclusions we can draw in the final chapter.

7
Conclusions

The following is a brief assessment of the theoretical implications of the social and linguistic data in this volume.

Regarding the terminology, theories and sociohistorical data discussed in chapters 1 to 3, we can conclude that sociolinguistic factors are essential parts of the definition of both pidgins and creoles. While one could draw up a list of structural features shared by most of the Atlantic creoles (cf. chapters 5 and 6), few would claim that these could be used to determine that a language is a creole without reference to its sociolinguistic history.

The validity of the theories put forward to explain the genesis and development of pidgin and creole languages crucially depends on whether these theories can satisfactorily take into account the many, various and complex sociolinguistic circumstances under which the known pidgin and creole languages came into being and developed. The social history of the speakers of the seven pidgin and creole languages surveyed in chapter 3 casts light on some of the major issues, particularly in the context of the broader survey in Holm (1988–9, vol. II). These issues include nativization and the role it plays in determining the structural complexity of creoles as opposed to the relative structural simplicity of pidgins. Another primary factor in defining pidgins has been their stability, but it now appears that this is irrelevant to the likelihood of a pidgin becoming a creole. While stability enables us to distinguish pidgins from jargons or pre-pidgin continua, creolization appears to depend instead on social factors, with either pidgins or jargons providing adequate input. Tertiary hybridization was thought to be crucial to a pidgin's stabilization, but counterevidence can be found in varieties such as Chinese Pidgin English, which appear to have stabilized without it.

The power and prestige relationships between the speakers of the languages involved in pidginization and creolization appear to be relevant in a number of respects, most importantly in determining which language becomes the source of the lexicon. However, the fact that Europeans have used pidgins based on indigenous languages in colonial situations in which the balance of power was quite clearly in their favour – e.g. Fanakalo, Bazaar Malay and Kisetla Swahili – indicates that relative power is not the only deciding factor. It has been suggested that colonialism or slavery might be key factors in the sociolinguistics of pidginization and creolization; while there are a number of counterexamples, the correlation is frequent enough to bear closer examination. The relevant factor would seem to be the degree of power of one group over another, since very powerful social forces are usually needed to counter the momentum of normal language transmission. Both colonialism and slavery represented a degree of power over others that permitted social engineering on a scale that could affect the genesis and development of a great number of pidgins and creoles from the fifteenth century onwards.

There is growing evidence that at the time of the creoles' early development Europeans often spoke them more fluently and played a greater role in their development and diffusion than has generally been assumed. A better understanding of the linguistic repertoires of colonial whites is also needed to advance research in an area that may long remain one of the biggest challenges to creolists: the genesis and development of semi-creoles. Some very basic questions have yet to be satisfactorily answered: is creolization an all-or-nothing kind of process? If different degrees of creolization can occur, is this simply the result of the ratio of superstrate to substrate speakers during the first generations of the speech community's existence, or are other factors of equal or greater importance, such as the social relationships between these groups? It is hard to imagine any progress being made in this crucial area of research unless structural features of the relevant languages are evaluated within the context of the social history of their speakers, and to do this we need to understand better the relationship between the two.

The lexical data (discussed in chapter 4) reflect more readily than data from other linguistic levels the social history of the speech communities that today use creole languages. Regionalisms in the lexical source language retained in the creoles can suggest patterns of immigration, as can words characteristic of superstrate social dialects. Lexical retentions and borrowings from substrate languages provide similar information, as do the less direct traces of substrate lexical influence such as creole semantic shifts, idioms, reduplications and other effects of calquing. The lexicons of the Atlantic creoles also provide some evidence of the importance of Portuguese in the Atlantic slave trade. The influence of adstrate languages (such as Amerindian and European languages other than the superstrate) appears to be confined solely to the level of lexicon in most Atlantic creoles. Morphological and semantic changes in creole words *vis-à-vis* their European etyma do not differ in kind from changes found between different stages of other languages, but the scale on which these changes occurred in the creoles – particularly morpheme boundary reanalysis – reflects the massive structural changes characteristic of pidginization and creolization.

The phonological data (discussed in chapter 5) suggest that at least the Atlantic creoles have what Stein (1984:102) calls a *Doppelzugehörigkeit*, a 'double belonging' to both the family of their lexical source language and their own family, the Atlantic creoles. While some of these creoles – and particularly post-creoles – share so many features with their lexical source languages that they might well be called Romance (or Germanic) languages of the second generation (1984:101), conservative varieties share a preponderant number of structural features with other conservative Atlantic creoles – of whatever lexical base – rather than any European language. Although the balance of European versus non-European features varies considerably from creole to creole, all varieties – even post-creoles and semi-creoles – share this double identity to some degree.

Perhaps the single most important factor shaping the phonology of the Atlantic creoles was the retention of substrate phonotactic rules tending to give syllables a CV structure. The seven-vowel system of many substrate languages had the effect of making the conservative creoles' vowel systems closer to one another's than to those of their lexical sources. Substrate languages also influenced other phonological patterns in the creoles, ranging from the nasalization of vowels to the palatalization of various consonants. While some aspects of the creoles' phonology were clearly affected by universal tendencies, substrate influence had to be the origin of certain phonological features in creoles that are completely absent in their lexical source languages, such as co-articulated or prenasalized stops, or phonemic tone.

The syntactic data (discussed in chapter 6) provide further evidence of the creoles' *Doppelzugehörigkeit* but also strengthen the case for the Atlantic creoles being a typological group of languages *sui generis*. While any claim of their genetic relatedness would have to rest on the genetic relatedness of their superstrates on the one hand and their substrates on the other, there would seem to be a strong case for parallel independent development, with greater likelihood of the diffusion of features within lexical-base groups. It is hardly controversial to observe that the Atlantic creoles arose among speakers of partially similar African languages learning partially similar European languages under partially similar social conditions.

The many syntactic features common to the Atlantic creoles fall into several categories: preverbal tense and aspect markers with similar meanings that combine in similar ways; different but corresponding words for 'be' determined by the following syntactic environment; parallel serial verb constructions, the second element of which corresponds to complementizers or prepositions in European languages; similar determiners and pluralizers in the noun phrase; the substitution of possessive adjectives by possessive pronouns for emphasis; and miscellaneous parallels in function words ranging from personal pronouns to phrasal prepositions.

While these syntactic structures are made largely of lexical building blocks from the lexical source languages (building blocks that carry with them syntactic and semantic elements from those languages), the model for many of these structures was clearly from the substrate. Some of these structures (e.g. serial verbs) are not rare among the world's languages and their universality may have made it easier for them to take root and develop in the creoles. Indeed, the presence of such features in non-Atlantic creoles such as Tok Pisin and Nubi points to the relevance of comparing the structure of their substrate languages with those of the Atlantic creoles. However, when structures are rare outside the Niger-Congo family (e.g. predicate clefting), their presence in the Atlantic creoles can hardly be explained by universals. Whatever evidence there is for universals seems to be in the Greenbergian sense of general parameters on possible structures or in the sense of universals in adult second language acquisition that played a role in pidginization and creolization (e.g. the isolating of grammatical elements). This study has uncovered no linguistic data that could be interpreted as unambiguous evidence of neurally based universals. There is, however, considerable evidence that creoles function like any other languages in developing a systematicity and complexity of their own which is, in the final analysis, something quite distinct from that of either their superstrate or their substrate.

Regarding the development of theory, progress in a number of areas of research bodes well for progress in pidgin and creole linguistics in general. First and foremost, linguistic descriptions of individual varieties are being written that are more frequently of high quality and sufficient detail, reflecting native-speaker sensitivity to nuance (e.g. DeGraff 1992). Secondly, considerable progress is being made in sociohistorical studies, not only of creole speech communities but also of the traffic in slaves and indentured labourers that brought people to these communities. This improved knowledge of creole speakers' ethnolinguistic origins, coupled with more detailed and rigorous studies of the relevant substrate languages themselves, promises a significant improvement in our understanding of the development of creoles. Together with broader comparative studies of universal grammar (e.g. Stassen 1985) and theoretical advances in other areas of contact linguistics, these will provide the means of uncovering the data to test and improve the theories that guide pidgin and creole linguistics.

REFERENCES

Abraham, R. C. (1962) *Dictionary of modern Yoruba*, Hodder and Stoughton, London.

Aceto, M. (1996) 'A new future marker emerges in the Panamanian West Indies', paper presented to the Society for Pidgin and Creole Linguistics, San Diego.

Achebe, C. (1969) *Things fall apart*, Fawcett Crest, New York.

Adam, L. (1883) *Les idiomes négro-aryen et maléo-aryen: essai d'hybridologie linguistique*, Maisonneuve, Paris.

Adamson, L. (ms.) 'Sranan', in Holm.

Aitchison, J. (1987) '"Bagaraps" in Tok Pisin', paper presented at the Seminar on Pidgin and Creole Languages, University College London.

Akers, G. (1981) *Phonological variation in the Jamaican continuum*, Karoma, Ann Arbor.

Alexandre, P. (1967) *Langues et langage en Afrique noire*, Payot, Paris.

Alleyne, M. C. (1971) 'Acculturation and the cultural matrix of creolization', in Hymes, pp. 169–86.

(1980) *Comparative Afro-American*. Karoma, Ann Arbor.

Allsopp, S. R. R. (1958) 'Pronominal forms in the dialect of English used in Georgetown (British Guiana) and its environs by people engaged in non-clerical occupations', unpublished MA thesis, University of London.

(1970) 'Critical commentary on the *Dictionary of Jamaican English*', *Caribbean Studies* 10(2):90–117.

(1972) 'Some suprasegmental features of Caribbean English and their relevance to the classroom', paper presented at the UWI/UNESCO Conference on Creole Language and Educational Development, University of the West Indies.

Anderson, R. (ed.) (1983) *Pidginization and creolization as language acquisition*, Newbury House, Rowley.

Anonymous (1854) *Kurzgefasste Neger-Englische Grammatik*, Bautzen. (1965 reprint, S. Emmering, Amsterdam.)

Arends, J. (1986) 'Internal and external factors in the development of the Sranan comparative', paper presented to the Society for Caribbean Linguistics, Trinidad.

(1993) 'Towards a gradualist model of creolization', in Byrne and Holm, pp. 371–80.

(ed.) (1995) *The early stages of creolization*, John Benjamins, Amsterdam/Philadelphia.

References

Arends, J., P. Muysken and N. Smith (eds.) (1994) *Pidgins and creoles: an introduction*, John Benjamins, Amsterdam/Philadelphia.

Arends, J., and M. Perl (1995) *Early Suriname creole texts: a collection of 18th-century Sranan and Saramaccan documents*, Vervuert, Frankfurt / Iberoamericana, Madrid.

Arens, H. (1969) *Sprachwissenschaft: der Gang ihrer Entwicklung von Antike bis zur Gegenwart*, Fischer Athenäum, Frankfurt.

Ariza, M. M. (1980) 'Stress and intonation in Haitian Creole', paper presented to the Society for Caribbean Linguistics, Aruba.

Aub-Buscher, G. (1970) 'A propos des influences du français dialectal sur un parler créole des Antilles', in *Phonétique et linguistique romanes: mélanges offerts à M. Georges Straka*, vol. I, Centre d'Etudes Romances, Strasbourg, pp. 360–9.

Bailey, B. L. (1965) 'Toward a new perspective in Negro English dialectology', *American Speech* 40. (Reprinted in Wolfram and Clarke (1971), pp. 41–50.)

(1966) *Jamaican Creole syntax: a transformational approach*, Cambridge University Press, Cambridge.

Bailey, R., and M. Görlach (eds.) (1982) *English as a world language*, University of Michigan Press, Ann Arbor.

Baissac, C. (1880) *Etude sur le patois créole mauricien*, Berger-Lerrault et Cie, Nancy.

Baker, P. (1972) *Kreol: a description of Mauritian Creole*, Hurst, London.

(1976) 'The problem of variability with special reference to Bickerton's study of Guyanese English', unpublished University of York exam-option paper.

(1984) 'The significance of agglutinated French articles in the creole languages of the Indian Ocean and elsewhere', in Sebba and Todd, pp. 19–29.

(ed.) (1995) *From contact to creole and beyond*, University of Westminster Press, London.

Baker, P., and C. Corne (1982) *Isle de France Creole: affinities and origins*, Karoma, Ann Arbor.

Bakker, P., and P. Muysken (1994) 'Mixed languages and language intertwining', in Arends, Muysken and Smith, pp. 41–84.

Bakker, P., and R. A. Papen (1997) 'Michif: a mixed language based on Cree and French', in Thomason, pp. 295–364.

Barry, M. V. (1982) 'The English language in Ireland', in Bailey and Görlach, pp. 84–133.

Bartens, A. (1995) *Die iberoromanisch-basierten Kreolsprachen*, Lang, Frankfurt am Main.

(1996) *Der kreolische Raum: Geschichte und Gegenwart*, The Finnish Academy of Sciences, Helsinki.

(1998) *Ideophones and sound symbolism in the Atlantic creoles*, The Finnish Academy of Sciences, Helsinki.

Bauer, A. (1975) *Das Kanton-Englisch: ein Pidginidiom als Beispiel für ein soziolinguistisches Kulturkontaktphänomen*, Lang, Bern.

Baugh, A. C. (1957) *A history of the English language*, Appleton-Century-Crofts, New York.

Baugh, J. (1980) 'A reexamination of the Black English copula', in W. Labov (ed.) *Locating language in time and space*, Academic Press, New York, pp. 83–106.

Bendix, E. H. (1983) 'Sandhi phenomena in Papiamentu, other creoles, and African languages', in Carrington, Craig and Todd Dandare, pp. 112–23.

Bentolila, A., P. Nougayrol, P. Vertict, C. Alexandre and H. Tourneux (1976) *Ti diksyonnè kreyòl–franse: dictionnaire élémentaire créole haïtien–français*, Editions Caraïbes, Port-au-Prince.

Berry, J. (1959) 'The origins of Krio vocabulary', *Sierra Leone Studies* 12:298–307.

Bertrand-Bocandé, E. (1849) 'Notes sur la Guinée portugaise ou Sénégambie méridionale', *Bulletin de la Société de Géographie* 12:57–93.

Bhattacharjya, D. (ms.) 'Nagamese', in Holm.

(fc.) *The genesis and development of Nagamese: its social history and linguistic structure*, Ph.D. dissertation, City University of New York.

Bickerton, D. (1971) 'Inherent variability and variable rules', *Foundations of Language* 7:457–92.

(1973a) 'The structure of polylectal grammars', in R. W. Shuy (ed.) *Sociolinguistics: current trends and prospects*, Georgetown University Press, Washington, pp. 17–42.

(1973b) 'On the nature of a creole continuum', *Language* 49:640–9.

(1974) Creolization, linguistic universals, natural semantax and the brain, *University of Hawaii Working Papers in Linguistics* 6(3):124–41. (Republished 1980.)

(1975a) *Dynamics of a creole system*, Cambridge University Press, Cambridge.

(1975b) 'Can English and Pidgin be kept apart?' in K. A. McElhanon (ed.) *Tok Pisin i go we?* (conference proceedings), *Kivung*, special publication no. 1 (University of Papua New Guinea): 21–7.

(1976) 'Creole tense–aspect systems and universal grammar', paper presented to the Society for Caribbean Linguistics, Guyana.

(1977a) 'Putting back the clock in variation studies', *Language* 53(2):353–9.

(1977b) 'Pidginization and creolization: language acquisition and language universals', in A. Valdman, pp. 49–69.

(1979a) 'Introduction' to Schuchardt (1979), pp. vi–xvii.

(1979b) 'The status of *bin* in the Atlantic Creoles', in Hancock, Polomé, Goodman and Heine, pp. 309–14.

(1980) 'Creolization, linguistic universals, natural semantax and the brain', in Day, pp. 1–18. (Reprint of Bickerton (1974).)

(1981) *Roots of language*. Karoma, Ann Arbor.

(1984) 'Creoles and universal grammar: the unmarked case?' paper presented at the winter meeting of the Linguistic Society of America, Baltimore.

(1986) 'Beyond Roots: the five-year test', paper presented at the Linguistic Society of America Summer Institute, City University of New York.

Bickerton, D., and A. Escalante (1970) 'Palenquero: a Spanish-based creole of northern Colombia', *Lingua* 24:254–67.

References

et al. (1984) 'The language bioprogram hypothesis', *Behavioral and Brain Sciences* 7:173–221.

Bilby, K. M. (1983) 'How the "older heads" talk: a Jamaican Maroon spirit possession language and its relationship to the Creoles of Suriname and Sierra Leone', *New West Indian Guide* 57(1–2):37–88.

Bird, C., J. Hutchison and M. Kanté (1977) *An ka bamanankan kalan: beginning Bambara*. Bloomington: Indiana University Linguistics Club.

Bloomfield, L. (1933) *Language*, Allen and Unwin, London.

Boas, F. (1933) 'Note on the Chinook Jargon', *Language* 9:208–13.

Bollée, A. (1977) *Le créole français des Seychelles*. Max Niemeyer, Tübingen.

(1978) 'Reduplikation und Iteration in den romanischen Sprachen', *Archiv für das Studium der neueren Sprachen und Literaturen* 215(1):318–36.

(1981) 'Le vocabulaire du créole haïtien et du créole seychellois: une comparaison', paper presented at the 3e Colloque International des Etudes Créoles, St Lucia.

(1984) 'Dictionnaire étymologique des créoles', in *Wörterbuch der deutschen Romanistik: Rundgespräche und Kolloquien*, Verlag Chemie GmbH, Acta humaniora, Weinheim.

Boretzky, N. (1983) *Kreolsprachen, Substrate und Sprachwandel*, Harrassowitz, Wiesbaden.

(1986) 'Verbkategorien im Fantse und im Jamaica Creole', ms.

Bouton, J. (1640) *Relation de l'establissement des françois depuis l'an de 1635 en l'isle de la Martinique*, Paris.

Brachin, P. (1985) *The Dutch language: a survey*, Stanley Thornes, Cheltenham.

Bradford, W. P. (1986) 'Virgin Islands Dutch Creole: a morphological description', *Amsterdam Creole Studies* 9:73–99.

Broch, I., and E. H. Jahr (1984) 'Russenorsk: a new look at the Russo-Norwegian pidgin in northern Norway', in P. S. Ureland and I. Clarkson (eds.) *Scandinavian language contacts*, Cambridge University Press, Cambridge, pp. 21–65.

Brown, R. W., and U. Bellugi (1964) 'Three processes in the child's acquisition of syntax', *Harvard Educational Review* 34:133–51.

Burling, R. (1973) *English in black and white*, Holt, Rinehart and Winston, New York.

Byrne, F. (1984) '*Fi* and *fu*: origins and functions in some Caribbean English-based creoles', *Lingua* 62:97–120.

(1985) 'Some aspects of the syntax of *fu* in Saramaccan', *Amsterdam Creole Studies* 8:1–26.

Byrne, F., and J. Holm (1993a) 'Perspectives on the Atlantic and Pacific . . . and beyond', in Byrne and Holm (1993b), pp. 1–22.

(eds.) (1993b) *Atlantic Meets Pacific: a global view of pidginization and creolization*. John Benjamins, Amsterdam/Philadelphia.

Carden, G., M. Goodman, R. Posner and W. A. Stewart (1990) 'A 1671 French Creole text from Martinique', paper presented at the annual meeting of the Society for Pidgin and Creole Linguistics.

Carden, G., and W. A. Stewart (1988) 'Binding theory, bioprogram, and creolization: evidence from Haitian Creole', *Journal of Pidgin and Creole Languages* 3(1):1–68.

Carr, E. (1972) *Da kine talk: from pidgin to standard English in Hawaii*, University Press of Hawaii, Honolulu.

Carrington, L., D. R. Craig and R. Todd Dandare (eds.) (1983) *Studies in Caribbean language*. Society for Caribbean Linguistics, St Augustine.

Carter, H. (1979) 'Evidence for the survival of African prosodies in West Indian creoles', *Society for Caribbean Linguistics, occasional paper 13*.

(1982) 'The tonal system of Jamaican English', paper presented to the Society for Caribbean Linguistics, Suriname.

(1983) 'How to be a tone language', in Carrington *et al.*, pp. 96–111.

(1987) 'Suprasegmentals in Jamaican: some African comparisons', in Gilbert, pp. 213–63.

Carter, H., and J. Makoondekwa (1976) 'An introductory Kongo reader', ms.

Cassidy, F. G. (1961) *Jamaica talk: three hundred years of the English language in Jamaica*, Macmillan, London.

(1964) 'Toward the recovery of early English-African Pidgin', *Symposium on multilingualism (Brazzaville)*, Commission de coopération technique en Afrique, publication 87, Conseil Scientifique pour Afrique, London, pp. 267–77.

(1994) 'The early pidgin/creole scene: some historical notes', paper presented to the joint meeting of the Society for Caribbean Linguistics and the Society for Pidgin and Creole Linguistics, Guyana.

Cassidy, F. G., and R. B. Le Page (1980) *Dictionary of Jamaican English*. Cambridge University Press, Cambridge.

Chapuis, D. (ms.) 'Dominican and Seychellois Creole French', in Holm.

(fc.) 'Aspects of restructuring in vernacular lects of Réunion French', Ph.D. dissertation, City University of New York.

Chaudenson, R. (1974) *Le lexique du parler créole de la Réunion*, Champion, Paris, 2 vols.

(1979) *Les créoles français*, Nathan, Evreux.

(1992) *Des îles, des hommes, des langues*, L'Hartmattan, Paris.

Chévillard, A. (1659) *Les desseins de son éminence de Richelieu pour l'Amérique*, Rennes.

Chomsky, N. (1965) *Aspects of the theory of syntax*, MIT Press, Cambridge, Mass.

Coelho, F. A. (1880–6) 'Os dialectos românicos ou neolatinos na Africa, Asia e América', *Bolletim da Sociedade de Geografia de Lisboa*. (Republished in J. Morais-Barbosa (ed.) (1967) *Estudos linguísticos crioulos*, Acadêmia Internacional de Cultura Portuguesa, Lisbon.)

Comhaire-Sylvain, S., and J. Comhaire-Sylvain (1955) 'Survivances africaines dans le vocabulaire religieux d'Haïti', *Etudes dahoméennes* 14:5–20.

Corne, C. (1977) *Seychelles Creole grammar: elements for Indian Ocean Proto-Creole reconstruction*, Gunter Narr, Tübingen.

(1995) 'A contact-induced and vernacularized language: how Melanesian is Tayo?' in Baker, pp. 121–48.

References

Corominas, J. (1967) *Breve diccionario etimológico de la lengua castellana*, Biblioteca románica hispánica, Madrid.

Couto, H. H. do. (1996) *Introdução ao estudo das línguas crioulas*, Editora da Universidade de Brasília, Brasília.

Craig, B. (1991) 'American Indian English', *English World-Wide* 12(1):25–62.

Crouse, N. (1940) *French pioneers in the West Indies, 1625–1664*, Columbia University Press, New York.

(1943) *The French struggle for the West Indies, 1665–1713*, Columbia University Press, New York.

Cruickshank, J. G. (1916) *'Black Talk': being notes on Negro dialect in British Guiana with (inevitably) a chapter on the vernacular of Barbados*, Argosy, Demerara.

Curtin, P. D. (1969) *The Atlantic slave trade: a census*, University of Wisconsin Press, Madison.

Daeleman, J. (1972) 'Kongo elements in Saramacca Tongo', *Journal of African Languages* 11(1):1–44.

Dalgado, S. R. (1900) *Dialecto Indo-Português de Ceylão*, Imprensa Nacional, Lisbon.

d'Andrade, E., and A. Kihm (eds.) (1992) *Actas do colóquio sobre crioulos de base lexical portuguesa*, Colibri, Lisbon.

d'Ans, A. M. (1968) *Le créole français d'Haïti*. Mouton, The Hague/Paris.

Day, R. R. (ed.) (1980) *Issues in English creoles: papers from the 1975 Hawaii conference*, Varieties of English Around the World G2, Groos, Heidelberg.

DeCamp, D. (1961) 'Social and geographical factors in Jamaican dialects', in Le Page, pp. 61–84.

(1964) 'Creole language areas considered as multilingual communities', *Symposium on multilingualism (Brazzaville)*, Commission de Coopération Technique en Afrique, publication 87, Conseil Scientifique pour Afrique, London, pp. 227–32.

(1971a) 'The study of pidgin and creole languages', in Hymes, pp. 13–42.

(1971b) 'Toward a generative analysis of a post-creole speech continuum', in Hymes, pp. 349–70.

(1977) 'The development of pidgin and creole studies', in Valdman, pp. 3–20.

DeCamp, D., and I. F. Hancock (eds.) (1974) *Pidgins and creoles: current trends and prospects*, Georgetown University Press, Washington.

DeGraff, M. (1992) *Creole grammars and the acquisition of syntax: the case of Haitian*, Ph.D. dissertation, University of Pennsylvania, University Microfilms International, Ann Arbor.

(ms.) 'Haitian', in Holm.

de Granda, G. (1978) *Estudios lingüísticos hispánicos, afrohispánicos y criollos*, Editorial Gredos, Madrid.

de Groot, A. (1984) *Tweedelig woordregister: Auka–Nederlands/Nederlands–Auka*, Artex, Paramaribo.

Dejean, Y. (1983) 'Diglossia revisited: French and Creole in Haiti', *Word* 34(3):189–204.

246

de Josselin de Jong, J. P. (1926) *Het huidige Negerhollandsch (teksten en woordenlijst)*, Verhandelingen der koninklijke Akademie van Wetenschapen te Amsterdam, Afdoeling Letterkunde 26:1–107.

de Kleine, C. (ms.) 'Negerhollands', in Holm.

(1999) *An analysis of Dutch as spoken by the Creole population of Paramaribo, Suriname*, Ph.D. dissertation, City University of New York, University Microfilms International, Ann Arbor.

den Besten, H. (1986) 'Double negation and the genesis of Afrikaans', in Muysken and Smith, pp. 185–230.

Denis, B. (1998) 'St Thomas French: a semi-creole?' paper presented to the Society for Caribbean Linguistics, St Lucia.

Devonish, H. (1986) 'The decay of neo-colonial official language policies: the case of the English lexicon creoles of the commonwealth Caribbean', in Görlach and Holm, pp. 25–32.

Dijkhoff, M. (1985) 'Some observations about the passive participle in Papiamentu', paper presented at the Workshop on Universals and Substrata in Creole Genesis, University of Amsterdam.

Dillard, J. L. (1972) *Black English: its history and usage in the United States*, Random House, New York.

(1976) *American talk*, Random House, New York.

(1979) 'Creole English and Creole Portuguese: the early records', in Hancock *et al.*, pp. 261–8.

Domingue, N. Z. (1977) 'Middle English: another creole?', *Journal of Creole Studies* 1(1):89–100.

Donahoe, W. A. (1946) *A history of British Honduras*, Provincial Publishing Co., Montreal.

Donicie, A., and J. Voorhoeve (1963) *De Saramakaanse Woordenschat*, Bureau voor Taalonderzoek in Suriname van de Universiteit van Amsterdam, Amsterdam.

Ducoeurjoly, S. J. (1802) *Manuel des habitans de Saint-Domingue*, Chez Lenoir, Paris.

Dwyer, D. (n.d. [1967]) *An introduction to West African Pidgin English*, [East Lansing] MSU African Studies Center [produced for the US Peace Corps], mimeo.

Eersel, C. H. (1976) 'A few remarks on some sound patterns of Sranan', paper presented to the Society for Caribbean Linguistics, Guyana.

Elliott, D., S. Legume and S. A. Thompson (1969) 'Syntactic variation as linguistic data', in R. Binnick *et al.* (eds.) *Papers from the 5th Regional Meeting of the Chicago Linguistic Society*, Chicago University Press, Chicago.

Faine, J. (1936) *Philologie créole: études historiques et etymologiques sur la langue créole d'Haïti*, Imprimerie de l'Etat, Port-au-Prince.

(1939) *Le Créole dans l'univers: étude comparative des parlers français-créoles*, vol. I, *Le mauricien*, Imprimerie de l'Etat, Port-au-Prince.

Faraclas, N. (1996) *Nigerian Pidgin*. London: Routledge.

(ms.) 'Tok Pisin', in Holm.

References

Favery, M., B. Johns and F. Wouk. (1976) 'The historical development of locative and existential copula constructions in Afro-Creole languages', in S. B. Steever, C. A. Walker and S. S. Mufwene (eds.) *Papers from the Parasession on Diachronic Syntax*, Chicago Linguistic Society, Chicago, pp. 88–95.

Feist, S. (1932) 'The origin of the Germanic languages and the Indo-Europeanizing of North Europe', *Language* 8:245–54.

Ferguson, C. A. (1959) 'Diglossia', *Word* 15:325–40.

    (1971) 'Absence of copula and the notion of simplicity: a study of normal speech, baby talk, foreigner talk, and pidgins', in Hymes, pp. 141–50.

Ferraz, L. (1974) 'A linguistic appraisal of Angolar', in *In Memoriam António Jorge Dias*, Instituto de Alta Cultura, Junta de Investigações Científicas do Ultramar, Lisbon, pp. 177–86.

    (1975) 'African influences on Principense Creole', in Valkhoff *et al.*, pp. 153–64.

Ferraz, L., and A. Traill (1981) 'The interpretation of tone in Principense Creole', *Studies in African Linguistics* 12(2):205–15.

Focke, H. C. (1855) *Neger-Engelsch Woordenboek*, Van den Heuvell, Leiden.

Forman, M. (1972) 'Zamboangueño with grammatical analysis', Ph.D. dissertation, Cornell University.

Fortier, A. (1885) 'The French language of Louisiana and the Negro French dialect', *Transactions of the Modern Language Association of America* 1:96–111.

Fought, J. (1982) 'The reinvention of Hugo Schuchardt', *Language in Society* 11:419–36.

Frajzyngier, Z. (1984) 'On the origin of *say* and *se* as complementizers in Black English and English-based creoles', *American Speech* 59(3):207–10.

Friedemann, N. S., and C. Patiño R. (1983) *Lengua y sociedad en el palenque de San Basilio*, Instituto Caro y Cuervo, Bogotá.

Fromkin, V., and R. Rodman (1993) *An introduction to language*, Harcourt Brace Jovanovich, New York.

Fyle, C. N., and E. D. Jones (1980) *A Krio–English dictionary*, Oxford University Press/Sierra Leone University Press.

Gibson, K. (1986) 'The ordering of auxiliary notions in Guyanese Creole', *Language* 62(3):571–86.

Gilbert, G. (1980) 'Introduction' to Schuchardt (1980), pp. 1–13.

    (1983) 'Focus on creolists: Hugo Schuchardt', *Carrier Pidgin* 11(1):4–5.

    (1984) 'The first systematic survey of the world's pidgins and creoles: Hugo Schuchardt, 1882–1885', in Sebba and Todd, pp. 131–40.

    (1985) 'Hugo Schuchardt and the Atlantic Creoles: a newly discovered manuscript "On the Negro English of West Africa"', *American Speech* 60(1):31–63.

    (1986a) 'The language bioprogram hypothesis: déjà vu?' in Muysken and Smith, pp. 15–24.

    (1986b) 'Oldendorp's *History* . . . and other early creole materials in the Moravian archives in Herrnhut, East Germany', *Carrier Pidgin* 14(1):5–7.

    (ed.) (1987) *Pidgin and creole languages: essays in memory of John E. Reinecke*, University Press of Hawaii, Honolulu.

Gilman, C. (1979) 'Cameroonian Pidgin English: a neo-African language', in Hancock *et al.*, pp. 269–80.

Givón, T. (1979) 'Prolegomena to any sane creology', in Hancock *et al.*, pp. 3–36.

Göbl-Gáldi, L. (1933) 'Problemi di sostrato nel creole-francese', *Revue de linguistique romane* 9:336–45.

(1934) 'Esquisse de la structure grammaticale des patois français-créoles', *Zeitschrift für französische Sprache und Literatur* 58:257–95.

Goilo, E. R. (1972) *Papiamentu textbook*, De Wit, Aruba.

Goodman, M. F. (1964) *A comparative study of creole French dialects*, Mouton, The Hague.

(1971) 'The strange case of Mbugu (Tanzania)', in Hymes, pp. 243–54.

(1985a) 'Review of Bickerton (1981)', *International Journal of American Linguistics* 51(1):109–37.

(1985b) 'The origin of Virgin Islands Creole Dutch', *Amsterdam Creole Studies* 8:67–106.

(1987) 'The Portuguese element in the American creoles', in Gilbert, pp. 361–405.

Görlach, M., and J. Holm (eds.) (1986) *Focus on the Caribbean*, Varieties of English Around the World G8, John Benjamins, Amsterdam/Philadelphia.

Grade, P. (1889) 'Bemerkungen über das Negerenglisch an der West-Küste von Afrika', *Archiv für das Studium der neueren Sprachen* 83:261–72.

Green, K. (1997) *Non-standard Dominican Spanish: evidence of partial restructuring*, Ph.D. dissertation, City University of New York, Ann Arbor, University Microfilms International.

Greenberg, J. H. (1966a) *The languages of Africa*, Indiana University Press, Bloomington/Mouton, The Hague.

(1966b) *Language universals*, Mouton, The Hague.

Greenfield, W. (1830) *A defense of the Surinam Negro-English version of the New Testament* . . . Bagster, London. (Reprinted in the *Journal of Pidgin and Creole Languages* 1(2):259–66ff.)

Grimes, J. E. (ed.) (1972) *Languages of the Guianas*, Summer Institute of Linguistics, University of Oklahoma, Norman, Okla.

Grion, G. (1891) 'Farmacopea e Lingua Franca del dugento', *Archivo glottologico italiano* 12:181–6.

Günther, W. (1973) *Das portugiesische Kreolisch der Ilha do Príncipe*, Marburger Studien zur Afrika- und Asienkunde, Marburg.

Guthrie, G. M. (1935) *Lingala grammar and dictionary*, Conseil Protestant du Congo, Léopoldville.

(1954) 'Lectures on Bantu tonology', unpublished ms.

Guttman, L. (1944) 'A basis for scaling qualitative data', *American Sociological Review* 9:139–50.

Hall, R. A., Jr (1948) 'The linguistic structure of Taki-Taki', *Language* 24:92–116.

(1950) 'The African substratum in Negro English: review of Turner (1949)', *American Speech* 25:51–4.

References

(1955) 'Sostrato e lingue creole', *Archivo glottologico italiano* 40:1–9.

(1958) 'Creole languages and genetic relationships', *Word* 14:367–73.

(1959) 'Neo-Melanesian and glottochronology', *International Journal of American Linguistics* 25:265–7.

(1962) 'The life cycle of pidgin languages', *Lingua* 11:151–6.

(1966) *Pidgin and creole languages*, Cornell University Press, Ithaca.

(1968) 'Creole linguistics', in Sebeok, pp. 361–71.

Hall, R. A., Jr, S. Comhaire-Sylvain, H. O. McConnell and A. Métraux (1953) *Haitian Creole: grammar, texts, vocabulary*, Memoir 74 of the American Anthropological Association, and Memoir 43 of the American Folklore Society, American Folklore Society, Philadelphia.

Hancock, I. F. (1969) 'A provisional comparison of the English-based Atlantic creoles', *African Language Review* 8:7–72.

(1971) 'A study of the sources and development of the lexicon of Sierra Leone Creole', unpublished Ph.D. thesis, University of London School of Oriental and African Studies.

(1977) 'Recovering pidgin genesis: approaches and problems', in Valdman, pp. 277–94.

(1979a) 'On the origins of the term pidgin', in Hancock *et al.*, pp. 81–8.

(1979b) 'The relationship of Black Vernacular English to the Atlantic creoles', working paper of the African and Afro-American Studies and Research Center, University of Texas at Austin.

(1979c) 'Review of W. Keller Vass, *The Bantu linguistic heritage of the United States* (University of California Press, 1978)', *Research in African Literatures* 12:412–19.

(1980) 'Lexical expansion in creole languages', in Valdman and Highfield, pp. 63–88.

(1984) 'Romani and Anglo-Romani', in P. Trudgill (ed.) *Language in the British Isles*, Cambridge University Press, Cambridge, pp. 367–83.

(1986) 'The domestic hypothesis, diffusion and componentiality: an account of Atlantic Anglophone creole origins', in Muysken and Smith, pp. 71–102.

(1987) 'A preliminary classification of the Anglophone Atlantic creoles', in Gilbert, pp. 264–334.

Hancock, I. F., E. Polomé, M. Goodman and B. Heine (eds.) (1979) *Readings in creole studies*, E. Story-Scientia, Ghent.

Harrison, J. A. (1884) 'Negro English', *Anglia* 7:232–79.

Heine, B. (1976) *A typology of African languages, based on the order of meaningful elements*, Reimer, Berlin.

(1982) 'The Nubi language of Kibera – an Arabic Creole: grammatical sketch and vocabulary', in B. Heine and J. G. Möhlig (eds.) *Language and dialect atlas of Kenya*, Reimer, Berlin.

Heinl, R. D., and N. G. Heinl (1978) *Written in blood: the story of the Haitian people, 1492–1971*, Houghton Mifflin, Boston.

Hellinger, M. (1985) *Englisch-orientierte Pidgin- und Kreolsprachen: Entstehung, Geschichte, und sprachlicher Wandel*, Wissenschaftliche Buchgesellschaft, Darmstadt.

Herskovits, M. (1941) *The myth of the Negro past*, Harper and Brothers, New York/London.

Herskovits, M., and F. S. Herskovits (1936) *Suriname Folk-lore* . . . Columbia University Contributions to Anthropology 37, Columbia University Press, New York.

Hesseling, D. C. (1897) 'Het Hollandsch in Zuid-Afrika', *De Gids* 60(1):138–62. (Reprinted in English in Hesseling (1979), pp. 1–22.)

(1899) *Het Afrikaansch: bijdrage tot de geschiedenis der nederlandse taal in Zuid-Afrika*, Brill, Leiden.

(1905) *Het Negerhollands der Deense Antillen. Bijdrage tot de geschiedenis der nederlandse taal in Amerika*, Sijthoff, Leiden.

(1910) 'Overblijfsels van de nederlandse taal op Ceylon', *Tijd* 29:303–12. (Reprinted in English in Hesseling (1979), pp. 23–30.)

(1928) 'Het perfektum in het post-klassieke Grieks: overblijfsels in de taal van heden', *Mededelingen der Koninklijke Akademie van Wetensehappen, Afdeling Letterkunde* (Amsterdam) 65A(6).

(1933a) 'Papiaments en Negerhollands', *Tijd* 52:265–88. (Reprinted in English in Hesseling (1979), pp. 47–61.)

(1933b) 'Hoe ontstond de eigenaardige vorm van het Kreools?', *Neophilologus* 18:209–15. (Reprinted in English in Hesseling (1979), pp. 62–70.)

(1934) 'Gemengde taal, mengeltaal, kreools en kreolisering', *Nieuwe Taalgids* 28:310–22.

(1979) *On the origin and formation of creoles: a miscellany of articles*, Karoma, Ann Arbor.

Highfield, A., and A. Valdman (eds.) (1981) *Historicity and variation in creole studies*, Karoma, Ann Arbor.

Hinskens, F. (1995) 'The Negerhollands word *sender* in eighteenth-century manuscripts', in Arends, pp. 63–87.

Holder, M. (1982) *Accent shift in Guyanese Creole: linguistic introduction and classified word lists*, Karoma, Ann Arbor.

Holm, J. A. (1976) 'Copula variability on the Afro-American continuum', paper presented to the Society for Caribbean Linguistics, Guyana.

(1978) *The Creole English of Nicaragua's Miskito Coast: its sociolinguistic history and a comparative study of its lexicon and syntax*, Ph.D. thesis, University College London, University Microfilms International, Ann Arbor.

(1980) 'African features in White Bahamian English', *English World-Wide* 1(1):45–65.

(1981) 'Sociolinguistic history and the creolist', in Highfield and Valdman, pp. 40–51.

(ed.) (1983) *Central American English*, Varieties of English Around the World T2, Groos, Heidelberg/John Benjamins, Amsterdam.

References

(1984) 'Variability of the copula in Black English and its creole kin', *American Speech* 59(4):291–309.

(1986) 'Substrate diffusion', in Muysken and Smith, 259–78.

(1987) 'Creole influence on Popular Brazilian Portuguese', in Gilbert, pp. 406–30.

(1988–9) *Pidgins and creoles*, Cambridge University Press, Cambridge, 2 vols.

(1992a) 'A theoretical model for semi-creolization', paper presented to the Society for Caribbean Linguistics, Barbados.

(1992b) 'Creole English lexicon common to the Atlantic and Pacific', *Language Sciences* 14(3):1–2.

(1998a) 'The study of semi-creoles in the twenty-first century', paper presented to the Society for Pidgin and Creole Linguistics, New York.

(1998b) 'Semi-creolization: problems in the development of theory', paper presented at the International Symposium on Degrees of Restructuring in Creole Languages, University of Regensburg, Germany.

(fc.) *Semi-creolization*, Cambridge University Press, Cambridge.

(ed.) (ms.) 'Comparative creole syntax', to appear as J. Holm and P. Patrick (eds.), Battlebridge Press, London.

et al. (1994) 'Relative clauses in Atlantic and non-Atlantic creoles', *Papia* 3(2):70–87.

et al. (1997) 'Passive-like constructions in English-based and other creoles', in E. W. Schneider (ed.) *Englishes around the world 1 (general studies, British Isles, North America): studies in honour of Manfred Görlach*, vol. I, John Benjamins, Amsterdam/Philadelphia, pp. 71–86.

et al. (1998) 'A comparison of serial verb constructions in Cape Verdean and other creoles', in K. Zimmermann (ed.) *Lenguas criollas de base lexical española y portuguesa*. Frankfurt: Vervuert/Madrid: Iberoamericana, pp. 297–319.

et al. (1999) 'Copula patterns in Atlantic and non-Atlantic creoles', in J. R. Rickford and S. Romaine (eds.) *Creole genesis, attitudes and discourse: studies celebrating Charlene Sato*, John Benjamins, Amsterdam/Philadelphia, pp. 79–119.

et al. (fc.) 'The creole verb: a comparative study of stativity and tense reference', in J. McWhorter (ed.) *Language change and language contact in pidgins and creoles*, Amsterdam/Philadelphia, John Benjamins, pp. 133–61.

Holm, J., and C. Kepiou (1993) 'Tok Pisin i kamap pisin gen? Is Tok Pisin repidginizing?' in Byrne and Holm, pp. 341–53.

Holm, J., G. A. Lorenzino and H. R. de Mello (1999) 'Diferentes grados de reestructuración en dos lenguas vernáculas: el español caribeño y el portugués brasileño', in Luís Ortiz (ed.) *El Caribe hispánico: perspectivas lingüísticas actuales*, Vervuert, Frankfurt, pp. 43–60.

Holm, J., with A. Shilling (1982) *Dictionary of Bahamian English*, Lexik House, Cold Spring, N.Y.

Homburger, L. (1949) *The Negro-African languages*, Routledge, London.

Hoyer, W. M. (1948) *Vocabulary and dialogues: English–Papiamento–Dutch*, Hollandsche Boekhandel, Curaçao.

Hudson, J. (1983) *Grammatical and semantic aspects of Fitzroy Valley Kriol*, Summer Institute of Linguistics, Australian Aborigines Branch, Darwin.

Hudson, R. A. (1980) *Sociolinguistics*. Cambridge University Press, Cambridge.

Hull, A. (1968) 'The origins of New World French phonology', *Word* 24(1–2–3):255–69.

—— (1974) 'Evidence for the original unity of North American French dialects', *Revue de Louisiane* 3:59–70.

—— (1979) 'On the origin and chronology of the French-based creoles', in Hancock *et al.*, pp. 201–16.

—— (1983) 'Créole louisianais et créole haïtien: ressemblances et différences', paper presented at the 4th Colloque International du Comité International des Etudes Créoles, Lafayette.

Huttar, G. L. (1974) 'Serial verbs in Surinam creoles', *University of North Dakota, Work Papers* 18:55–66.

—— (1975) 'Sources of creole semantic structures', *Language* 51(3):684–95.

—— (1981) 'Some Kwa-like features of Djuka syntax', *Studies in African Linguistics* 12(3):291–323.

Hyman, L. (1975) *Phonology: theory and analysis*, Holt, Rinehart and Winston, New York.

Hymes, D. (ed.) (1971) *Pidginization and creolization of languages*, Cambridge University Press, Cambridge.

Instituto Lingwístiko Antiano (1984) 'The standardization of Papiamentu: problems and possibilities', paper presented to the Society for Caribbean Linguistics, Jamaica.

Ivens Ferraz, L. (1979) *The creole of São Tomé*, Witwatersrand University Press, Johannesburg.

—— (1985) 'Review of Holm with Shilling (1982)', *African Studies* 44(1):109–13.

—— (1987) 'Portuguese Creoles of West Africa and Asia', in Gilbert, pp. 337–60.

Jacobs, K. (1932) 'Notes on the structure of Chinook Jargon', *Language* 8:27–50.

Jansen, B., H. Koopman and P. Muysken (1978) 'Serial verbs in the creole languages', *Amsterdam Creole Studies* 2:125–59.

Jespersen, O. (1922) *Language: its nature, development, and origin*, Allen and Unwin, London.

Jeuda, D. (1982) 'The elaboration of Papiamentu grammar', paper presented to the Society for Caribbean Linguistics, Suriname.

Joubert, S. M. (1976) 'El papiamento, lengua criolla de Curazao, Aruba y Bonaire', *Kristof* 3:12–19.

—— (1991) *Dikshonario Papiamentu–Hulandes/Handwoordenboek Papiaments–Nederlands*, Cromotip, Curaçao.

Kahane, H., R. Kahane and A. Tietze. (1958) *The Lingua Franca in the Levant: Turkish nautical terms of Italian and Greek origin*, University of Illinois Press, Urbana.

References

Kay, P., and G. Sankoff (1974) 'A language-universals approach to pidgins and creoles', in DeCamp and Hancock, pp. 61–72.

Keesing, R. (1988) *Melanesian Pidgin and the Oceanic substrate*, Cambridge University Press, Cambridge.

Kihm, A. (1980) 'Aspects d'une syntaxe historique: études sur le créole portugais de Guiné-Bissau', Thèse de doctorat de 3e cycle, Université de Paris III, Sorbonne Nouvelle.

(1984) 'Les difficiles débuts des études créoles en France (1870–1920)', *Langue française* 63:42–56.

Koelle, S. (1963 (1854)) *Polyglotta Africana*, Fourah Bay College, Sierra Leone.

Koopman, H. (1986) 'The genesis of Haitian: implications of a comparison of some features of the syntax of Haitian, French and West African languages', in Muysken and Smith, pp. 231–58.

Kramp, A. (1983) 'Early creole lexicography: a study of C. L. Schumann's manuscript dictionary of Sranan', unpublished Ph.D. thesis, University of Leiden.

Krapp, G. P. (1925) *The English language in America*, Century, New York.

Labadie Solano, J. (1982) 'Reaching out for help: can Antilleans cooperate . . . ?', paper presented to the Society for Caribbean Linguistics, Suriname.

Labov, W. (1969) 'Contraction, deletion and inherent variability of the English copula', *Language* 45(4):715–51.

(1972) *Language in the inner city: studies in the Black English Vernacular*, University of Pennsylvania Press, Philadelphia.

(1982) 'Objectivity and commitment in linguistic science: the case of the Black English trial in Ann Arbor', *Language in Society* 11:165–201.

Lalla, B. (1986) 'Tracing elusive phonological features of early Jamaican Creole', in Görlach and Holm, pp. 117–32.

Larsen, J. (1950) *Virgin Islands story*, Muhlenberg Press, Philadelphia.

Lawton, D. (1963) 'Suprasegmental phenomena in Jamaican Creole', unpublished Ph.D. dissertation, Michigan State University.

Lefebvre, C. (1993) 'The role of relexification and syntactic reanalysis in Haitian Creole: methodological aspects of a research program', in Mufwene, pp. 254–79.

Lefebvre, C. (1998) *Creole genesis and the acquisition of grammar: the case of Haitian Creole*, Cambridge University Press, Cambridge.

Lenz, R. (1928) *El papiamento, la lengua criolla de Curazao (la gramática más sencilla)*, Balcells y Cia, Santiago de Chile.

Le Page, R. B. (1955) 'The language problem of the British Caribbean', *Caribbean Quarterly* 4(1):40–9.

(1957–8) 'General outlines of Creole English dialects in the British Caribbean', *Orbis* 6:373–91; 7:54–64.

(ed.) (1961) *Creole language studies II*, proceedings of the Conference on Creole Language Studies (University of the West Indies, Mona, 1959), Macmillan, London.

Le Page, R. B., and D. DeCamp (1960) *Jamaican Creole: Creole studies I*, Macmillan, London.

Le Page, R. B., and A. Tabouret-Keller (1985) *Acts of identity: creole-based approaches to language and ethnicity*, Cambridge University Press, Cambridge.

Lichtveld, L. (1927) 'Afrikaansche resten in de creolentaal van Suriname', *West-Indische Gids* 10:391–402.

Loftman, B. I. (1953) 'Creole languages of the Caribbean area: a comparison of the grammar of Jamaican Creole with those of the creole languages of Haiti, the Antilles, the Guianas, the Virgin Islands, and the Dutch West Indies', unpublished MA thesis, Columbia University.

Lorenzino, G. (1993) 'African vs Austronesian substrate influence on the Spanish-based creoles', in Byrne and Holm, pp. 399–408.

(1998) *Angolar Creole Portuguese: its grammar and sociolinguistic history*, Ph.D. dissertation, City University of New York, University Microfilms International, Ann Arbor. Lincom Europa, Munich.

(ms.) 'Angolar', in Holm.

Maduro, A. (1971) *Ensayo pa yaga na un ortografia uniformá pa nos papiamentu*, Scherpenheuvel, Curaçao.

Mafeni, B. (1971) 'Nigerian Pidgin', in Spencer, pp. 95–112.

Magens, J. M. (1770) *Grammatica over det creolske sprog, som bruges paa de trende Danske Eilande, St Croix, St Thomas, og St Jans i Amerika*, Gerhard Giese Salikath, Copenhagen.

Maher, J. (1985) *Contact linguistics: the language enclave phenomenon*, Ph.D. dissertation, New York University, University Microfilms International, Ann Arbor.

Makhudu, D. (1993) 'The location of Flaai-Taal within the Afrikaans creole continuum: a different view', paper presented to the Society for Pidgin and Creole Linguistics, Amsterdam.

Markey, T. L. (1982) 'Afrikaans: creole or non-creole?', *Zeitschrift für Dialektologie und Linguistik* (2):169–207.

Marques, A. H. de Oliveira (1976) *History of Portugal*, Columbia University Press, New York.

Marroquim, M. (1934) *A língua do Nordeste (Alagôas e Pernambuco)*, Companhia Editora Nacional, São Paulo.

Matthews, W. (1935) 'Sailors' pronunciation in the second half of the 17th century', *Anglia* 59:192–251.

Maurer, P. (1986) 'Le papiamento de Curaçao: un cas de créolisation atypique?', paper presented at the 5th Colloque International des Etudes Créoles, La Réunion.

(1995) *L'angolar: un créole afro-portugais parlé à São Tomé. Notes de grammaire, textes, vocabulaires*, Helmut Buske Verlag, Hamburg.

(1998) 'Papiamentu', in Perl and Schwegler, pp. 140–217.

McWhorter, J. (1995) 'Sisters under the skin: a case for genetic relationship between the Atlantic English-based creoles', *Journal of Pidgin and Creole Languages* 10(2):289–333.

References

(1998) 'Identifying the creole prototype: vindicating a typological class', *Language* 74(4): 788–818.

Mead, M. (1931) 'Talk Boy', *Asia* 31:141–51, 191.

Megenney, W. W. (1978) *A Bahian heritage: an ethnolinguistic study of African influences on Bahian Portuguese*, University of North Carolina Press, Chapel Hill.

(1982) 'La influencia del portugués en el palenquero colombiano', *Divulgaciones Etnológicos* (Universidad del Atlántico, Barranquilla, Colombia) 2:25–42.

(1984) 'Traces of Portuguese in three Caribbean creoles', *Hispanic Linguistics* 1(2):177–89.

Meijer, G., and P. Muysken (eds.) (1977) 'On the beginnings of pidgin and creole studies: Schuchardt and Hesseling', in Valdman, pp. 21–48.

Meillet, A. (1967) *The comparative method in historical linguistics*, Champion, Paris.

Meintel, D. (1975) 'The creole dialect of the island of Brava', in Valkhoff *et al.*, pp. 205–57.

Mello, H. Ribeiro de (1997) *Brazilian Vernacular Portuguese: evidence of partial restructuring*, Ph.D. dissertation, City University of New York, University Microfilms International, Ann Arbor.

Mercier, A. (1880) 'Etude sur la langue créole en Louisiane', *Comptes rendus de l'Athénée louisianais* 1(5):378–83.

Michel, A. (1992) 'The preverbal markers of Papiamentu in Curaçao: *ta, tabata, a, o*', paper presented to the Society for Pidgin and Creole Languages, Philadelphia.

(ms.) 'Papiamentu', in Holm.

Migeod, F. W. H. (1972 (1911)) *The languages of West Africa*, Kegan, Paul, Trench, Trubner, Freeport, N.Y.

Mitchell, K. (1997) 'CUNY leads in degrees granted to people of color', *Envoy* (Hunter College) 53:1:4.

Mufwene, S. S. (1986a) 'Universalist and substrate theories complement one another', in Muysken and Smith, pp. 129–62.

(1986b) 'Number delimitation in Gullah', *American Speech* 61(1):33–60.

(1994) 'On decreolization: the case of Gullah', in M. Morgan (ed.) *Language and the social construction of identity in creole situations*, Center for Afro-American Studies, UCLA, Los Angeles.

(1996) 'The founder principle in creole genesis', *Diachronica* 13:83–134.

(1997) 'Jargons, pidgins, creoles, and koines: what are they?', in Spears and Winford, pp. 35–70.

Mufwene, S. S. (ed.) (1993) *Africanisms in Afro-American language varieties*, University of Georgia Press, Athens, Ga./London.

Mühlhäusler, P. (1976) 'Samoan Plantation Pidgin English and the origin of New Guinea Pidgin: an introduction', *Journal of Pacific History* 11:122–5.

(1979) *Growth and structure of the lexicon of New Guinea Pidgin*, Pacific Linguistics C (52), Research School of Pacific Studies, Australian National University, Canberra.

(1982) 'Tok Pisin in Papua New Guinea', in Bailey and Görlach, pp. 439–66.

(1986) *Pidgin and creole linguistics*, Basil Blackwell, Oxford.

References

Mühlhäusler, P., and T. Dutton (1977) 'Papuan Pidgin English and Hiri Motu', in Wurm, pp. 209–23.

Muller, E. (1975) *Naar een papiamentstalige basisschool op de Nederlandse Antillen*, Instituut voor Algemene Taalwetenschap, Universiteit van Amsterdam, Amsterdam.

(1980) 'Variants in the use of Papiamentu words: some directives concerning language planning', paper presented to the Society for Caribbean Linguistics, Aruba.

(1989) *Inleiding tot de sintaxis van het papiamentu*, Ph.D. dissertation, University of Amsterdam.

Muysken, P. (1981) 'Creole tense/mood/aspect systems: the unmarked case?', in Muysken, pp. 181–200.

(ed.) (1981) *Generative studies on creole languages*, Foris, Dordrecht.

(1985) 'The syntax and morphology of P in the creole languages', paper presented at the Workshop on Universals and Substrata in Creole Genesis, University of Amsterdam.

Muysken, P., and G. Meijer (1979) 'Introduction' to Hesseling (1979), pp. vii–xix.

Muysken, P., and N. Smith (eds.) (1986) *Substrata versus universals in creole genesis*, John Benjamins, Amsterdam.

Nagy, N., C. Moisset and G. Sankoff (1996) 'On the acquisition of variable phonology in L2', *University of Pennsylvania Working Papers in Linguistics*.

Naro, A. J. (1978) 'A study on the origins of pidginization', *Language* 54(2):314–49.

Neumann-Holzschuh, I., and E. W. Schneider (eds.) (fc.) *Proceedings from the conference on degrees of restructuring in creole languages, University of Regensburg, Germany*, John Benjamins, Amsterdam.

Ogunbọwale, P. O. (1970) *The essentials of the Yoruba language*, Hodder and Stoughton, London.

Oldendorp, C. G. A. (1777) *Geschichte der Mission der evangelischen Brueder auf den caraibischen Inseln S. Thomas, St. Croix und S. Jan*, C. F. Laur, Barby.

Owens, J. (1977) *Aspects of Nubi syntax*, Ph.D. thesis, University of London.

(1980) 'Monogenesis, the universal and the particular in creole studies', *Anthropological Linguistics* 22(3):97–117.

(1985) 'The origin of East African Nubi', *Anthropological Linguistics* 27(3):229–71.

Owens, J., and C. Khamis (ms.) 'Nubi', in Holm.

Park, J. (ed.) (1975) *Ogii sani di pasa anga Da Kelema* by Da Kelema Asekende, Summer Institute of Linguistics, Paramaribo.

Parsons, E. C. (1933–43) *Folklore of the Antilles, French and English*, American Folklore Society, New York, 3 vols.

Patrick, P. (1992) *Linguistic variation in urban Jamaican Creole: a sociolinguistic study of Kingston, Jamaica*, Ph.D. dissertation, University of Pennsylvania, University Microfilms International, Ann Arbor.

(ms.) 'Jamaican', in Holm.

Peck, S. M., Jr (1988) *Tense, aspect and mood in Guinea-Casamance Portuguese Creole*, Ph.D. dissertation, University of California, Los Angeles, University Microfilms International, Ann Arbor.

References

Pelleprat, P. (1655) *Relation des missions des pp. de la Compagnie de Jésus*, Paris.

Perl, M., and A. Schwegler (eds.) (1998) *América Negra: panorámica actual de los estudios lingüísticos sobre variedades hispanas, portuguesas y criollas*, Vervuert, Frankfurt/Iberoamericana, Madrid.

Peters, A. Boero de (1982) 'The phoneme /r/: articulatory variation in Aruba Papiamento', paper presented to the Society for Caribbean Linguistics, Suriname.

Pollard, V. (1983) 'The social history of Dread Talk', in Carrington *et al.*, pp. 46–62.

—— (1984) 'Rastafarian language in St Lucia and Barbados', in Sebba and Todd, pp. 253–63.

—— (1986) 'Innovation in Jamaican Creole: the speech of Rastafari', in Görlach and Holm, pp. 157–66.

Pompilus, P. (1969) 'Le français en Haïti', in *Le français en France et hors de France*, Centre d'Etudes des Relations Interethniques, Nice, pp. 37–42.

Poyen-Bellisle, R. (1894) *Les sons et les formes du créole des Antilles*, Ph.D. dissertation, University of Chicago, John Murphy, Baltimore.

Pringle, I. (1985) 'More on the origin of *say* and *se* as complementizers in English-based creoles', ms.

Raidt, E. H. (1983) *Einführung in die Geschichte und Struktur des Afrikaans*, Wissenschaftliche Buchgesellschaft, Darmstadt.

Rawley, J. A. (1981) *The transatlantic slave-trade: a history*, Norton, New York/London.

Reinecke, J. E. (1937) *Marginal languages: a sociological survey of the creole languages and trade jargons*, Ph.D. dissertation, Yale University, University Microfilms International, Ann Arbor.

—— (1969) *Language and dialect in Hawaii: a sociolinguistic history to 1935*, (ed.) S. Tsuzaki, University Press of Hawaii, Honolulu.

—— (1977) 'Foreword' to Valdman (ed.) pp. vii–xi.

—— (1983) 'William Greenfield: a neglected pioneer creolist', in Carrington *et al.*, pp. 1–12.

Reinecke, J. E., and A. Tokimasa (1934) 'The English dialect of Hawaii', *American Speech* 9:46–58, 122–31.

Reinecke, J. E., S. M. Tsuzaki, D. DeCamp, I. F. Hancock and R. E. Wood (eds.) (1975) *A bibliography of pidgin and creole languages*, University Press of Hawaii, Honolulu.

Rens, L. L. E. (1953) *The historical and social background of Surinam's Negro English*, academisch proefschrift, North Holland, Amsterdam.

Révah, I. S. (1963) 'La question des substrats et superstrats dans le domaine linguistique brésilien: les parlers populaires brésiliens doivent-ils être considérés comme des parlers "créoles" ou "semi-créoles"?', *Romania* 84:433–50.

Richardson, L. A. (1972) 'Ensayo de etimología de algunas palabras del papiamento: las partes del cuerpo humano y algunas funciones del mismo', proefschrift, Rijksuniversitair Centrum, Antwerp.

(1977) 'The phrasal conjunctor and the comitative marker in Papiamentu', *Amsterdam Creole Studies* 1:55–68.

(1979) 'Towards a language education policy in the Netherlands Antilles', paper presented at the Conference on Theoretical Orientations in Creole Studies, St Thomas.

Rickford, J. (1977) 'The question of prior creolization in Black English', in Valdman, pp. 190–221.

(1980) 'How does *doz* disappear?', in Day, pp. 77–96.

(1986) 'Social contact and linguistic diffusion: Hiberno English and New World Black English', *Language* 62(2):245–89.

(1987) *Dimensions of a creole continuum*, Stanford University Press, Stanford.

(1992) 'The creole residue in Barbados', paper presented to the Society for Pidgin and Creole Linguistics, Philadelphia.

Rickford, J., and S. Romaine (eds.) (fc.) *Creole genesis, sociohistory and discourse: studies celebrating Charlene Sato*, John Benjamins, Amsterdam.

Riego de Dios, M. I. (1979) 'The Cotabato Chabacano (CT) verb', Papers in Pidgin and Creole Linguistics no. 2, Pacific Linguistics A-57, Research School of Pacific Studies, Australian National University, Canberra.

Robertson, I. E. (1979) 'Berbice Dutch: a description', unpublished Ph.D. dissertation, University of the West Indies, St Augustine.

(1986) 'Substratum influence in the grammar of Berbice Dutch', paper presented to the Society for Caribbean Linguistics, Trinidad.

Robins, R. H. (1967) *A short history of linguistics*, Indiana University Press, Bloomington/London.

Romaine, S. (1988) *Pidgin and creole languages*. Longman, London.

Römer, R. (1977) 'Polarization phenomena in Papiamentu', *Amsterdam Creole Studies* 1:69–79.

Rotimi, O., and N. Faraclas (ms.) 'A dictionary and grammar of Nigerian Pidgin'.

Rountree, S. C. (1972a) 'The phonological structure of stems in Saramaccan', in Grimes, pp. 22–7.

(1972b) 'Saramaccan tone in relation to intonation and grammar', *Lingua* 29:308–25.

Rountree, S. C., and N. Glock (1982) *Saramaccan for beginners: a pedagogical grammar of the Saramaccan language*, Summer Institute of Linguistics, Paramaribo.

Rowlands, E. C. (1959) *A grammar of Gambian Mandinka*, School of Oriental and African Studies, University of London, London.

(1969) *Teach yourself Yoruba*, English Universities Press, London.

Russell, T. (1868) *The etymology of Jamaica grammar, by a young gentleman*, DeCordova, MacDougall and Co., Kingston.

Ryan, P. A. N. (1985) *Macafouchette: a look at the influence of French on the dialect of Trinidad and Tobago*, Port of Spain, Trinidad.

Sabino, R. (1986) 'Towards a phonological description of Negerhollands: an overview', ms.

References

Saint-Jacques-Fauquenoy, M. (1972) 'Le verbe *être* dans les créoles français', in *Langues et techniques, nature et société*, Klincksieck, Paris, pp. 225–31.

Saint-Quentin, A. de (1872) *Etude sur la grammaire créole*, Maisonneuve, Paris.

Sandoval, Padre A. de (1627) *De instauranda Aethiopum salute*. Seville.

Sankoff, G. (1980) *The social life of a language*, University of Pennsylvania Press, Philadelphia.

Sankoff, G., and P. Brown. (1976) 'The origins of syntax in discourse: a case study of Tok Pisin relatives', *Language* 52(3):631–66.

Santoro, S. (ms.) 'Zamboangueño', in Holm.

Sato, C. J., and A. Reinecke (1987) 'John E. Reinecke: his life and work', in Gilbert, pp. 3–22.

Sawyerr, H. A. (1940) 'The Sierra Leone Patois: a study of its growth and structure with special reference to the teaching of English in Sierra Leone', unpublished M.Ed. thesis, University of Durham.

Schneider, E. W. (1989) *American Earlier Black English: morphological and syntactic variables*. The University of Alabama Press, Tuscaloosa/London.

(1993) 'Africanisms in the grammar of Afro-American English: weighing the evidence', in Mufwene, pp. 209–21.

Schneider, G. D. (1960) 'Cameroons Creole dictionary', unpublished ms., Bamenda.

(1966) *West African Pidgin English: a descriptive linguistic analysis with texts and glossary from the Cameroon area*, Ph.D. thesis, Hartford Seminary Foundation. Athens, Ohio, University Microfilms International, Ann Arbor.

Schuchardt, H. (1881) 'Review of Coelho (1881)', *Zeitschrift für romanische Philologie* 5:580–1.

(1882a) 'Kreolische Studien. I. Ueber das Negerportugiesische von S. Thomé (Westafrika)', *Sitzungsberichte der kaiserlichen Akademie der Wissenschaften zu Wien* 101(2):889–917.

(1882b) 'Kreolische Studien. II. Ueber das Indoportugiesische von Cochim', *Sitzungsberichte der kaiserlichen Akademie der Wissenschaften zu Wien* 102(2):799–816.

(1883a) 'Kreolische Studien. III. Ueber das Indoportugiesische von Diu', *Sitzungsberichte der kaiserlichen Akademie der Wissenschaften zu Wien* 103(1):3–18.

(1883b) 'Kreolische Studien. IV. Ueber das Malaiospanischen der Philippinen', *Sitzungsberichte der kaiserlichen Akademie der Wissenschaften zu Wien* 105(1):111–50.

(1883c) 'Kreolische Studien. V. Ueber das Melaneso-englische', *Sitzungsberichte der kaiserlichen Akademie der Wissenschaften zu Wien* 105(1):151–61. (Reprinted in English in Schuchardt (1979), pp. 18–25; (1980), pp. 14–23.)

(1885) *Ueber die Lautgesetze: gegen die Junggrammatiker*, Oppenheim, Berlin. (Reprinted and translated in T. Vennemann and T. Wilbur (1972): 'Schuchardt, the neogrammarians, and the transformational theory of phonological change', *Linguistische Forschungen* 26. Athenäum, Frankfurt.)

References

(1887) 'Review of Da Costa and Duarte (1886) *O creôl de Cabo Verde*', *Literaturblatt für germanische und romanische Philologie* 8:132–41.

(1888a) 'Kreolische Studien. VII. Ueber das Negerportugiesische von Annobom', *Sitzungsberichte der kaiserlichen Akademie der Wissenschaften zu Wien* 116(1):193–226.

(1888b) 'Beiträge zur Kenntnis des kreolischen Romanisch II. Zum Negerportugiesischen Senegambiens', *Zeitschrift für romanische Philologie* 12:301–12.

(1888c) 'Beiträge zur Kenntnis des kreolischen Romanisch III. Zum Negerportugiesischen der Kapverden', *Zeitschrift für romanische Philologie* 12:312–22.

(1888d) 'Kreolische Studien. VIII. Ueber das Annamito-französische', *Sitzungsberichte der kaiserlichen Akademie der Wissenschaften zu Wien* 116(1):227–34.

(1889a) 'Beiträge zur Kenntnis des kreolischen Romanisch IV. Zum Negerportugiesischen der Ilha do Principe', *Zeitschrift für romanische Philologie* 13:463–75.

(1889b) 'Beiträge zur Kenntnis des kreolischen Romanisch V. Allgemeineres über das Indoportugiesische (Asioportugiesische)', *Zeitschrift für romanische Philologie* 13:476–516.

(1889c) 'Beiträge zur Kenntnis des kreolischen Romanisch VI. Zum Indoportugiesischen von Mahé und Cannanore', *Zeitschrift für romanische Philologie* 13:516–24.

(1889d) 'Beiträge zur Kenntnis des englischen Kreolisch I', *Englische Studien* 12:470–74. (Translated in Schuchardt (1980), pp. 30–7.)

(1889e) 'Beiträge zur Kenntnis des englischen Kreolisch II. Melanesoenglisches', *Englische Studien* 13:158–62. (Translated in Schuchardt (1979), pp. 7–14; (1980), pp. 23–9.)

(1890) 'Kreolische Studien. IX. Ueber das Malaioportugiesische von Batavia und Tuga', *Sitzungsberichte der kaiserlichen Akademie der Wissenschaften zu Wien* 122(9):1–256.

(1891) 'Continuation of Schuchardt (1890)', *Literaturblatt für germanische und romanische Philologie* 12:199–206.

(1893) 'Review of I. Vila. 1891. Compendio de la doctrina cristiana en Castellano y fa d'Ambú . . . ; Elementos de la gramática ambú ó de Annobón', *Literaturblatt für germanische und romanische Philologie* 14:401–8.

(1909) 'Die Lingua Franca', *Zeitschrift für romanische Philologie* 33:441–61. (Translated in Schuchardt (1979), pp. 26–47; (1980), pp. 65–88.)

(1914a) *Die Sprache der Saramakkaneger in Surinam*. Johannes Müller, Amsterdam. (Preface, pp. iii–xxxvi translated in Schuchardt (1979), pp. 73–108; (1980), pp. 89–126.)

(1914b) 'Zum Negerholländischen von St Thomas', *Tijdschrift voor nederlandsche taal- en letterkunde* 33:123–35. (Translated in Schuchardt (1979), pp. 48–58.)

References

(1979) *The ethnography of variation: selected writings on pidgins and creoles*, ed. and trans. T. L. Markey, Karoma, Ann Arbor.

(1980) *Pidgin and creole languages: selected essays*, ed. and trans. G. G. Gilbert, Cambridge University Press, Cambridge.

Schultze, E. (1933) 'Sklaven- und Dienersprachen (sogen. Handelssprachen); ein Beitrag zur Sprach- und uuanderungs-Soziologie', *Sociologus* 9:377–418.

Schumann, J. H. (1978) *The pidginization process: a model for second language acquisition*, Newbury House, Rowley, Mass.

Sebba, M. (1984) 'Serial verb or syntactic calque: the great circuit of *say*', paper presented to the Society for Caribbean Linguistics, Jamaica.

Sebba, M., and L. Todd (eds.) (1984) *Papers from the York Creole Conference, 24–27 September 1983*. York Papers in Linguistics 11, Department of Language, University of York.

Sebeok, T. A. (ed.) (1968) *Current trends in linguistics*, vol. IV, *Ibero-American and Caribbean Linguistics*, Mouton, The Hague.

Shilling, A. (1976) 'Negation in Bahamian English', paper presented to the Society for Caribbean Linguistics, Guyana.

Siegel, J. (1987) *Language contact in a plantation environment: a sociolinguistic history of Fiji*, Cambridge University Press, Cambridge.

(1997) 'Mixing, levelling, and pidgin/creole development', in Spears and Winford, pp. 111–49.

Singler, J. V. (1981) *An introduction to Liberian English*, Michigan State university African Studies Center / Peace Corps, East Lansing.

(1984) 'Variation in tense-aspect-modality in Liberian English', unpublished Ph.D. dissertation, University of California at Los Angeles.

(1985) 'The story of *o*', paper presented at the 16th Conference on African Linguistics, Yale University.

(1986) 'African languages and Caribbean creoles', course at Linguistic Society of America Summer Institute, City University of New York.

Slomanson, P. (fc.) 'Language contact and syntactic change in the evolution of Afrikaans', Ph.D. dissertation, City University of New York.

Smith, I. (1979) 'Convergence in South Asia: a creole example', *Lingua* 48:193–222.

Smith, M. G. (1972) 'The plural framework of Jamaican society', in P. Baxter and B. Sansom (eds.) *Race and social difference*, Penguin, Harmondsworth, pp. 257–74.

Smith, N. S. H. (1987) 'The genesis of the creole languages of Surinam', unpublished Ph.D. dissertation, University of Amsterdam.

Smith, N. S. H., I. Robertson and K. Williamson (1987) 'The Ijo element in Berbice Dutch', *Language in Society* 16:49–90.

Sonesson, B. (1977) 'El papel de Santomas en el Caribe hasta 1815', *Anales de Investigación Histórica* 4(1–2):42–80.

Spears, A. K., and D. Winford (eds.) (1997) *Pidgins and creoles: structure and status*, John Benjamins, Amsterdam/Philadelphia.

Spencer, J. (ed.) (1971) *The English language in West Africa*, Longman, London.

Sprauve, G. (1976) 'Chronological implications of discontinuity in spoken and written Dutch creole', paper presented to the Society for Caribbean Linguistics, Guyana.

(1981) 'Pre- and post-emancipation language development in the Virgin Islands', in *Freedom's flame*, Bureau of Libraries, Museums and Archeological Services, St Thomas.

Sprauve, G. A. (ed.) (1985) 'Maritšimát en Stendifi, the story of Black Witch and Ground Dove as told by Mrs. Alice Stevens', cassette and transcription in Negerhollands and English, College of the Virgin Islands, St Thomas.

Stassen, L. (1985) *Comparison and universal grammar*, Oxford University Press, Oxford.

Stein, P. (1984) *Kreolisch und Französisch*, Niemeyer, Tübingen.

(1986a) 'Les premiers créolistes: les frères moraves à St Thomas au 18e siècle', *Amsterdam Creole Studies* 9:3–17.

(1986b) 'The documents concerning the Negro Dutch language of the Danish Virgin Islands, St Thomas, St Croix and St John – Negerhollands – in the Unitäts-Archiv (Archives of the Moravian Brethren) at Herrnhut. A commented bibliography', *Amsterdam Creole Studies* 9:19–31.

Stewart, W. A. (1962) 'Creole languages in the Caribbean', in F. A. Rice (ed.) *Study of the role of second languages in Asia, Africa and Latin America*, Center for Applied Linguistics, Washington, pp. 34–53.

(1967) 'Sociolinguistic factors in the history of American Negro dialects', *Florida FL Reporter* 5. (Reprinted in Wolfram and Clarke (1971), pp. 74–89.)

Stolz, T. (1984) 'Two chapters in Negro-Dutch etymology', *Amsterdam Creole Studies* 7:35–52.

(1986) *Gibt es das kreolische Sprachwandelmodell? Vergleichende Grammatik des Negerholländischen*, Europäische Hochschulschriften 21:46, Peter Lang, Frankfurt/Bern/New York.

Stolz, T., and P. Stein (1986) 'Social history and genesis of Negerhollands', *Amsterdam Creole Studies* 9:103–22.

Sylvain, S. (1936) *Le créole haïtien: morphologie et syntaxe*, Imprimerie de Meester, Port-au-Prince, Wetteren.

Taylor, D. R. (1953) 'Review of Hall *et al.* (1953)', *Word* 9:292–6; 10:91–2.

(1956) 'Language contacts in the West Indies', *Word* 13:399–414.

(1957) 'Spanish contact vernaculars in the Philippine Islands', *Word* 13:489–99.

(1959) 'On function words versus form in "non-traditional" languages', *Word* 15:485–9.

(1960) 'Language shift or changing relationship?', *International Journal of American Linguistics* 26:155–61.

(1963) 'The origin of West Indian creole languages: evidence from grammatical categories', *American Anthropologist* 65:800–14.

(1971) 'Grammatical and lexical affinities of creoles', in Hymes, pp. 293–6.

(1977) *Languages of the West Indies*, Johns Hopkins University Press, Baltimore.

References

Teyssier, P. (1959) *La langue de Gil Vicente*, Klincksieck, Paris.

Thomas, G. (1698) *An historical description of the province and country of West-New-Jersey*, London.

Thomas, J. J. (1869) *The theory and practice of Creole grammar*. (1969 reprint. New Beacon Books, London.)

Thomason, S. G. (1980) 'On interpreting "The Indian interpreter"', *Language in Society* 9:167–93.

(1984) 'Is Michif unique?', unpublished ms.

(1997a) 'Ma'a (Mbugu)', in Thomason (1997b), pp. 469–88.

(ed.) (1997b) *Contact languages: a wider perspective*, John Benjamins, Amsterdam/Philadelphia.

Thomason, S. G., and A. Elgibali (1986) 'Before the Lingua Franca: pidginized Arabic in the eleventh century AD', *Lingua* 68:407–39.

Thomason, S. G., and T. Kaufmann (1988) *Language contact, creolization, and genetic linguistics*, University of California Press, Berkeley.

Thompson, R. W. (1961) 'A note on some possible affinities between the creole dialects of the Old World and those of the New', in Le Page, pp. 107–13.

Tinelli, H. (1981) *Creole phonology*, Mouton, The Hague / Paris / New York.

Todd, L. (1974) *Pidgins and creoles*, Routledge and Kegan Paul, London/Boston.

(1984) *Modern Englishes: pidgins and creoles*, Basil Blackwell, Oxford.

Todd Dandare, R. (1979) 'Analyzing variation in creole languages: the Papiamento case', paper presented to the Conference on Theoretical Orientations in Creole Studies, St Thomas.

Turner, L. D. (1949) *Africanisms in the Gullah dialect*. (1974 reprint, University of Michigan Press, Ann Arbor.)

Valdman, A. (1970) *Basic course in Haitian Creole*, Indiana University Press, Bloomington.

(ed.) (1977) *Pidgin and creole linguistics*, Indiana University Press, Bloomington.

(1978) *Le créole: structure, statut et origine*, Klincksieck, Paris.

(1983) 'Creolization and second language acquisition', in Anderson, pp. 212–34.

(1984) 'The linguistic situation in Haiti', in C. R. Foster and A. Valdman (eds.) *Haiti – today and tomorrow*, University Press of America, Lanham, Mo., pp. 77–99.

Valdman, A., and A. Highfield (eds.) (1980) *Theoretical orientations in creole studies*, Academic Press, New York.

Valdman, A., with R. Rosemond and P. Philippe (1988) *Ann pale kreyòl*, Indiana University Creole Institute, Bloomington.

Valdman, A., S. Yoder, C. Roberts and Y. Joseph (1981) *Haitian Creole – English – French dictionary*, Indiana University Creole Institute, Bloomington.

Valkhoff, M. (1966) *Studies in Portuguese and Creole with special reference to South Africa*, Witwatersrand University Press, Johannesburg.

(1972) *New light on Afrikaans and Malayo-Portuguese*, Peeters, Louvain.

Valkhoff, M., W. Bal, J. Morais Barbosa, L. Ferraz, S. Frusoni, D. Meintel, M. Nunes Nabarro, P. E. Raper and M. Valença (eds.) (1975) *Miscelânea*

Luso-Africana: colectânea de estudos coligidos, Junta de Investigações Científicas de Ultramar, Lisbon.

Valls, L. (1981) *What a pistarckle! A dictionary of Virgin Islands English Creole*, St John, US Virgin Islands.

van der Merwe, E. (1993) 'Orange River Afrikaans: post-creole or not?', paper presented to the Society for Pidgin and Creole Linguistics, Amsterdam.

van Diggelen, M. (1978) 'Negro-Dutch', *Amsterdam Creole Studies* 2:69–100.

van Dyk, P. (1778) *Niewe en nooit bevoorens geziene onderwijzinge in het Bastert Engels* . . . Jacobus van Egmont, Amsterdam.

van Ewijk, P. A. H. (1875) *Nederlandsch–Papiamentsch–Spaansch woordenboekje*, Arnhem.

van Ginneken, J. (1913) *Handboek der Nederlandsche taal* . . . 1, *De sociologische structuur der Nederlandsche taal*, Malmberg, Nijmegen.

van Name, A. (1869–70) 'Contributions to creole grammar', *Transactions of the American Philological Association* 1:123–67.

van Rossem, C., and H. van der Voort (1996) *Die Creol Taal: 250 years of Negerhollands texts*, University of Michigan Press, Ann Arbor.

van Wijk, H. L. (1958) 'Orígenes y evolución del Papiamentu', *Neophilologus* 42:169–82.

Vendryes, J. (1921) *Le langage: introduction linguistique à l'histoire*, Renaissance du Livre, Paris.

Volker, C. A. (1982) 'An introduction to Rabaul Creole German (Unserdeutsch)', MA thesis, University of Queensland.

Voorhoeve, J. (1953) *Voorstudies tot een beschrijving van het Sranan Tongo (Negerengels van Suriname)*, Noord-Hollandsche UM, Amsterdam.

(1957) 'The verbal system of Sranan', *Lingua* 6:374–96.

(1961) 'Le ton et la grammaire dans le Saramaccan', *Word* 17:146–63.

(1962) *Sranan syntax*, North Holland, Amsterdam.

(1970) 'The regularity of sound correspondences in a creole language (Sranan)', *Journal of African Languages* 9:51–69.

(1971) 'Church creole and pagan cult languages', in Hymes, pp. 305–16.

(1973) 'Historical and linguistic evidence in favor of the relexification theory in the formation of creoles', *Language in Society* 2:133–45.

Waher, H. (1993) 'Derivation in a variation of pre-standardized Afrikaans', paper presented to the Society for Pidgin and Creole Linguistics, Amsterdam.

Warantz, E. (1983) 'The Bay Islands English of Honduras', in Holm pp. 71–94.

Warner, M. (1971) 'Trinidad Yoruba: notes on survivals', *Caribbean Quarterly* 17(2):40–9.

Washabaugh, W. (1977) 'Constraining variation in decreolization', *Language* 53(2):329–52.

(1980) 'From preposition to complementizer in Caribbean English Creole', in Day, pp. 97–110.

(1983) 'The off-shore island creoles: Providencia, San Andrés and the Caymans', in Holm, pp. 157–79.

References

Weinreich, U. (1953) *Languages in contact: Findings and problems*, Mouton, The Hague.

Welmers, W. B. (1973) *African language structures*, University of California Press, Berkeley.

Westermann, D., and M. Bryan (1952) *Handbook of African languages*, vol. II, *Languages of West Africa*, Oxford University Press, Oxford.

Whinnom, K. (1956) *Spanish contact vernaculars in the Philippine Islands*, Hong Kong University Press, Hong Kong.

(1965) 'Contacts de langues et emprunts lexicaux: the origin of the European-based creoles and pidgins', *Orbis* 14:509–27.

(1971) 'Linguistic hybridization and the "Special case" of pidgins and creoles', in Hymes, pp. 91–116.

(1977) 'Lingua Franca: historical problems', in Valdman, pp. 295–312.

Williams, J. P. (1983) 'White Saban English: a sociohistorical description', MA thesis, University of Texas at Austin.

Williamson, K. (1965) *A grammar of the Kolokuma dialect of Ijo*, Ibadan.

Wilson, W. A. A. (1962) *The Crioulo of Guiné*, Witwatersrand University Press, Johannesburg.

Winford, D. (1997–8) 'On the origins of African American Vernacular English: a creolist perspective', *Diachronica* 14:(2): 305–44 (1997); 15(1): 99–154 (1998).

Wolfram, W., and N. Clarke (eds.) (1971) *Black–White speech relationships*, Center for Applied Linguistics, Washington.

Wood, R. E. (1972a) 'New light on the origins of Papiamentu: an eighteenth-century letter', *Neophilologus* 56:18–30.

(1972b) 'The hispanization of a creole language: Papiamentu', *Hispania* 55(4):857–64.

Wright, J. (1895–1905) *English Dialect Dictionary*, Oxford University Press, London, 6 vols.

Wullschlägel, H. R. (1856) *Deutsch-Negerenglisches Wörterbuch*. (1965 reprint, S. Emmering, Amsterdam.)

Wurm, S. A. (1977a) 'The nature of New Guinea Pidgin', in Wurm (1977b), pp. 511–32.

(ed.) (1977b) *Language, culture, society and the modern world*, vol. III, *New Guinea area languages and language study*, Pacific Linguistics, C 40, Australian National University, Canberra.

Yansen, C. A. (1975) *Random remarks on Creolese*, Thanet Press, Margate.

Yillah, S. (1992) *Temne phonology and morphology*, Ph.D. dissertation, City University of New York.

(ms.) 'Krio', in Holm.

Zimmermann, K. (ed.) (1998) *El Segundo Colóquio Internacional de Lenguas Criollas de Base Española y Portuguesa*, Vervuert, Frankfurt.

Zinzendorf, N. von. (1742) *Büdingische Sammlung einiger in die Kirchen-Historie einschlagender Schrifften*, vol. I, Stöhr, Büdingen. (1965 reprint, Olms, Hildesheim.)

Zyhlarz, E. (1932–3) 'Ursprung und Sprachcharakter des Altägyptischen', *Zeitschrift für Eingeborenen-Sprachen* 23:25–45, 81–110, 161–94, 241–54.

INDEX

Page numbers in *italics* refer to maps; headings in **bold** are languages (or varieties). The following abbreviations are used: def., defined; P/C, pidgin and/or creole; see also key to maps 1 and 2.

267

Lingala, *xx*, 39, 69, 101, 113
Lingua Franca, *xx*, 14–16, 30, 46, 102
lingua francas, 41, 83, 96, 103
Língua Geral, *xx*, 39, 102
literacy and P/C speakers, 4, 19, 89
literature in creoles, 19, 21, 24, 89
liturgical languages, 20, 114
loan translations, *see* calquing
locative 'be', 179, 199–200, 205
  and progressive aspect, 180–1, 199–200
locative preposition, general, 108, 123
  meaning 'from', 229
Lorenzino, G., 66, 75, 174, 223
Louisiana, 102
Louisiana CF, *xix*, 24, 28, 85

Ma'a (*see also* Mbugu), 11
Macanese CP, *xix*, 27–8, 72
Macao, 27
Macro-Chibchan languages, 125
Madagascar, 85
Madeira, 71, 125
Magens, J., 19, 83
Mahdist revolt, 103
Makhudu, D., 66
Makista or Macaísta, *see* Macanese CP
Malacca, 72, 102
Malagasy, 28–9, 215, 224
Malay, 215
Malay, restructured (*see also* Baba Malay, Coastal Malay), *xx*, 97–8, 102
Malayo-Portuguese, *xix*, 20, 30, 35, 46, 213, 215
Malaysia, 81
Malinke, 87, 172
Manchuria, 102
Mande languages, 87, 144–5, 154–5, 172–3, 206, 233
Mandinka, 157, 181, 192–3, 198–200, 218, 230–1
Mano, 233
map of Caribbean area, *xxi–xxii*
map of world, *xix–xx*
Marathi, 220
marginal languages, 38
Maridi Arabic, 14, 15
markedness, 59–60, 139
maroon creoles, 41, 92, 114
Maroons, 73–4, 76, 92–4, 114 (def.)
Martinique, 17, 18, 87
Martinique CF, *xxii*, 17, 24, 85
masking, 115 (def.)
mass nouns, 135
Maurer, P., 67, 74, 76, 78, 164
Mauritania, 15
Mauritian CF, *xx*, 24, 29, 38, 63, 85, 219, 224
Mbugu (*see also* Ma'a), 11

Mbundu, *see* kiMbundu
McConnell, O., 89
McWhorter, J., 49, 66
Mead, M., 6, 99
Meillet, A., 34
Melanesian PE, 6, 30, 42, 96
Mello, H., 4, 66, 70
Mende, 157, 188, 233
mengeltaal, 35–6 (def.)
mesolect, 10 (def.), 51, 140, 185, 204, 209, 236
  and zero copulas, 199
metaphor and semantic shift, 134
metathesis, 143 (def.)
Michel, A., 174
Michif, 11, 66
Middle English, 15
  a creole? 15–16, 22
Miskito, 126, 135
Miskito Coast CE, *xxi*, 135, 192, 194, 204, 214–15, 217, 221, 230, 234, 236
  preceding pidgin, 135
missionaries, 17–19, 21, 83, 88, 97, 99
Missouri French, 11
mixed languages, 2, 11, 34–6
mixing slaves by language, 113–14
mnemonic devices, 131
Mobilian Jargon, *xx*, 39, 102
modality, 188
Mongolia, 102
monogenesis of creoles, 32, 35, 44–9, 58, 61, 106, 123
  of all languages, 21
monophthongization, 148
Montserrat, *xxii*
Moravians, 18–22, 83
morpheme boundary reanalysis, 107, 127–30, 239
morphemes, new combinations, 79
morphological changes, 127–32, 238
morphophonemic rules, 59
Motu, 102
Mozambique, 74
Mufwene, S., 63, 65
Mühlhäusler, P., 5, 96–9, 101, 107
multidimensional continuum, 54, 56
multifunctionality, 108 (def.), 135
multilingualism, 40, 54, 56, 79
Muslims, 103–4
mutual intelligibility, 47, 54, 85, 104
  of French-based creoles, 47, 85
  of Jamaican E/CE, 54
  of Juba and Nubi Arabic, 104
Muysken, P., 66

Nagamese, *xx*, 39, 102, 198, 204, 228, 233, 235
Nahuatl, 126

Index

pitch, 164–5
pitch-accent languages, 165 (def.), 169
pitch polarity, 169
plantation creoles, 40, 91–2
playforms, 134
pleonastic pronouns, 121
plosives, 154
plural forms, 28, 215–16
  as etyma, 128–9, 215
plural marker, 19, 24, 28, 79, 84, 214–17, 240
polygenesis, 47–9, 58, 61, 106
polylectal grammars, 55, 192
polysemy, 108 (def.)
Pompilus, M., 45, 88
Popular Brazilian Portuguese, *see* **Brazilian Vernacular Portuguese**
Portugal, 71–2
Portuguese, 77–8, 80, 125, 180, 193, 201, 238
  creolist literature in, 65
  influence on Atlantic creoles, 123–4
Portuguese, Pidgin, 16, 46, 71, 77, 218
Portuguese-based P/Cs, *xix*, 27–8, 30, 37, 57, 71–2, 86, 123–4
Portuguese empire, 71–2, 81
possession, 212, 217–22
possessive adjectives, 90, 218, 221–2, 226, 240
  with phrasal prepositions, 231
possessive particle, 80, 84, 90, 219–20
possessive pronouns, 90, 220–1
  as emphatic possessive adjectives, 220–1, 240
post-clitics, 127
post-creoles, 4, 10 (def.), 33, 50, 51, 55, 92, 235, 239
post-nominal determiners, 17, 28
postpositions, 128, 231–2
postverbal markers, 128, 176
power relationships, 6, 68–70, 106, 237
predicate clefting, 32, 201–2, 211–12, 240
predicate marker, 211–12
prefix, 127
prenasalized stops, 100, 139, 153, 155–7, 239
pre-pidgin, 8, 42, 68–9, 95, 107, 237
prepositions, 79, 240
  general locative, 123, 229; meaning 'from', 229
  indicating possession, 218
  omission of, 218, 230
  phrasal, 230–1
  versus postpositions, 231
present participle, 180
  as etymon, 129
present tense, 175, 177
  'historical present', 177
Pressoir, C., 89
prestige, 69, 76, 79, 89, 90, 98, 100, 144, 237

preverbal markers, 17, 19, 32, 50, 79, 104, 117, 174–97, 239
  ordering, 179, 190–2
previous creolization, 3
primary language, 7
Príncipe CP, *xix*, 30, 73, 154, 166, 210, 212, 215, 223, 227, 229–32, 235
private domains, 116
progressive aspect, 28, 84, 101, 123, 129, 175–6, 179–84, 186, 188, 197, 201
  and habitual, 183
  and locatives, 180
  in superstrates, 180–1
progressive nasalization, 149 (def.), 150
pronouns, 222–6
  case, 222
  gender, 216
  inclusiveness, 223–4
  interrogative, 226
  number, 222
  personal, 222–6
  possessive, 220–1
  quasi-reflexive, 225–6
  relative, 226
  variation, 55
prostitutes, 112
prothesis, 142 (def.)
proto-creole, 49, 51
Providencia CE, *xxi*
punctual, 183 (def.)

quantification of variables, 27
quantifiers, 129
quasi-modal, 194
quasi-reflexives, 25, 29, 225–6
Queensland, 96, 98
question markers, 59, 234–5
questions, 234–6
  embedded, 235–6
question words, 234
  bimorphemic structure, 61, 120, 226
  with highlighter, 202–3

/r/, /l/ alternation, 32, 161–2
Rabaul, 97–8
racism, 22–3
'radical' creoles, 62–3, 140
Rastafarians, 94
ratio of native to non-native speakers, 238
reanalysis, 107, 115, 117
recopying, 32, 201–2, 211–12, 234
reduced pidgin, *see* early pidgin
redundancy
  in compounds, 131
  in pidgins, 59
redundancy convention, 54
reduplication, 28, 59, 101, 104, 107, 121, 238